# The Empire
of the Great Mughals

# The Empire
# of the Great Mughals

## History, Art and Culture

Annemarie Schimmel

Translated by Corinne Attwood

Edited by Burzine K. Waghmar

With a Foreword by Francis Robinson

REAKTION BOOKS

Published by REAKTION BOOKS LTD
79 Farringdon Road
London EC1M 3JU, UK

www.reaktionbooks.co.uk

First published in English 2004

This is a revised edition of a book published in 2000 by Verlag C. H. Beck under the title *Im Reich der Grossmoguln: Geschichte, Kunst, Kultur* by Annemarie Schimmel © Verlag C. H. Beck oHG, München 2000

English-language translation © Reaktion Books 2004

The publication of this translation was subsidized by a grant from INTER NATIONES, Bonn

This edition is published with the assistance of the Al-Sabah Collection, Kuwait

British Library Cataloguing in Publication Data
Schimmel, Annemarie, 1922–2003
    The empire of the great Mughals : history, art and culture
    1. Art, Mogul  2. Mogul Empire  3. Mogul Empire - Civilization
    I. Title
    954'.025
    ISBN 1 86189 185 7

# Contents

1. 'The Ottoman Sultan Bayazid in a cage at Timur's court', *c.* 1680, gouache with gold on an album leaf.

# Foreword

*by* Francis Robinson

Supporting an estimated 100 million people and producing cash crops and textiles for export, the Mughal empire, which was ruled from 1526 to 1707 by a series of remarkable men, was the greatest of the Muslim gunpowder empires of the early modern era. It outstripped by far the Uzbek state of Central Asia with its five million people, Safawid Iran with six to eight million, and the Ottoman empire with its roughly twenty-two million people scattered across its Asian and European territories. Indeed, at the time the Mughal empire was rivalled only by the Ming empire of China. From the perspective of the present, the Mughal empire led to major geopolitical outcomes: although in no way proselytising, it continued the framework of Islamic power in South Asia, set up from the thirteenth century by the Delhi Sultanate, which enabled the massive conversion of South Asian populations to Islam to the point that they now represent one third of the Muslim world; through this development the centre of gravity in the Muslim world has shifted so that in the twenty-first century more Muslims live east of Afghanistan than to the west; and thus from the eighteenth century to the present, South Asia has increasingly become a source of new ideas and new organization for the Muslim world as a whole.

From the perspective of the early modern era, the Mughal empire in South Asia was the arena in which Mongol traditions of rule and empire, which reached back through Timur to Chingiz Khan (Mughal is an arabized transliteration of Moghol, the Persian term for Mongol), and the high culture of Iran and Central Asia long patronized by Mongol and Timurid rulers, came to be united with the wealth and the talents of South Asian peoples. The outcome was an extraordinary period of power and patronage in which persianate high culture was brought to a new peak. Thus, India for seventeenth-century Europe was a vision of riches; the word Mughal to this day is loaded with a sense of power; and the Taj Mahal is arguably the most admired building of the past four centuries.

No scholar was better equipped to evoke the cultural achievement of the Mughals than Annemarie Schimmel, who died in January 2003. For her fellow scholars she was, as the Mughals might have declared, 'the wonder of the age'. Born in Erfurt, Germany, in 1922, from early on her prodigious gifts were evident. Drawn to the world of Islamic culture by Goethe's *West-östlicher Divan* and by Friedrich Rückert's translations of Arabic and Persian poetry, she began to learn Arabic aged fifteen. She left school two years early, aged sixteen. By the age of nineteen she had completed her first doctoral thesis, and by the age of twenty-four her *Habilitationsschrift* (post-doctoral) thesis. By this time she was already teaching at Marburg University. From 1954 she taught at the University of Ankara, and from 1967 to her retirement in 1992 she held the chair of Indo-Muslim Languages and Culture in the Department of Near Eastern Languages and Civilizations at Harvard University, where young scholars would come from all over the world to sit at her feet. Annemarie Schimmel was a linguist of uncommon gifts. Apart from Latin and Greek, and half a dozen modern European languages, she knew Arabic, Persian, Turkish, Urdu and Pashto well enough to write and lecture in them. These gifts, moreover, were put to good effect in supporting an extraordinary scholarly output. So numerous were her books that different obituarists stated their number as being 50, 80, nearly 100, and 105, the last estimate probably being closer to the mark. At the heart of her scholarship was her pursuit of an understanding of Sufism, its expression in classical Persian poetry, and in the persianate languages of the Muslim world. Along with these essential tools for understanding persianate high culture that goes back to a book on the Mughals she wrote and illustrated aged sixteen was an immersion in its physical remains that was supported by museum consultancy and annual visits to the subcontinent over forty-five years.

The emphases in Annemarie Schimmel's extraordinary erudition are evident in *The Empire of the Great Mughals*. She does not tell us much about the politics or economies of the empire, but when it comes to religion, the world of women, the imperial household, literature and the arts, we are given a dazzling display of learning.

Mughal princesses are brought to life. The role of clothes, books, jewels, drugs, animals, etc., are elucidated. We learn how men and women of the court travelled, how a daily supply of ice was achieved, and the pastimes courtiers enjoyed. A remarkable world of connoisseurship in the arts is explained, and frequently, but not too frequently, Schimmel draws on her unrivalled store of poetry to reinforce a point. The Mughals left many writings of their own, as did their courtiers and Western visitors to the court. Schimmel uses these voices to guide us through their world. Throughout, she deploys her sources with a sensitivity and sureness of touch that came from a profound knowledge of, and respect for, the Mughals and their achievement. I recall, over thirty years ago, R. A. Leigh, who spent a lifetime producing an edition of the correspondence of Jean Jacques Rousseau, musing on the loss to the world each time a great scholar died. *The Empire of the Great Mughals* could only have been written by Annemarie Schimmel. It is hard to imagine that we shall see anyone capable of producing such a book again.

# Editorial Notes

*by* Burzine K. Waghmar

The original German edition of the present work was published in 2000, two years prior to Annemarie Schimmel's untimely death, and almost a decade after her retirement from Harvard University. Although she had earlier examined the poetics, calligraphy and religion of the Mughal era in various scholarly papers, *Im Reich der Grossmoguln: Geschichte, Kunst, Kultur* was the only volume on the Mughals in her vast *œuvre* spanning over half a century.

It is hoped that this edition will be both instructive and appealing to an English-speaking readership, especially students of Indo-Islamic history, for whom no comprehensive treatment is currently available of daily life during the Mughal era. This is because in the expanding corpus of Mughal literature, one observes, in the main, either monographs by specialists (fiscal administration, architecture, etc.) or *histoire événementielle* narratives embellished with illustrations depicting Mughal splendour, also popularly evinced in miniatures, tourist brochures, cuisine and those ornately painted arched palace windows on the national carrier, Air India.

Corinne Attwood carefully translated this work; my task has chiefly been to scrutinize her translation and the quoted extracts from German and oriental literary sources; factual inconsistencies embedded in the German original have also been rectified insofar as fundamental details are concerned. Matters of interpretation – such is the nature of scholarship – constitute an author's prerogative, and one is loathe to tamper with a posthumous edition. Numerous illustrations of relatively lesser-known paintings and *realia* have been added to complement those included in the original edition. Both the glossary and the map have been extensively revised. A note explaining Islamic dating and orthography is included below.

For illustrations I acknowledge the personal co-operation of Dr Madhuvanti Ghose, SOAS, University of London; Dr Jennifer Howes, The British Library, London; and Alison Ohta, Royal Asiatic Society, London. The copyright permission and support of J. C. Grover and Dr W. Siddiqui of the National Museum and Rampur Raza Library respectively towards despatching slides from India is also noted. All other individuals and institutions have been appropriately acknowledged separately (see the Photo Acknowledgements). My thanks to Dr Giles Tillotson, who through Hilary Smith, initially suggested that I consider acting as editor for this project proposed by Reaktion

Books. I would like to thank the Reaktion staff for their help. Professor J. Michael Rogers, a colleague of the late Annemarie Schimmel, read the first draft of the translated typescript. I am indebted for his comments, which very wholly and substantially facilitated this endeavour.

## ISLAMIC DATING AND ORTHOGRAPHY

Islamic dates cited here precede their Gregorian counterparts. Muslims reckon their years on the basis of a lunar or *hijri* (AH) calendar beginning with the prophet Muhammad's flight from Mecca to Medina in 622 CE; and their year is shorter falling generally between two consecutive years of the Common Era. For example, AH 1425 = 2004–05 CE. A convenient reference guide is G.S.P. Freeman-Grenville, *The Islamic and Christian Calendars AD 622–2222 (AH 1–1650): A Complete Guide for Converting Christian and Islamic Dates and Dates of Festivals* (Reading, 1995).

A compromise rather than a standard system of transliterating Islamic and Indo-Pakistani languages is necessary in a work not exclusively written for scholars. It would be superfluous for specialists already aware of the discussed terms and beguiling to others. A lack of uniformity will be discernible, but generally all diacritics have been dispensed with except the *ayn* (ᶜ) and *hamza* (ʾ), the voiced pharyngeal fricative and glottal stop respectively. Also, the letters *yā* (y) and *waw* (w) have been transcribed with certain qualifications. The semivowel *y* denoted the long vowels ē and ī whose phonemic distinction, unlike that in modern Persian, is still maintained in Afghan and South Asian pronunciation thus *Zeb un-nisa* instead of *Zib un-nisa*. In most cases, contemporary Persian usage has been adopted here where all

long vowels are transcribed as *i*, but with exceptions, such as *Bedil* not *Bidel* and Sher Khan not Shir Khan, lest it imply a different name when really referring to the same person. The letter *w* represents the semivowel *w* or the long vowels ō and ū. The traditional distinction of these phonemes is still retained in Afghanistan and South Asia, though all long vowels, as in modern Persian, are generally transcribed here as *u*. The letter *w* has been preferred instead of *v*, as for example, *wazir* rather than *vezir* or the somewhat quaint *vezier*. The dipthong *aw* is modified to *au* because *Aurangzeb* is familiar in English and *Awrangzib* would be excessively pedantic. All geographical names are expressed by their regular English spellings, hence *Delhi* and not *Dihli*. The correspondence between the Hindi-Urdu feminine ending and the Persian adjectival suffix *–i* will be noticed in certain constructs such as the honorific *Maryam–i makani*. All terms in the Glossary, as in the original edition, have been transliterated for the benefit of the student with some knowledge of Islamic or Indo-Pakistani languages. Titles of books and articles remain unmodified.

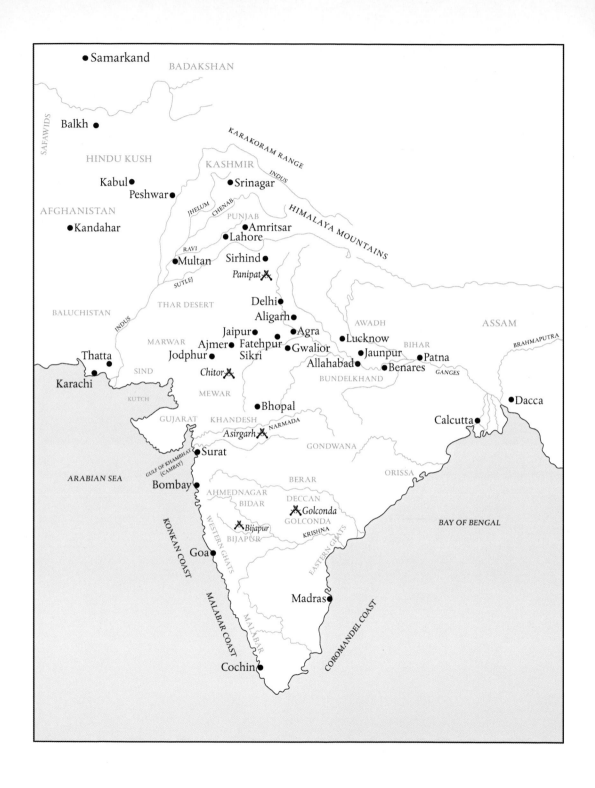

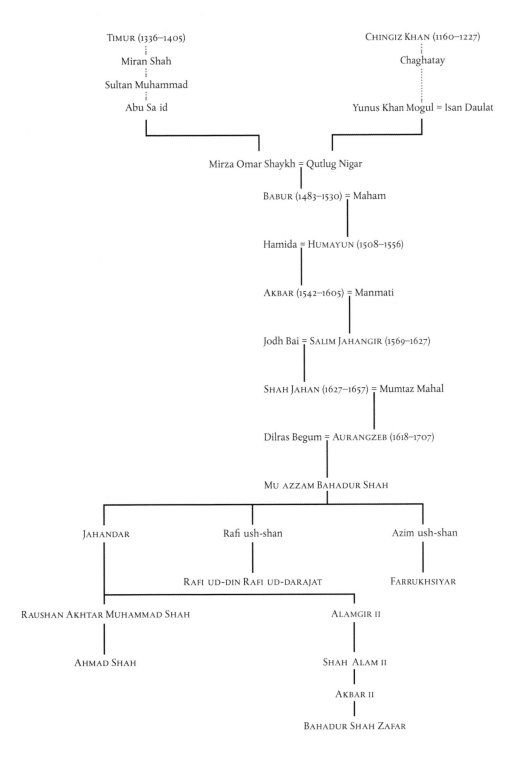

TIMUR (1336–1405)                CHINGIZ KHAN (1160–1227)

Miran Shah                Chaghatay

Sultan Muhammad

Abu Sa id             Yunus Khan Mogul = Isan Daulat

Mirza Omar Shaykh = Qutlug Nigar

BABUR (1483–1530) = Maham

Hamida = HUMAYUN (1508–1556)

AKBAR (1542–1605) = Manmati

Jodh Bai = SALIM JAHANGIR (1569–1627)

SHAH JAHAN (1627–1657) = Mumtaz Mahal

Dilras Begum = AURANGZEB (1618–1707)

MU AZZAM BAHADUR SHAH

JAHANDAR        Rafi ush-shan        Azim ush-shan

RAFI UD-DIN RAFI UD-DARAJAT        FARRUKHSIYAR

RAUSHAN AKHTAR MUHAMMAD SHAH        ALAMGIR II

AHMAD SHAH        SHAH ALAM II

AKBAR II

BAHADUR SHAH ZAFAR

# Prologue

Our judgment of the past is not immutable. The reputations of all great historical figures fluctuate in the assessments of later generations, and there is never a final verdict.

History books reveal more about the writers and their age than about their subject matter. We know little enough about our own deep motives, or the people close to us, let alone about our contemporaries, whom we observe directly; yet we delude ourselves that we can learn the truth about generations and individuals in the far distant past from whatever evidence happens to be available.

Carl J. Burckhardt, 'Thoughts Regarding Charles V', in *Portraits* (1958)

In Milton's *Paradise Lost*, the great Mughal cities of Agra and Lahore are revealed to Adam after the Fall as future wonders of God's creation.

For Europeans in the seventeenth and eighteenth centuries, the Great Mughal Empire seemed like a wonderland of fabulous riches, priceless jewels and golden treasure. The word *Mughal* still retains something of this connotation, denoting a man of immense power and 'exotic' wealth. However, Mughal is in fact an Arabization of the Persian word for Mongol, and was originally synonymous with barbarian. The Mughals called themselves The House of Timur, after the conqueror of Central Asia, who died in 1405.

Babur, the founder of the Mughal empire, was a direct descendant of Timur, being descended from the Mongol ruler Chingiz Khan through the maternal line.

No other dynasty in the Islamic world has left behind more comprehensive historical documentation than the Mughals. Two of the great rulers, Babur and his great-grandson Jahangir, kept personal diaries recording their lives, their adventures and their loves. There are official and unofficial historical records detailing not only great events but also the minutiae of daily life at court and in the political sphere, such as Princess Gulbadan's vivid stories about her brother Humayun, or

2. Govardhan, 'Timur handing the imperial crown to Babur in the presence of Humayun', a leaf from a dispersed album made for Shah Jahan, *c.* 1630, gouache and gold on paper.

Bada'uni's acerbic chronicle of life in Akbar's time, contrasting with the overblown hagiography of his contemporary and theological opponent Fazl, whose detailed descriptions of court administration and household fittings are so comprehensive as to include even a few mouth-watering imperial recipes. Numerous court chronicles were compiled in the following decades, many of them illustrated, such as the *Baburnama*, which was embellished with delightful vivid miniature paintings by artists at the court of his grandson, Akbar. The 'Windsor *Padshahnama*' and other great historical works from the time of Shah Jahan (1628–58) also contain many exquisite pictures.

The relatively little information we have about the common people of the time is derived mainly from the accounts of foreign visitors, such as Portuguese Jesuits at the court of Akbar, and news bulletins from European ambassadors like Sir Thomas Roe, who sent a number of rather critical reports about Jahangir. Somewhat later, many other foreigners, including the French physician Bernier, the French jeweller Tavernier and the Venetian physician Manucci, recorded their sometimes highly imaginative impressions of the private lives of the upper classes and various aspects of daily life. These portrayals created such a dazzling image of the Mughal empire that an early eighteenth-century German jeweller, Johann Melchior Dinglinger, was inspired to create a masterpiece for Augustus the Strong, *Aurangzeb's Birthday Celebrations*, which is now on display in Dresden's Green Vault.

The arts were cultivated under the Mughals. During the century from Akbar's time to that of Shah Jahan, artists painted miniature portraits of all the great ones at court with almost photographic accuracy. The arts of weaving and textiles flourished, costly vessels were produced from jade and nephrite, glittering weapons were embellished with precious stones, manuscripts were richly decorated and magnificently bound.

In the sixteenth century, poems were written in praise of rulers and courtiers in classical Persian, which had been refined over centuries. Mystical poetry was composed in regional languages such as Sindhi, Punjabi, Pashto, and also Hindi. Sanskrit played an important role, while the Turkic language, the Chaghatay-Turkish of the Central Asian regions, was used by the Mughal royal family at home, as was Persian.

Numerous studies by Indian and Western historians have been devoted to Mughal systems of administration, to the complicated social hierarchy of the nobility, their education, agriculture, system of government and many other aspects of life. Countless documents relating to these subjects lie gathering dust in the archives of various Indian states and in private collections. It is extremely difficult to unravel the complex family relationships and ever-changing political and military offices, especially since a change of office or a new title often entailed an additional name.

The interrelationship among the Indian religions has primarily interested both admirers and critics, many finding themselves mired in the many shades of Islam, from the strictest fundamentalism to ecstatic Sufism. The majority of the population were Hindus, but the Christian, Jewish, Parsi, Jain and many other religions contributed threads to the colourful tapestry of a multi-faith empire.

Of all the great Mughals, it is Akbar to whom the most studies have been devoted. Because of his apparent renunciation of Islam he was damned by orthodox Indo-Muslim historians, but revered as the 'shadow of God on earth' and the greatest of all the Indo-Muslim rulers by the mystically inclined and by members of a peace movement founded on a belief in the essential unity of everything. In the case of Akbar's grandson Aurangzeb, this judgement was reversed.

Even people who know nothing of the history and culture of the Mughal dynasty have heard of the Taj Mahal in Agra, the mausoleum of the wife of Shah Jahan, the mother of his fourteen children, who died in childbirth in 1631. This almost translucent-seeming building has become a symbol for the whole world of beauty and love.

The empire maintained its splendour for almost two centuries, until Aurangzeb's death in 1707 ushered in a century and a half of slow and painful decline, culminating in the failed uprising of 1857. The 'Mutiny' consolidated British rule over the former Mughal domains, and in 1858 Queen Victoria became the Empress of India.

I have been interested in the Mughals since my childhood. I wrote a book on Islamic culture at the age of sixteen, which I illustrated with my own drawings, some showing the Taj Mahal and I'timad ad-daula's mausoleum, and portraits of twelve Mughal rulers. During the course of almost annual visits to India and Pakistan since 1958, I have had the opportunity to visit all of the buildings mentioned in this book, and, thanks to the generosity of my hosts, to experience the continuity of the fine traditions of the Mughal period in contemporary extended family life. I have often met individuals who reminded me of a face in a Mughal miniature, as if the many races and human groups were still alive to this day. There, for instance, is a girl with a lock of hair over her ear just like Jahangir, who looks exactly like him in profile – she must be descended from the Mughals; a colleague in Lucknow looks just as if he had come from Bukhara; a man at the university looks just like a handsome Rajput prince I have often encountered in pictures. So I came to feel that I had actually experienced Mughal culture for myself.

During the time that I held the chair for Indo-Muslim culture at Harvard University from 1967 to 1992, I was primarily interested in the religious and literary life of the Mughal period. I was also fortunate to be able to work for a decade as a special consultant in the Islamic department of New York's Metropolitan Museum of Art.

During my teens, one of my most treasured possessions was Ernst Kühnel's beautiful catalogue titled *Islamic Miniatures from the State Museums of Berlin*, so I was delighted to be able to assist with the preparation of the magnificent exhibition entitled *INDIA!* in the summer of 1985. It was a source of tremendous joy to me to be able to work with Stuart Cary Welch, with whom I collaborated on many publications.

It has been my privilege to meet virtually everyone involved with Mughal art. Ebba Koch and I have travelled together through old Delhi. Many of my students have shed new light on aspects of the Mughal period over the years. During my time at Harvard, the great symposium on Fatehpur Sikri was held there, in 1989. It was always a pleasure to discuss Deccani art and precious *Bidri*-ware with Mark Zebrowski, who, alas, passed away all too soon.

In India, I am indebted to Jagdish Mittal's wonderful collection in Hyderabad, in the Deccan, and to the wealth of information on Mughal administration and traditions from my good friend Dr Zia A. Shakeb, who has long since settled in London. London became practically my second home too, thanks to the ever-hospitable Philippa Vaughan, with whom I used to discuss Mughal painting and artistic patronage, commencing over breakfast. The museums and libraries in London are treasure troves of all kinds of Indian objects, and my colleagues there – Robert Skelton, Michael Rogers and Jeremiah Losty – were most helpful to me, as were the directors of the Royal Asiatic Society.

In Germany, Dr H. O. Feistel at the Staatsbibliothek Preussischer Kulturbesitz, and Dr Volkmar Enderlein at the Islamic Museum in Berlin, were ever willing to give advice and show photographs, as were the staff of the Museum für Völkerkunde in Munich, and the Linden-Museum in Stuttgart. I am grateful to Dr Dorothea Duda in Vienna for the *Kataloge der österreichischen Miniaturmanuskripte*, also for detailed information concerning the Millionenzimmer in the palace of Schönbrunn. Finally, Dr Eberhard Fischer at the Rietberg Museum in Zurich has always been a source of help and inspiration.

Many friends in Lahore, Karachi, Peshawar and Islamabad were able to throw light on the history and art of the Mughal period by means of symposia and publications of innumerable Persian and Urdu works. I am indebted to them for much advice and information over the years. My friends in various museums in the USA have been constant sources of stimulation and also of gifts – in particular Daniel Walker, the head of the Islamic Department of the Metropolitan Museum of Art, who provided me with access to his work on Mughal carpets, as well as an introduction to the Cincinnati Art Museum.

Thanks are also due to my former students at Harvard, among them Wheeler M. Thackston, whose numerous new translations and editions of the most important Mughal texts have provided historians with readable versions in modern American English; also to Ali S. Asani for his painstaking research in obscure sources outside Germany.

Friends in Bonn have replied to my queries relating to their own spheres of work in science and medicine, among them Clas Naumann, the director of the Museum König, and Christian Kellersmann. Stefan Wild and his assistants at the Oriental Seminar at Bonn University provided practical assistance with unfailing amiability. Gudrun Schubert in Lörrach proofread the manuscript and contributed to its development during frequent telephone discussions. It was a great pleasure to work with my editors at C. H. Beck, Dr Marla Stukenberg and Angelika Schneider.

# ONE

# Historical Introduction

Some background knowledge of the history of the Mughals is an essential prerequisite to a study of Mughal culture, in the broadest sense of the word; however, the subject-matter is too vast to permit more than a brief overview. There is a great deal of source material, and conflicting interpretations by experts. The difficulties readers encounter are compounded by the fact that readers are continuously confronted by new names, titles and offices, the incumbents of which are forever becoming entangled in intrigues and changes of side. As a consequence, the history of the Mughal rulers can appear to be an all but hopelessly tangled skein, petering out ignominiously in the eighteenth century. Innumerable battles were fought, some in which the outstanding bravery of the first generations of heroes triumphed over all manner of enemies, but others in which cowardice and weakness coupled with cruelty led to unexpected and sometimes unmerited defeat.

No attempt has been made to chronicle all of these facts or to disentangle the webs of intrigue, for an intrigue of some kind is behind almost every development. The lives of Akbar's amirs, as described by Pilloth in his new edition of the English translation of Abuʾl Fazl's ʿAʾin-i Akbari are just as confusing as the more than seven hundred biographies in Shamsham ad-daula's Maʾathir al-umara.

I have been able to provide little more than a brief sketch of my own particular area of interest – family relationships and Mughal marriages. Although the latter were always contracted to serve dynastic interests, they were nevertheless often great love stories.

Fortunately there are portraits of almost all the Mughal rulers, a few of which are included to illustrate this historical outline.

3. The Emperor Babur, *c.* 1630–40, gouache on paper, from an album of Dara Shikoh.

## ZAHIR UD-DIN BABUR, *firdausmakani*

'he whose realm is paradise' (1483–1530)

No authentic portraits of the first Mughal ruler are known. The illustrations accompanying his fascinating journals date from the time of his grandson, Akbar, when his autobiography was translated into Persian, and copies were made in three exquisite calligraphies. The illustrators naturally tended to portray the face of the founder of the dynasty with features somewhat resembling those of Akbar, with perhaps a hint more Turkish in them. In the manuscripts of the *Baburnama* he appears as a vigorous young hero, a dashing knight, a conqueror who laid the foundations of his Indian empire in 1526, only four years before his untimely death in a fall at the Purana Qila in Delhi.

After his death, Babur's body was taken from Hindustan, where he had been revered rather than loved, and returned to Kabul, the scene of his early triumphs, where most of his children were born. There he was laid to rest in a small open pavilion.

'In Ramadan 899 (June 1494) at the age of twelve (= lunar years) I became ruler of the province of Ferghana', wrote Zahir ud-din Babur in his autobiography, one of the most important works of

Chaghatay-Turkish literature. His father was ʿUmar Shaykh, a direct descendent of Timur, who as a true Timurid bore the title *Mirza*. The Mughals ('The House of Timur') maintained their strong connections with Central Asia. To the end of his life Jahangir used to question visitors from Samarkand about the condition of the Gur Amir, Timur's mausoleum, and sent gold to pay for its upkeep.[1]

Babur's mother was the daughter of the Mughal Yunus Khan, a descendent of Chingiz Khan. After his death his dynamic widow devoted her energies to her grandchildren. Babur's relatives, who ruled more or less independently over most of central Asia and the land now known as Afghanistan, did not make life easy for the young man. His autobiography, in which family relationships are delineated in great detail, may well have been written partly in order to clarify his right to rule as the successor both to Timur and, on his mother's side, Chingiz Khan.[2]

Babur's early years were taken up with campaigns to subjugate new territories. At the age of fourteen he besieged Samarkand and won it, only to lose it not long afterwards to a relative. After a second unsuccessful siege he wandered for a time as a refugee, or more accurately, a knight errant. He may have felt more at home in the nomadic Mughal traditions than among his urbanized Timurid relatives. In his diary he describes with some pleasure the honour of being presented with nine standards and a Mughal gown during a Mongolian yak tail ceremony.

In 1504 Babur left Farghana for good and set off for Khorasan, where, he writes, he 'shaved for the first time', and so came to maturity. He mentions with pride the fact that his mother, who was almost as active as his grandmother in her day, accompanied him on many of his expeditions. Once, during particularly difficult circumstances,

his mother was given use of the only tent that he and his small troop possessed.

In the same year he took Kabul, which became and remained his favourite place. Kabul was then an important trading centre on the route from India to Central Asia, and there were succulent fruits and excellent wines. Babur was amazed at the many different races of people he saw there, and the many languages and dialects that he heard.[3]

In 1506 Babur paid his first visit to Herat, the residence of his distant uncle Husayn Bayqara, who died not long afterwards. Babur was something of a poet himself, and was somewhat critical of his uncle's poetry. Babur was fascinated by Herat, and his descriptions of the city still make interesting reading today. Among his notable finds there was a pavilion with murals depicting the heroic deeds of the Timurid Abu Saʿid Mirza. Later, during the Mughal period in India, murals were a prominent feature of castles and palaces. Babur describes the large drinking parties held by his relatives, where even the men danced; he admits that he did not know how to cut up a goose breast during a celebration feast. Unfortunately, it was at Herat that he acquired the taste for alcohol that was to become the bane of the Mughal family.

Babur set off back for Kabul, battling through snow and ice. There he created his first garden, in the classic Persian *charbagh* style, a garden divided into four by small canals. In miniatures he is depicted overseeing the gardeners as they water the flowers.[4] Gardening was to become a favourite activity with his descendants.

In January 1505 Babur made his first journey to India, traversing Kohat and Bannu (known today as the tribal area in north-west Pakistan) with a small troop to reach the Indus. They fought the Afghans, who surrendered 'with grass between their teeth', by which he meant in abject humiliation. Although these were primarily raids of pillage for booty, such as the nomads' plump sheep, rather than campaigns of conquest, Babur upheld Timur's tradition of constructing towers with the skulls of vanquished enemies on these occasions. Discipline in his encampments was harsh: anyone who missed the night watch had his nose split in two.

By this time Babur had several wives, and on 6 March 1508 his son Humayun was born in Kabul to his favourite wife, Maham. From this time on the proud father took the title *Padshah* instead of *Mirza*. Unfortunately, the important years 1509 to 1519, during which he secured his position in Afghanistan and dealt harshly with lawbreakers, are missing from the chronicles.

From this time on, his incursions into India intensified. In 1519, when another son was born to him, as a good omen he called the child by the Turkish name Hindal, which means 'Take India!'. In Kallarkahar in the Salt Range he made his followers swear an oath to remain loyal to him during future campaigns. In his journals he describes the advance towards Hindustan, the region beyond the land of the five rivers.

In 1526 Babur's 1,500 soldiers attacked the estimated 100,000 cavalry and 1,000 elephants of the Lodi rulers at Panipat, a broad, rather flat region near Delhi, where Babur's army won a decisive victory for the Mughal empire. Afterwards Babur travelled to Delhi to visit the mausoleums of the two great holy men of that city, the Chishti master Nizamuddin Auliya, who died in 1325, and his fellow order member Qutbuddin Bakhtiyar Kaki, who died in 1235 and who, like the conqueror himself, was from Ush in Central Asia. (In 1556 and 1761, Panipat was yet again the site of decisive battles with many casualties, when 'the spirit birds of many fled the cages of their bodies, whilst the wings of others were clipped by the blades of double-edged swords'.)

The conqueror's detailed descriptions of the flora and fauna of India are fascinating, in some cases amusing. Babur marvelled at the sight of elephants and rhinoceroses, but considered that 'the screeching of parrots is as hideous as the sound of broken porcelain being scraped across a metal plate'. He liked mangoes and bananas, but compared jackfruit to the 'revolting' intestines of sheep. He learned that schnaps (toddy) was made from the Palmyra palm, and that the leaves of this tree could be used to write on, and much more. However, on the whole he found India to be a 'not very attractive place'.

Babur's soldiers did not like India either; one of his most loyal officers, Khwaja Kalan, composed the following verse:

If I pass the Sind safe and sound,
May shame take me if I ever again wish for Hind!

Babur replied, in verse, naturally, that he should, in fact, be grateful:

Return a hundred thanks, O Babur, for the bounty of the merciful God
Has given you Sind, Hind, and numerous kingdoms;
If unable to stand the heat, you long for cold;
You have only to recollect the frost and great cold of Ghazni!

Babur himself threw himself into improving India. In Agra, which became his imperial seat, he constructed a garden that included a cascading fountain and a *hammam*, the typical Islamic bath that was then unknown in India.

4. James Atkinson, 'The Tomb of the Emperor Baber' near Kabul, 1839–40, watercolour, from a series of *Sketches in Afghaunistan.*

Meanwhile, his enemies were not idle. Rana Sangha enthroned another Lodi prince, who was then defeated in battle by Babur at Khanwa in 1527. After this victory over the most powerful Hindu prince of the region, Babur then added to his name the title *ghazi* – fighter for the faith. He composed the following verse in Chaghatay:

> For the sake of Islam I became a vagabond,
> I fought with Hindus, and with many
>   heathens,
> I was ready to die as a martyr,
> But thanks be to God! I became a hero of
>   the faith!

Babur later mentioned a meeting with the mystic Muhammad Ghauth Gwaliari (died 1562), the highest authority on the invocation of the name of God, whose brother Shah Phul later became Humayun's adviser.

Babur continued his travels and conquests. During a visit to Gwalior, he was disturbed by the sight of the enormous statues of naked Jain holy men, which can still today be seen on the ascent to the fortress.[5]

After a victory against Rana Sangha, Babur devoted himself somewhat more to his family. In 1528 the women of the harem travelled from Kabul to India, and ten-year-old Hindal received some beautiful presents: a jewelled inkwell, a footstool inlaid with mother of pearl, a short robe of his father's, and an alphabet. Humayan, the successor to the throne, received only a reprimand for his complicated letter-writing style and spelling mistakes. For Babur was also a man of letters, whose works on the metre of Persian poetry, on *Hanafi* law and other themes are important works of Chaghatay-Turkish. He even invented his own form of writing, the *khatt-i baburi*.

As a sign of his possession of India, Babur had the route from Agra to Kabul surveyed and marked with milestones. Then he began to set his sights on the east. He had a ship built, with several decks and equipped with a cabin, which he named *Asayish*, 'peace'. It was probably this boat which provided the model for many fanciful miniatures, among them a delightful painting of Noah's Ark with all the animals of the world on its numerous decks.[6]

The athletic Babur boasted of having swum across the Ganges with only thirty-three strokes in each direction, indeed of having swum across every river he had ever encountered.

He reached Bengal in 1529, the same year that Sher Khan Suri, 'on whom I had conferred my patronage only the previous year', pledged his country's allegiance to the rebellious Afghans. The Sur family were Pashtuns, and it was this same Sher Khan who barely a decade later would drive Babur's favourite son Humayun out of India.

At the end of the decade Humayun became danagerously ill. Babur carried out the full ceremonial rites to cure his son by taking his son's illness upon himself. On 26 December 1530 Babur died at the age of forty-six, and Humayun became the next ruler – and the envy of his brothers Kamran, Hindal and ᶜAskari.

5. Nasir ud-din Humayun in a tree-house, detail from the border of a Jahangir Album, c. 1608–18, painting on paper.

## NASIR UD-DIN HUMAYUN, *jannat ashiyani*

'he who is nested in heaven' (1508–1556)

Humayun's great interest in the arts encouraged the first Iranian artists to move to Kandahar and Kabul, and from there to Agra and Delhi. Their portraits of the king depict him as rather lean, with a narrow face, usually wearing an elegant Chaghatay hat with an upturned broad brim. The most beautiful and, of course, true to life portraits depict him in a romantic landscape, and allude to his interest in spiritual matters, in astrology and magic, rather than his liking for sensual pleasures – women and opium. Anyone looking at these portraits must wonder how such a delicate-looking prince could first lose, and then regain, his father's empire before his untimely death in the Purana Qila in Delhi.

Historians have been so impressed by Babur's steadfast bravery, his literary talent and his earthy sense of humour, and they have heaped so much praise on his grandson Akbar, that Humayun has been put in the shade by both father and son. But one historian's conclusion, that he 'stumbled into death as he had stumbled through life', is certainly too harsh an epitaph.

Humayun was not a hero like his father. His interests lay primarily in the spheres of mysticism, magic and astrology, which played a central role in his life. He always chose the appropriate day for any activity by reference to the constellations of the stars, and he would only receive certain classes of underlings on specific days. Long after Humayun's death, one of his loyal servants presented his grandson with a manual written by Humayun, containing prayers, astronomical observations and similar texts.

Humayun was intensely religious. His piety went to such lengths that he would only utter one of the names of God in a state of ritual purity, even when the name formed only part of a person's surname – for example, someone by the name of *Abdul Karim*, which means 'servant of the Merciful One', would be addressed simply as *Abdul*; *Karim*, being one of the names of God, would be dropped.

Two biographies portray Humayun as a peaceable and very humane ruler. One of these was written by his half-sister Gulbadan, at the request of her nephew Akbar. The other is the journal of his 'ewer bearer', *aftabji* Jauhar, who accompanied the ruler everywhere for more than twenty years as his trusted valet.

There was a great celebration for Humayan's coronation in 1530, during which he distributed twelve thousand robes of honour, among them two thousand gold brocade tunics with gilt buttons.

Humayun's half brothers Kamran, ʿAskari and Hindal were plotting to seize power for themselves;[1] Humayun, however, tried to follow his father's request to do nothing to harm his brothers.

He did not take advantage of an opportunity to attack the ruler of Gujarat during that ruler's unsuccessful siege of Chitor. In 1532 Humayun let the Pashtun leader Sher Khan Suri take the strong fortress of Rohtas in Bihar by cunning, smuggling in his soldiers disguised as women, perhaps because he was unaware of what was happening.

Not long afterwards Gaur, Bihar and Jaunpur – the region of the lower Ganges – also fell into the hands of the clever Pashtun leader.

A report by Jauhar concerning an early military foray reveals Humayun's character:

At Mandu a deserter presented himself. The officers wanted to torture him to make him reveal where the enemy had hidden its treasure. Humayun replied: 'Since this man has come to me of his own free will, it would not be magnanimous to use force against him. If success can be achieved by means of kindness, why use harsh measures? Order a banquet to be prepared. Ply the man with wine, and then ask him where the treasure is hidden.'

In 1538 Humayun set off for Bengal, 'and unfurled the carpet of pleasures'; in other words, he abandoned himself to a lengthy period of carefree living in the lap of luxury. Meanwhile, his brothers were starting their rebellion. Hindal had the mystic and magician Shah Phul, Humayun's spiritual guide, called to Benares and killed. He then had the Friday sermon in Agra recited in his own name instead of Humayun's. As Humayun was making his way over the Ganges with a weak army, his way at Chausa was barred by Sher Khan. The two armies confronted each other for three months, then after an apparent declaration of peace, battle commenced on 25 June 1539. A bridge collapsed and many people drowned, 'dragged by the crocodile of death down into the waters of annihilation', a number of women among them. The Mughal army was decimated. Now Sher Khan had the Friday sermon in Bengal recited in his name, and took the title Sher Shah. Shamsuddin Atga of Ghazna, who saved Humayun from drowning, was later honoured by having his wife, Jiji Anaga, appointed as a nurse to his son

Akbar. Shamsuddin Atga himself later became one of the most powerful of men under Akbar.

The same year, 1539, Babur's cousin Mirza Haydar Dughlat went to India; his historical work *Tarikh-i rashidi* is a valuable source of information on the situation in the north of the subcontinent at the time.

Humayun's brothers now pressed their advantage. Kamran Mirza and Hindal travelled to Lahore from Kandahar, where there was a strong Mughal garrison. A Mughal army was defeated by Sher Shah. Kamran and ᶜAskari then advanced on Kabul. Humayun had no option but to flee.

Sher Shah's rule in the north of the subcontinent is famous as an interlude of order and good government. The Pashtun ruler built the Grand Trunk Road that today still links Bengal with Peshawar. He had 1,800 caravanserais and numerous fountains set up between Sonargon in Bengal and the Indus. On the Jhelum river, not far from present day Islamabad, he constructed the mighty fortress of Rohtas along the lines of his citadel in Bihar. Criminals were severely punished, and it was safe to travel along the roads. Badaᵓuni, who was undoubtedly impartial, was full of praise for the ruler in his chronicle. However, Sher Shah and his son Islam Shah persecuted the Mahdawi sect mercilessly. In 1545 Sher Shah was killed in a gunpowder explosion, and his son succeeded him as ruler.

Babur's sons now spread out across the country. Hindal took Mewat, the region near Delhi, Kamran took the Punjab, ᶜAskari got Sanbhal, whilst Mirza Sulayman, a cousin, established himself in Badakhshan. Humayun fled from his brothers and Sher Shah to Sind. For seven months he laid siege to Sehwan on the lower Indus without success. His friends deserted him, and for a while he was close to starving. For months he wandered between Sind and Rajasthan with his small group of faithful allies, including the women of the harem. During a sojourn in Sind he found a new love, the fourteen-year old Hamida, of Persian extraction, who gave birth to his son Akbar on 15 October 1542 in Umarkot. At his birth, the proud father smeared the child with musk so that his scent would permeate the world. Still the ruler without a country continued his peregrinations, which were becoming ever more arduous. He decided to make for Kandahar, which Hindal had taken and then given to his brother ᶜAskari. They crossed the mountain range, where it was so cold that Jauhar Aftabji complained that 'the soup freezes as it is being poured from the pot onto the plate'.[2] Gulbadan described the problems Humayun's troops experienced with camels:

> In seven, no, seventy generations they had seen neither city nor load nor any human beings ... As soon as a camel was mounted, it tossed the rider to the ground and made off into the woods. Every pack camel, when it heard the sound of horses' hooves, reared and bucked and threw its burden down and bolted. If the pack was so securely fastened that the camel couldn't throw it off, the animal would race off with its burden. This was the state of affairs as the ruler set out for Kabul ...

The situation was to deteriorate still further when they had put the Indus Valley behind them. They passed one night in the snow, weak from hunger, so the emperor ordered a horse to be killed. There was no cooking pot, so everyone cooked a piece of meat in their helmets, and they roasted some of it. They lit fires on all four sides, and the emperor roasted some meat with his own blessed hand, and then ate it. He said, 'My head is completely frozen from the cold.' In the morning they saw a pair of wild Baluchis, whose language is the tongue of the demons of the desert . . .[3]

Humayun saw that his only hope of salvation lay in seeking asylum in Iran. Little Akbar had been placed in the care of Humayun's eldest wife, and had been taken to Kabul under extremely difficult circumstances. In 1554 Humayun and his young wife Hamida reached Iran, and were taken in by Shah Tahmasp, the son of the founder of the Safawid dynasty. The couple visited a series of holy shrines, among them the mausoleum of Hamida's ancestor the great Sufi Ahmad-i Jam (died 1141). On 29 December 1544 Humayun had the following Persian verse inscribed on one of the walls of the mausoleum:

Oh Thou whose mercy accepts the soul of all,
The mind of everyone is exposed to thy
    Majesty,
The threshold of thy gate is the *qibla* of all
    people,
Thy bounty with a glance supports everyone.
Muhammad Humayun,
The wanderer in the desert of destruction.[4]

There are detailed descriptions, especially by Jauhar Aftabji, of the enjoyable as well as the trying aspects of Humayun's journey through Iran. The fleeing ruler is said to have approached the Iranian emperor with the following verse, which contains a pun on his name 'Humayun':

Everyone takes refuge in the *huma* shade –
Now see before you the *huma*, coming under
    your shadow!

It was believed that anyone on whom the shadow of the *huma* bird fell would become the emperor.

Shah Tahmasp, who had been made ruler at a young age by the death of his father Shah Isma'il in 1524, was apparently somewhat volatile. He had recently undergone a period of 'sincere penitence', and he now tried by various means to convert Humayun to Shi'i Islam. Aftabji relates that Tahmasp asked the fugitive Humayun to fetch him a pile of firewood. Tahmasp then informed Humayun that if he did not convert to Shi'i Islam, then he would use this stack of firewood for his funeral pyre. It ended amicably when Humayun signed the Shi'i doctrine as requested. They parted with an exchange of valuable gifts, at which Humayun presented the Iranian ruler with an enormous diamond.

Fortunately for Humayun, in the course of his wanderings he came upon Bayram Khan, one of his father's soldiers from the Turcoman Qaraqoyunlu clan, who joined forces with him. After travelling through Sistan and Meshed, they succeeded in wresting Kandahar from Kamran's reign of terror, despite the fact that little Akbar was in his keeping at the time, and Kamran threatened to place the infant on the city wall so that Humayun's troops could not fire on the citadel. There are many accounts of the scene when the infant Akbar and his mother were reunited.[5] Kabul became once more a centre for the Mughals, as it had been in Babur's time. Humayun was able to attract some of the best artists of the Safawid empire to Kabul, since their capital Tabriz was no longer a congenial environment for artists following Tahmasp's period of 'sincere penitence'.

Humayun travelled by river raft from Jalalabad to Peshawar, and with Bayram Khan's help succeeded in winning back the territory bequeathed him by his father. He was reconciled with his brother Hindal, who was later fatally wounded during a nocturnal attack by Kamran. Gulbadan,

6. Humayun's tomb, Delhi, 1560s.

his sister, mourned him deeply.[6] In 1552 Kamran fled to the Suri prince Islam Shah. Disguised in a *burqa*[c], he sought refuge with Adam Ghakkar, who ruled the region surrounding the fortress of Rohtas on the Jhelum river in the Punjab, where Kamran was later captured. Humayun could not bring himself to kill his own brother, so he had Kamran blinded instead. Jauhar relates that this was carried out in a horrific way, which caused the prince terrible suffering. Kamran and his wife were sent on a pilgrimage to Mecca, where he died in 1557.

Humayun made his way eastwards, overcoming a detachment of Suri fighters to the east of Lahore. He made Delhi his capital, installing himself in Purana Qila, the ancient castle. There he met his end a few years later, falling from the roof of the library pavilion. Bayram Khan had taken the fourteen-year-old Akbar with him on a military campaign, and allowed the youth to pay homage to his father. The chronicler paid the following tribute to Humayun: 'His angelic character was adorned with every manly virtue; his knowledge of astrology and mathematics was without equal.'

Work soon commenced on Humayun's mausoleum in Delhi near the Jumna, under the supervision of his eldest widow. Construction was completed within eight years, in 1569. It later became a dynastic centre and place of pilgrimage for the Mughals, extolled by Shah Jahan's court poet Kalim.[7]

7. A portrait sketch of Jalal ud-din Akbar, *c.* 1600, drawing on paper.

## JALAL UD-DIN AKBAR, ᶜ*arsh ashiyani*

'he whose nest is on the divine throne of God'
(1542–1605)

Akbar is regarded by many as the greatest of the Mughal rulers of the Indian subcontinent, and more books have been devoted to him than to any other Mughal prince. He has been compared to the Buddhist Emperor Ashoka, while being regarded by orthodox Muslims as a heretic. His face is familiar from numerous paintings, which portray him with typically Turkish high cheekbones and rather narrow eyes. There is also a description of his appearance by his son Jahangir: 'He was of medium stature but inclining to be tall; his complexion was wheaten or nut coloured, rather dark than fair; his eyes and eyebrows dark black and the latter running across into each other; with a handsome person, he had a lion's strength which was indicated by an extraordinary breadth of chest and the length of his arms and hands. On the left side of his nose there was a fleshy wart, about the size of half a pea, which in contemporary eyes appeared exceedingly beautiful, and was considered auspicious of riches and prosperity. His voice was loud and his speech elegant and pleasing, especially when making speeches and issuing proclamations. His manners and habits were different from those of other people, and his visage was full of godly dignity.'[1]

At the age of fourteen, Akbar became the ruler of the small part of India bequeathed him by his father. He was a keen athlete and a fearless and tireless rider. Although he was taught by the best of tutors and became a passionate lover of books and pictures, he had little time for study.

Akbar's reputation as *ummi*, illiterate, has for the most part been taken as fact. He liked to be read to in the evening, he had an incredible memory for poetry and dates, and he even composed a few Persian verses himself in the classical style, none of which, however, rules out the possibility that perhaps he could neither read nor write. In recent times it has been suggested that he might have been dyslexic.[2] However, there is another possible explanation for Akbar's reputed illiteracy. *Ummi*, which is used in the Qur'an (*Sura* 7:157) of Muhammad, has been interpreted by Muslims as meaning 'illiterate', because the Prophet may not be led astray by his intellectual knowledge into confusing his own thoughts with the inspirational knowledge bestowed on him. Thus *ummi*, in the tradition of Islamic mysticism, has come to mean an inspired mystic. Many Sufis have been deemed to be *ummi* by their followers, even though they were the authors of dozens of learned works in Arabic, Persian and other languages, and it is in this sense that the word should be interpreted. Abu'l Fazl, Akbar's venerating biographer, doubtless used the word to portray Akbar as one possessed of ʿilm laduni (*Sura* 18:65), 'knowledge directly from God'. Akbar himself insisted that 'The prophets were all illiterate. Therefore parents should allow one of their sons to remain in this state.'[3] *Ummi*, therefore, perhaps testifies to Akbar's greatness, not to any deficiency. Furthermore, there is one small note written by

him in clear Arabic letters; it is understandable if he did not bother much with writing or reading later in life.

There are two lengthy chronicles about Akbar, as well as a number of small ones. It is clear from the extravagant eulogies by Abu'l Fazl, the son of Akbar's confidant Shaykh Mubarak and brother of the poet laureate Faizi, that he was honoured as a great hero, whose every little act from childhood onwards was interpreted as a sign of divine influence. Akbar's hagiography assimilated the Mongolian legend of Alanquwa, a virgin who was impregnated by a deity, to whom she bore triplets, one of whom was an ancestor of Chingiz Khan's nine generations before, and from whom the Mughals themselves were descended.[4] A light was said to have emanated from Hamida's face before Akbar was born. Indeed, divine glory, *farr-i izadi*, surrounded and permeated him. According to the hagiography, even when Akbar was at play, his movements were interpreted as divine gestures through which he was secretly influencing the course of events in the world.[5]

Abu'l Fazl's great chronicle, the *A'in-i Akbari*, provides a welcome contrast to the reader weary of the overblown hagiographic style of the *Akbarnama*. The three volumes contain the most comprehensive information about the organization of the Empire and the army, down to the number of employees in the fruit storerooms, and the food that was given to the best hunting leopards (cheetahs). Even though much of it is idealized, the *A'in* is nevertheless an incomparable guide to Mughal administration. (A miniature painting survives of the chubby-faced Abu'l Fazl presenting Akbar with the second volume of his chronicle, bound in leather and embossed in gold.[6])

For a more critical viewpoint, there is the *Muntakhab at-tawarikh* by Bada'uni. This book, which deals with the period up to 1595, and was not publicized until Jahangir's day, provides another counterbalance to the hyperbole of Abu'l Fazl's *Akbarnama*. Bada'uni, a theologian, translator, and former friend of Mubarak and his sons, criticizes Akbar mercilessly towards the end of his work. Bada'uni is anti-Hindu, against the sects, especially the Shi'a, and opposed to the dilution of Islam. What Abu'l Fazl considers to be intellectual freedom in Akbar's day is intellectual anarchy as far as Bada'uni is concerned.

Other works include the *Tarikh-i alfi*, written by Ahmad Thattawi (who was murdered in 1585) to commemorate the approaching end of the first millennium of the Islamic calendar; the useful *Tabaqat-i Akbari*, from which Bada'uni derived much of his information; also the interesting personal observations of Asad Beg, who was employed as Abu'l Fazl's secretary, and as special ambassador for Akbar in the last years of his life.

Bayram Khan had considerable influence over Akbar during his early years as ruler. In his first year on the throne he succeeded in defeating his dangerous enemy, the Hindu Hemu Vikramaditya, at the second battle of Panipat (1556). Within the palace walls, however, a group of women made life difficult for Akbar and the loyal Bayram Khan. Akbar remained emotionally very close to his chief nurse Maham anaga, whose son Adham Khan was a member of the government. His ambitious mother would have liked him to occupy Bayram's position, for 'her heart was pricked by the thorn of envy'. Adham Khan played an active part in the siege and conquest of Mandu, but failed to carry out Akbar's order to send the captives and booty back to him. Apart from a few elephants, he kept everything for himself. All of the captives, except for young girls from the harem, were slaughtered, among them many Muslims. Akbar was furious when he heard about this, and ordered Adham Khan to hand over the booty. However, he still secretly kept two beautiful young girls captive for himself. When Akbar discovered the deceit, Adham Khan's mother murdered the two beautiful slave girls instantly to cover up his offence. Adham Khan, who was thoroughly 'drunk on the intoxicating wine of worldly success', then had the audacity to stab Akbar's prime minister Shamsuddin Muhammad Atga, the husband of one of Akbar's nurses and the father of Mirza 'Aziz Koka, in the palace. On 16 May 1562 Akbar seized Adham Khan and singlehandedly threw him from the palace veranda. Adham survived the fall, whereupon Akbar hurled him down a second time. From then on he was his own master. 'Everything which was said of Adham was bad. He excelled, just like his mother, in defamation, and he did everything in his power to poison Akbar's thoughts against the best of his Amirs.' Bayram, 'who accomplished everything, while Akbar was occupied with pursuits which had nothing to do with his royal duties', had been recalled from his post a few months before Adham's death. He set off on a pilgrimage to Mecca, as was the custom, during the course of which he was murdered, on 31 January 1561. 'The time of Bayram was the best of times, when India was like a bride', sighed Bada'uni, and the author of the *Ma'athir al-umara'* agreed with him wholeheartedly. Bayram Khan's widow, the daughter of a Mewati prince, managed to flee with her four-year-old son, 'Abdu'r Rahim. Bayram's second wife, Salima, Humayun's half-sister, then married Akbar. The young 'Abdu'r Rahim was soon called to the court and Akbar treated him almost like his own son. He rose very rapidly to the highest ranks, and proved his mettle during the conquest of Gujarat and Sind and in the battle for north Deccan. He was not only a great general, *khankhanan*, but a poet in Persian, Turkish and especially Hindi. He translated Babur's memoirs into Persian, and was the greatest patron of poets in the entire Mughal period.[7]

In 1562, the year in which Adham Khan had been killed and his mother Maham anaga had died after losing her son, Akbar went to war. Adham Khan had already subjugated Malwa, and now it was the turn of Gondwana (1564) and Chitor (1568). Around thirty thousand Rajputs were killed during the difficult conquest of this hitherto impregnable Rajput fortress.[8] Afterwards the great victory was commemorated in history books, in imperial proclamations and in paintings. The following year, 1569, the conquests of Ranthambhor and Bundelkhand added to the territory under Mughal rule. The conquest of Gujarat in 1573 was another important victory, despite the subsequent rebellion. The Mughals made their way towards Bengal, reputed to be 'the home of unrest',[9] 'where the climate favours the lowly, and the dust of dissent ever rises'. The Mughals had little liking for Bengal – the marshes and the fish and rice diet of the inhabitants were not congenial to a highlands people.

The rivalry between the Mughal princes continued. Akbar's youngest half-brother, Hakim Mirza, who ruled Kabul, besieged Lahore in 1565. Akbar was reluctant to punish him, as his loyal followers urged, because he reminded him of his beloved father. The Kabul region of Afghanistan remained a constant irritant throughout Akbar's rule.

During the 1560s Akbar had the fort of Agra constructed, with stones as 'red as the cheeks of fortune'. He wanted to improve the integration of the Hindu majority of his expanding empire, and he undertook to achieve this with an effective system of government. In 1564 he abolished the *jizya*, the poll tax imposed on non-Muslims. To further his integrationist aims Akbar married a Rajput princess, Manmati, the daughter of Raja Bhagwandas of Amber, who first provided him with a long-awaited son, and then with twins. When the twins died, Akbar followed the Muslim custom of consulting a friend of Allah. The emperor had previously undertaken a pilgrimage to Ajmer, to the tomb of Khwaja Muʿinuddin Chishti, the founder of the Chishti order. Now he visited Salim Chishti, a holy man living near Agra, who promised that Akbar would soon be given a son. On 31 August 1569, 'the unique pearl of the caliphate emerged from the shell of the mussel and reached the shore of existence'. Akbar's gratitude was boundless. The infant boy was named Salim, after the Chishti shaykh, although he would later rule under the name of Jahangir. Akbar made regular pilgrimages to Ajmer over the next few years, and soon two more princes were born, Murad, in 1570, and Danyal, who was born in Ajmer on 9 September 1572.

In gratitude for Salim's birth, Akbar built the city of Fatehpur Sikri, a huge construction of red sandstone, near the shaykh's residence.[10] Salim Chishti's mausoleum lies in the court 'like a white pearl'. During Akbar's fifteen years of residence in Fatehpur, he constructed the ʿIbadat-khana, where religious debates were held on Thursday evenings, initially between Muslim theologians, then later also with Hindus and Parsis. In 1580 Jesuits also took part. The scholarly and strictly orthodox Badaʾuni describes the debates between the narrow-minded theologians, which doubtless contributed to Akbar's later aversion to orthodox Islam:

Suddenly the theologians of our time became highly disputatious, and noise and confusion prevailed. His Majesty became very angry at their rude behaviour, and said to me, 'In future report to me if any of the theologians talk nonsense and don't behave themselves.

8. An engraving of the mausoleum of Shaykh Salim Chishti in Fatehpur Sikri, 1571–81.

I'll see to it that they leave the room!' I said quietly to Asaf Khan, 'If I carry out this order, the majority of them will have to leave the room.' His majesty suddenly asked me what I'd just said. He was pleased with my reply and repeated it to those sitting near him.

Indeed, when 'learned men wield the sword of the tongue on the battlefield of mutual disagreement', it could lead to 'the moustache of the emperor bristling like that of a tiger'.[11]

Akbar's religious fervour encompassed all religions. He honoured the image of the Madonna in the chapel in the presence of Jesuits, and also took an interest in the rites of the Parsis, particularly their cult of fire. Above all he strove for a profound understanding of Hinduism, and to this end he encouraged the translation of the most important Sanskrit texts. He invited a Persian philosopher, Fathullah-i Shirazi, to his court, whose students subsequently developed an important philosophical school, which was later to play a significant

role in the Firangi Mahal in Lucknow during Aurangzeb's time.[12]

The subject of polygamy was a contentious one, since Akbar and his descendents certainly had more wives than the four permitted under Islamic *shariᶜa* law. Finally a compromise was agreed, whereby it would be considered that he had married the subsequent wives in a form permitted by Shiᶜa called *mutᶜa*, or 'temporary marriage' (which could be legitimated by means of a contract valid for up to ninety-nine years).

Akbar's religious views, which had been strengthened by the debates in the ᶜIbadat khana, were greatly affected by a mystical experience he had while out hunting on 22 April 1578, when looking at the enormous number of animals that had been slain; he then put a stop to the killing. Although there are some who have classified this moment as an epileptic seizure, it was certainly a *jadhba*, a spiritual 'calling' of a kind not uncommon among mystics. Afterwards Akbar took up various yogic and Sufi practices and rites, had his hair cut, became a vegetarian, and his leanings towards religious syncretism became even more pronounced. An attempt of his to recite the Friday sermon, however, was not a success. These developments culminated in 1579 with the famous *mahzar*, an edict that has erroneously been called 'the decree of infallibility'. The *mahzar*, signed in Shaykh Mubarak's own handwriting, proclaimed the ruler to be the 'the refuge of all people, the prince of the faithful'. It accorded him the right of *ijtihad*, according to which Akbar would have the deciding say in case of disagreement among the learned about the meaning of any part of the Qur'an. (One can see the negative influence of the *cibadat khana* debates!) However, the *sultan-i cadil* ('the just sultan') was supposed to have knowledge of Sharica law, which Akbar lacked.[13] The two highest religious dignitaries, the *shaykh ul-islam* cAbdu'l Nabi and the *makhdum ul-mulk*, were forced to sign the decree against their will.

These two dignitaries, who had long been in Akbar's service, were not, apparently, models of piety. cAbdallah Sultanpuri *makhdum ul-mulk* 'served his country', had been appointed by Humayan, had subsequently served his enemy Sher Shah, but he had been taken back by Akbar. He and cAbdu'l Nabi, who could not stand one other, were primarily interested in enriching themselves. In 1579 Akbar sent them off on a pilgrimage to Mecca. They returned without permission, whereupon they met their deaths in mysterious circumstances, although Abu'l Fazl was said to have been responsible for the death of cAbdu'l-Nabi.[14]

That same year, Akbar carried out a remarkable experiment to determine whether children could learn to speak without being taught. He arranged for a number of infants to be raised together, and forbade their nurses to speak to them. When the children were examined a few years later, they were found to be dumb and mentally retarded.

Akbar left Fatehpur Sikri in 1585 and made Lahore his seat for the following fourteen years. Although the Mughals were used to a nomadic existence and seldom remained in one place for long, in this instance the motive for their departure for Lahore may have been to bring the northwest of the subcontinent under better control. At the border they were attacked by the Raushaniyya, a politically motivated group of mystical Pashtuns with a great many supporters in the mountainous region. Man Singh, Akbar's best Rajput general, managed to defeat the Raushaniyya on this occasion, but they continued to pose a threat until the beginning of the seventeenth century.

Yusuf Sarfi, the ruler of Kashmir, who was married to the poetess Habba Khatun, was an admirer of the theosophy of Ibn cArabi. In January 1580 political tension in Kashmir drove him to Akbar, and in 1586 Kashmir and Swat were incorporated into the Mughal empire. In the following decades Kashmir became the Mughals' favourite summer retreat, despite the rather arduous two-week journey there from Lahore. During this period Akbar found time to visit Kabul and pay homage at the tombs of his grandfather Babur and his uncle Hindal.

During his years in Lahore, the emperor's time was strictly regulated, and he set himself a specified number of administrative tasks to accomplish each day. He also carried out a complete renovation of the city fort, where the finest works of early Mughal painting were subsequently produced.

Akbar's religious ideal of *sulh-i kull*, 'at peace with all', did not restrain him from further conquests, for, as Abu'l Fazl wrote, 'he regarded additions to the region under his rule to be a means of honouring God, and ruling to be a form of serving God.'[15] He launched another attack on Gujarat, which had been subjugated for the first time in 1575, this time under Bayram Khan's son

ʿAbduʾr Rahim, later the *khankhanan*. The Sindhi historian Mir Maʿsum Nami and Daulat Khan Lodi (whose son Khan Jahan Lodi was to become a political rival of ʿAbduʾr Rahim) also took part in the fighting. ʿAbduʾr Rahim celebrated his victory in September 1583 in grand style, giving away all the spoils of victory, and creating the *Fathbagh*, a 'victory park', in Ahmedabad.

While he was in Lahore, Akbar decided to send the army to Kandahar to attack the fortress that had always been a bone of contention between Iran and Mughal India, and also to subjugate Sind, the lower Indus valley. Since 1520 Sind had been ruled by the Arghuns, a family of Chaghatay-Turkish rulers to whom Akbar was closely related, and their followers, the Tarkhans. The *khankhanan* travelled by ship down the Ravi and then to the Indus river, finally conquering Thatta after a series of harrowing adventures along the way. The captured prince Jani Beg Tarkhan was taken back to Lahore. The prince, who was also a lover of music and wine, got on extremely well with Akbar and became a member of the *din-i ilahi*, the religious movement founded by Akbar. Still, Akbar would have preferred to be able to annex Kandahar to the empire instead of Sind.

There are widely varying interpretations about the *din-i ilahi*. Akbar's opponents considered it to be merely an ersatz religion, and it does appear to have been a kind of esoteric club for select members. There was only one Hindu member, a former singer and entertainer called Raja Birbal, who was highly honoured by Akbar. Man Singh refused politely but firmly to give up his Hindu faith for something unknown. The rest of the membership was made up of Muslims drawn from the different schools of Islam, who prostrated themselves before the ruler just as Sufis prostrate themselves before their Master.

The aspirant had to swear an oath that he would remain loyal to the ruler through thick and thin, and be prepared to sacrifice his life, property, honour and faith to him. They observed rituals which Akbar had drawn from a number of other religions, including paying homage to the sun. One modern critic has described the *din-i ilahi* as 'a crazy hotchpotch of different rituals performed with great pomposity'.[16] Akbar was mistaken if he thought that he had come up with a substitute for Islam. Despite Badaʾuni's criticism of Akbar for his anti-Islamic attitude, the reports of the time are so contradictory that it is impossible to judge whether or not this is justified. However Badaʾuni also asserts that Akbar used the *dhikr* formula *ya huwa, ya hadi*, 'O He, O Guide!'; he even dubbed Badaʾuni's son ʿAbduʾl Hadi, 'Servant of the Guide'.

However, it was not only Badaʾuni's view that Akbar went too far in his attempts to further religious tolerance. Quite a few members of the upper class were not happy about it, including the *khankhanan* ʿAbduʾr Rahim, and Mirza ʿAziz Koka, one of Akbar's foster brothers. Mirza ʿAziz Koka, Akbar's favourite foster brother, left Lahore secretly to go to Mecca, and Akbar wrote him a letter telling him how annoyed he was about this. Although Akbar did not punish his foster brother, against the advice of many courtiers, he could not resist teasing him for growing a beard, which was not the custom at that time: 'You're late! Clearly the hair of your beard is weighing you down.' Akbar ordered Mirza ʿAziz to return from Mecca, after which he stayed close to Akbar. However he played a prominent part in the disputes over Akbar's successor, since his daughter was married to Jahangir's son Khusrau, whom he consequently supported.

After the conquest of Sind in 1591, Akbar's next project was the conquest of the Deccan, the south Indian Muslim states. Since 1327, when Muhammad Tughluq sent a group of eminent intellectuals from Delhi to Devagiri (Daulatabad), there had been a series of Muslim states and a number of significant cultural developments in the region. Among the states which existed in Akbar's time were Ahmednagar, the most northerly, also Golconda and Bijapur. From 1580 to 1612 Golconda was ruled by Muhammad-Quli Qutubshah, who was an excellent poet in Dakhni-Urdu, and whose verses were admired for their freshness and elegance. The neighbouring state of Bijapur was ruled by Ibrahim ᶜAdil Shah II (1580 to 1627), who had been enthroned as a child, and brought up under the guardianship of his aunt Chand Bibi from Ahmednagar. Chand Bibi was a heroic princess who had played a central role in the defense of Ahmednagar. The princess who had fought so bravely in battle was later murdered by her own people, and so Ahmednagar fell in 1600 to the Mughals.

Ibrahim ᶜAdil Shah, like his neighbour Muhammad-Quli, was an artist, a poet in Dakhni-Urdu, and a lover of paintings, and both courts vied with Agra and Lahore in the production of beautiful works of art.[17] Golconda was the richest source of diamonds, so the Mughals were keen to get their hands on it. Furthermore the Shiᶜi form of Islam predominated in the Deccan at that time, and the kingdom enjoyed a very good relationship with Iran, whereas the problem of Kandahar was always a sticking-point in the relationship between the Mughals and Iran.

Akbar now despatched his best general, the *khankhanan* ᶜAbduʾr Rahim, to the Deccan, assisted by Akbar's second son Murad, who turned out to be more of a hindrance than a help. Murad was a difficult character whose temperament was made still worse by his addiction to alcohol and drugs, the bane of the Mughals, which killed him in 1599.

The *khankhanan* and his men had their headquarters in Burhanpur, on the Tapti river, the true northern frontier of the Deccan.[18] ᶜAbduʾr Rahim had constructed a magnificent extension to this city; he employed more than a hundred writers, illustrators, bookbinders and others in his library, to which all the minor and major poets of the land, whether they wrote in Persian or Hindi, contributed works. The ruins of that enormous library still stand. The *khankhanan* also embellished the city with an elegant *hammam* and numerous gardens. In 1540 weavers from Sind migrated to Burhanpur, which became a centre for silk and wool weaving. The region of Burhanpur was named after the great Chishti holy man Burhanuddin Gharib, who died in 1338. In Akbar's time it was a centre of Sufism as well as for the Satpanthi Ismaᶜilis.

The chief objective of the Mughals was to capture the fortress of Asirgarh about twenty kilometres to the north of Burhanpur,[19] in which around 34,000 people had taken refuge. The assault troops accomplished the incredible feat of scaling cliffs and then walls together totalling three hundred metres, and in November 1600 Asirgarh fell. It is hard to imagine that they could have achieved this without resorting to bribery or without the assistance of betrayal from some quarter on the other side.

Abuʾl Fazl, who had slowly been ascending the military career ladder, was among those who had taken part in the siege. After their victory over the fortress, he set off slowly northwards to report to Akbar. As he was making his way through Bir Singh Bundela's territory he was attacked and killed. Bir Singh was later promoted to high rank by Jahangir, on whose orders the murder had been carried out. At that time Jahangir was only the governor of Allahabad, but he had set his sights on becoming emperor, and Abuʾl Fazl had reported some of the crown prince's youthful indiscretions.' After he came to the throne, Jahangir wrote very coolly: 'Although this deed caused great anger in the breast of the then king, it enabled me to kiss the threshold of my father's palace without having to put myself to undue trouble.' Akbar fainted when he learned of the murder of his loyal friend in 1602. That same day he wrote the following verse:

> When our Shaykh came, overwhelmed by longing, he came, longing to kiss my foot, without head and feet![20]

Akbar's last years were gloomy ones. Murad died of *delirium tremens*, and Danyal – who had married for the first time only in 1588 – suffered the same fate, shortly before the arrival in Burhanpur of the Bijapuri princess he was about to marry against her will.

'Akbar could subdue wild elephants, yet he had enormous difficulties with his son and heir Salim.'[21] While the crown prince was going his own way in Allahabad, the ruler became ever more distrustful, fearing he would be poisoned. Soon many of his officers were openly stating that they would prefer to see Salim's oldest son Khusrau (born in 1587) as Akbar's successor. Khusrau and his brother Khurram, the later Shah Jahan, were at that time being held almost as hostages in Akbar's court. Fortunately, in 1603, Hamida (titled Maryam Makani), Akbar's mother, was able to bring about a reconciliation. Akbar placed his turban on Salim, confirming his position as successor to the throne. Akbar died on 15 October 1605, and a huge mausoleum in an unusual mixture of styles was erected for him in Sikandra, not far from Agra.

9. A portrait of Nurud-din Jahangir as a youth, *c.* 1620–30, gouache with gold on paper.

# NURUD-DIN JAHANGIR

'Seizer of the World' (1569–1627)

After mounting the throne, Salim changed his name to Jahangir. The son of a Rajput princess, he was the first Mughal ruler whose mother was not from a Turkish or Persian family. He appears in miniatures as an imposing, elegant individual, whose handsome profile displays a felicitous blend of Turkish and Indian features. In the vivid descriptions of him by foreign visitors, Sir Thomas Roe's, for example, he comes across as the quintessential Great Mughal – a refined ruler who never wore a ring, or shoe, nor any item of clothing that would not grace a museum collection today.

Jahangir had a demonic temper coupled with a streak of cruelty. Stefan George's poem in his collection *Algabal* could apply to Jahangir:

> Look, I am as soft as apple blossom
> and gentle as a newborn lamb
> Yet iron, stone and tinder
> Lie dangerously together in my turbulent
> heart . . .

Like his great-grandfather Babur, Jahangir wrote memoirs, which he commenced after he 'had made the dust of Akbar's feet into a salve for my eyes' and 'when the throne had been honoured by my succession'. His *Tuzuk* is an invaluable account of the ideas, desires and sensibility of the ruler under whom Mughal art reached its zenith, for 'his thwarted energies were channelled into wine, women, song and patronage of the arts'. Jahangir had many wives, including a number of Rajputs, and fathered numerous children (on one occasion three daughters were born to him in one night!).

Jahangir is described by historians as indolent and uninterested in financial or political matters.[1] Soon after his accession he had to put down a rebellion by his eldest son Khusrau, who hoped, with the help of Man Singh and Mirza 'Aziz Koka, to seize his grandfather Akbar's inheritance. In 1605 the prince fled to Delhi, with his father in pursuit. Jahangir took advantage of this opportunity to visit the two spiritual centres of the city, the tomb of Humayun and the mausoleum of the Chishti holy man Nizamuddin Auliya. Khusrau and his allies were severely punished by Jahangir, who now bestowed his affections on Khurram, his son by Jodhi Bai, the daughter of the 'fat Raja' Uday Singh. Khurram many difficult years later succeeded to the throne as Shah Jahan.

There were constant uprisings along the eastern and western borders of the empire, in Bengal and in what is today called Afghanistan. However, Jahangir's main military objective was to expand his territory southwards. The skirmishes that began under Akbar were continuing and becoming ever fiercer, primarily due to the tactical skill and subterfuge of the Abyssinian eunuch Malik Ambar, who occasionally succeeded in defeating the Mughal army. The *khankhanan* 'Abdu'r Rahim had briefly fallen out of favour because he did not appear to be attacking the Deccan with sufficient zeal. He now returned to the head of the imperial army and attempted to drive the Deccanis away from Burhanpur using subterfuge rather than outright attack. His son Iraj Shahnawaz played a successful part in the action.[2] The extent of Jahangir's hatred for the black rebel can be seen in one of the allegorical portraits fashionable at the time. The picture portrays him in heaven, surrounded by angels, shooting an arrow at Malik Ambar's decapitated head.[3]

There were frequent outbreaks of unrest in Kandahar. Jahangir was concerned to establish good relations with Iran, so in 1611 he sent a high-ranking embassy to his 'brother Shah 'Abbas', bearing gifts. The portrait painter Bishndas, a nephew of the painter Nanha, was a member of this embassy, so there are numerous paintings of the Safawid ruler. In one allegorical portrait he is depicted in the glow of Jahangir's nimbus, being embraced, almost crushed, in the Mughal ruler's arms.[4]

Jahangir's memoirs make fascinating reading because he took an interest in everything, especially art, of which he was a connoisseur. He also wrote detailed observations of the flora and fauna of the country, especially of Kashmir. The court artists also painted pictorial records of everything that happened, from finding rare plants, to meetings between the ruler and Sufis, and especially *yogis* such as Gosain Jadrup.

The fact that Jahangir was able to live a life of luxury and devote himself almost exclusively to art and science, concerning himself very little with matters of government, was thanks to his wife Nur Jahan. She was the daughter of one of his Persian *mansabdars*, Mirza Ghiyath Beg, who later, as I'timad-ad-daula, enjoyed almost limitless power. Her brother, Asaf Khan, also became a very powerful man in the state. Mihr un-nisa, 'Sun among Women', was married to one of Jahangir's officers, who was shot in somewhat

10. 'Shah ᶜAbbas I of Iran holding a falcon', brush drawing on paper, early 19th century, after a 17th-century Mughal original.

During these years, there was ever increasing contact between Mughal India and the European powers. Akbar's initial dealings were with the Portuguese, who since 1498 had been settling in a number of areas on India's west coast, particularly in Goa. Now the British entered the picture. In 1603 the merchant John Mildenhall reached Agra and presented Akbar with a letter from Elizabeth I, who was hoping to secure assistance for British traders. Although Akbar did not reply, the British East India Company, which had been founded in 1600, began trading during Jahangir's reign. We have Sir Thomas Roe to thank for some vivid descriptions of life at court, also of the daily difficulties which the British had to contend with, such as the quantity of gifts they should be giving to the ruler and the officials in order to get anything accomplished. Nevertheless, despite the difficulties which the superintendent of the most important harbour, Surat, caused for the British by impounding Roe's crates of baggage containing mostly presents for the emperor, Jahangir was enchanted by many of the things which the British did manage to introduce, such as wine, unusual games, even a carriage for Nur Jahan. Above all else Jahangir was interested in European paintings.

The European presence was becoming steadily more tangible. As well as establishing themselves on the west coast of India, the British and the Dutch were constructing factories in Dacca in Bengal, while in Hooghly near Calcutta, wealthy Portuguese were building residences.

Jahangir's love for his son Khurram appeared to be boundless. In 1617 he bestowed upon him the title Shah Jahan, by which he would later come to be known. Nur Jahan arranged the marriage between Khurram and the daughter of her brother Asaf Khan, Arjumand Banu. She later became known as Mumtaz Mahal, 'the Elect of the Palace', and it is to her that the Taj Mahal is dedicated.

mysterious circumstances in Bengal. At her marriage in 1611 she was granted the title *Nur Mahal*, 'Light of the Palace', which was later elevated to *Nur Jahan*, 'Light of the World', and coins were minted in her name. The clever, athletic and competent woman, together with her father and brother, wielded the power behind the throne. Salih Kanboh suspects that because of Jahangir's overwhelming love for Nur Jahan, 'he trusted her in all respects, so that after he had loosened his grip on the reins of power, all kinds of problems began to surface in the country, and great weaknesses and irregularities in political and economic affairs were revealed.' [5]

11. Mahabat Khan, 1630–35, a tinted drawing with gold on an album leaf.

Just as Salim had rebelled during his father Akbar's last years, now Shah Jahan in his turn became disobedient after a victory against Malik Amber. For the first time Jahangir refers to his beloved son in his diary as *bi-daulat*, 'the wretch', apparently because in 1622 he had had his oldest brother Khusrau killed in Burhanpur.

Khurram went on the run for years, turning up in the Deccan, then in Bengal, then Sind, accompanied throughout by his young wife, who bore him a child almost every year. The *khankhanan* ꜥAbduʾr Rahim acted as mediator in this difficult situation.

Mahabat Khan, whose face is familiar from numerous *durbar* scenes painted by court artists, also played a very important part in these intrigues. He came from Kabul, changed his name from Zamana Beg, and enjoyed a meteoric ascent up the career ladder. He became *ahadi*, then, as a reward for killing a man whom the emperor disliked, he was elevated to the rank of 500-*zat* officer, despite the regulations prohibiting the promotion of *ahadis*. After Jahangir's enthronement, Mahabat Khan was promoted to 1,500-*zat* officer, and also to the rank of *bakhshi* (Treasurer) for the private privy purse. Under Jahangir's weak rule, Mahabat Khan, who hated Asaf Khan, rose ever higher.

Nur Jahan initially supported Shah Jahan's claim to succeed as crown prince. It is not clear why she suddenly shifted her allegiance first to her stepson Shahriyar, and then to Jahangir's grandson, Khusrau's son Dawarbakhsh.

In the summer of 1627 Jahangir paid another visit to his beloved Kashmir. As the imperial couple were camped by the Jhelum, Mahabat Khan suddenly arrived from Deccan with Jahangir's second son, Parviz, and surrounded the camp. Nur Jahan fled, and organized reinforcements for her husband. Mahabat Khan fell out of favour for some time afterwards, while *khankhanan* ꜥAbduʾr Rahim, who had been *persona non grata* because of his support for Shah Jahan, was grateful to be received back at court. However he died shortly after his rehabilitation. On 27 October 1627, when Jahangir 'mistook this temporal house for the palace of eternity', his brother-in-law Asaf Khan was in league with his son-in-law Shah Jahan, assisting him to seize power. The blood of many of their relatives was shed during the following turbulent months, and many pretenders to the throne had their eyes put out.

Jahangir was an extremely complex character, a connoisseur and an aesthete, whose tendency to outbursts of cruelty was exacerbated by opium and alcohol, which he enjoyed to excess. As punishment for a slight misdemeanour or oversight he was capable of shooting a man on the spot, or having him flayed. Yet he was so distraught at the death of a granddaughter that he was unable to write about the event, and had to let his secretary report it.

There were no significant political or military developments during Jahangir's reign, and the empire stayed within the boundaries which had been established under Akbar.

12. A portrait miniature of Shah Jahan in old age, c. 1655, gouache on paper.

## SHAH JAHAN, *sahib qiran, Sulayman makani*

'Lord of auspicious conjunction who occupies Solomon's place' (1627–1657)

Shah Jahan was also the son of a Rajput, Jodh Bai. In miniatures he looks imposing, like a noble statue. In profile his features appear sharp, with scarcely any trace of Turkic. He was a great builder during a time when white marble and gold were the building materials of choice – the Taj Mahal was constructed in honour of his beloved queen Mumtaz Mahal. Although under his rule the Mughal empire reached its zenith, the cracks were already visible.

While his father was still alive, Shah Jahan had taken part in a battle with the Abyssinian Commander-in-Chief Malik Ambar shortly before the latter's death in 1626. He resolved at that time to conquer the Deccan.

After his coronation in February 1628 he spent a lot of time in Burhanpur and the surrounding region, and it was there that his beloved wife died on 17 June 1631 while giving birth to her fourteenth child in sixteen years. The emperor was inconsolable, grieving and wearing white mourning clothes for a long time afterwards.

The pleasures of worldly rule and kingship, which were mine with her by my side, have

13. 'Shah Jahan
enthroned, with
Mahabat Khan
and a Shaykh',
c. 1629–30, from
the Late Shah
Jahan Album,
gouache and
gold on paper.

now become burdens and increasing sources of grief![1]

His oldest daughter Jahanara, scarcely eighteen years old, took the place of her mother as the First Lady of the empire.

At Shah Jahan's court previously unheard of luxury prevailed. Whereas his father Jahangir had been a connoisseur of fine paintings and golden artifacts, his great obsession was with building. No longer content with the enlargement of towns and fortresses (as in Agra and Lahore), his goal was to construct an entire city which would bear his name: *Shahjahanabad*, a new addition to the old residential city of Delhi, with the Red Fort, the large mosque and spacious houses for the nobility.

As the site of the mausoleums of Humayun and Nizamuddin, Delhi had always been a spiritual centre for Indian Muslims, but from this time on it became the centre of Indian Islam.

Shah Jahan then commissioned the construction of the Peacock Throne, on which his best goldsmiths worked for seven years. The completed throne inspired poets to compose verses praising it with ever more hyperbole, and visitors to the court from France, Italy and England were completely overwhelmed at the sight of it.

The Persian architect ᶜAli Mardan Khan was inspired by the gardens in Kashmir to create the Shalimar Gardens in Lahore,[2] for which he had to construct a canal more than a hundred miles long to carry water from from the mountains to the city. ᶜAbduʾl Hamid Lahori wrote the *Padshahnama* in praise of his ruler. When he presented Shah Jahan with a few passages of the work, he was rewarded with his weight in gold, plus an additional three thousand rupees.

Shah Jahan had no further grand plans for the conquest of new provinces, so he was now able to indulge his passion for building. Only Kandahar remained a problem, but neither Dara Shikoh nor Aurangzeb were able to take the fortress away from the Persians.

Aurangzeb, the third of Shah Jahan's surviving sons, gained a reputation for heroism during his youth. Painters of miniatures and poets recorded depicted an occasion when the fifteen year old subdued a wild elephant, saving those present from danger.[3] In 1636, at eighteen years of age, he had been made governor of the province of the Deccan, after which he was in constant confrontation with the increasingly powerful kingdoms of Golconda and Bijapur. He could easily have annexed them to the empire during his governorships in 1655 and 1657; however, his father instructed him merely to demand tributes. Perhaps that to some extent explains the relentlessness with which he fought these two kingdoms when he himself attained the throne.

Aurangzeb was apparently envious of his oldest brother, the artistic crown prince Dara Shikoh (born 1615). The crown prince, who was married to the daughter of his uncle Parwez, Nadira Begum, was an aesthete like his grandfather Jahangir. Like his great grandfather, Akbar, he was drawn to mysticism.[4] His goal was to achieve the 'confluence of the two oceans', i.e. mutual tolerance between Islam and Hinduism, and he wrote numerous works in Persian devoted to this end. He was far more interested in writing a biography of his guru Mian Mir (died 1635) and translating Hindu texts than he was in fighting with the sword and spear, or in dealing with matters of administration. In miniatures he is often portrayed in the company of wise men. Dara Shikoh's transliteration of fifty of the *Upanishads* into Persian was translated into Latin at the beginning of the nineteenth century by Anquetil-Duperron, and provided an important stimulus for European idealistic philosophy.

14. Bhawani Das, 'The Sons of Shah Jahan Enthroned: Shah Shujaᶜ, Dara Shikoh, Muradbakhsh, Aurangzeb and Aᶜzam Shah', leaf from an album, *c.* 1680, gouache and gold on paper.

It is not surprising that the brothers did not get on well together. Aurangzeb was jealous of Dara Shikoh, who was so obviously their father's favourite. However, Dara Shikoh was harshly criticised by his contemporaries and by Mughal historians because he 'beat the drum of conceit and egoism'.[5] He might also have been jealous of Shah Shujaᶜ (born 1617), the favourite of his grandfather Jahangir. Not much has been said of the youngest, Muradbakhsh. When Princess Jahanara, who had taken the place of the brothers' mother after her death, suffered for months from severe burns, it became apparent just how much Shah Jahan loved his daughter. Her younger sister Raushanara was particularly close to Aurangzeb.

Although Delhi and the Red Fort were still gleaming in all their splendour, the wealth of the empire was steadily dwindling. The cost of all of the incredible luxury at court, which, at great expense, the *mansabdar*s had to keep up with, was steadily draining the treasury's coffers. The figures presented by the chronicler are astounding: 'The treasury cried out, "Don't touch me!"'[6]

Then the empire was struck by famine, which was particularly severe in the Deccan. The influence of the European powers gradually, almost imperceptibly, grew ever stronger. The reports of the goldsmith Tavernier and of Bernier, as well as those of the doctor Manucci, give a good idea of the precarious situation in the empire.

At the end of 1657 when the rumour began spreading that the emperor was seriously ill, Aurangzeb saw that his time had come. Although Shah Jahan soon recovered, it still seemed to him to be the opportune moment to seize the throne. It is a sad story, how Aurangzeb, suffering from cholera and thirsting for revenge, finally captured his father and imprisoned him together with his daughter Jahanara in the fortress of Agra, where from his window the former emperor could gaze on the Taj Mahal.

Dara Shikoh went into battle against his brother at Samugarh, near Agra, but lost because of his own foolhardiness. In yet another battle the crown prince was defeated and had to flee. Accompanied by his wife Nadira and an ever diminishing group of loyal followers, he travelled around, like his ancestor Humayun, to Sind and then into Baluchistan, where Nadira Begum died. Darah Shikoh sent her corpse with his few remaining soldiers to Lahore, so that she could be buried near the mausoleum of Mian Mir. Her small tomb is still within the present-day cantonment of the city. Dara Shikoh was betrayed and brought to Delhi, and paraded around the city riding backwards on a donkey. He was finally executed in 1659, after his sons had been killed in front of him. Then Aurangzeb, who had taken the throne name ʿAlamgir, turned his attention to his brother Muradbakhsh, who he imprisoned with his beloved wife in Gwalior. Muradbakhsh died there in 1661, whilst Shah Shujaʿ met his death in Arakan.[7]

Shah Jahan lived on until 1666 in his palace prison, in the company of his beloved daughter Jahanara. Her younger sister Raushanara fell out of favour with their brother Aurangzeb because whilst he was ill she took over the Great Seal and signed decrees in his name. She died in 1671, and Jahanara outlived her by a decade.

15. Aurangzeb in old age, *c.* 1700, gouache with gold.

## Aurangzeb ᶜAlamgir, *khuld makan*

'he whose residence is eternal paradise'
(1618–1707)

The sharp features of his father Shah Jahan appear sharper still in portraits of Aurangzeb. After he had imprisoned his father and had his three brothers killed, Aurangzeb succeeded in expanding the Mughul empire still further – in fact to such an extent that it exhausted its power. The empire collapsed in 1707 when Aurangzeb died, not long before his ninetieth birthday, having ruled for nearly half a century. Aurangzeb was not interested in the arts or luxurious living like his forefathers. His primary concern was the survival of the Islamic way of life, not one of universal brotherhood based on mystical illusions. The *Fatawa-yi ᶜalamgiri*, a collection of laws passed during Aurangzeb's reign, is a valuable record of the legal system in his time.

The enthronment of Aurangzeb brought about a rift in Mughal history. 'Piety was his calling', as one historian put it,[1] and Aurangzeb attempted to live his life as a model of new ideals, conducting his personal life according to these precepts in every respect. Every year he completed a *chilla* – a long meditation retreat – and he used to spend time copying out the Qurʾan and sewing caps – a humble and therefore holy occupation.[2] In the thick of battle he would dismount from his horse to recite the evening prayers. As a young man he had been active for a time in the Deccan, then in Gujarat, in Balkh and in Multan, had fought in vain for Kandahar, then returned in 1652 to the Deccan. When he finally became ruler, he was crowned for the second time, this time officially, in May 1659, and he began to introduce his severe decrees and laws. The ban on alcohol was strictly enforced (although Christians were allowed to produce wine), and gradually pleasures such as musical concerts disappeared from life. Poetry too was slowly supressed. Although numerous miniature pictures and illustrated chronicles were produced in Aurangzeb's time – and the harsh ruler had many portraits of his imprisoned son sent to him from the prison[3] – artists no longer received the encouragement and support they had hitherto enjoyed. More and more powers were conferred on the *muhtasib*, the supervisor of the market-place, or, more accurately, the censor of morals, and life became ever more joyless.

It was not possible to change the traditional policies with regard to the Hindus, although the *jizya*, which had been repealed by Akbar, was reintroduced. However the number of Hindu-*mansabdar*s was not reduced. Even Aurangzeb could not do without the Hindu soldiers, especially now, when the empire was being menaced by a new danger, emanating not from the two weakened kingdoms which Aurangzeb had finally managed to conquer, Bijapur, which he conquered in 1686, and Golconda, conquered the following year, but from the Deccan, from the Marathas. They had invaded the north in Shah Jahan's time, and their leader, Shivaji, had reached Shah Jahan's court in 1659, only to flee from it. When Shivaji died in 1680, he was succeeded by other leaders skilled in the art of conquest. Throughout the eighteenth century the history of India was dominated by the Marathas, who gradually advanced towards the north, and who later participated in Delhi politics.

Aurangzeb's primary goals as ruler were not only the consolidation of the empire externally, but also the improvement of Muslim education and culture. His greatest achievement with regard to the latter was the creation of the Firangi Mahal, which was established in Lucknow in 1691, and developed into one of the most important Muslim educational centres.[4]

The empire was now threatened by enemies both internally and externally. The greatest threat as ever was from the north-west province. For a short time, Cooch Bihar and Arakan in the east of India were included in the Mughal empire. Initially Aurangzeb and the Pashtun leader Khushhal Khan Khatak co-existed in a spirit of amicable mutual cooperation. However, then the Pashtun leader was captured by the Mughals and imprisoned for a few years in the notorious gaol at Gwalior. After his return to his homeland near the Indus river, Khushhal called on the Pashtuns to war against the Mughal ruler, giving vent to his feelings in a famous Pashto poem:

> I know Aurangzeb's sense of justice very well:
> A Muslim who always follows the
> commandments,
> Yet he imprisoned his own father for many
> a year
> And shed his own brothers' blood
> mercilessly.
> A man might bow his head to the ground a
> thousand times
> And fast until his navel touches his spine,
> Yet if his motives are not as pure as his actions
> All is in vain, no merit will accrue from
> his pious actions.

16. Attributed to
Bhawani Das,
'Aurangzeb', from
an album assembled
for Shuja$^c$ ad-daula,
1707–12, pigment
and gold on paper.

17. 'Prince Aurangzeb spearing an excited elephant in the presence of his father and brothers', mid-17th century, watercolour with some gouache and line drawing.

If he says one thing out loud but secretly
  thinks otherwise,
His heart is split asunder, his liver turns to
  blood!
The snake's body gleams and shimmers
  wondrously,
But is poisonous inside! Be on your guard!
The coward does little but speaks volumes.
The brave man says little; he shows his
mettle in deeds.
Here my strength is of no avail against the
  tyrant,
Do not forgive him, Oh Lord, on judgment
  day!

Before his death in 1689, Khushhal commanded that he be buried out of earshot of the hooves of the Mughal nags.

For twenty-six months, assisted by a few Rajput princes, Aurangzeb waged war unsuccessfully. When his five sons began to rebel, they were thrown into prison immediately. His main problem now was financial. All sources of support had dried up, and the treasury coffers were now empty. The emperor was even forced to melt down the household silver. This dire state of affairs was not immediately apparent to foreign observers, who were presented as always with the fabulous splendour of the ruler's palace, the peacock throne and the jewels. In fact it was the reports from the court of Aurangzeb which inspired one of the greatest German goldsmiths to create his masterpiece, 'Aurangzeb's Birthday Celebrations', which represents the splendours of Aurangzeb's court with dainty silver figurines.[5]

However, visitors who stayed for a longer time noticed the wretched and indisciplined state of the army (Aurangzeb was unable even to maintain discipline among his troops), and that one or another prince was always starting an uprising.

The fact that Aurangzeb never returned to Delhi or Agra during the last thirty years of his reign testified to the fact that the true heart of the empire was not important to him; that it was even perhaps alien. His letters reveal him to be a disappointed father and ruler. In one of his letters he mentioned that his horoscope had foretold that his own life would be successful, but that after his death misfortune would befall the empire. Like all his ancestors, Aurangzeb believed in the role of the stars in human life. Whether his took this prophecy seriously or whether he was astute enough to realise what would happen after his death, he had little hope that one of his sons would rule successfully.

In miniatures of Aurangzeb painted towards the end of his life, he is always portrayed bent over the Qurʾan, or praying with his rosary. When Aurangzeb died in 1707, he was nearly ninety years old, and his sons were really too old and worn out to take over the government of an empire beset with so many problems. This was the case even with Kambakhsh, Aurangzeb's youngest and favourite son, who had been born to him in 1667 by Adaipuri Mahal.

In his will, Aurangzeb specified that he wished to be buried by the mausoleum of the Sufi Zaynuddin, in the Deccan, Khuldabad, near Aurangabad. There his modestly enclosed grave lies out the open air – just as Babur, the founder of the dynasty, was laid to rest in an open grave in Kabul.

Aurangzeb's death was the beginning of the end for the Mughal empire. During the following 150 years the Mughal dynasty declined steadily, with only occasional glimmers of its former glory, until in 1857 it collapsed in ruins.

18. Attributed to Ghulam ᶜAli Khan, *The Emperor Bahadur Shah II enthroned*, 1838, watercolour and gold on paper.

# THE TWILIGHT OF THE MUGHAL EMPIRE (1707–1857)

Whereas the first six rulers and their families are depicted in numerous portraits, many of them great works of art, pictures of the following rulers are fewer in number and poorer in quality. For one thing, artists were hampered by the rapid changes of ruler after Aurangzeb's death, if they were even able to obtain any commissions for their work. Furthermore, portraiture was no longer regarded as an official manifesto of power, as it had been particularly in the time of Jahangir and Shah Jahan. Later pictures were typically private ones, such as those of Muhammad Shah Rangela,[1] the 'pleasure addict', who was painted not only in a sedan chair carried by eight women, but also in the act of making love. There are some gloomy portraits of the blinded Shah ᶜAlam II Aftab, poet and 'blind sun', seated on his throne.[2] In one picture of the last Mughal ruler, Bahadur Shah Zafar, although the somewhat puny prince is seated on a golden throne, the lions supporting the throne look more like poodles, and even the large pearl necklaces worn by the prince and his sons cannot conceal the poverty of the court. The most deeply moving picture is a photograph of the old man in exile in Rangoon, where he died destitute in 1862.

As had been foretold by the horoscope, after Aurangzeb's death the empire began to fall. Of his five sons, only three survived, and a fight over the succession broke out among them in March 1707. Ja'far Zatalli, who was known for his frivolous verses (and who was killed in 1713 because of one ironic verse), complained in one of his poems:

Where would we find another such ruler,
Accomplished, magnanimous, wise?
Now the world weeps tears of blood,
Gentle sleep no longer comes to anyone
Through the noise of guns and cannons,
Everywhere nothing but slashing, striking,
Everywhere violence and death
And cudgels, axes, daggers . . .

During the last ten years of Aurangzeb's rule, the soldiers had been paid three years in arrears, if at all; however, there was still a great deal of gold left in the treasury in Agra, which the three rival brothers divided up among themselves before they started fighting. The middle brother, A'zam, son of the proud and vivacious Persian Dilras Banu, and the youngest, Aurangzeb's favourite Kambakhsh, both lost their lives during the infighting. The oldest of the surviving sons, Mu'azzam (born in 1643) had spent seven years in prison. Now at last, at the age of sixty-four, he succeeded in ascending the throne in Delhi under the throne name Bahadur Shah.

The victor, who had a reputation for generosity, had a difficult time of it during the first years of his rule. During the Friday prayers in Lahore in February 1711, he alienated devout Sunni members of the congregation by following the Shi'i custom of referring to the fourth Caliph 'Ali ibn Abi Talib as *wasi*, 'heir' (to the Prophet). There had been tensions with the Sikhs even in the time of Akbar's successor. Aurangzeb had had their Guru, Tegh Bahadur, put to death in 1675. Three years after Bahadur Shah came to power, the tenth guru,

19. Bahadur Shah I, *c.* 1710–15, drawing on paper.

Gobind Singh, was murdered, which stirred up a Sikh rebellion led by a brigand called Banda. They began committing the most appalling atrocities in Sirhind and the surrounding region, extending the area of their activities until Banda was captured and executed in 1716 after years of fighting.

Bahadur Shah died in February 1712, and, predictably, his four sons went to war with one another. Jahandar succeeded his father after a short battle with his brother 'Azim, who had a reputation for being idle and irresponsible.

However, Jahandar himself proved to be dissolute, and completely under the thumb of his mistress Lal Kumar. The people sang the following ditty:

The owl is living in the eagle's nest
The crow has usurped the nightingale!

Jahandar's frivolous way of life, enlivened by singing, dancing and entertainment, turned Aurangzeb's surviving daughter Zinat un-nisa (died 1721) against him. The people of Delhi were shocked when Jahandar, at the age of more than fifty, bathed naked with his favourite wife in the pool at the shrine of *Chiragh-i Dihlawi* in Delhi. It is hardly surprising that he was strangled to death after barely a year of 'rule'. He was replaced by Farrukhsiyar, the second son of ᶜAzim ush-shan, born in 1683, who was at that time the governor of Patna. The Sayyids of Barha, Husayn Khan and ᶜAbduᵓllah Khan, entered the political arena at this stage. Their family had played a major role in Indian politics since Akbar's time, and their round faces are depicted in numerous portraits.[3] They were to be the royal family for the next few years, during which time they were mocked by Delhi poets:

They were altogether just like an hourglass:
The heart full of dust, yet pure of face!

In 1717 three Mughal princes were blinded as a precaution, to eliminate them as potential pretenders to the throne.

One man who was to play an important role in the future began to rise to prominence at this stage. This was Chin Qilich Khan, whose title was *Nizam ul-mulk*, who was put in charge of the administration of the Deccan. The Nizam's grandfather was from Samarkand, and he himself had proved his mettle during his father's lifetime. Despite having lost his eyesight due to an illness, he achieved the rank of 7000-*zat*. Qilich became the governor of Bijapur, but he withdrew from political life after the death of ᶜAzim ush-shan, and supported Farrukhsiyar.

The reign of the bull-necked Farrukhsiyar was beset by problems,[4] among them his own ill health. Warfare with the rebellious Sikhs continued unabated until Banda's death in 1716. No sooner had this danger ceased than the Jats rose up and began to recruit brigands in the Punjab and the south of Delhi, terrorising the country in a rampage of destruction. The situation soon began to appear so hopeless that the Sayyid brothers stormed the palace on 27 February 1719. They blinded the ruler they themselves had placed on the throne, threw him into a miserable hole, and two months later strangled him. The poet Bedil (died 1731) found a chronogram, with the text: 'The Sayyids were disloyal to their King'. It recorded the year of his death as 1131, according to the Muslim calendar.

During the search for a new ruler, the twenty-year-old Rafiᶜ ud-darajat, a son of Rafiᶜ ush-shan, was found quite by chance in the palace, and placed on the throne for want of anyone better. Before his death only a few months later, the weak and probably consumptive young man recommended his older brother Rafiᶜ ud-daula to the Sayyid brothers as his successor. However, like his brother, he had become addicted to, and weakened by, opium. He only ruled from 11 June to September 1719, before, in his turn, departing this transitory world.

The next successor was a grandson of Bahadur Shah, Raushan Akhtar, who ascended the throne as Muhammad Shah. He was 'good looking and (above all) fairly intelligent'.[5] His first act as ruler was to pay a visit to the mausoleum of Muᶜinuddin Chishti in Ajmer. Nizam ul-mulk had returned to the Deccan, and now the time had come to settle matters with the Sayyid brothers. They were killed in 1720, and one year later Nizam ul-mulk took over the position of the *wazir* in Delhi. He stood down only two years later in order to concentrate on establishing his fiefdom in the Deccan, and founding the Asafjahi Dynasty of the Nizams of Hyderabad.

There were numerous other enemies to plague the indolent ruler Muhammad Shah, who was primarily interested in art and women, not the problems of government. In the northwest of Delhi the Rohillas, a Pashtun group, seized power. They were to play an important political role in the second half of the century. The Marathas, who under their clever leader Shivaji had made life difficult for Shah Jahan and even more so Aurangzeb, now took advantage of the weakness of the Delhi government to increase their sphere of influence. Soon they had control of the harbour at Surat as well as Burhanpur and Malwa. During the 1730s, their power increased to such an extent that Raja Rao was able to sack the suburbs of Delhi in 1737. 1729 saw the first popular uprising against the Hindus. The rebellion was started by shoemakers, who were enraged by a small incident involving a prominent Hindu. They started clamouring for the protection of Islam, then occupying the mosque. However, the ruler 'did nothing whatsoever apart from sitting on the throne and wearing the crown'.

Muhammad Shah was under the influence not only of his wife Qudsiyya Begum, a former dancer, but also of a strange 'holy man', the supposed dervish ᶜAbduˀl Ghafur from Thatta. He entered the women's quarters dressed as a milk-maid, and curried favour by delivering private messages and acting as a wonder healer and interpreter of dreams. The ruler had also fallen even more strongly under the influence of Koki Jiu, a woman who gained access to him by claiming to be a foster sister, or *koki*, of his. Her father was a *rammal*, a geomancist.

Even though the Mughal empire was in dire straits, both internally and externally, it still maintained its image as a region of fabulous riches, and this reputation attracted an Iranian conqueror, Nadir Shah. This strongly self-disciplined man, born in 1688, the son of a poor Turcoman, had defeated the Afghan rulers of Iran after a series of fierce battles. In 1737 he marched east and conquered Kandahar. At the beginning of November 1738, he advanced on India, reaching Peshawar with his army. When Lahore was conquered on 30 January 1739, the government in Delhi had no idea what to do. The three chief advisers of the ruler, the Shiᶜi Saᶜadat Khan, governor of Awadh and *wazir*, the Sunni Nizam ul-mulk, the *wakil*, and Shamsham ad-daula, the *bakhshi*, could not agree on how to resist this well-equipped and experienced enemy. They assembled all the soldiers they could find – about a million men – as well as numerous horses and other animals. This was such a huge assembly that there was no room for them all on the broad plain of Karnal, to the north of the traditional battlefield of Panipat. Inevitably the battle on the 13 February 1739 ended with the defeat of the Mughal army. Even though the Mughals had been using firearms since the time of Babur, they were less well equipped than Nadir Shah's army.

At first Nadir Shah was willing to negotiate. Since he was able to speak Turkish with Muhammad Shah (and also Nizam ul-mulk), it seemed as if it would be easy for them to come to an agreement. However, the situation was made far more complicated by conflicting suggestions and intrigues between the three rival advisors. On 9 May the people of Delhi were attacked by Persian troops, and the command was given to pillage the city. At least thirty thousand men and women were killed or took their own lives. Afterwards Nadir Shah carried an enormous amount of booty back to Iran on seven hundred elephants: gold and silver, jewels, the Peacock Throne and nine other thrones, cannons and implements, with a combined worth of seven hundred and fifty *crore* rupees – a *crore* being ten million. In addition they took elephants, around ten thousand horses and as many camels. The population of Iran did not have to pay taxes for the next three years.

Nadir Shah's thirst for power grew in proportion to his brutality, until he was finally murdered in June 1747.

Delhi remained in a state of devastation. Muhammad Shah had survived the massacre, but he died not long afterwards, on 26 April 1748, and was buried in the garden of the mausoleum of Nizamuddin Auliya. Afterwards the devout inhabitants of Delhi decided that disaster had befallen their city because the tomb of the irresponsible Muhammad Shah had been placed between those of Nizamuddin and of his beloved youth, the poet Amir Khusrau, separating the master and the youth, the lover and the beloved.[6] Over the following decades the city suffered a great deal more misfortune.

In 1748 Nadir Shah's successor, the Afghan Ahmad Shah ᶜAbdali Durrani, started a series of regular invasions of India, and succeeded in annexing the Punjab for a while. Muhammad Shah's successor, Ahmad Shah, 'a well-meaning fool', had been raised among women, and had received no education or military training. However thanks to the intrigues of his adoptive mother Qudsiyya Begum, he was placed on the throne,[7] only to be blinded by Ghazi ud-din ᶜImad ul-mulk, the grandson of Nizam, in 1754. That same year Delhi was attacked by the Jats and

20. Nadir Shah, mid-18th century, ink on paper.

partially destroyed. ᶜAlamgir II (1754–59),[8] a son of Jahandar Shah, was killed by ᶜImad ul-mulk, but his son managed to flee. Ahmad Shah ᶜAbdali carried out regular attacks on northwest India. He allied himself with the leader of the Rohillas, Najib ud-daula, who was in power in Delhi at the time, where he was praised by theologians such as Shah Waliullah for his preference for the orthodox Sunni form of Islam. ᶜAbdali conquered the Marathas at the third battle of Panipat in 1761, which was almost as catastrophic as the sacking of Delhi by Nadir Shah a good twenty years previously. The poet Mir Taqi Mir described the events:

> The Afghans and Rohillas commenced their destruction and pillaging, breaking down doors and slaying anyone they found inside, in many cases beheading them or burning them alive. Everywhere there was bloodshed and destruction, and this barbarism lasted three days and three nights . . . Men who had been pillars of the state were annihilated, men of noble rank were reduced to penury, family men were robbed of their loved ones. Most of them drifted along the streets, humiliated and degraded. Women and children were captured, and the murder and robbery continued unabated . . .[9]

Infighting intensified between the different factions at court, fuelled by the longstanding mutual antipathy between the 'Turani' Sunni faction and the 'Irani' Shiʿi faction. A ruler by the name of Shah Jahan II was enthroned for a short while (1759–60), while another group supported a son of ʿAlamgir II (born in 1728), who was known by the throne name of Shah ʿAlam II. However after he was enthroned in 1759, he chose to remain in exile. He spent some time in Lucknow, which under Safdar Jang (the nephew of Saʿadat Khan) and his son Shujaʿ ud-daula, had become an important state in which the Shia form of Islam gradually came to dominate. The *nawwab*, or ruler, the enterprising Ghaziuddin Haydar, received the title 'King' from the British in 1819.

Shah ʿAlam II made his way eastwards, to Allahabad, and attempted to secure part of Bengal for himself. However, he was defeated by the British at Baksar in 1763.

This point marks the beginning of the end for the Mughal leadership. In 1757 the British, whose East India Company was operating in Bengal, won their first decisive victory over the Mughal governor at Plassey, to some extent thanks to the treachery of Mir Jaʿfar. They were now in a position to consolidate their Bengal possessions. Calcutta became their political and cultural centre, and the weak Shah Alam II was made to hand over the revenue of the country. Astonishingly, the government in Delhi and their spiritual advisor, Shah Waliullah, failed to realise the danger threatening in the east from the British. Najib ud-daula died in Delhi in 1770. One year later Shah Alam II returned to the old capital. He was for the most part a puppet of the leader of the Marathas, Sindhia, who enjoyed the support of the British. With the help of the Shiʿi Nawwabs of Awadh, the British overcame the Rohillas, the compatriots of Najib ud-daula. Their great leader, Hafiz Rahmat Khan, who was defeated in 1774, was very interested in religion and literature. His priceless library with thousands of handwritten texts in Arabic, Persian, Urdu and Pashto was moved to Lucknow, where eighty years later the Austrian orientalist Aloys Sprenger catalogued the remnants of the collection.[10]

In Delhi the situation in the royal household had become unbearable. The fort was overpopulated with hundreds of princes, for whom there was insufficient food. Foreign visitors reported that they could hear cries of hunger coming from the quarters of the *salatin*, the princes, 'like the howling of beasts of prey in an abandoned zoo'. The more enterprising of the princes sought a way out, and one of them, Azfari Gurgani, managed to escape. He earned his living afterwards by compiling a grammar of Turkish grammar. With the royal family suffering such hardship, the condition of population at large can hardly be imagined.

Shah ᶜAlam II, who wrote poetry under the *nom de plume* Aftab, 'Sun', was a frequent guest at social gatherings with religious music arranged by the mystical poet Khwaja Mir Dard in his own house. He too, like his ancestors, took refuge in opium, which he solicited for himself and his ministers from the British in Patna.

The victory which the British and the Nawwab of Awadh had achieved over the Rohillas led to adverse consequences. Najib ud-daula's grandson Ghulam Qadir attacked the palace in 1788. After attempting to form a pact with the chief widow of Muhammad Shah, Malika-i Zaman, he commenced on a round of atrocities, killing twenty-one princes and princesses in two days. The most appalling cruelty was perpetrated against members of the Mughal family, culminating in the blinding of the ruler on 10 August, the 'blind sun' lamented in a Persian poem:

The icy storm of fate
Rose up to humiliate me
Blowing to the wind the foliage
And the flowers of rulership.
I was the sun of the spheres
Raised high in the kingdom
But alack alas: this fall
Brought me to the night of cessation.
My eyes were put out
By cruel fate
Yet it is better that I do not see
What has become of my domain.
I committed sins
For which this was the punishment.
So I hope that now my guilt
Will finally be expiated.
The young Afghan, he cast
The splendour of the kingdom to the wind.
Who but God was there
To show me some friendship?

I nourished the snake with milk
I raised its offspring myself
It grew stronger and grew
And drank, oh calamity! my blood.
And princes and rajas and counts
And landlords and the destitute . . .
What a disaster! Not one of them was there
To share my troubles.
Aftab, in heaven I have seen
Powerful portents today!
God will perchance tomorrow
Restore your head and your power![11]

Although this hope was never to be realised, the blind man ruled under British 'protection' until 1806, even though under *shariᶜa* law, the ruler must be physically intact. The British described themselves as 'servants of the Emperor Shah ᶜAlam', although they paid him not so much as a farthing from the revenues of the country which they were supposedly administering on his behalf.

One of Shah ᶜAlam's seventy children, his son Akbar II, succeeded him, but there is little else to relate concerning him.[12]

The last Mughal ruler, Bahadur Shah Zafar, attained the throne in 1837. He was a calligrapher and poet, who composed enchanting songs in Urdu. He was also very interested in mystical practices, and so Mehrauli, the mausoleum in the quarter of Bakhtiyar Qutbuddin Kaki, which had been venerated for centuries, became his unofficial seat. Many of the nobility established themselves there also. Against his will, the elderly ruler became involved in a military uprising, the so-called Mutiny of 1857. After this was put down, all of India, with the exception of the principalities, came under British rule. Bahadur Shah died in penury in exile in Rangoon in 1862, at the age of eighty-eight.[13]

After the sacking of Delhi in 1739, the important

21. 'Akbar Shah II with Mirza Jahangir greets the British Resident', c. 1815, gouache and gold on paper.

political and cultural developments of Muslim India occurred elsewhere. In the province of Awadh, Urdu achieved its finest flowering, and the Shi'ite festivals were celebrated lavishly. The last ruler, Wajid 'Ali Shah, was forced into exile when Awadh was annexed by the British in 1856. He moved to Calcutta with his large entourage of women and his well-stocked zoo.

In the Deccan, the Asafjahi dynasty was formed by the descendents of Nizam ul-mulk. They helped to foster Islamic traditions and literature, so that until 1948, when the Nizam of Hyderabad's territo-ry was annexed by the Indian Union, it was one of the most important centres of Islamic tradition.

Lahore, which first fell to the Sikhs and then in 1849 came under British rule, attempted to retain its classical heritage. Muslim rulers in south India offered strong resistance to the British, among them Tipu Sultan, who was finally defeated in 1799 at Srirangapatnam.

When it finally came to an end, the era of the Great Mughals seemed like an amazing and enchanting dream, which would forever be remembered with wonder.

22. ' ʿAbduʾl Hadi, *mir bakhshi* to Shah Jahan', from the Small Clive Album, *c.* 1630–40, gouache and gold on paper.

# TWO

# At Court

## THE *DURBAR*: AUDIENCE WITH THE GREAT MUGHAL

Three times a day he (Jahangir) takes his seat in three different places:
once to watch his elephants and other animals fighting; then from four
to five or six o'clock to converse with all his visitors; then at night, from
nine to midnight, with those of his dignitaries in whom he has complete
trust. I visited him during the second session, at which I found him in a
courtyard, sitting like a king in a theatre, with all of his nobles and myself
seated lower down and rather less magnificently on a stage covered with
carpets; but the canopies above his head, and two men standing on the
heads of two wooden elephants to keep the flies away . . .

This was Thomas Roe's description of one of
Jahangir's receptions. Although Persian sources
give somewhat different times for these sessions,
it is clear from all descriptions of life at court
that the ruler followed a strict routine, which he
attempted to adhere to even when he was feeling
unwell.

Ideally, he would perform his morning prayers
before sunrise. Then after sunrise he would
appear on a small balcony facing the Jumna river
(in the case of Agra and Delhi; in Lahore it was
the Ravi). Below, on the riverbank, a crowd of all
kinds of people would be waiting to greet him and
receive his blessing. Apparently there were a great

many who would not even commence their daily
work until they had seen the ruler first thing in the
morning. After no more than an hour, the ruler
withdrew to the *diwan-i ᶜamm*, the public audience
hall. This hall was supported largely by columns,
and in the middle of the wall separating it from the
rest of the palace was the *jharoka*, a small alcove,
from which the ruler showed himself to those
present, granting them *darshan*, a 'view' of himself.
He took his seat on a cushioned throne; to his left
stood standard bearers with their backs to the
wall; behind the throne were eunuchs fanning
him with peacock feather fans and yak hair fly-
whisks, the latter often dyed red. He was

surrounded by bodyguards (who are usually not clearly portrayed in miniature paintings), who were often burly Uzbeks. The executioner was nearby so that grievous offences could be punished on the spot. The throne was surrounded by an expanse of wood, beyond which was an area overlaid with silverwork, where the nobility were arranged according to rank. It was the duty of all officials to participate twice daily, morning and evening, in the *durbar*, the audience, or else be punished with a fine. However, many nobles concocted excuses: 'Asaf Khan's son absented himself from his duty at the imperial court by feigning ill health, and spread out the carpet of comfort.'[1]

Everything in the *durbar* was controlled down to the last detail. No one was allowed to sit in the presence of the ruler, or to leave his place without permission. There are numerous pictures showing the precise order in which the nobles, often identified by name, were positioned around the throne. In the rooms opposite the entrance to the audience hall, bands of musicians, *nauba*, played in honour of the ruler – drums, double drums, and five groups of trumpets announced the presence of the emperor, whose worthiness to rule was symbolized by the *chatr*, an umbrella set with precious jewels, and the *aftabgir*, the bearer of the oval parasol, beside the throne. Jahangir's standard bore the emblems of the sun and a lion.

Miniatures of the earlier periods depict a colourful array of costumes. However, Aurangzeb the Great forbade the wearing of red or yellow clothing by his nobles as religious law stipulated that these colours were unsuitable for men. They were also not allowed to wear clothes with either short or half-length sleeves, nor scarves. The popular habit of chewing betel was forbidden in the ruler's presence, as spittoons, however beautifully worked, were not permitted in the *durbar*, so spitting out the red juice would stain the floor or the walls.

They then got down to business. The *bakhshi*, the Paymaster General, presented officers who had been selected for promotion to the ruler, and the groups of petitioners presented their petitions, which had to be handed to the ruler by officials.

When someone was receiving an honour, he had to perform the official form of greeting (*taslim* or *kurnish*), bowing three times as he approached the throne, bending down to the ground so that the back of his right hand touched the ground. Then, as he stood up, he touched his forehead with the back of this hand. The *sijda*, the same prostration as in ritual prayer, was also customary for a time. However, the devout maintained that one should only prostrate oneself before God, so the custom of *zaminbus*, 'kissing the ground', was introduced, whereby the right hand was laid on the ground and the back of the hand was then kissed, instead of actually kissing the ground. One reads frequently, 'I had the good fortune to be allowed to kiss the ground in honour', or: 'He was honoured by being permitted to kiss the ground.'

Foreign visitors were impressed by these highly regulated receptions. Their hierarchical arrangement produced a profound psychological effect, and pictures of the *durbar* convey some idea of the majestic presence of the emperor. Furthermore, the slightest infringement of etiquette was strictly punished on the spot.

An Amir of Aurangzeb's who was about to kiss his right foot accidentally touched the ruler's cushion, and was harshly criticised by Aurangzeb for his poor eyesight. For three days afterwards he was made to wear glasses.

A young man who appeared drunk in Akbar's presence in broad daylight was tied to the tail of a horse and dragged through the town . . .[2]

23. Ghulam Murtaza Khan, *Emperor Akbar Shah II and four of his sons, c.* 1810, gouache with gold on card.

When the proceedings and nominations were over, the elephants were led past the ruler so that he could see that they were being well looked after. If time allowed, horses and other animals were also presented, and the hunting dogs appeared, caparisoned in red. Sometimes the *durbar* would be followed by an elephant fight, which was the exclusive privilege of the ruler.

On special occasions the *diwan-i ʿamm* would be adorned with carpets and wall hangings, and, from the time of Shah Jahan, the Peacock Throne would be brought out. It was topped by a pearl-fringed canopy supported by gold columns decorated with precious stones. On such rare occasions the highest ranking amirs were permitted to sit on cushions covered with deep red cashmere shawls. Fragrant water was sprayed in the air, and there might also be a performance by dancing girls.

All of this took place in the first couple of hours after sunrise. Towards ten o'clock the ruler made his way to the *diwan-i khass*, the room where he held private audiences and discussed confidential matters with select persons. Requests were examined; tax officials presented their accounts; sometimes alms were distributed to the poor, and occasionally the ruler would view the works of highly regarded artists and artisans, building plans and so on.

Towards eleven o'clock, the most highly confidential matters were discussed by a select few in the Shahburj, or *ghuslkhana*, as it had formerly been called. The *ghuslkhana* was in fact the bath area, situated between the *diwan-i khass* and the women's quarters of the palace. Very few people were allowed into this region of the palace, so there were rooms in which absolute security could be guaranteed.

At noon the ruler held the midday prayer session in the women's quarters of the palace. He was received by the women, who gave him presents and presented him with petitions and requests for help. The ruler also had something to eat during this time. Towards three o'clock he performed the afternoon prayers, and, if necessary, held another audience (as mentioned by Thomas Roe).

In the evening the *diwan-i khass* was illuminated by perfumed candles set in rich holders. Shah Jahan is known to have listened to music there for a while, and other rulers possibly did also. At about eight o'clock the evening prayers were performed. If there was any more business to attend to, it was dealt with in the Shahburj, the innermost secure room. The ruler spent the rest of the evening in the women's quarters, where he listened to music and ate a little. Then he retired to his bed, and a reader or reciter read to him until he fell asleep.

This was the ideal daily routine, at least for Jahangir and Shah Jahan; when necessary, it would be amended.

The granting of titles to men of merit was an important aspect of protocol. A man's ascent through the court hierarchy could be traced through the various titles which he held. In the case of a Muslim, the title Khan would first be appended to his name, and/or a name derived from his particular achievement: *Ma<sup>c</sup>mur Khan* (from the Arabic root *amara*, 'built on', as is *mi<sup>c</sup>mar*, architect) was the honorific title of a leading architect; *Warzish Khan*, 'Sir Sport', that of a fencing master; *Naubat Khan* was the conductor of the military band, *nauba*. *Khushkhabar Khan*, 'Sir Good Tidings' was bestowed on someone who brought good news to the ruler, such as a military victory or the birth of a son. A eunuch in charge of the treasury was very appropriately titled *I<sup>c</sup>timad Khan*, 'Sir Trustworthy'. The title *Asaf Khan* for one of the highest ministers originated with Asaf, the legendary minister of the prophet-king Sulayman (Solomon). An individual's personal characteristics could also provide the inspiration for titles, for example *Salabat Khan*, 'Sir Steadfast', was awarded the title on account of his enormous stature and impressive strength. Jahangir even named one individual whom he had banished from the court *Mardud Khan*, 'Sir Rejected'. For Hindus, the title *Rana* was used, or *Rai* for lower ranking individuals, or *Maharaj* for the highest Rajputs. Doctors, poets and artists received names appropriate to their talents. Sometimes a name was awarded by itself without the addition of *Khan*: *barq andaz*, 'Lighning Striker', was bestowed on the Chief of Artillery, whilst *sher afghan*, 'Lion Conqueror', denoted a brave hunter.[3]

A few dignitaries inherited their titles from their fathers, but this was rare.

It was related that a noble who had inherited

the title *Amir Khan* from his father was reminded by Aurangzeb that his father had originally held the title *Mir Khan*, and that for the letter *a*, which converted *mir* into *amir*, he had paid not less than one *lakh*, the equivalent of 100,000 rupees.[4]

So it was evidently possible to procure titles by means of small gifts...

Titles were usually bestowed during festivals, such as a coronation, or *Nauruz*, the spring new year. However, in special cases, a title could be granted immediately. For example, a soldier who carried the head of a feared enemy to the court would be awarded with the honorary name *Bahadur*, 'Hero', on the spot.

Other awards included the *khil°a*, the robe of honour, which was customary in all Islamic empires from their earliest days. The *khil°a* was a garment which had been worn by the donor and thereby imbued with his benediction. In the time of the Mughals, clothing which had been worn by the ruler himself was designated as *malbus-i khass*, 'special costume'. In the Mughal wardrobe there was a plentiful supply of robes of honour, consisting of suits of three, five, or seven pieces, which were selected according to the rank of the recipient. There are accounts of rulers presenting bereaved *mansabdars* with a special robe of honour at the end of the forty-day period of mourning, after which they were able to discard their mourning clothing. One gift, the *sarapa*, 'head to foot', consisted of a tunic, a turban and a ceremonial sash, *shash*; it was sometimes complemented with jewels or horses.

There were various other honours that were only awarded under precisely determined circumstances, or only to certain classes of Amirs.

Under Shah Jahan the *mahi-i maratib* was introduced as the highest distinction, which would only be accorded to amirs of more than seven thousand *zat*. The standard to be carried by the amir displayed two steel balls and a goldfish. The *'alam* was a standard awarded to thousand-*zat* amirs. Anyone receiving this had to prostrate himself in the *taslim*. Amirs of upwards of two thousand *zat* (or three thousand, according to some sources) were entitled to have military music played in their houses on special occasions, but great care had to be taken not to beat the huge kettle drums when the ruler was within earshot.

Jewelled ornaments were often given as gifts, but the lotus blossom set with jewels, the *padma-i murassa*, was only given in exceptional circumstances.

The *sarpech-i yamani*, the Yemeni turban ornament, was another rare gift, which was only given to amirs of more than three thousand *zat*. A sapphire ring engraved with the recipient's title was a highly valued gift. Valuable ceremonial daggers and swords were awarded more frequently, racehorses less so. Elephants were the most highly prized of all. Anyone who received an animal had to pay a certain 'bridle fee' to the Head Stableman, a custom which was abolished by Jahangir (although for how long is not known).

Receiving such honours was a far from simple matter. Chandar Bhan Brahman, writing during Shah Jahan's time, relates that anyone receiving an office, a promotion, or a fief, had to perform the official salutation, the *taslim*, four times, after which jewels would be placed on his head. Armbands or rosaries and similar objects would be placed in his hand or around his neck, after which he had to bow. If he were receiving weapons, a sword would be hung from his neck, a dagger would be placed upon his head, a quiver upon his shoulder. A shield would be placed on his neck, a coat of mail on his shoulders.

In the case of horses or elephants, the horse's saddle equipment or the elephant handler's

24. Payag, 'Jahangir presents his son, Prince Khurram (Shah Jahan), with a jewelled turban ornament', *c.* 1640, gouache on paper; from Shah Jahan's *Padshahnama* ('Chronicle of the King of the World').

hook, *ankus*, would be placed upon his shoulders. Each time four *taslim* would have to be performed, after which he was entitled to carry and use the objects.

Gifts or promotions were rarely as easily come by as in the story of the exorbitant amir mentioned earlier. For, as Bernier remarked, 'one does not approach a Great One empty handed'. The custom of *pishkash*, of gifts to the ruler (and to all the nobility), was the norm at all levels. In addition there was a specified sum of money, the *nazr* (*nadhr*), which could actually be fairly small. Bada'uni, who only possessed a few hectares of land, went to some trouble to present Akbar with just forty rupees during the Festival of Nauruz.

The *pishkash* could, however, be a substantial sum of money. In order to become the Governor of Bengal, an amir had to pay the fixed sum of 500,000 rupees to Jahangir and Nur Jahan. The chronicles record the amount of costly pearls and rubies or, less frequently, horses and especially fine elephants which the nobility brought to court. Jahangir always reported with satisfaction how much had been brought by whom, and how he had picked out the best gifts in honour of the donor, whilst the rest were returned to the givers. No wonder this system gradually ruined the country's finances.

Portable gifts such as jewellery were presented in a ceremonial cloth, the *rumal*, which was adorned with silk embroidery or painting.

The custom of 'gifts' also applied to foreigners. Sir Thomas Roe was amazed at the many gifts received by Jahangir, whilst the ruler was equally amazed at the paltry gifts presented by the British. Reports by Tavernier and the British East India Company, which was gradually increasing its sphere of operations, both state that enormous sums of money had to be paid to the ruler for every concession. The company had to pay 200,000 rupees to the ruler, and a further 100,000 to his officials, in order to secure its freedom of operations.

Sir Thomas Roe was deeply disappointed when a ring he had given to Asaf Khan as a gift, not merely as a bribe but in friendship, was returned to him as too cheap, being worth merely four hundred rupees.

OFFICES

There were a huge number of employees, ranked in a hierarchy, to assist the ruler in carrying out his daily routine of pomp and duties.

The highest position under the ruler was that of the *wakil*, who was in charge of the administration of the imperial household. Since there was no distinction between private and official in the household, the *wakil's* authority was all-inclusive. Sometimes his duties were connected or interchangeable with those of the *wazir*, who was in charge of the various central offices. The best known and certainly the most powerful Mughal *wazir* was I'timad ad-daula, Jahangir's father-in-law.

There were three offices to deal with financial matters; the *diwan-i kull* dealt with the entire financial administration, the *diwan-i khalisa* with all revenues, and the *diwan-i tan* with the stipends of the *mansabdars* and the princesses, as well as all other outgoings. There was also the ancient office of the *mustaufi*, the chief comptroller of the imperial domains. In texts from the period there are many references to the *bakhshi*, the highest administrative officials dealing with all military matters, who were also responsible for *mansabdars* and soldiers and their upkeep.

The *mir saman* was responsible for the *buyutat*, which comprised the residential quarters of the palace and, primarily, the workshops, the *karkhana* (plural *karkhanaha*), connected to the palace, where the finest textiles, miniature paintings, metalwork and jewellery were produced. When a particularly skilled craftsman was discovered anywhere in the country he would be despatched to the imperial workshop. Each of the *karkhanas* was arranged according to rank, and the ruler of the time – especially Akbar and Jahangir – took a great interest in the works of art which were produced there, and inspected them regularly.

Abu'l Fazl (*A'in* I, 5f.) details still more court offices. There was the keeper of the seal (although the most important seal was kept in the women's quarters, i.e. the ruler's own private quarters); the *bar-begi* or *mir-i ᶜarz*, brought petitions; the *qur-beg* carried the imperial insignia on festive occasions; whilst the *mir-i tuzak* was master of ceremonies.

The *mir-i barr* was in charge of the fleet, consisting for the most part of the boats which plied the great rivers, for the Mughals had little interest in seafaring or in maritime trade.

The *mir-i bahri* was responsible for the forests, and the *mir-i manzil* was the Major Domo.

The *khwansalar* was in charge of the kitchens and the numerous cooks, kitchen boys, and food tasters, and many others.

The hunting as well as the ornamental birds were the province of the *qush-begi*, while the royal stud was the domain of the *akhtabey*. The *atbegi*, 'Horse Master', who had overall responsibility for the thoroughbred horses, was selected from among the highest-ranking *mansabdars*.

There were innumerable other specialists of all kinds, including the fourteen *waqiᶜa-nawis*, perhaps best described as court chroniclers, whose task it was to record everything that happened down to the most trivial occurrence. The *mir munshi* was in charge of the chancellery. He was supposed to be distinguished by the nobility of his correspondence, for the better the style, the more profound the impression created by a letter from the ruler, whether to a friend or foe. There was also a post office.

In addition there were the religious dignitaries, who were subordinate to the *sadr as-sudur*. The *qadi al-qudat*, the highest judge, was the defender of the *shariᶜa*, and the *qadi*s in the provinces and towns were under his authority. Then there was the leader of the *diwan al-mazalim*, who in classical Islam resolved cases which could not be judged according to *shariᶜa* law. In Mughal India he was the representative of the executive, who also acted in the capacity of a judge in some respects. The third important official was the *muhtasib*. His original duties were to oversee the market and inspect prices, and to supervise the conduct of subordinates (seeing to it that they did not imbibe too much wine). The *muhtasib*, well known to readers of the verses of Hafiz as the supervisor of morals, often assumed the role of censor, which made him quite unpopular with the majority of the population.

From the fifteenth century on there was also the *shaykh ul-islam*, who was responsible for religious administration and the distribution of alms as sanctioned by the religious authorities (to widows, orphans, for the building of schools and help for the needy). He was the ultimate religious authority and as such should precede the *qadi al-qutar*.

The imperial seal, which was used on all important documents, played a central role in *durbar* meetings. Jahangir or Shah Jahan are often depicted in miniatures holding this seal, which Abu'l Fazl writes about in great detail in *A'in* I, no. 20.[1]

There were various other seals, some of which were made of metal or carnelian, and also various inscriptions in a variety of styles (e.g. *riqaᶜ*, *nastaᶜliq*). The genealogical seal was especially important. It was round, with the name of the ruler in the centre surrounded by the names of all his ancestors, with Timur's name at the top. This seal was originally guarded by the highest dignitary, however later it was kept in the harem, where Nur Jahan, Mumtaz Mahal and Jahanara were allowed to use it.

The *uzuk* (*yüzük* in Turkish) seal was used for important edicts by the ruler, but was originally reserved for letters to foreign rulers. For legal transactions there was a concave seal with the following Persian verse engraved around the name of the ruler:

Justice earns the approval of God –
I have seen no one stray from the right path
(and be lost).

Akbar used a square seal with the inscription *Allahu akbar jalla jalaluhu* – 'God is Greater (than everything), may his majesty be exalted' – this text being often wilfully misread by the emperor's devotees as referring to Akbar's 'godly' being.

Every edict issued by the palace had a particular name. *Hukm* was the imperial edict (*hukam* is still today the correct form of address for a Maharaja). A *nishan* was issued by members of the imperial family; simple imperial orders were called *parwanche*; a *sanad* was an agreement to an allocation of land or conferment of office. There was also the *yad-dasht*, an official memorandum, and the ᶜ*arz chahra*, in which particular things or situations were described. There was naturally an appropriate type of paper, style of writing and arrangement of text for every type of edict.

Abu'l Fazl describes some typical examples of the work of the chancellery, giving a description of the complicated procedures for important appointments, involving multiple folds and seals applied to a *farman-i thabti*. In extremely urgent and important circumstances, a *farmani-i bayazi* had to be sent (*A'in* II, no. 14).

The *farman* is folded so that both corners touch, then a paper knot is tied and then sealed in so that the contents are not visible. The sealing gum is made from the sap of *kunar*, *bar*, *pipal* and other trees, which, like wax, becomes soft when warmed, but hardens when cold. After the *farman* has been sealed, it is placed in a golden envelope, for His Majesty regards the use of such external signs of greatness as a service to God.

These *farmans* were conveyed to the recipient by *mansabdars*, *ahadis* or regular soldiers. When an official received such an order, he had to approach up to a certain distance, perform various displays of honour, then place the document upon his head, prostrate himself and reward the messenger in the manner appropriate to his standing or connections. When the ruler wanted to show special honour to someone, for example notifying a Rajput prince of his pardon, he might also put his fingerprint on the document.

There were a group of scribes – fourteen in Akbar's time – in the ruler's service, with two on duty each day. All applications and documents presented to the court, and all orders and enquiries from the ruler, were written down by the particular scribe responsible, to be read out in court the following day. No imperial order could be executed without confirmation from the scribe that the case had been presented to the ruler as recorded. This confirmation then had to be recorded in the *farman*: 'It was witnessed that the command recorded in this *farman* was duly proclaimed by the ruler, whilst this and that scribe was on duty.' The correct transcription of the *farmans* on the appropriate paper and with the designated seal could take days, even months. If the ruler wished to amend something or express his opinion, he would write this diagonally over the text.

Everything that had been dealt with in the day's sitting would be recording on a sheet of paper with the heading *akhbarat-i durbar-i mu^calla*, 'News from the Exalted Court', followed by the date. Papers found in archives in Jaipur and elsewhere reveal that all kinds of events were recorded, such as multiple births, presents given or received by the ruler, conferment or rescindment of titles, stipends and so on and so forth. Many *akhbarat* from the time of Aurangzeb record that the ruler enquired after the health of an officer. The deaths of important personages and the arrangements for the care of their family were noted, even dreams which someone considered significant – everything was related in the *durbar*. These papers provide an insight not only into dry administrative problems, they also permit glimpses into the private life of the ruler and his underlings.

DIPLOMATIC RELATIONS

The maintenance of diplomatic relations with neighbouring states was an important task of the ruler.[1] Only the most trustworthy amirs were chosen for the office of ambassador, and they were then promoted to a higher rank of *mansab*.

The ruler would write a letter for his ambassador to give to the ruler of the country to which he was being posted, emphasizing the high standing and position of trust of the bearer. Scientists or men from religious orders were sometimes engaged as ambassadors, but *sayyids*, descendents of the Prophet, were particularly favoured, especially when the Mughals wished to impress their Iranian neighbours, as honour for the Prophet's family occupies a central role in Shi^ci Islam. Furthermore, Persian was the language of literature and culture, and it was used for all important documentation.

The ambassador was expected to foster friendship between the countries and especially the rulers, sometimes negotiating treaties, and of course he had to send a stream of reports on the political and economic conditions of the host country. Secret agents were often used as messengers, to ensure that the report was delivered to the ruler without the contents being revealed to others. The Mughals employed clever merchants for this role, as trade relations were extremely important, especially with Iran.

Mughal embassies contained between fifty and five hundred members of staff, for the larger the embassy, the greater the impression it made upon the ruler of the country. The highest official was the *tahwildar*, who was responsible for the embassy's gifts and expenditure, as well as being the official spokesman. When Jahangir sent Khan ^cAlam to Iran, he was accompanied by seven or eight hundred servants leading ten elephants with gold and silver harnesses, as well as other valuable animals.[2] There was also an artist, Bishndas, among the entourage, who took advantage of his position to make a number of portraits of Shah ^cAbbas. If the predilections of the host were known in advance, these would be taken into consideration when choosing gifts. The Central Asian rulers knew that the Mughals were keen hunters, so they would sometimes send a *mir shikar*, 'hunt master', with doves, birds of prey, or similar gifts.

Gifts played an important role in mutual relations. The Mughal rulers made careful note of all presents they received, and designated scribes compiled meticulous lists of them. Jahangir also always assessed the value of all presents given to him.

The Iranians often gave thoroughbred Arabian horses which had been bred in Iraq, as these were considered to be the very best; also jewellery, costly vessels and textiles. It was a sign of great honour if the ruler gave his counterpart loot taken during a recent military campaign, or booty from a vanquished prince. The Iranians gave Russian furs to the Mughal court as a sign of their high esteem – ninth-century records reveal that these had been prized by Muslims since the early Middle Ages. Nadir Shah gave the Czar in St Petersburg prize booty from the sacking of the Mughal treasury at Delhi in 1739.

Once all the preparations had been completed, the ambassador was despatched with a letter to the ruler of the host country, along with verbal instructions. The letters were from the highest *munshi*, the head of the chancellery, and written in a very complex style. In Akbar's time it was often Abu'l Fazl's task to compose such letters in his inimitable florid style. A number of different versions would be drafted, from which the ruler selected the one he liked best. This would then be transcribed in artistic calligraphy.

In each province through which the ambassador travelled, he would be received with the highest honours. As he approached the capital or current residence of the ruler, he was greeted by members of the nobility, and provided with ample money so that, as a guest of the ruler, he would not be out of pocket.

On the ambassador's arrival at his destination, the ruler would despatch a *mihmandar*, a sort of Chief of Protocol, who was to attend to the guests and their accommodation. Sometimes the *mihmandar* was himself a former or future ambassador. A date would be fixed for his official reception – the sooner he was received, the higher the honour. Ambassadors from less important regions might have to wait weeks or months, during which time they attempted to speed things up by means of small, or not so small, gifts to influential men at court.

Sometimes a whole series of ambassadors would arrive in Delhi or Agra in quick succession.

In 1664 Bernier witnessed their arrival from Mecca, Yemen, Basra, Ethiopia and Uzbekistan. This last, who brought lapis lazuli, horses and fruits, was described by the observant French doctor as being 'somewhat unclean', and he was probably not the only one who was repelled by Uzbek eating habits (also their penchant for horse flesh).

When the ambassador was finally presented at court, there was the problem of the appropriate form of greeting, which often led to disputes. The Persian custom was to clasp the hands in front of the chest, rather than bowing deeply or kissing the ground. Sir Thomas Roe obstinately refused to perform the full greeting, employing the European form instead. He then shocked both the ruler and the court by demanding a chair and refusing to stand throughout the entire *durbar*. It was no easy matter, especially for older or corpulent men, to bow as deeply as directed, and many miniatures depict a visitor being supported by the waist whilst bowing.[3]

The reception ceremony at the Mughal court took place in the *diwan-i ʿamm*. After a brief conversation, the ambassador's letter of introduction would be handed to the ruler by a court official. Only rarely would an ambassador be permitted to pass the letter to the ruler himself. After some discussion, the ambassador produced a few valuable gifts, and was then given a robe of honour. Whilst a complete inventory of his presents was being prepared, a date would be fixed for their presentation, the ruler selecting the ones which pleased him. If the ambassador had also brought a few small gifts of his own, this would increase his standing. Sometimes the ruler would then converse with the ambassador – Jahangir especially enjoyed this, often over a glass of wine. A gift of fine wines would always win the approval of the Mughal princes.[4]

The ambassador then received invitations from the nobles. He was obliged to take part in

25, 26. Sur Das, 'Akbar receiving ambassadors from Badakhshan in 1561', from the *Akbarnama*, c. 1603–5, pigment and gold on paper.

hunts and attend festivities such as the ceremonial weighing of the ruler, weddings, firework displays, in fact on all occasions when the power of the ruler was on display.

Ambassadors tended to remain for a fairly long time in Agra or Delhi – the minimum stay was three to four months, although some were detained at the Mughal court for more than a year. Only in cases of emergency would they be sent home after a month.

In addition to a robe of honour and other presents, the ambassador would be given a considerable sum of money – between 50,000 and 100,000 rupees. Many of them earned an additional income from trade. They brought goods from Iran or their homeland and bought large quantities of Indian goods which were transported over the borders duty free in diplomatic bags. The East India Company was naturally extremely angry about this trade, which deprived them of considerable profits.

At the end of his stay, the ambassador was provided with another robe of honour and more presents, and sent home with a festive farewell.

All in all, it was a protracted and costly business, so less expensive ambassadors, such as travellers and merchants who were travelling that way in any case, were also used for specific purposes. This might involve conveying urgent messages and information, or gifts between statesmen and other non-royal personages, for there were many vital diplomatic connections in these circles as well.

If an official ambassador happened to arrive during a period when diplomatic relations had been suspended, he would nevertheless be treated very cordially, although he would not be allowed to visit the ruler. He would be accompanied to the border, and 'there is not a single instance in the records of Indo-Persian relations of any ambassador being treated badly; however bad diplomatic relations might be, and however unwelcome the contents of his letters.'[5]

If the Mughal ambassador returned to court having been successful in his mission, he would be rewarded with a promotion and money; if not, then he could be demoted and even banished from the court.

THE TRAVELLING COURT

The daily work of the ruler was very exacting, and it was planned down to the last detail. Since most miniatures portray him seated on the throne, it is easy to forget that he spent a great deal of his time on the move, and more than merely shuttling between Fatehpur Sikri and Lahore, or just moving from one residence to another. Although their culture was highly refined, the Mughals appear to have retained their traditional nomadic way of life. They made regular journeys between Lahore and Kashmir, their favourite summer resort from the sixteenth century onwards, and frequently left one palace and moved to another, and not just for a holiday or to reduce the pressures of work, since they took the entire court and all its accoutrements with them.

When the ruler issued the command to leave for Kashmir or Kabul, the superintendent of the *farrashkhana*, where materials, tents, carpets and such were stored, was advised to choose the location for the first camp. There were two identical sets of equipment in the *farrashkhana*, which were used in alternation. Like the ruler, the Amirs had all their equipment in duplicate, since they had to have everything they needed with them in any new location. A camp was set up in one location, whilst a second camp was being prepared with the other set of equipment at the next stop. No wonder the chief of the *farrashkhana* bore the title *Pishraw Khan*, 'Sir Going On Ahead'.

An astrologically auspicious date for departure was determined, then the ruler prepared himself for the journey in the presence of the amirs. He dipped his finger into a pot of yoghurt then drew it across a fish, which was supposed to ensure good luck for a journey. His sword, quiver and bow were placed on him, and finally he mounted his elephant and rode off to the sound of timpani, being greeted by elephant handlers on either side. Servants went in front of the procession leading a camel laden with white shrouds. These would be used to cover any human or animal corpses that might be encountered along the way, so the sovereign would not be disturbed by the sight of them.

Water carriers sprinkled the ground so that the dust would not rise up and cover him.

The European ambassadors who took part in such processions wrote detailed accounts of their experiences. The Cornish traveller Peter Mundy (in India 1628–34) mentions the retinue of thirty-five thousand horses and ten thousand infantrymen that accompanied the ruler. The cavalcade of numerous elephants was preceded by drummers, trumpeters, canopy carriers, and standard bearers. There were usually nine changes of horse for the ruler, a number favoured by the Turks. Next came the ruler and his entourage, with servants, guards and so on bringing up the rear.

Mundy describes Shah Jahan's return journey from the Deccan. There were twenty wagons at the head of the train, two of them pulled by Kutch horses, the rest by enormous oxen. Then came a thousand knights, followed by around twenty state elephants in full regalia, complete with sedan chairs and standards. Nobles carrying silver rods rode ahead of the ruler. The emperor, who on such occasions was mounted on a dark grey steed, followed the crown prince, Dara Shikoh. Next came more knights with gleaming lances, and the officers' elephants, 'like a flotilla of ships at sea'. Sir Thomas Roe reports that there were three palanquins of gold decked with red satin and adorned with rubies and emeralds among the baggage, and that the artillery was transported on elephants. There were travel guides to provide information about the regions they journeyed through, and people whose job it was to measure the distance covered each day, and the stretch to be traversed on the next march.

The enormous troop travelled in short stages, covering scarcely more than ten miles a day. When the ruler was seated on his elephant, the Amirs followed behind on horseback. If he was mounted, they went on foot. When the ruler reached the

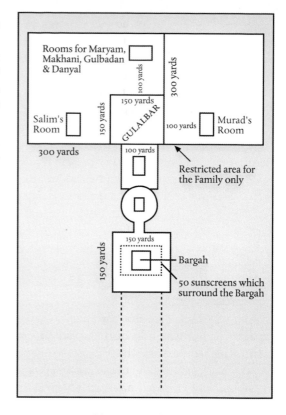

27. Encampment of the Great Mughuls, c. 1580.

camp, the band began to play. All the *mansabdar*s decorated their tents very lavishly, and the ruler entered the camp from either side, selecting for himself whatever of their valuable finery appealed to him, according to Bernier.

Military and armoured elephants cleared the way until he reached his own tent, greeted all along the way by salutations. After he had washed his hands he withdrew, and was joined by the women, who had arrived ahead of him, having taken a short cut – however, considering the steep pathways leading to Kashmir, it is difficult to imagine that they could have taken a quicker and more convenient route than the one taken by the king.

The camp was very spread out. The imperial tent occupied an area 1,450 to 1,500 m in length and 350 m in width, surrounded by a fence of cloth. The cloth fence and the tents themselves were often decorated with patterns, such as cypress trees. The women's tent was on the east side of the imperial tent.

The ground was covered with carpets. In the middle was a platform covered by a huge canopy. This was the *mahtabi*, where the ruler held confidential conversations at night. There were also other tents and canopies reserved for particular purposes.[1] In the centre of the entire complex was a tall mast with a large lamp hanging from it to light the way for anyone who became lost in the tent town. Special heavily guarded tents were reserved for the women, especially the queen mother, and also for the princes. These were cordoned off, and a strip of land about ninety metres wide separated them from the rest of the encampment, where the armoury, wardrobes, fruit stores and, most important, the kitchen were located. There was a complete bazaar with everything they could possibly need for sale. Aurangzeb's procession to Kashmir in 1662 included camels laden with gold as well as fifty kitchen camels and fifty milch cows. The guards spent two days each week on duty.

There are no exact figures relating to the size of the camps, but Sir Thomas Roe states that it was one of the greatest rarities and wonders that he had ever set eyes on. Even cheetahs – hunting leopards – and other animals had been brought along.

The ruler adhered to his normal routine in the camp, just as at home; he performed his prayers, presented himself to the *mansabdar*s and to the people, for his twice daily appearance was a

28. An embroidered silk and metal thread canopy, *c.* 1700.

formality which could not be neglected under any circumstances. The camp must indeed have been a magnificent sight, especially during the evenings, when the nobility paid a visit to the ruler, and an uninterrupted stream of lanterns or torches was moving through the tent city. It must seem incredible to modern readers that this enormous structure was dismantled and then reconstructed only a few miles further on. It must have been a terrific burden on the inhabitants of these areas (if also an honour), to have such a huge crowd of people and animals in the vicinity. In addition to the ruler, the officers, the women, and the men responsible for the well being of the household, such as cooks and water carriers, there was also an entire army of craftsmen to assemble and dismantle the tents; smiths and ironworkers, and even, according to Abuʾl Fazl, 150 sweepers to keep the pathways clear, and similar workers.

It took them several weeks to reach their destination. Since they liked to be in Kashmir in the springtime, they travelled there in late winter, so they were often hampered by rain and snow. However they hoped to be able to celebrate *Nauruz*, the vernal equinox, at the spring garden in Kashmir, in luxurious tents erected for the purpose.

A final note about the tents.[2] It is no doubt difficult for the modern reader to visualize these enormous tents, which, according to Abuʾl Fazl, it took a thousand *farrash* a week to erect. However, on the sub-continent the technical skills necessary to erect tents for up to ten thousand people have been retained to this day.

It is even more difficult to imagine the luxury of an imperial tent, since practically all of the components have been destroyed over time.[3] However, the exhibition INDIA! held in New York in 1985 gave some idea of its luxury for the first time. In 1658 the Rajput prince Jaswant Singh captured a tent during a battle against Aurangzeb and his brother Shah Shujaᶜ. Since that time it had been kept safe in the palace at Jodhpur, and the Maharaja of Jodhpur lent it to the Metropolitan Museum of Art for the exhibition. It was the centrepiece of the exhibition – 3.3 metres in height and 7.34 to 7.44 metres in width. It was made of red silk velvet embroidered with gold, and could well have been the *chubin rawati* mentioned by Abuʾl Fazl (*Aʾin* I, no. 21).

# THREE

# The Empire

People from many races (Arabs, Persians, Turks, Tajiks, Kurds, Iranians, Tatars, Russians, Abyssinians and so on) and from many countries ('Rum', i.e., Turkey, Egypt, Syria, Iraq, Arabia, Persia, Gilan, Mazandaran, Khurasan, Sistan, Transoxiana, Kurdistan) – in fact, different groups and classes of people from all races and all human societies – have sought refuge in the imperial court, as well as different groups from India, men with knowledge and skills as well as warriors, for example, Bukharis and Bhakkaris, *Sayyids* of genuine lineage, *Shaykhzadas* with noble ancestry, Afghan tribes such as the Lodis, Rohillas, Khweshgis, Yusufzay etc. and castes of Rajputs, who were to be addressed as *rana, raja, rao* and *rayan* – i.e., Rathor, Sisodias, Kachhawas, Haras, Gaurs, Chauhans, Panwars, Bhadurias, Solankis, Bundelas, Shekhawats and all the other Indian tribes , such as the Ghakkar, Langar, Khokar, Baluchis and others who wielded the sword, *mansab*s from one hundred to one thousand *zat*, from one to seven thousand *zat*, and from one hundred to *ahadi*, likewise landowners from the steppes and mountains, from the regions of Karnataka, Bengal, Assam, Udaipur, Srinagar, Kumaon, Bankhu, Tibet and Kishtwar and so on – whole tribes and groups of them have been privileged to kiss the threshold of the imperial court.

Chandarbhan Brahman

The Mughal empire, which encompassed innumerable tribes and races of widely varying origin, had no hereditary nobility, as the term is understood today. The status of a man was derived from the military rank, *mansab*, he held. Although some status would pass to the son of an amir, i.e., a commander of upwards of 500-*zat* or 1,000-*zat* (see below), titles were usually not inherited, only granted to individuals, and only a small amount of property could be inherited, for all land belonged to the crown.

There was, however, one great social distinction—membership of the *ashraf*, the nobility. This class was descended from Muslim families who had migrated from the eastern side of the border of the subcontinent, from the Arabian, Persian or Turkish-central Asian regions, whether as soldiers or conquerors (as was the case with many families of Turkish or Pathan origin), or Sufis, who came with the intention of gradually converting the land to Islam. *Sayyids*, descendants of the Prophet Muhammad, enjoyed the highest status of all.

Muslims were a small minority of the population of India, relative to the Hindu majority. Muslims of Turkish and Pashtun descent formed the government, or at least part of it. During Akbar's rule, the martial Hindu Rajputs were permitted for the first time to participate in the running of the state, and to hold high office.

What exactly was a *mansabdar*? The word denotes 'someone possessed of a certain rank, *mansab*'. Therefore everyone who held any rank at all in the military hierarchy was a *mansabdar*. However it is not clear what the qualifications for these ranks were, and what these confusing titles actually mean. What was a 5,000-*zat* / 3,000-*suwar* officer? Did he have command of 5,000

soldiers and 3,000 cavalrymen with horses? In fact, it was far more complicated than that.

Abu'l Fazl delineates the ideal structure of the army. The divisions of the soldiers were organized decimally; the lowest rank was the *dih bashi*, 'Leader of Ten', and above that was the seldom mentioned *bisti*, 'Leader of Twenty'. Above that was the *yüzbashi*, 'Leader of a Hundred', and this was further elaborated in very complicated ways. The holder of a rank of 500-*zat* and above was called an *amir* (plural *umara*). Among these were the *omrah*, which are mentioned in reports by European travellers. Above these were the officers from 1,000-*zat* (*mingbashi*) to the 7,000-*zat*. The highest ranks of all – up to 12,000-*zat* – were reserved for the princes, who at a very tender age held high office and had 'command' of between 7,000 to 10,000 troops. There was a general tendency to inflate titles and ranks, so that under the rule of Shah Jahan and Aurangzeb there was even a rank of 36,000-*zat*. Various insignia distinguished the ranks, for example an amir of more than 2,000-*zat* received a kettle-drum. Flags with one to three yak tails, *tüman tügh*, were also used to differentiate the ranks.

The word *zat* (from the Arabic *dhat*, 'being, person') signified a man's personal rank, not the number of soldiers under his command, whereas the title *suwar*, 'cavalry officer', indicated the number of horses and riders he was supposed to provide. He received a salary, usually the revenue from a village or a district, from which he had to meet the expenses of his cavalry. This was his *jagir*, which means much the same as 'fief'.

The army received monthly salaries, but not always for every month of the year. Although many received a twelve-monthly salary, others might be paid for only eight or five months a year. This was calculated not in silver rupees, but in the smallest denomination of copper coins, the *dam*:

forty *dam* equalled one rupee, so astronomical sums were involved. The most important official, the *bakhshi*, 'Military Paymaster', had the unenviable task of sorting it all out.

Abu'l Fazl provides an illustration: a normal *yüzbashi* received (in theory) 23,000 *dam* a month, i.e. 700 rupees. From that he had to pay 20 rupees to each of the ten men for whom he was responsible. From the remaining 500 rupees he had to pay for the upkeep of ten horses (which were also ranked according to breeding), three elephants, ten camels and five transport wagons, which altogether amounted to 313 rupees. That left only 187 rupees for his personal expenses, however it was possible to live quite well on that amount at the time.[1]

Understandably, the *mansabdars*, especially the highest ranks, attempted to have as few soldiers as possible to maintain, since they were only necessary in times of war. So when someone had a rank of 3000-*zat* 1500-*suwar*, this did not always mean that he was actually maintaining 1500 cavalrymen, and any surplus salary went into his own pocket. This was also the case with horses, so Akbar introduced the regulation that horses had to be branded, so that when the troops were inspected it would be clear whether or not the *mansabdar* had really brought his own horses or whether he had borrowed someone else's just to pass muster.[2] To further complicate matters, among the *suwar* of a *mansabdar* were not only normal cavalrymen, there were also *du aspa* and *sih aspa*-soldiers, who had not merely *one* horse, but two or three.

There was a special group of soldiers called *ahadi*, who could not usually become *mansabdar* – nevertheless, from time to time one of them would succeed in making a career for himself, such as Mahabat Khan in Jahangir's time. They were directly beneath the ruler in rank, and had special duties to perform. Many of the artists in Akbar's studios were *ahadi*s. They usually had a horse, however sometimes two or even three of them had to share one horse between them (*nim aspa*). Contemporary sources give the impression that, being entrusted with special duties, they occupied a position of honour. However, in later times they mostly stayed home awaiting the call to duty. Still today there is an Urdu expression *ahadipan*, 'to act like an *ahadi*', meaning laziness, indolence.[3]

Anyone who became a *mansabdar* had to place his life entirely at the disposal of the ruler and do whatever he was commanded to do, even if the order had nothing to do with his qualifications. Abu'l Fazl, the court chronicler, was a man with absolutely no military experience, yet he was entrusted with an important task during the Deccan war. There were of course precise rulings as to which posts corresponded to which *zat-suwar* rank, and how many *jagirs* in Jaunpur were equivalent to one in Sind, because the level of remuneration varied widely. Asaf Khan, for example, received 50 *lakh* per annum, equivalent to five million rupees, from his *jagir*. *Mansabdars* could be suddenly transferred from one post to another, so that it was highly unlikely that they could develop a real relationship with the inhabitants of their region. The frequent changes of *jagir* incumbents were also bad for the economy, since for many *mansabdars* the chief purpose of their administration was to amass as much wealth as possible for themselves, not to improve the living conditions of the inhabitants.

The promotion of *mansabdars* appears to have been somewhat arbitrary. Someone could be promoted for distinction on the field of battle, or, as is particularly evident from Jahangir's accounts, for performing a personal service for the ruler or doing him a favour. *Mansabdars* could also be punished or demoted. A fief could be subdivided to punish the holder. However, 'their error could be cleansed with the pure water of forgiveness' – those punished could be restored to office and could sometimes rise up again to high ranks.

On the death of a *mansabdar*, his territory reverted to the crown. However, some provision was made for his descendants, provided the *jagir* was not mired in debt. The debts might be settled, and the remainder passed on to his heirs. The penniless son of a man who had fallen in battle might receive a small *jagir* in recognition of his father's bravery. One typical case was that of a long-serving Commander-in-Chief, Mun'im Khan, who, at the age of eighty, remained in Bengal despite a raging epidemic, and 'no-one dared to remove the cotton wool of ignorance from his ears'. He died in 1575, and, 'since he had no heir, all of his wealth was seized by officials for the imperial treasury, all that he had taken so many years to amass . . .'4

Sometimes a *mansabdar* who felt his end approaching would quickly pay his soldiers a year or two's salary so that they would not suffer under his successor.

The household employees of the highest *mansabdars* were as stratified as those of the ruler, from the *bakhshi*, paymaster, to the head chef, from the chief of the office responsible for all copies, receipts and letters, to the 'secret scribe'. Each had their own secret duties, which was particularly useful in time of war. *Mansabdars* gave small or more lavish 'gifts' to those of higher rank to resolve difficulties, for instance so that the ruler did not have to be informed of any wrongdoing on their part, as they would be harshly punished if it came to the attention of the court. Curiously, Aurangzeb, who was otherwise known for his severity, was astonishingly lenient with his *mansabdars*.

A man had to wait a long time to be awarded an office – it took weeks, even months, until he actu-

ally had the *farman* authorising the new *mansab* in his hand. If he lived in the capital, he would usually wait patiently until he could take the document home. If he was not able to wait for some reason or other, he received a certified copy of the *farman*, issued by the scribe responsible, together with the supplementary order of the financial administration relating to the fief he was to receive. The certified copy had to be presented to the tax official of that region, also an affidavit that the imperial order was being prepared and would soon be delivered. Then he had to guarantee that he would assume responsibility for any loss, in case the order did not come. Since *mansabdars* were so frequently promoted or transferred, such matters must have taken up a considerable amount of their time.

Many *mansabdars*, especially in later times, became prosperous merchants. A position such as Superintendent of the harbour at Surat was an attractive one because it offered ample opportunity to profit from import and export. It rarely happened that a merchant achieved the rank of *mansabdar*, however Mir Jumla, a Persian groom, became a diamond trader and finally, under Shah Jahan and Aurangzeb, a highly influential *mansabdar*. (An earlier example is that of Mahmud Gawan of Gilan, who for thirty years, as 'King of the Merchants', ruled the kingdom of Bidar on behalf of the minor or incompetent Bahmanid sultan, before being murdered in 1481.) Mir Jumla was especially interested in diamond and maritime trading, and at about the same time, Shayasta Khan was able to create a salt emporium, trading primarily with Bengal. Just as there were court *karkhanas*, 'workshops', for fabrics, clothing, vessels and so on, many of the *mansabdars* had their own workshops.

Artists who had been dismissed from the court by Jahangir for not meeting his exacting standards, often withdrew to the provinces and found employment with the nobility, from where they promulgated Mughal artistic ideals.

Evidently there were no fixed regulations about salaries, and the Mughals were rather lax about paying their artists, and, more crucially, their soldiers. Consequently officers had to keep concocting stories about forthcoming payment for fear that their soldiers would otherwise desert. Nevertheless, many of the great amirs managed to complete worthwhile projects – they constructed lodgings, bridges, reservoirs, gardens, and mosques for the benefit of the populace. *Langars*, which provided free food for the poor, were established not only by the rulers, but also by many of the amirs.

The award of a *mansab* always had a military connotation, even if the *mansabdar* only served at court, but there were alternative ways of honouring a man of merit. The ruler could give him an *in<sup>c</sup>am*, which was either a sum of money or the revenue from a particular district.

*Suyurghal*, or *madad-i ma<sup>c</sup>ash*, 'income support', was important particularly for civilians. This was also either in the form of cash, or, more usually, lands, the income from which was tax-free. In general, the recipient of *suyurghal* would be allotted an area of virgin land, to be cultivated by peasants (*ayma, ima*), thereby increasing the area under cultivation. According to numerous documents, *madad-i ma<sup>c</sup>ash* were primarily awarded to members of religious orders, to mullahs or preachers. They were also given to Muslim women, for whom they were particularly important. There are many references to the widows of religious dignitaries or especially devout women receiving such gifts. Such stipends were sometimes used to establish free schools. The learned or pious also received a pension, *tankhwah*. The *madad-i ma<sup>c</sup>ash*, unlike the *jagirs*, could be bequeathed.

Jahangir introduced the *al tamgha*, 'red seal'. This was a fief which, in contrast to the normal *jagirs*, could be granted for an extended period of time.

Whilst the thousands of *mansabdar*s and their troops formed the secular army of the Mughals, pensioners, both male and female, constituted a *lashkar-i du<sup>c</sup>a*, a sort of 'Prayer Army'.

## MARTIAL ARTS AND WARFARE

'A monarch should always be engaged in conquest, otherwise his neighbours will aim their weapons at him. The army should always be waging war so that it does not become soft from lack of exercise.'[1] This was the view of Akbar, who was praised as a prince of peace. But what was the Mughal army like? When Babur first set off for India, bows and arrows and swords were still very much in use as the weaponry of war. The Central Asian Turks were renowned and feared for their skill with bows and arrows and for their sudden attacks, retreats and unexpectedly renewed attacks. In great battles, the Mughals also adopted the strategy of outflanking. Miniatures depict various types of strong bow, which were often tipped with poison.

Swords were an important part of the weaponry. Although there are references to the sharpness of the *sayf-i hindi*, the Indian sword, even in classical Arabian poetry, in Jahangir's time the English merchant William Hawkins found 2,200 German swords in the Mughal treasury. In addition to various types of dagger, the ruler was armed with a sword, which he carried at all times in a red sheath, either at his side or behind him. Especially valuable swords were even given names, such as *sarandaz*, 'decapitator', or *shahbacha*, 'child of the king'. However, the Mughals soon realised the

29. Attributed to Hashim, *khankhanan ʿAbduʾr Rahim*, *c.* 1620–25, ink and gold on paper.

need for firearms. From the late fifteenth century, the Ottomans were the leading Muslim producers of firearms, and thanks to them the use of cannon, mortars, and muskets was widespread in the Middle East. Consequently, the commander of the Mughal artillery often bore the title Rumi Khan, even though he may not have been an Ottoman Turk.

Babur also occasionally used a musket, and he relates with amusement that the inhabitants of the central Indus region, which he invaded in 1519, were not frightened by the sound of shooting, on the contrary: 'they laughed and made obscene gestures'. They evidently thought that the attackers were afflicted with flatulence! Not long afterwards (in 1525), Babur began making use of mortars. The first attempts failed, and 'Master ᶜAli was almost at the point of throwing himself into the mould with the molten bronze'.[2] The next attempt was successful, but Babur had not yet got the hang of it entirely, and in India in October 1527, a mortar exploded, killing or wounding a number of people. About fifteen years previously, in Cairo, the Mamluk Sultan Qansuh al-Ghuri, who had also been trained in the use of cannons by the Ottomans, had suffered a similar calamity.[3]

Firearms had improved considerably by the time of Akbar, and he often went shooting. Abuʾl Fazl relates (Aʾin I, 37) that the ruler's rifles were catalogued according to weight, the source of the iron, the manufacturer and place of manufacture as well as the date of casting. The muskets were organized into different categories, and brought to Akbar in a particular order. These weapons were extremely beautifully made, inlaid with gold and enamels. Two generations later, Shah Jahan's poet laureate wrote verses on the ruler's muskets:

The Emperor's musket incinerates the enemy,
Annihilates his opponent's life at once:

Like thunder and lightening, a dark cloud
Shoots from the ruler's thunderous hand![4]

Miniatures show the imperial marksman supporting his very long musket either on the shoulder of a man kneeling in front of him, or on a sort of metal pitchfork. Even when he was firing from the back of an elephant, the weapon would be supported on the shoulder of the elephant driver sitting in front, and the recoil could hardly have made his job of steering the animal any easier.[5]

Muskets tended to overheat rather rapidly, and were very slow to reload; hence, a large number of musketeers was necessary to guarantee an effective line of attack. Akbar apparently had 12,000 musketeers.

The army was divided into the infantry, cavalry, and artillery, the most important of which was the cavalry. A soldier's greatest fear was losing his horse in battle, since he would be liable for the loss.

Miniatures depict the troops in the field of battle wearing a narrow cap-like helmet with a neck protector. The ruler wore one made of gold, or gilded. They also wore armbraces and leg armour,[6] those of the higher ranks being very costly. The armbraces for the ruler and the nobility reached the elbow and were lined with velvet. Miniatures in the *Padshahnama* depict some knee shields in the form of a human face.

They carried slightly convex leather shields which were often lavishly decorated with inlay, and sometimes with exhortations repeated several times on the inner edge, such as *ya fattah!*, 'Oh Opener!' (one of the 99 Names of God), *ya ᶜAli!* , 'Oh ᶜAli!' The rest of their equipment, including their swords, also bore religious inscriptions.

The coat of mail worn by the ruler and the high-ranking amirs reached down to the knee, and was decorated with gold bands. Underneath they might wear a 'talisman garment', a cotton or linen smock with appeals to God, verses from the Qur'an and the like written on it. The high-ranking amirs carried standards with yak tails, *tüman tügh*. Many miniatures depict a wonderfully orderly forest of standards, all edged with golden scallops with white yak tails hanging from them. Before the start of battle the lances carried by some army divisions were also arranged, if pictures are to be believed, as regularly as an iron railing fence.[7]

Horses also wore armour made up of several separate pieces, which covered their entire bodies except for their legs, and was sometimes decorated with gold or gilt chains. They had chamfrons, and their braided manes were pulled through openings in their neck armour.

The higher-ranking officers were provided with kettle drums. The sound of the beating of these drums was the sign of a strong army unit, for they were only permitted to *mansabdars* of more than 2,000 (or 3,000) *zat*.

As the artillery came to play an increasingly important role, the equipment of the officers and soldiers was mentioned less frequently by the chroniclers. Manucci observed that the soldiers wore no uniform, unlike their European counterparts.

The Mughals sought the help of Turks, and also increasingly of Europeans, especially Portuguese and Italians, with their heavy artillery. Akbar attempted to enlist Christian marksmen in Surat, and under Aurangzeb the number of European marksmen increased. Those who were competent in this profession were extremely well remunerated.

Cannons, catapults and rockets were also used. The great cannons were sometimes real works of art, but transporting them was a major problem. The cannonballs were initially made of stones weighing around 540 pounds, so the cannons had to be very solidly constructed to be able to fire them. During one siege in 1527, Babur used fourteen heavy cannon, which fired balls weighing from 225 to 315 pounds. 700 to 800 porters were needed to help carry all this equipment uphill, whilst on level ground they used 200 pairs of oxen as well as several elephants to pull it. Initially these cannons could only fire eight shots a day, but this was gradually increased to sixteen.

At the Battle of Kanauj in 1540, Babur's son Humayun used 700 guns, each carried on a wagon pulled by four oxen. The cannonballs weighed about five pounds each. There were also twenty-one heavy cannons pulled by eight pairs of oxen. The lead cannonballs weighed about 46 pounds and had a range of one *farsakh*, approximately 62 kilometres. During sieges they used the wagons to form fortifications.

In all military campaigns, the role of pioneers was crucial. Among their many accomplishments, these resourceful men were able to construct pontoon bridges so strong that even wild elephants could run across them.

One of the most famous miniatures from Akbar's time depicts the siege of Chitor in 1567,[8] and clearly shows the incredible effort it took for the army to pull the heavy cannons up the steep hill to the fort. The oxen could hardly move the wooden-wheeled carriages. The preparation for the manoeuvre was as follows:

> First of all a *sabad* is laid out. This is a wall starting just within musket shot from the enemy fortress, continuing up to fairly near the parapet, and if possible, to a greater height. The guns are fired over the *sabad* to create breaches in the walls of the fort, and under their cover the troops storm the citadel down to the last man. For the construction of these fortified walls, they use cylindrical wicker baskets

covered with buffalo hide and filled with earth. The sappers roll this portable defence into position in front of themselves so that they can work behind it safe from enemy fire . . .

Then trenches were dug and explosives were laid, which was a difficult job in hard ground:

> Five thousand men were used for the digging alone, and every day on average about two hundred of them were killed. However, they were all volunteers, for the emperor would not permit compulsory labour to be used for this work, preferring to pay the men so handsomely that there were always new workmen to take the place of those who perished on the job . . .
>
> The emperor ordered that the *sabad* of the communication trench was to be high enough that a warrior seated on the back of an elephant and holding a lance could not be seen from the citadel, and wide enough that ten cavalrymen could ride along it side by side. This tremendous preparation took about three weeks, including laying two mines not far from each other.[9]

As the assault commenced on 13 December, the second mine exploded prematurely, blowing up friend and foe alike. The siege lasted until the end of the following February, when Chitor surrendered. Those trapped inside the city committed *jauhar*, immolating themselves. Bada'uni, who would have liked to take part in the battle himself, quotes the following verse:

> And what a great day it was for the vultures and crows –
> Praise be to Him, Who feeds his creatures so abundantly![10]

30. Miskina and Paras, 'The siege of Ranthambhor', from the *Akbarnama*, 1568, gouache and gold on paper.

The conquest of Chitor was achieved at the cost of thousands of lives. It was represented by the chronicler as a struggle again the infidel, and Akbar as a hero of Islam. It should be remembered that only twelve years previously Akbar had achieved victory over Hemu in the second battle of Panipat, and after the battle he constructed a tower with the skulls of the slain enemy, as his forefather Timur had often done, and Babur also, according to reports.

31, 32. Miskina, with Bhura (left panel) and Sarwan (right panel), 'A mine explodes during the siege of Chitor (1567)', *c.* 1590-95, colour and gold on paper.

During the siege of Chitor, elephants were driven through the breaches in the walls of the fort, to trample the inhabitants in the streets. They had been trained not to be alarmed by the noise of rockets and cannons, and had weapons fixed to their trunks. Their tusks were encased in iron, and they had steel plates on their brows to use as battering rams. Sometimes the animals were festooned with yak tails and animal pelts to make them appear even more fearsome. In Shah Jahan's time a good war elephant was worth 100,000 rupees.

The following passage was written by Shamsham ad-daula about the battle of Kalpi in Shah Jahan's time:

> An *Ahriman*-like elephant broke the gate down . . . and their lily-white swords made the dark Indus tulip-coloured (i.e., red) and painted the face of bravery with rose-coloured victory . . .

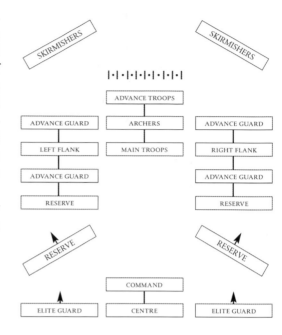

33. Aurangzeb's order of battle at Meerut.

The use of elephants was not without its drawbacks. They sometimes took fright on the battlefield and turned around and trampled their own troops. And whereas it was in some respects an advantage for the army general to be highly visible seated on his elephant, it also made him an easy target. During the Battle of Samugarh in 1658, Dara Shikoh, acting on the bad advice of a false friend, got off his elephant and mounted a horse, with catastrophic consequences. His soldiers thought that he had been shot, and took flight. After this disaster it was decided that it would be better if the ruler himself did not take part in the battle, but remained in his headquarters to receive communiques on the number and names of the fallen and the wounded and so on.

The officers were given orders regarding the distance to be marched each day, which was decided according to the prevailing circumstances. They marched no more than 25 kilometres each day, so a distance of 180 km. involved ten overnight stops.

Catering for the army was quite a problem, especially since many officers and soldiers took their families along with them, increasing the burden on supplies. An entire bazaar accompanied the troops to provide food and drink. When they had to travel long distances, small rest camps were set up at fairly regular intervals. Raja Man Singh, who was a Hindu, had special tents erected for mosques and baths for his Muslim soldiers, and provided them all with a daily meal.

In the first century and a half of Mughal rule discipline appears to have been fairly strict, and soldiers were punished if they started looting before victory had been achieved.

Akbar's forces apparently comprised four million soldiers, divided between different *mansabdars*. They included wrestlers, *shamsherbaz*, 'sword players', and other kinds of sportsmen. The active combatants were recorded on muster rolls, and there was a *bitikchi*, army scribe, to oversee everything. Even more important was the *bakhshi*, the paymaster, for salaries were often paid by the *mansabdars* very haphazardly. In the early days, the soldiers received a few months' advance on their salaries before a campaign. If the *mansabdar* was out of funds, the state made a contribution. However, with the passage of time, payments became increasingly irregular, and it was quite unusual for a *mansabdar* to pay his men regularly. By the middle of the eighteenth century the soldiers were in a miserable condition. Even before that time, European visitors to the Mughal court shook their heads in dismay at the appalling situation of the soldiers. The satirist Sauda (who died in 1781) wrote a long poem in Urdu, *Tazhik-i ruzgar*, 'The Most Ridiculous Creature of our Day', describing the clapped out nag belonging to one impoverished soldier, to draw attention to the terrible state of the army.

The Mughal army specialized in land battles, during which 'the plain was made into a tulip garden by the blood of the slain', and where the enemy 'hastened into the pit of annihilation', and the Mughal heroes sometimes 'drank the nectar of martyrdom'.

There was no Mughal navy, although in Akbar's time a couple of grabs were constructed, from the Arabic *ghurab*, meaning 'raven', which were large cruising vessels, usually two-masted, with an armoured prow, equipped with guns. Aurangzeb also equipped a few ships with cannons. However, an ocean battle was out of the question, whether against the Portuguese in the Indian Ocean or against the British or Dutch in the Bay of Bengal, where there were also pirates adding to the hazards. The lack of an effective navy which could stand up to the increasing encroachment of the European powers was the Achilles' heel of the Mughal empire.

## PUNISHMENT

When Jahangir ascended the throne, he installed a gilded chain 30 *gaz* (yards) long hung with sixty golden bells, so that anyone with a grievance could call him.[1] During Humayun's brief reign he used a 'drum of justice'. Sir Thomas Roe reported that Jahangir always listened patiently to the complaints of his subjects, and that he and the other Mughal rulers would continue to administer justice whilst they were on their travels. A Berlin miniature of 1618 depicts Jahangir's throne with a European-influenced figure of 'Justice' portrayed on the backrest.

In general, legal problems were settled quickly. Muslims followed *shariʿa* law, which was administered by the *qadis* (*kazi*), as is customary in Islamic countries. The same laws applied to Hindus, who were considered to be *dhimmis*, 'people under the protection of the law'; they were subject to Islamic laws, but tried by their own judges. However, they were permitted to lodge their complaints with the *qadis*, as was often the case with Christians and Jews in the Near East. In the countryside, many cases were settled by the village assembly, the *panchayat*. In the *Fatawa-yi ʿalamgiri* (a compendium of legal judgments, compiled in Aurangzeb's time) it states that *dhimmis* 'do not have to bow down before the law of Islam, whether in religious matters such as fasting and prayer, or in secular matters, such as selling wine or pork, which are proscribed by Islam but are legal for them. We (Muslim lawyers) are commanded to allow them freedom in matters covered by their own laws.'

When Jahangir came to the throne he repealed many laws, particularly those concerning punishment. From then on, a guilty man was not to have his nose and ears cut off, a punishment which was previously quite common, as evidenced by the number of men with the Turkish nickname *burunsuz*, 'noseless'. Jauhar Aftabji reports that there was a man in Humayun's time who had had his entire ear cut off, not only the earlobe, but afterwards it was successfully sewn back on again.

However, many other harsh punishments remained in force, with hardly any alteration, although at one time Jahangir did moderate the trial by fire, which involved the accused grasping a red hot iron. Apparently there was also a trial which involved walking through fire, for Akbar proposed to the Jesuit Fathers that they and a number of leading Muslim theologians undergo this trial together, in order to determine which was the true religion, but the Jesuits refused. However, at a later date, a politically active member of the Barha Sayyids, on whose genealogy aspersions had been cast, is supposed to have stood for an hour up to his knees in fire in order to prove his legitimacy, without being harmed . . .[2]

Hawkins refers to the fact that an executioner and a police officer were present during the *durbar*, although they are rarely depicted in large paintings of *durbars*. This was also the custom in earlier times, including the reign of Muhammad Tughluq (ruled 1325–54).

The smallest lapses of protocol were harshly punished. If anyone touched the ruler's foot or approached too close to his throne, at the very least he risked a few days of house arrest. If a man who had been judged to be a sinner or criminal came to the court, he had to place a white cloth around his neck as a sign of repentance. This *mandil* was also practiced at the Mamluk court in Egypt and elsewhere.[3] The hands of criminals were bound behind their backs. High ranking prisoners of war had their swords hung around their necks. When Prince Khusrau was brought before his father Jahangir after his rebellion, he was in chains and had to approach the throne from the left. Sometimes the ruler 'drew the bow of pardon over the crime' of the guilty man. At other times, however, 'the noble ruler placed him in the school of correction', i.e. prison.

The most important prison, especially for political prisoners, was the mighty Gwalior fort. Its pleasant external appearance gives little indication of the many hundreds, even thousands of prisoners who have languished within. The great, if also rather eccentric, mystical theologian Ahmad Sirhindi reported that he had a mystical vision and felt the might and power of God whilst inside. Many prisoners, especially members of the royal household, were forced to drink a large glass of water every morning in which an opium poppy head had been infused overnight, so that they were gradually physically weakened and mentally deranged, and thereby rendered harmless.

Shah Jahan once, with a stroke of his pen, magnanimously freed

> all prisoners who were confined in the black house of fate, suffering in appalling gloomy conditions with no sight of heaven or earth.[4]

Rebels were always put to death brutally, being either hanged or impaled. Such scenes were occasionally depicted in miniatures, for instance the hanging of Abu'l-Maʿali. This elegant but treacherous man, who had once been Humayun's closest friend, was found guilty of the murder of Humayun's widow Mahchuchak.[5]

Jahangir's punishment for those who had supported his rebellious son Khusrau was especially gruesome. They were impaled, and Khusrau was made to ride on an elephant between the two rows of stakes while the dying men called out 'Your chosen servants pay homage to you!'[6]

The ruler often 'released someone from the burden of his body'. This saying was well illustrated by the verse composed by Sarmad in 1661 when he was about to be beheaded for his crimes. He greeted his executioner with the verse:

He made short work of it
Else the headache would've lasted long!

It is often reported in historical sources, or depicted in miniatures, that the ruler paid a bounty to anyone bringing him the decapitated heads of his enemies. The elite *khankhanan* ᶜAbduᵓr Rahim was punished especially gruesomely for his part in the wars of succession at the end of Jahangir's era – the head of his only surviving son was served up to him like a melon.

Theft was usually punished according to *shariᶜa* law by cutting off the right hand. Other variations include cutting off the right hand and the left thumb, or else both thumbs (this was done to one man for illegally chopping down a *champa* tree, a variety of jasmine). Someone who had stolen shoes had his foot cut off. The Achilles tendon was sometimes severed. One officer who had failed to defend his fort was paraded through Agra on an ass, after which his hair and beard were cut off because of his 'womanly behaviour'.[7]

One Hindu was punished extremely harshly, not only by having his tongue cut out, but also being made to eat with dogs and pariahs. His crime was keeping a Muslim dancing girl captive in his house, also killing her parents and burying them under the house.[8]

Humiliating someone by thrashing them with shoes was still a widespread punishment until just a few decades ago, one that was also common within families.

Bastinado (beating the soles of the feet with cudgels) was as common in Mughal India as in other oriental countries, and it was not uncommon for a man found guilty to be beaten to death. Curiously, Aurangzeb was very reluctant to impose a death sentence of any kind, even when it was merited.

Sometimes prisoners were placed in the stocks. Someone who had been disobedient to the ruler might be stabbed – 'his arrogance was enlightened by the gleam of Indian daggers'. Instances of throttling with leather strips are also recorded. People who had merely fallen out of favour were sometimes walled up alive, even though they might be quite innocent of any crime. The victims suffered a slow and painful death from suffocation, which was the fate of both sons of the Sikh Guru Hargobind in 1612.

Jahangir had two of his rebellious son's supporters sewn up in the skins of a freshly slaughtered ox and ass, their heads taking the place of the animals' tails. One of them died as a result of this torture. The other survived, but as a reminder of his punishment he was given the nickname *khar*, 'ass'.[9] (He was later restored to favour.) One illustration in the *Akbarnama* shows a group of rebels being led before the emperor partially sewn up in hides.

Princes or other more distant relatives were often blinded to put them out of the running for the throne, since a prerequisite for rulership was to be free of all physical disability. The first, but by no means last, incidence of this was the blinding of Humayan's half-brother Kamran Mirza, who was in constant rebellion against him. The ruler hesitated for a long time before yielding to pressure from his amirs to carry it out. Shah ᶜAlam II, who had been blinded by his youthful Rohilla enemy in 1788, was able to continue to rule; however, this was largely thanks to the support of the British, who were the *de facto* rulers during the declining years of the Mughal empire. Sometimes the blinding was unsuccessful, according to reports. The surest method was with red hot needles, otherwise it could be both very painful and still not completely effective, as was the case with Kamran Mirza.

Punishments were often out of all proportion to the crime, especially during the time of Jahangir, who often flew into a rage when under the influence of drink and drugs. A man could be flayed alive for the smallest offence in the presence of the ruler. Someone who accidentally scared off a nilgay just as Jahangir was taking aim at it would be shot on the spot. Anyone who entered the *qamargah*, the enclosed hunting grounds, risked the same fate or enslavement.

Trampling to death by elephants was the most common method of execution during the Mughal era. Illustrations show that the victim's hands were first tied together behind his back. The elephants often began by lifting him up by his arms with their tusks and playing with him for a while before trampling him. Akbar had a man thrown to the elephants for five days, during which they were not permitted to kill him.[10] Then, when he was probably more than half dead from fear, he was pardoned. Bernier was appalled to note that Jahangir derived great pleasure from watching such executions – the realistic depictions of them in miniature pictures are quite horrific enough.

No wonder many condemned men sought to avoid such punishments by committing suicide. Not only Hindus but also Muslims took their own lives, even though this violates the spirit as well as the law of Islam. The Gujarati prince Muzaffar slit his own throat after being taken prisoner. A prison guard took his own life after the escape of an important prisoner; a *mansabdar* who had embezzled money from the government also committed suicide. Less surprising is the suicide of Jahangir's Rajput wife, who took an overdose of opium. There is a vivid miniature picture of a man who had hanged himself. This might have been the work of the painter Daswanth, one of the great masters at Akbar's court, who is said to have become mentally deranged in the end and to have committed suicide himself in 1584.[11]

ECONOMY

There are numerous Indian and British books on the Mughal economic system, varying according to the politics and historical perspective of the author. Not being an economist, it is difficult for me to provide a complete picture of the subject; however, a few details will help to clarify the situation somewhat.

The total population of the Mughal empire was somewhere between 100 and 125 million. Large areas of land were undeveloped, and far more of it was then under forest. However the Mughals were not much interested in the upkeep of the forests, which provided shelter for brigands and wild animals.

European travellers were astonished at the great Mughal cities, which were comparable to the great cities of Europe, the populations of which were no more than 200,000. Visitors estimated that in Jahangir's time Lahore was larger than Istanbul, the capital of the Ottoman empire, renowned for its greatness and beauty. Agra was said to be greater than London, and Delhi not much smaller than Paris. There were a few other major cities at the time, such as Burhanpur, long the seat of Mughal viceroys. However, these cities only displayed their full splendour when the ruler and his court were actually in residence, being rather less impressive at other times.

The villages all tended to be somewhat similar, consisting of simple huts without much furniture. The dwellings of the urban lower classes were also extremely modest.

The empire was divided into provinces, *suba*, of which the *subadar* was the highest civil and military authority. The next administrative unit was the district, *sarkar*, after which came the sub-district, *pargana*. Within this there were *balda*, towns, and *mahalla*, urban districts, the smallest units. Everywhere in the empire there was the same hierarchical structure as in the centre. The *diwan* was the central secretariat, and the *kotwal*, magistrate, was responsible for administration, especially for security. If there was a robbery in his district, he was responsible for the capture and punishment of the robber.

The administration of justice was the province of the *qadi* (*qazi*). The *qadi* took difficult cases to the *mir-i*ᶜ*adl*, who would take them to the *subadar* if necessary, and thence to the chief *qadi* at the court. If need be, he would present these cases to the ruler himself.

In the villages, however, the traditional *panchayat* system prevailed, whereby disputes and problems were resolved by the village elders.

In Akbar's time, the provinces of Allahabad, Agra, Awadh, Ajmer, Gujarat, Bihar, Bengal, Delhi, Kabul, Lahore, Multan and Malwa were under his rule. During his reign Kashmir and Khandesh were officially incorporated into the empire, followed by Berar and Ahmednagar after military victories in the northern Deccan. The central provinces such as Agra, Lahore and Delhi were naturally the most desirable postings for governors, whilst Bihar and Bengal were rather less popular.

All of these administrative units had to pay taxes, which were calculated according to the solar year, rather than the Islamic lunar year, as Akbar inaugurated the *Ilahi* era in 1556, with the year commencing at the start of spring, *Nauruz*. The tax system was extremely complex. Working out the *mansabdars'* salaries alone was a difficult arithmetical problem, all the more so because they were calculated in *dams*, i.e. one-fortieth of a rupee, so the sums involved were enormous. No wonder highly skilled mathematicians were needed for this task. Akbar's most competent Finance Minister was a Hindu by the name of Todar Mal. The lower levels of financial administration had for some time been in the hands of Hindus, who had proved themselves to be accomplished calculators. Todar Mal succeeded in thoroughly reorganising the financial system, and he also accomplished something else very important – changing the language of financial administration from Hindi to Persian.

It is not possible to calculate the exchange rate of the Mughal currency with complete accuracy. What is certain is that extremely fine coins were minted at the empire's zenith, for one of the essential signs of rulership of an Islamic empire was that the ruler had his name imprinted on the coins (the other prerogative was having the Friday prayers said in his name). Both Badaʾuni and Abuʾl Fazl devoted lengthy treatises to the various coins and their inscriptions. There were three main types of coins, made of copper, silver and gold respectively. The copper coins, such as the aforementioned *dam*, were the smallest denomination. However, the unit of coinage most often referred to is the silver rupee. Sir Thomas Roe gives its value as two and a half (Jacobean) shillings. However, its value rose or fell with changing economic conditions. Abuʾl Fazl gives the exact prices of the most important staple foods and other goods. Apparently the *muhr*, a valuable gold coin, would purchase two or three days' supply of wheat.

The Mughals liked coins as they could easily be hoarded and did not take up much space. For this reason they insisted that European merchants make all payments in silver.

Choosing the design of new coins was a prerogative of a new ruler. At the start of his reign, Jahangir had coins minted with signs of the zodiac. On New Year's Day in the year 1000 (= 1591–2), his father Akbar had the silver and gold coins of previous rulers melted down and new coins minted with his seal.

Jahangir's coins were given appropriate names. The gold coins, whether round or square, had religious creeds or verses inscribed on one side, and on the reverse side there might be a verse with the date of minting as a chronogram. Jahangir had coins minted with the name of his wife Nur Jahan, proof that he had invested all his authority in her.

Abu'l Fazl describes the production of coins in detail in *A'in* I, no. 5. The *darugha*, the Superintendent of Coins, first checked the purity of the metal. The engraver had the important and difficult task of engraving the text on steel blocks in mirror writing. Then the round or square coin pieces were placed between the blocks, and the text pressed onto them. Like almost everyone at court, the engraver had a military rank. He was *yüzbashi*, Commander of One Hundred.

One of Akbar's greatest achievements was the standardisation of weights and measures, so that incomes and outgoings could be calculated accurately. He also standardised the measurement of area, although the smallest unit of land, the *bigha*, continued to fluctuate in size. For measuring distances, the *kos* was used, which Akbar set as approximately equivalent to 2.5 miles or 4.5 kilometres. The *ilahi gaz*, the yard, corresponded to 33 inches or 80 cms. For the division of agricultural regions, the traditional Islamic categories of *ushri*- and *kharaji*-land were used, *ushri* being land that

had been in Muslim hands since ancient times. In India, therefore, only a very small fraction of the land was designated *ushri*, most of it being *kharaji* land. Akbar also introduced an improvement to the way the harvest tax was assessed. Instead of calculating it afresh each time according to the harvest, dependent as this was upon the weather, he introduced the *dahsala*, which was based on the average yields of the past ten years.

There was a special kind of taxation for orchards. Jahangir relates in his *Tuzuk* (II, 52), how he arrived at the theory that land is more fruitful the less it is taxed, with the result that just one pomegranate could produce the juice of five or six fruits. Furthermore, 'whoever lays out a garden on arable land will not be liable for tax'.

The system of weights was rectified somewhat, so that one *ser* was equivalent to 933 grams, or nearly one kilogram, and one *man* was made up of 40 *ser*, or 37,324 kg. There were of course still some fluctuations, but at least when Abu'l Fazl records that a first class hunting cheetah received 5 *ser* of meat a day, the reader can have some idea of how much this was.

Potatoes have been cultivated in India since the time of Akbar, although they are still not all that popular there. New World guavas (which are very common today) and soft custard apples (which have large kernels) both first appeared in the second half of the sixteenth century. The Portuguese introduced the pineapple, and Jahangir encouraged the cultivation of different varieties of grape.

The honeydew melon was first cultivated in India under Shah Jahan, and this very popular fruit was highly profitable for the producers. The primary agricultural products were grains of all kinds, also legumes. These are still the staple foods of India today, *dal* (lentils) and rice being the most popular.

Abu'l Fazl provides exact figures for the tax due on different types of produce. Each type of agricultural produce was taxed differently, according to the amount that was sown, and not according to how much was actually harvested. This resulted in great hardship in cases of harvest failure, locust infestation, or floods. Curiously, indigo was the most highly taxed item, followed by poppies, which were used in the production of opium. The tax on sugar cane was twice the tax on wheat.

The farmers were not serfs, although they usually worked their land for the *jagirdars*. It is typical of Jahangir that at the beginning of his reign he ordered the *jagirdars* not to take land away from peasants to cultivate it for themselves. Although farmers were allowed to leave their land and move elsewhere, their lives were far from easy. In historical accounts there are a number of intimations of peasant uprisings against taxation. Because *jagirdars* were frequently transferred, they had little interest in improving conditions for the farmers. This speech by the ever critical Bernier expressed the *jagirdars'* attitude:

Why should we be troubled by the neglected state of the countryside? And why should we waste our time and money trying to make it fruitful? It could be taken away from us in the blink of an eye, and then all our efforts would bring no benefit to ourselves or our children. So let's just take as much profit as we can from the land, even if the peasants starve or disappear, and leave it as a desolate wasteland when we're ordered to leave.

Even the farmers themselves were reluctant to cultivate the land to the best of their abilities, since someone from a neighbouring area might come along and covet it and take it away from them on some pretext or other.

Similarly, many merchants disguised themselves as poor and needy in the hope of evading taxation.

Akbar used to advance money to destitute farmers, but it is not known whether his successors did the same.

Sometimes there were unforeseen misfortunes – not only natural catastrophes, but also as a result of human negligence. Tavernier reports that the state elephants were sometimes turned out to graze on the distraught farmers' land, trampling it completely. Also, during the great hunting parties, the ruler's *ahadis* were unable to prevent the horses and elephants from trampling the crops. So it is hardly any wonder that, according to Bernier, there was a flight from the land in the seventeenth century, with adverse consequences for the entire economy.

In 1610 there was an uprising in Bihar because the burden of taxation had become so heavy.[1]

Life for the rural population was made extremely hard not only by the irresponsible *mansabdars*, but also by frequent famines, when 'that black-breasted *amah*, "the spring cloud", and the fiery cloud both deny the milk of rain to the seedlings.'

The chroniclers record many such catastrophes, especially in Gujarat, Malwa and Berar. Their descriptions of the great famine of 1631 in the Deccan are especially dramatic. Shah Jahan's poet laureate composed a long poem about this famine, containing the following verses:

When a scrap of cloud appeared in the sky
It contained no water, being just like wind
    paper . . .
Like a sandglass both worlds were
Full of the dead and bereft of the living.[2]

As Salih Kambuh wrote: 'It was not possible to count, let alone list the dead, and the words "weep" and "howl", "shroud" and "grave" faded . . . as every day caravan after caravan hastened to the valley of annihilation . . . '. Worse still, the famine was so severe that not only did people resort to eating ritual animals (if they could find any), but 'fathers and mothers even ripped the darling little hearts from their dear children and ate them raw . . . '. A decade later the northern Deccan was plagued by famine, so that the inhabitants would have given *jane bi nane*, 'a life for a piece of bread', and would have sold *sharife bi raghife*, 'a nobleman for a loaf of bread'.[3]

During such terrible famines, the government tried to help by setting up more facilities for the distribution of free food to the poor, in addition to those which had already been established in times of plenty. However, the death toll was still extremely high.

Maccrab [Muqarrab] Khan desires various things to be procured in England and despatched on the next ship to Surat for the Great Magor [Mughal]: a. Two complete suits of armour, strong yet light and easy to wear. b. Curved swords, broad. Difficult to obtain, for they test them on their knees, and if they withstand this, then they don't want them. c. Knives of the best quality, large, long and so thin that they can be bent round into a circle and then spring back when released. d. Satin, red, yellow, green, and tawny. e. Velvet, the best, in red, yellow, black, and green. f. All kinds of toys to keep the king happy. g. Fine cloth of the best quality, which does not show marks, in yellow, red, and green. h. All kinds of women's toys. i. Pictures on linen, not wood. k. Perfumed leather. l. Flemish tapestries, with pictures. m. The largest mirrors obtainable. n–o. Figures of animals, birds or other forms made of plaster, silver,

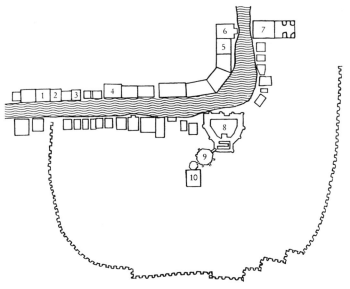

34. Sketch-plan of the city of Agra, *c*. 1700.

1 Bagh-i Nur Afshan
2 Bagh-i Jahanara
3 Mausoleum of Afzal Khan
4 I'timad ad-daula's Mausoleum
5 Chahar Bagh
6 Mahtab Bagh
7 Taj Mahal
8 Fort
9 Bazaar
10 Great Mosque

brass, word, iron, stone, or ivory . . . in addition, mastiffs, greyhounds, spaniels and small dogs, three of each . . . a good supply of writing parchment and parchment.[1]

This is part of an order sent to London in 1614 by Nicholas Downton of the East India Company, to which he added a few comments. He advised, for example, substituting cheaper goods in some cases, or else there would be no profit; and also warned that 'dogs are difficult to transport'.

The list reveals what British merchants had to do to find favour with the Mughal government. The British had been trying to establish trading relations with India since Mildenhall first presented a letter from Queen Elizabeth I to Akbar in 1583 (she never received a reply). India's trade with Europe had been steadily increasing since the first Portuguese merchants had set foot on Indian soil, and it was proving very difficult to compete with these accomplished traders with their long-standing experience of the Mughals, who also had the benefit of support from the Jesuits. Not long afterwards the Dutch also established themselves as a third trading power.

The Indian domestic market was also very important. Bada'uni and Abu'l Fazl both write about the great trade roads connecting the provinces, as well as the overland routes to Central Asia and the Near East.

The route favoured by the traders, especially for transporting imports, led from Surat, the only fully functioning harbour, to Agra via Burhanpur. Another route went from Surat to the capital via Gwalior. Two roads led out of the country from Delhi, one the northern route to China via Lahore and Kabul, the other the road to Kandahar and Iran by way of Lahore and Multan. Caravans could travel to Ladakh, Yarkand and Kashgar from the Punjab. Equally important was the route along the Ganges from Allahabad and Benares to Bengal, and on to their trading partners the other side of India – Pegu (Arakan) and Burma. The Ganges itself was also a trade route.

Foreign merchants complained about the difficulties of the journey to the court at Agra. Many of them travelled from Surat to Ahmedabad and Ajmer, from where it was easy to get to Agra. However the usual route went via Burhanpur, 'a disgusting town', as Finch wrote in 1608, despite efforts to beautify the town at that time. The journey to the capital took around ten weeks, the caravans being stopped frequently at checkpoints, especially to collect road tolls.

There were all kinds of tolls, although officially the dues were very small. Transit tolls, which had to be paid on long journeys through several provinces, were based on the quantity of goods rather than their value, and also the distance travelled. They usually had to bribe the officials so that they did not charge them too much money or hassle them unduly. When a river had to be crossed, as at Narmada *en route* to and from the north, there were toll ferries. Fortunately these were controlled by Indians or Iranians and Mongols, so British merchants were less likely to be attacked by brigands, as once happened to the enraged Finch. The jungle provided perfect cover for robbers, who were harshly punished if they were ever caught. At Panipat, Finch witnessed 'the heads of a few hundred robbers who had recently been caught and impaled on stakes'.

Foreign merchants had the novel experience of dealing with Hindu tradesmen, the *banyas*, whose prowess is still legendary to this day. Finch complained that they were 'as cunning as the devil', a 'crafty and clever race', who controlled a major part of private sector trade and finance.

The travellers may also have encountered Indian corn dealers, who travelled the land in groups, peddling their wares along the way, and supplying soldiers stationed in the country. They lived in tents, and were organised in a quasi-military fashion themselves. Even in times of war they were allowed to go on their way unimpeded, for they were neutral and only concerned with their trade, which was essential for the country.

Indian domestic trade was very important, and Mughal historians have provided a wealth of information regarding the products of the different provinces and states.

The province of Agra was the primary source of copper, silver, and iron. Gold and silverware, embroidery and carpets were produced in the city of Agra, which was known for its numerous bazaars. During the time when Agra was the capital, the imperial workshops were located there, producing everything needed at court.

The residence town of Fatehpur Sikri was connected to Agra by a great trade route. When it was made the capital, the workshops were also relocated there. In other times, however, the town was known chiefly for its great quarry, which produced the red sandstone which was the ideal building material for the town itself and other Mughal palaces.

Gujarat was a particularly rich province, producing velvet and all sorts of other fine materials, especially in Ahmedabad, where there is now a calico museum exhibiting the textile arts of the province. Perfumes and weapons were also produced. Boats were built in Sarkhej, near Ahmedabad. This region is also mentioned in connection with the production of indigo, which enhanced the dark blue, red and white coloured cotton material made in the west of the subcontinent (*ajrak*). The primary state for the production of indigo was Bayana, near Agra. Nur Jahan owned some large fields there, which accounted for a considerable part of her fortune, for the indigo trade was highly lucrative. William Finch describes the production of this valuable pigment, which was transported overland from Bayana to Cambay, where it was sorted and packed into balls if good quality, or flat packets if of lesser quality, then exported to Europe and Iran. Shah Jahan is said to have cultivated indigo in Patna as well.

Gujarat, the location of the important harbours of Cambay, Surat and Broach, was also internationally renowned for its beautiful cabinets and cupboards, which were adorned with precious mother of pearl and ivory inlay.

Jute was produced in Bengal, as well as rice and sugar cane – 'Bengal sugar' is mentioned in the fourteenth century in a verse by the great Persian poet Hafiz. The sugar cane was transported along the water routes.

One of the most valuable products was salt, one source of which was Lake Sambhar, near Ajmer. However, the salt mines in Khewra, in the Salt Range between the Jhelum and the Indus, were a far richer source, and salt is still extracted there to this day. In the Mughals' time 'many skilful artists fashioned trays, plates and lamps' from Khewra salt. In the broad gallery of the salt mine, there is a small mosque constructed entirely out of colourful rock salt.

Lahore, a stopover for the numerous Armenian merchants,[2] was renowned for its textiles. It had long been a centre for weaving velvet, and later began to rival Gujarat in the production of exquisite fabrics. Since the time of Akbar, if not before, it was also a flourishing centre for the production of carpets. Kashmir was famous for its gossamer-fine shawls, which were woven in the mountainous regions and also in Lahore, the nearest large town.

Calico fabric was named after the Indian town of Calikut. The production and export of cotton fabrics was one of the most important sources of revenue of the Mughal empire. Weaving was ubiquitous, and cotton fabric was produced and exported in ever greater quantities, either in a plain bleached state, or dyed, printed and finished as chintz. The Portuguese shipped the fabric to north and west Africa. Between 1619 and 1625, British exports increased from 14,000 to 200,000 lengths of fabric, each measuring two to fifteen yards.

Silk fabric was also exported. Raw silk was produced in Bengal. Two and a half million pounds of cocoons were produced each year in the province, around a quarter of which were exported, chiefly by the Dutch.

Sind, on the other side of the Mughal empire, was the source of the best dromedary camels, as well as fish and fish oil. It was also known for a particular kind of floral carpet during the Mughal era, and the lower Indus region still has a reputation for interesting weaving.

Bihar, especially Rajgir, was a centre for the production of paper. It was even more famous, at least in earlier times, for its 'ud, aloe wood. This is a soft wood with a strong aroma which was used as incense, which had been highly prized in the Arab world since the early Middle Ages.[3]

Saltpetre was extracted in the region around Agra. Later on, after Jahangir's time, Patna also became a centre for the trade in saltpetre.

Abu'l Fazl mentions that fine muslin was produced in Sironj, whilst glassware came primarily from Alwar. He also writes that Benares produced wonderful fabrics, and the tradition of costly Benares saris has survived to this day.

Towards the end of Akbar's reign, tobacco was introduced at court, after which it was imported by Jahangir. Imports increased during Shah Jahan's reign; however, Aurangzeb prohibited smoking.

There was another product which was universally popular: *charas*, cannabis, which was exported from Kashmir and Kabu. Opium was also consumed in enormous quantities, and the

northern region of the subcontinent, and Malwa and the Benares area, became important centres for the cultivation of poppies. *Pust*, a mixture of spices and opium, was especially popular. Opium was also one of India's export products.

Saffron, another highly sought-after product, was only found in Kashmir. Akbar loved the saffron fields of Kashmir, with their apparent infinitude of flowers, like a kind of crocus. However, the acrid smell of the flower fields gave Jahangir a headache.[4] Saffron was among the valuable gifts which the governor of the province used to send to the court. A document for the appointment of the superintendent of saffron production contains the following advice to the incumbent of this vital position:

> [He] should not for a moment relax his vigilance and care. He must be attentive and alert in his work whilst the flowers are blooming, whilst they are being harvested and dried; whilst establishing their price, which is dependent upon the abundance or scarcity of supply, and whilst trying to maximise the profit for the state . . .
> He must ensure that no one dares to deceive the buyers or adulterate the saffron, and that the buyers pay the full price for the saffron, leaving absolutely no outstanding arrears. [5]

Saffron was highly profitable to export, but not easy to handle. The plants are at their best after three years. They remain fruitful for six years, after which they have to be ploughed under to make room for new plants, which will reach their maximum fruitfulness after another three years. Mu'tamad Khan, the *bakhshi* and loyal companion of Jahangir, relates the following:

> Eating saffron makes one laugh, and if one eats

35. A portable organ which had been given to Akbar, detail from the border of a Jahangir Album, c. 1608–18, painting on paper.

too much, one laughs so much that one is in danger of laughing oneself to death. [In the last year of his life] Jahangir had a prisoner who had been sentenced to death brought before him, and gave him 40 *mithqal* [around 30 g.] of saffron to eat. Nothing happened. The next day he gave him twice this amount, but his lips remained unmoved by laughter. But what on earth did he have to laugh about?' [6]

Exports to foreign countries, as already mentioned, could be transported either by sea or along overland routes. Lahari Bandar in Sind was primarily used by Arabian and Persian ships, whilst Surat was the primary landing stage for ships from all over the world. Cambay was the main export station for ivory and for spices from Malacca, Mozambique and Indonesia. Carnelian, granite, agate, chalcedony and hematite were also loaded in Cambay.

The Portuguese organised their trade on the west coast of India very cleverly. Every year four or five ships sailed from Lisbon to India, then continued on via Goa to China and Japan, then back again. One of the reasons for this circuitous route was that in Mughal India payments always had to be made in cash, with silver coins, but the export of silver coins was forbidden. In Japan, however, there was no limitation on the export of precious metals. So they could improve their profits in the course of buying and selling by taking such an apparently roundabout route.

Trade with Nepal was conducted via Patna. Rhinoceros horn, birds of prey and also dyes came from Nepal. From Pegu came the best elephants, among them the highly prized albino varieties, as well as rubies and sapphires. Trade with Pegu – corresponding roughly to Burma today – was conducted via Bengal, which was problematic, since the most important harbour, Chittagong, was not

36. A European couple
in Elizabethan costume,
c. 1620–30, gouache with
gold on paper, from the
Grindley's Bank Darah
Shikoh Album.

under Mughal rule before 1664. Pirates in the Gulf of Bengal presented an additional hazard.

The Portuguese and then the British introduced new products to the Mughal empire, such as wine from Shiraz. Despite the flourishing textile production in India, Persian silks and carpets were increasingly in demand at court. Pedigree horses were imported from the Arab world, and also coffee, from the last decade of the sixteenth century. Various African countries traded in ivory, ebony and slaves. The latter, especially Abyssinians, were often castrated, after which they could rise to positions of great responsibility at court as eunuchs.

In Sylhet, young boys were often castrated, and for a time Bengal paid its taxes in eunuchs,[7] a practice which Jahangir attempted to stamp out.

In Jahangir's time the Dutch established themselves along the Indian coastline, taking over a major part of the lucrative spice trade.

Trade with China was conducted overland as well as by sea. Muslims had long been purchasing Chinese porcelain, especially the blue and white ware, as can be seen in miniatures. In deference to their Muslim customers, the Chinese produced a kind of porcelain inscribed with pseudo-Arabic writing, testifying to the importance of porcelain exports. Later on crackleware came to India, which is referred to as 'hairy' porcelain in many poems from the end of the seventeenth century.

Toys were among the most popular European import items, especially from Britain (as seen at the beginning of this section). It is astonishing how much delight the Mughal rulers took in pretty little objects, among them perhaps the chamber organ depicted in the miniature. This instrument, given to Akbar by the Portuguese, is supposed to have enchanted all the animals with its sound.

Jahangir loved European pictures, and wanted to have as many of them as possible. Some of the pictures brought by Sir Thomas Roe were copied down to the last detail in the palace studios. Sir Thomas even brought a picture of his wife as a present for the Great Mughal and his consorts. The influence of European painters is clearly visible in landscape paintings and in embroidery after 1600. Nur Jahan loved English handicrafts, especially all kinds of embroidery, which had a great influence on Mughal art, introducing new motifs into weaving and providing inspiration for all the handicrafts. Some time later, around 1630, there was a reverse flow as a great many Mughal miniatures went to Holland, where they served as models for Rembrandt and other painters.

Foreign trade expanded steadily from the time of Akbar onwards. The skill of the East India Company in this sphere laid the ground for its later gradual takeover of India. This was not an easy process. The merchants did not enjoy territorial rights; if they were lucky, their rights were established by imperial *farmans*. The price of goods for export to the west was increased by the long and arduous journeys they had to make, and even more so by the necessity of making all payments in silver coins. Pepper and other spices were sold in Europe for five times their purchase price. Successful merchants had to keep their wits about them and their eyes open as they travelled the land. They had to make the effort, however reluctantly, to learn the customs regarding 'gifts'. Consequently, their reports provide far more detailed information about Mughal administration and the country and its people than the writings of native authors, who took such matters for granted – and who also did not wish to tarnish the reputation of the court.

FOUR

# Religion

It is impossible to understand religious developments in Mughal India without some knowledge of their historical background. The basis for the relationship between the Muslim minority and the Hindu majority was established in 711, when a part of the subcontinent, to the south of what is today Pakistan, converted to Islam. The young conqueror Muhammad ibn al-Qasim gave both Hindus and Buddhists, who were still numerous at that time, the same status as the Christians, Jews, and Sabaeans in the Near East. They were all *dhimmi*, 'protected people'; they were self-governing in matters of religion and jurisprudence, and not to be regarded as heathens who had to be subdued. Non-Muslims had to pay the *jizya*, a poll tax, as 'People of the Book', which was increasingly resented. When considering the religious situation of the Mughal empire, it has to be borne in mind that Hindus regarded Muslims, like all non-Hindus, as *mleccha*, unclean.

After the conquest of northwest India by Mahmud of Ghazna (reigned 999–1030), the great historian al-Biruni (died 1048) made a study of Hindu culture in the conquered territory. His was the first work of comparative religious history, providing an accurate and objective overview of Hinduism.

The history of Islam in the subcontinent really begins with Mahmud's conquest. Over the course of centuries, the attitude of the Muslim conquerors alternated between what I have termed, for want of better expressions, 'India-oriented, mystical and inclusive', and 'Mecca-oriented, prophetic and exclusive'. Of course every Muslim is orientated towards Mecca, in the sense that he turns towards the Kaʿba during his prayers. However, what is meant here is the feeling of not being at home in India, but of having one's roots in the Arab or Turko-Persian world (as was in fact the case for the majority of the later elite). In the middle of the eighteenth century, the great reformist theologian Shah Waliullah remarked that he was living 'in exile', although his ancestors had settled in India centuries before. However, his contemporary Azad Bilgrami (died 1785) attempted in his Arabic work *Subhat al-marjan* to show that India was the true homeland of the Prophet. This tension is revealed in the fourteenth century in the contrast between the poet and musician Amir Khusrau (died 1325), a representative of the 'Indian' tendency, and the historian Ziaʾuddin Barani (died after 1350), a hardliner. It is even more marked in the contrast between Shah Jahan's sons, the mystical Dara Shikoh and the orthodox Aurangzeb. It was evident in the twentieth century in the two great Indian thinkers Abu'l Kalam Azad and Muhammad Iqbal, and it is to some extent behind the present division of the subcontinent.

After Mahmud's seventeen incursions into northwest India, Lahore was made the capital city of the Indo-Ghaznavid Empire. It was also a centre for the study of theology and law, which were essential subjects for administration. In the following two centuries the Muslims extended their rule to Rajasthan. In 1206 it was extended to Delhi, and almost at the same time to Bengal. During this period of expansion, a number of theological seminaries, the *madrasas*, were established, which emphasized the study of traditional Islamic law and tradition. The foundation work was Saghani's *Mashariq al-anwar*, an enlightened work of instruction and popularisation of the two most important *hadith* works. The 'noble *Mashariq*' was taught until the late nineteenth century in the leading *madrasas*. In addition, there was Baghawi's *Masabih as-sunna* and Tibrizi's *Mishkat al-masabih*. In the time of the Mughals there was a celebration when students completed the study of Bukhari's *Sahih* and the *Mishkat*. Even more important was the study of law, for which Marghinani's *Hidayat al-mubtadi'* was the standard work until the time of the British. There was also Pazdawi's *Usul al-fiqh* and the manual of Hanafi law, the *Quduri*. Both works remained in use for centuries, for most of the Indian rulers of Turkish extraction were associated with the Hanafi school of law. In the later Mughal period, popular mystical poets used to mock the *kanz quduri kafiya*, regarding these three works of Hadith literature and law and of Arabic grammar to be hindrances on the path to God.

The Turkish ruler of Delhi, Iltutmish (reigned 1206-1236) established the office of the *shaykh ul-islam* to deal with religious problems, administration and delegation of the religious duties of

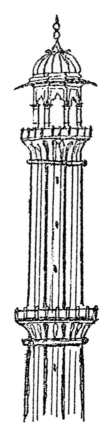

37. A sketch by the author of a typical Mughal minaret.

the rulers (payments to preachers and muezzins etc.), and the support of dervishes and Sufis.

A century later ʿAlaʾaddin Khalji (died 1316) created the office of the *sadr as-sudur*, the highest authority in disputes regarding religious law. It also administered the *auqafs*, the religious foundations. These tax-free foundations were able to play an important role and gradually expanded during the following centuries, largely thanks to their tax-free status.

These two offices continued unchanged during Babur's brief reign. Under Humayun, who spent a long time away from India, the offices and dignitaries still remained the same. The bigot Makhdum al-Mulk, whom Humayan had installed as the *shaykh ul-islam*, kept his office during the years of Sher Shah Suri's interregnum, during which he occupied himself with the persecution of heretics.

New personalities came to the fore under Akbar. After Humayun's return, Gada'i, a poet and the son of a poet, was appointed by Bayram Khan, a Shi'i. Akbar then appointed 'Abdu'n Nabi as *sadr as-sudur*. The latter was a grandson of the Chishti-Sabiri master 'Abdu'l Quddus Gangohi, a descendant of the great teacher of law Abu Hanifa (died 767). However, he was clearly not all that interested in following the religious traditions of his family, for it was the Chishti-Sabiri themselves who, from their beginnings at the end of the thirteenth century, had rejected any co-operation with the government – they regarded going to the sultan as being on a par with going to the devil. Makhdum ul-Mulk remained in office at the same time, despite the fact that he had served the opposing faction, the Suris, for many years. He retained his authority over all imperial edicts concerning the *madad-i ma'ash*, 'pension'. It was no surprise when his estate was found to be enormously wealthy after his death in 1584. Indeed, Bada'uni made a pun about a *mufti*, saying that he would never give a *fatwa*, legal response, *muft*, 'for nothing'. The mutual animosity between Makhdum ul-Mulk and the *sadr* was certainly one of the reasons for Akbar's gradual aversion for the representatives of the official Islamic tradition.

Akbar repealed the *jizya* in 1564, the year of his first pilgrimage to to Mu'inuddin Chishti's shrine in Ajmer. A mystical experience whilst out hunting in 1578 had strengthened his conviction that he had a religious vocation. Soon afterwards the *mahzar* was decreed, according religious authority to the emperor. Two years later the *din-i ilahi* was founded, which can be regarded as more of a religious cult than a new religion. In Bada'uni's view, the ruler's narrow-mindedness blinded him to Bada'uni's virtues, and so he tended to exaggerate the ruler's faults. He relates that the ruler prohibited the ritual prayers, did not permit pilgrimages, and that in his time 'the mosques were as empty as the wineries during Ramadan'.

After Akbar's death, he was succeeded by Salim Jahangir, who attempted to adhere to some of his father's ideals. However, he had both the Sikh guru Arjan and the Shi'i Qadi Nurullah Shushtari executed, which demonstrates how different he was from Akbar. However, he took a great interest in Sufis and *yogis*. After Jahangir's marriage to Nur Jahan, the Shi'a gained in influence and political strength.

Shah Jahan continued putting his father's policies into practice. He attempted to levy the pilgrimage tax on Hindus once more, which led to protests by the Brahmans of Benares. The rank of the *sadr as-sudur* was increased to 4000 *zat*, so that he occupied an important position among the *mansabdars*. A miniature depicts an occasion when the ruler extended an invitation to the religious dignitaries, who are seated before the throne, all dressed in gleaming white. There are also two black men among them. The *sayyids*, the descendants of the Prophet, are recognisable by their green turbans. All are smiling to themselves at being flattered in this way. Men with gilded clubs and swords are standing guard in front of the partitioned area to ensure that all protocol is strictly adhered to.[1]

The dual nature of Indian Islam is clearly manifested in Shah Jahan's sons, Dara Shikoh, the mystic, and Aurangzeb, who would be regarded as a fundamentalist today. Aurangzeb wanted to make India a truly Islamic nation. He would only permit those forms of punishment and taxation

كل در بر ومی برکف و معشوق بگا       سلطان جهانم خس روز غلام آت

در مجلس ملا ماه رخ دوست نمای شمع میار بد درین جمع که امش       لو
در مذهب مابا ده حلالست ولیکن       پی نرکس محمور زوای شمع حرا مس

38. 'Prince embracing a lady' in a scene from the *Diwan-i Hafiz*, early 17th century, miniature, gouache on paper.

which were sanctioned by Islamic law. The complete collection of *Fatawa-yi ʿalamgiri*, or *fatwas*, which were decreed during his reign, provide some insight into the way legal and religious problems were resolved or dealt with. In 1679 the *jizya* was reinstated, and the *muhtasib*, the Market Overseer, or Censor, gained more power. He not only inspected the salesmen in the bazaar and the quality of their wares, but also ensured that the ban on alcohol was enforced. For this reason

Aurangzeb prohibited the poetry of Hafiz, at least for a time, since so much of it was about wine. The following verse by Hafiz seems to apply to Aurangzeb's reign:

> The wine gives pleasure
> The wind scatters roses
> Do not drink to the sound of the harp!
> The censor is very powerful! [2]

Music was discouraged, even though Aurangzeb had formerly enjoyed it, and the painting of miniatures and the compiling of court annals were no longer highly valued. In 1697 the Shiʿi Muharram procession was prohibited.

Aurangzeb's attitude undoubtedly hardened as he grew older, and his regime is criticised by both liberal Muslims as well as Indian and European historians. However Pakistani historians praise Aurangzeb for his righteousness, and his rule for being scrupulously based upon *shariʿa* doctrine.

Aurangzeb's death in 1707 ushered in a period of political instability during which it was impossible to evolve a new and constructive religious policy. The rivalry at court between the Sunnis and Shiʿa played as great a role as the power of other religious groups in the fall of the empire and the rise of the principality (later kingdom) of Awadh, in which the Shiʿa predominated. Sufism remained an important element of Mughal society, and its customs and ideas remained very much alive after 1857.

NON-ISLAMIC RELIGIONS

HINDUISM

The status of the Hindus after 711 was that of *dhimmi*s, 'protected people'. However, every

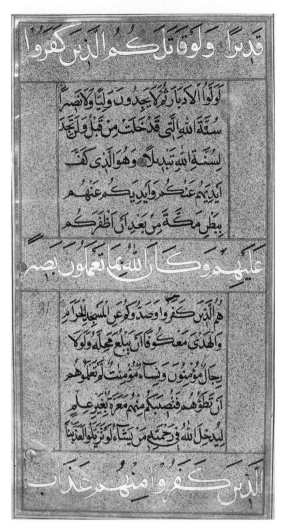

39. Page from the Qur'an (*Sura* 48, verses 22–25) in Aurangzeb's handwriting.

communal meals), and this attracted them to the basic Muslim beliefs and practices. In records of conversations of the time, such as the *Jawami^c al-kilam*, compiled by the great Sufi Gesudaraz of Gulbarga (died 1422), there are accounts of his attempts to convince Hindus to follow 'the true way',[1] as well as his theories on economic inducements for conversion. New converts were sometimes regarded with suspicion. The ultra-orthodox historian Barani (died *c*. 1350) was reluctant to entrust a newly converted Hindu with a position of authority. Only men of Turkish extraction, trained in the Hanafi school of law, were suitable for high office. Although this is an extreme case, prejudice certainly existed.[2]

In Akbar's time, the general position of Hindus underwent a change. Whereas before his reign there were hardly any Hindus in higher state offices, in the list of provincial finance ministers between 1594–94 there are no fewer than eight Hindus, constituting three quarters of the total. Hindus were known to be especially competent in mathematical and financial matters, and the money-lending system was almost totally in their hands. Many illustrations depict a Hindu moneylender holding a lengthy list. In fact during the time of the Mughals, noblemen in financial difficulties were advised to go to the humble, polite Hindus rather than to the downright offensive Muslim financiers!

There was one group of Hindus who had long played an important role in India – the astrologers, who were consulted on every occasion, and who are often depicted in miniatures.

For the first time in history, Akbar allied himself militarily with the Rajputs. Raja Man Singh of Amber, a Kachhawa Rajput, stood out among his contemporaries and military allies, and proved his mettle in battle with the Raushaniyya sect. Even Bada'uni referred to him in verse:

dynasty differed in the way it dealt with the majority of the population of the subcontinent. It would be interesting to know how frequently conversions occurred, and for what reasons. More than a century previously, Sir Thomas Arnold mentioned the role of the Sufis in this process. In the centres of Sufism, Hindus (low castes and untouchables) enjoyed a commonalty they had never experienced before (for instance

A Hindu is wielding the sword of Islam![3]

To this day the town of Mansehra, in the foothills of Kashmir, and the garden of Wah, near Hasan Abdal on the old Mughal route from Lahore to Kashmir, both display evidence of the influence of Man Singh in the northwest corner of the sub-continent. Another noteworthy Hindu was Todar Mal, the Finance Minister, who compiled a work on Hindu teachings and customs for Akbar. According to Bada'uni, on his return from war he 'hurried into the place of hell and torment, to be eaten by snakes and scorpions in the deepest abyss of hell'.[4]

The same historian directed more invective at Akbar's close friend, the Raja Birbal, a musician and court entertainer, the only Hindu to join the din-i ilahi, until he too 'trod the path of the hounds of hell'.

Under later Mughal rulers there was also a considerable number of Hindus in the adminis-tration and the military, sometimes even more than under Akbar. However, it is more significant that Akbar married a few Rajput princesses, among them the daughter of Bhagwan Das, the adoptive father of Man Singh, who was to become the mother of his first surviving son, Salim Jahangir. Later, as the queen mother, she bore the title Maryam az-zamani. Such marriages were quite common in the following decades, and portraits of the Mughal rulers show the transition from the strongly Central Asian facial features of Babur, and even Akbar, to more sharply chiselled features and darker skin.

As far as Akbar and his successors were con-cerned, it was quite natural for the Rajput princesses to introduce their customs and prac-tices to the palace. It was even permissible under religious law for a Muslim to take a wife who was 'under the protection of the law'. It is unclear whether any of the wives converted to Islam; however, several of them had mosques construc-ted. The last such marriage was the one between Farrukhsiyar and the daughter of Raja Ajit Singh of Marwar.

Because of his desire for 'peace with all', Akbar repealed the jizya early on his reign, which did not please the strongly Sunni factions at court and elsewhere. Akbar's rationale for this was that since the Rajputs had distinguished themselves in battle, they could not be considered dhimmis, 'protected people', and since the jizya was to some extent a dispensation from military service, any-one who paid it did not have to fight for the Muslim ruler. This line of reasoning was – con-sciously or unconsciously – later reversed. Akbar also repealed the pilgrimage tax which had been levied on Hindus since 1351.

There is also some evidence of anti-Hindu attitudes among the amirs. One Husayn Khan compelled the Hindus in his district to sew yel-low patches, tukri, onto their clothing to identify themselves. He came to be known consequently as 'Tukriya Khan'.[5] Orthodox Shi'a displayed an even stronger aversion to Hindus (Shi'is are renowned for their extreme regulations regarding purity). One particularly pious Shi'i, Muhammad Amin Hafiz, would permit no Hindus to come near him. If a great Rajput called on him, after-wards he would have his house thoroughly cleaned, the carpets taken out, and he would change his clothes. [6]

Official conversions by Hindus, like that of one of Shivaji's officers in 1667, were quite rare.

Co-operation between Muslims and Hindus was at its strongest in the sphere of the fine arts. A large number of miniature painters were Hindus, so if a synthesis of these two cultures existed in any sphere, it was in painting. The masterly pic-tures by Basawan or Govardhan of yogis[7] reflect the appeal which mystical Hinduism held for Akbar and his successors. These lifelike pictures depict *yogis* smeared with ashes, with their long fingernails, which had never been cut, and their long hair either twisted into a turban or falling loose. There are also many images of the *Kanphat yogis* with their large round earrings. The rapprochement between the two religions is especially evident in *bhakti*, a mystical strain of piety expressed in moving songs, similar to those of the Sufis. In fact in popular literature it is sometimes difficult to determine from which tradition a mystical folk song originated. There were more difficulties with Akbar's efforts to introduce his Muslim subjects to the Hindu scriptures. An Arabic translation of the *hatha* yoga tract *Amrtakunda*, 'Sea of Immortality", had been in existence since the thirteenth century, and in Akbar's time a new Persian version appeared among the adherents of the Sufi Muhammad Ghauth Gwaliari (died 1562). However, the ruler wanted more than this. Abu'l Fazl wrote:

Being aware of the fanatical hatred between Hindus and Muslims, and being convinced that this arose out of mutual ignorance, the enlightened ruler sought to dispel this ignorance by making the books of each religion accessible to the other. He chose the *Mahabharata* to begin with, as this is the most comprehensive and enjoys the highest authority, and arranged for it to be translated by competent men from both religions. In this way he wished to demonstrate to the Hindus that a few of their erroneous practices and superstitions had no basis in their classics, and also to convince the Muslims that it was absurd to ascribe a mere 7,000 years of existence to the world.

Bada'uni and a number of other scholars were entrusted with the arduous task of translation, which was completed by 1587, followed three years later by the *Ramayana*. However, in the year 1002/1594 Bada'uni composed a commentary on the Qur'an for a holy man's tomb, 'in the hope that, having distanced himself from the heresy of earlier books, this (i.e. the Qur'an) will be his friend in this life and his advocate after his death.'

Akbar and his son and grandson enjoyed meetings with Hindu ascetics. Ganga Rishi visited Akbar whilst he was staying in Kashmir. After the conquest of Asirgarh, Akbar met the *yogi* Gosain Jadrup, who was sitting in a pit, dressed only in a loincloth. Jahangir met this wise man no fewer than three times in Ujjain.[8] On a number of occasions, when referring to him, Akbar commented that 'the wisdom of Vedanta is the wisdom of Sufism'. In fact there is a strong accord between Vedanta and Sufism, especially in the form developed by Ibn ʿArabi.

For all his respect for Hinduism, however, Akbar was averse to a few of its customs, especially *sati*, the burning of widows. Poets wrote verses expressing their horror as well as admiration for the self-immolation of Indian women as the highest expression of absolute love. Akbar also admired widows who wished to be cremated with their deceased husbands. However, in 1583 he ruled that no woman was to be compelled to commit *sati*, and Abu'l Fazl quoted the emperor:

It is a strange commentary on the magnanimity of men that they seek their own salvation by means of the self-sacrifice of their wives![9]

Nevertheless, so far as I am aware, the only epic poem in the Persian language on the theme of a loving wife who follows her husband onto his funeral pyre was composed during Akbar's reign. The poet Nau'i (died 1610 in Burhanpur) dedicated his epic *Suz u gudaz*, 'Burning and Melting', to Akbar's son Danyal. In the early seventeenth century it was copiously illustrated.[10]

The situation changed somewhat under Jahangir. He enjoyed many discussions with Gosain Jadrup, and a new, illustrated translation of the *Yoga vasishta* appeared in his time,[11] but he was sometimes repelled by their practices. He visited Hardwar on the Ganges, was very well informed about the Durga Temple in Kangra, was knowledgeable about the Hindus' ideals, and their four stages of life.[12] However, when visiting *yogis* in Peshawar, he observed that they 'lacked all religious knowledge, and I perceived in their expressions only darkness of spirit'. He also reported that he broke a statue of Vishnu's incarnation as *Eber*, whilst disparaging the 'worthless Hindu religion'. He was also not exactly tactful in remarking that he had encountered a *sanyasi* standing as immobile 'as a fossil', and that 'any number of glasses of spirit made no difference whatsoever'.

Jahangir ordered that no temples should be destroyed, other than in times of war; however, no new temples should be constructed either.

His son Shah Jahan prohibited any proselytising on the part of the Hindus. However, during his reign there were a significant number of converts to Hinduism, and a whole department of the administration was established to deal with this issue. Hindu poets and painters lived in harmony at his court and played an important role there, for example Chandarbhan Brahman, the court secretary and friend of Dara Shikoh.

Dara Shikoh made another attempt to bridge the chasm between the two great religious cultures of the empire.[13] He held a number of discussions with Baba Laldas in Lahore in 1653, trying to gain a clearer understanding of Hindu terminology. In 1803, a translation of fifty of the *Upanishads*, which he had completed with the help of a few *pandits*, was published in Latin under the title *Oupnek'hat, id est secretum tegendum* by A. H. Anquetil-Duperron. This translation aroused strong interest among European philosophers, especially German Idealists. It contributed to their view of India as 'the home of so many useful arts, and no harmful ones' (Schlegel), and also helped foster a longstanding European idealisation of India.

In Dara Shikoh's view, the *Upanishads* were among the works alluded to by the Qur'an, which makes a number of references to the fact that no race of people is 'without The Book' (*Sura* 17:16; 53:22; 57:25). His efforts to effect a rapprochement between Vedanta and Sufism were astutely titled *Majma' al-bahrayn*, 'Confluence of the two Seas' [i.e. of salt and sweet water] (*Sura* 18:60).

His younger brother Aurangzeb considered such enthusiasm for mysticism to be politically dangerous. However, even though Aurangzeb remained true to the *shari'a*, he could not do without his Hindu officers, and large numbers of Rajputs as well as Marathas were among his *mansabdar*s. Any attempt to dispense with this contingent would have caused the break up of the empire. Even though the ruler had prohibited or at least demeaned a number of Hindu customs, and reintroduced the *jizya* in 1679, the dignitaries of both religions continued to meet frequently at holy shrines, for 'the Sufi shrine unifies, the Mosque divides'.[14]

Furthermore, Mughal princes occasionally took part in the festivals of non-Muslim groups. Numerous miniatures testify to their enjoyment of the Hindu festivals of *Holi* and *Diwali*; Akbar used to celebrate *Shivratri*; and sometimes they even wore *rakhis*, holy commemorative bands.[15]

Theoretical expositions of Hinduism are rare in Indo-Persian literature, and there is scarcely any mention of Hindu literature in that of the Muslims. Akbar was more interested in Hindu literature than philosophy. Few thinkers of the Mughal period immersed themselves more fully in Hindu philosophy than had al-Biruni, six centuries previously. The Naqshbandi master Mirza Janjanan of Delhi (died 1781) attempted to locate Hindus in the Muslim scale of values. He maintained that Hindus were basically monotheists, not idolators; however, their religion, along with all others, had been abrogated by the appearance of the Prophet Muhammad.

## JAINS

The Jains were, and still are, a relatively small religious group in Gujarat. The commandments of the Jain religion, which was founded around six centuries before Christ, are not to kill, not to steal, sexual abstinence, absolutely no possessions, and fasting. Followers attempted to adhere to these ascetic practices, which are also a feature of early Buddhism. Jains were strict vegetarians who wore face masks in order not to swallow any organisms inadvertently. Babur shuddered somewhat when reporting about the mighty stone figures near the fortress of Gwalior, which had been erected by the Jains.

Akbar admired the Jains for their strict vegetarianism. On 7 June 1583, a group of 67 *svetambaras*, 'white robed ones', appeared in Fatehpur Sikri; however, nothing is known of their contribution to any subsequent discussions. Muslims denounced the Jain sect known as *digambaras*, 'clothed in air', who wandered the land naked, which is forbidden by *shariᶜa* Islam. A few Jain scholars were rewarded by Akbar for writing

40. Govardhan, 'Emperor Jahangir playing *Holi* with his Noblemen', painting from a Jahangir Album.

works in Sanskrit. One of them wrote 128 verses in Sanskrit in praise of the ruler. Another was honoured for his services to knowledge by being dubbed *jagat guru*, 'teacher of the world'.

The one great conflict between the Mughals and the peaceful Jains had political causes. During Jahangir's time, Rai Singh of Bikaner rebelled against him because of a Jain prophecy that the emperor would be overthrown. Consequently, Rai was punished and the Jains were banished from the Mughals' territories.

The Jains had been merchants from earliest times, since the prohibition on killing made it difficult for them to follow any other profession.

It was Jain bankers who provided Aurangzeb with financial support to the tune of 550,000 rupees during the war of succession in 1658.

## PARSIS

From the middle of the seventh century on, after the Muslim conquest of Iran, Zoroastrians from Iran had been settling on the west coast of India. They arrived in Gujarat and later also Bombay. Karachi, which only later achieved some significance as a trading harbour, still has a small but active Parsi population. The Parsis were initially farmers, then later on primarily merchants. Bada'uni once referred to them as the 'fire worshippers from Gujarat'. Akbar met Dastur Mehrjee Rana in Surat and invited him to Agra. He went there in 1578, took part in discussions in the *ibadatkhana*, and received *madad-i ma*ash* (pension).

Akbar appears to have been very impressed with the industriousness, the cleanliness and the practicality of the Parsis. More importantly, however, their worship of fire and light were in accord with his own inclinations. Akbar kept a flame burning in the palace at all times, which a Zoroastrian had brought from Iran. Abu'l Fazl was entrusted with tending this flame. The veneration of light played a part in Akbar's religious devotions, which he performed at sunrise, midday, in the evening and at midnight. Abu'l Fazl relates that one hour before sunset, twelve white candles would be lit in the palace. Akbar was also fascinated by the dualistic nature of Zoroastrianism, and the emphasis on the eternal struggle between Good and Evil. It is certainly possible that a few aspects of the *din-i ilahi* were influenced by Zoroastrianism. The concept of *farr*, 'divine glory', which Abu'l Fazl attributes to his ruler, is derived from the ancient Iranian concept of *khwarena*, the 'divinely sanctioned kingship'.

Akbar was held in high esteem by the Zoroastrians, and there was apparently no tension or conflict between the Mughals and the Parsis. One Parsi played an important role in the delineation of the religious situation in India in the seventeenth century. This man, who called himself Mubad Shah, was the author of a work in Persian called *Dabistan*, which provided a somewhat confusing overview of religious problems in India. This frequently consulted work was also available in a number of more or less accurate translations. It has now been conclusively (in my view) established that this was the work of a Parsi author and not a Sufi.

Not long before the end of the Mughal era, the Parsis began to play an active and very successful part in the cultural and economic life of India, as they still do to this day.

## JEWS

There was also a small but important Jewish community, since the west coast of India was easily accessible from Central Europe. However, in contrast to the Parsis, the Jews migrated to Gujarat before the rise of Islam. Still today there is a notable Jewish community in Bombay. There is no mention of this group taking part in discussions in the *ibadatkhana*, to my knowledge.

However, a remarkable character of Jewish extraction appeared in Shah Jahan's day, namely Sarmad, a Persian Jew. This man had studied in Shiraz under the great Muslim philosopher Mulla Sadra (died 1640). He travelled to India as a merchant, where he fell in love with a Hindu youth in Thatta, Sind, which shocked him to such an extent that he became a wandering dervish, roaming

41. 'The last Zoroastrian monarch, Yazdgird, hiding in the mill', a scene from Firdawsi's *Shahnama*, copied *c.* 1440–45, gouache on paper.

around stark naked. He then attached himself to Prince Dara Shikoh. His quatrains, *ruba'iyat*, are steeped in gloomy melancholy, and he felt a special affinity with the mystic al-Hallaj, who had been executed in 922 in Baghdad. Like his exemplar, he was executed in 1661. It is not clear, however, whether this was due to anti-semitism. W. Fischel has attempted to disentangle Sarmad's Jewish roots and influences, trying to find evidence that he had not completely dissociated himself from his inherited tradition. However, Shamsham ad-daula, in his historical work, views Sarmad's close friendship with Dara Shikoh as the main reason for his subsequent persecution – 'because there were thousands of ecstatic naked men like him wandering in every back alley and street'.

Recently, a few Jewish authors from Bombay have attempted to revive Sarmad's memory, and they commemorate his anniversary beside his modest, newly renovated tomb near the Friday Mosque in Delhi.

## SIKHS

India is rich in syncretistic movements. It was primarily mystics from the Hindu and Muslim religions who attempted to foster mutual understanding between their two traditions, for example Kabir (died 1518), who wrote poetry in which he spoke out against the caste system, and for non-idolatrous worship of God. Kabir, who was a weaver, is claimed by both Hindus and Muslims as a member of their own faiths.[1]

The movement started by Guru Nanak (1460–1537) grew out of similar efforts. He declared himself to be neither Hindu nor Muslim, and his followers described themselves as *sikh*, 'students'. Akbar was very well disposed towards the Sikhs and their mystically inclined thinking.

In 1565 he visited Guru Amardas, and gave the city of Amritsar as a fief to his successor Guru Ramdas. Since that time the town, with its Golden Temple, which was completed in 1601, has remained the religious centre of the Sikhs. In 1598 Akbar visited the prolific Guru Arjan, who compiled the holy book of the Sikhs, the *Adi Granth*, which is a collection of prayers, religious texts and poems not only by Sikh poets but also Muslims. It is written in an early form of Punjabi, which is not always easy to understand, as well as a few related northwest Indian languages.[2] The *Granth* is as revered by the Sikhs as the Qur'an is by Muslims. This strong veneration for books is certainly due to Islamic influence.

The Sikhs are still recognizable today by their distinctive trappings: they conceal their uncut hair under tightly bound turbans, are bearded, wear steel bangles and carry knives. They are probably the only religious community to have begun as a mystical movement emphasising peace and the equality of all religions, and to have evolved into a group of militant fighters.[3] The cause of this reversal was their participation in uprisings against the central government. In 1606, shortly after ascending the throne, Jahangir had Guru Arjun executed (he considered him to be a 'Hindu'), because when Jahangir's firstborn son rebelled against his father, he had been supported by Guru Arjan, for which the ruler naturally wanted revenge. Then in 1612 Guru Har Gobind was imprisoned for political reasons in Gwalior, and both his sons were put to death in very gruesome ways, also primarily for political motives, in which the increasing militarisation of the Sikhs was also implicated. The situation deteriorated still further in Aurangzeb's day. In the struggles over the succession to the Peacock Throne, the Sikh Guru Har Rai initially took Dara Shikoh's side, but later withdrew his support. His successor, Guru Tegh Bahadur, was executed in 1675 at Aurangzeb's command, which led to an uprising. In 1699 the *Khalsa*, the 'Society of the Pure', was founded, with the aim of ending Muslim rule in India to ensure their own survival. In 1710, three years after Aurangzeb's death, the tenth guru, Gobind Singh, was murdered. He was said to be the last human guru. At his death, religious authority was derived exclusively from the holy book, the *Granth Sahib*. In the subsequent confusion, a rebel, Banda, took command of a number of Sikhs, who then began carrying out appalling atrocities against both Muslims and Hindus in the Punjab. Because of the increasing weakness of the central government in Delhi, the Sikhs succeeded in establishing themselves in the Punjab, their homeland. In 1799, Ranjit Singh took Lahore, then three years later the holy shrine in Amritsar. The British made Ranjit Singh ruler of the Punjab before incorporating the province into the territory under their own rule in 1849, after two bitter Anglo-Sikh wars.

## CHRISTIANS

The earliest Christian settlements in India go back to the first century AD. Christian groups entered the subcontinent in the south as well as the northern regions. Since the fourth century a group known as the Christians of St Thomas has distanced itself from the mainstream. The Mughals' first encounter with the Portuguese was in 1573, under Akbar, when the Portuguese began establishing settlements on India's west coast. The first conflicts occurred three years later with the siege of Surat. Three years later Akbar was in communication with two Jesuits who were active in Bengal. For the Indian Muslims, the presence of non-Muslim Europeans was a problem, as they increased the pressure on the west coast harbours, which were used as places of embarkation by pilgrims setting out on the dangerous sea voyage to Arabia, to Mecca.

Akbar took a great interest in everything which appeared to him to be worthwhile and important, particularly in religious matters, which led him to send the following letter in 1578 to the Portuguese in Goa:

In the name of God
To the High Priest of the Order of St Paul
Let it be known to you and I am a great friend of yours. I am sending my ambassadors ᶜAbdullah and Domenico Perez herewith, to invite you to send two of your learned men back with them, bringing with them law books, also especially evangelical ones, because I honestly and sincerely desire to acquire a full understanding of them.
I urgently beseech you once more to let them accompany my ambassadors with their books, for I would derive great solace from their arrival. Be so good as to comply with my request, and I shall receive them with every possible honour.

In September 1579 Akbar's embassy reached Goa, where it was received with great courtesy by the Portuguese, for the totally unexpected invitation from the mighty ruler had raised their hopes that he might be ripe for conversion.

The three Jesuit priests who were soon afterwards sent to Agra had been selected to serve the ends of Portuguese missionary zeal as well as political aims. Their leader was Rudolfo Aquaviva, and he was accompanied by Antonio Monserrate, whose letters and drawings constitute a vital historical record. There was also a Muslim convert to Christianity, Francesco Enrique, who acted as interpreter.

On 17 November 1579 the Jesuits set out from Goa. They travelled to Surat, where they stopped for a month before continuing their journey on 5 January 1580. They did not travel alone, but were accompanied by an entire caravan of merchants carrying Chinese silk and other wares for sale in the Mughal territory. They took the overland route via Mandu and Gwalior, and reached Fatehpur Sikri after an arduous journey lasting forty-three days.

Akbar had the men brought to him immediately on their arrival, and talked with them well into the night. His small sons – between eight and eleven years of age – were dressed in clothing inspired by Portuguese fashion. The ruler offered his guests large quantities of gold and silver, which they declined, as their vows of poverty only permitted the bare minimum of possessions necessary for their survival. This astonished the ruler, as giving and receiving monetary gifts was the generally accepted custom.

On 3 March 1580 the missionaries brought a particularly finely bound copy of a polyglot Bible (in Hebrew, Chaldean, Latin and Greek) that had been printed between 1569 and 1572 for Philip II of Spain. The guests reported that Akbar 'handled the holy text with the deepest respect, took off his turban, touched the volume to his head and then kissed it'. They also gave him a Persian work on the lives of the Apostles. The Bible and its illustrations apparently had some influence on Mughal painting, for soon afterwards biblical scenes began to appear in Mughal albums.

A chapel was constructed in the palace. Prince Murad, Akbar's second son, ten years old at the time, and a few other boys from noble families were taken to the priests for instruction in Portuguese and in Christian morality. The priests had free access to Akbar and were allowed to proselytize. Many paintings show them taking part in discussions in the cibadatkhana. With their pale faces and rather long pointed noses, and dressed in their black soutanes, they appear strangely alien among the colourfully dressed courtiers.[1]

No wonder the priests were so amazed at Akbar's tolerance, coming as they did from a world where the Inquisition and the persecution of heretics was in full swing. They were also astonished at the reverence which the emperor displayed towards pictures of Jesus and Mary – they were not aware of the affection and respect with which the Qur'an refers to Jesus, son of Mary, or its emphasis on the virgin birth, nor that the Prophet Muhammad decreed that pictures of Jesus and Mary were not to be destroyed when the Ka'ba in Mecca was in the process of being cleansed of all 'idols'. So it is understandable that Mughal painters produced so many pictures of the Madonna. The Christian images brought by the missionaries fired their imaginations to such an extent that they even painted pictures of the crucifixion of Jesus,[2] apparently disregarding the fact that this is strictly denied in the Qur'an (*Sura* 4:156) (although of course many of the painters were Hindus).

Understandably, the Portuguese guests assumed that Akbar was renouncing Islam and was on the way to becoming a Christian. This erroneous assumption was no doubt strengthened by Bada'uni's accounts of Akbar's difficult relationship with the narrow-minded orthodox *mullahs*, which appeared to be further proof of his un-Islamic attitude. The Jesuits were disappointed when they realised that Akbar's intense search for the truth was motivated by his mystical leanings and did not indicate a desire to convert to another religion, even though he did attend the Portuguese mass at Christmas.

In one discussion in the cibadatkhana it was suggested that they test the truth of both religions by means of a trial by fire. Akbar agreed, but Father Aquaviva refused.

In 1581, after a successful military campaign in Kabul, the Afghan highlands were added to the Mughal empire. Aquaviva was ill in Fatehpur Sikri at the time, but after his recovery he had a meeting with Akbar. Unfortunately the Jesuits' failure to follow the rules of etiquette, especially with regard to the Prophet, often deeply offended the Muslims and turned them against the Christians, and even Akbar was unable to smooth things over. For their part, the Jesuits were gradually giving up hope of converting the ruler and a large number of the nobles, even though Akbar had been present at the consecration of a church in Agra.

In 1583 Aquaviva asked for permission to return to Goa, and also to take with him a Russian family who were prisoners of war. They had been put in the service of the Queen Mother Hamida Banu Begum, during which time they had converted to Islam. Akbar granted the priest's request, despite his mother's opposition. Unfortunately, only two months later Aquaviva was murdered by Hindus seeking revenge for the destruction of some of their temples by missionaries.

Akbar's religious tolerance was still evident even after the departure of the Jesuits. In 1590 a Greek Orthodox priest appeared at court and talked to the emperor about the possibility of preparing translations of Christian books. A decade later ᶜAbduᵓs Sattar ibn Qasim wrote a biography of Jesus and the apostles for Akbar and dedicated the completed work to Jahangir (Mirᵓat al-quds). A *farman* of 1603 granted the Christians the right to preach and gain converts, and to erect churches not only in Agra and Lahore but also in Bombay and Thatta. Three sons of Akbar's youngest son Danyal, who died in 1605, were even christened, although they soon reverted to Islam. This had in fact been a political ruse, to prevent the youngsters from contending for succession to the throne.

Nevertheless, there was increasing tension between the Mughals and the Portuguese – and by extension the Christians. The increasing numbers of 'hat wearing' Europeans – Dutch and British as well as Portuguese – led to increasingly frequent skirmishes and a deterioration of the religious climate. This is very evident from a description of the siege of Hooghly in Bengal at the start of Shah Jahan's reign in 1631,[3] according to which ten thousand Europeans and a thousand Muslims perished. In 1664, after a number of lengthy battles, Chittagong was annexed to the Mughal empire.

## ISLAMIC SECTS

### THE MAHDAWIYYA

Throughout history there have been men who have declared themselves to be the promised Messiah, the one who was to appear at the end of time 'to replenish the earth with righteousness, just as it has been filled with unrighteousness'. Muslim peoples have gradually woven together the story of the second coming of Jesus, who at the end of the reign of the Antichrist, *dajjal*, would fight and conquer and bring about a glorious Islamic finale, and the story of the appearance of the *Mahdi* from the family of the Prophet Muhammad. This started with the Shiᶜa, but was subsequently taken up by the other factions. These self-declared messiahs, fired with conviction, tended to appear during times of political crisis, and especially at the turn of centuries or the millenium. A prime example is the *Mahdi* of Sudan, who took up the fight against the British and their associates shortly before the start of the fourteenth century of the Islamic calendar.

42. Nar Singh, 'Akbar presiding over a religious debate in the *ibadatkhana* with the Jesuit Fathers Rudolph Aquaviva and Francis Henriquez in the city of Fatehpur Sikri in 1578', *c.* 1578–9, pigment and gold on paper.

In India there are many records of apocalyptic religious leaders, such as Sayyid Muhammad Kazimi, whose name reveals him to be a descendant of the seventh Shiʿi Imam Musa al-Kazim. At the end of the eighth century of the *Hijira*, in 1494, whilst on a pilgrimage to Mecca, he declared himself to be the *mahdi*. No one in Mecca took much notice of his declaration, but on his return to India Sayyid Muhammad was attacked. He took flight and died in 1505 in Farah, not far from Herat, in what is today part of Afghanistan.

Sayyid Muhammad succeeded in attracting many followers because he and his close associates led exemplary lives strictly in accordance with *shariʿa*. For him, *dhikr*, the contemplation of God, was of primary importance. The disciples met twice daily, not in the mosque but in the *daʾira*, a simple meeting place where they intoned the name of God together hundreds of times. They also practiced *habs-i dam*, holding the breath for long periods. The most notable characteristic of the Mahdawis was their voluntary poverty, inspired by the saying attributed to the prophet: 'My poverty is my pride'. Disciples had to give away all their property. They were also characterised by their trust in God and their community of likeminded friends. In many ways they resembled early ascetic Sufis, for music and dancing were strictly forbidden. Historical sources record that many devout people in the country were impressed by the sincere and dutiful conduct of the Mahdawis. Badaʾuni relates that the pious theologian Shaykh ʿAlaʾi

renounced the customs of his ancestors
and his duties as a *shaykh* and religious
leader, trampled his self-regard and his self-
consciousness underfoot, and devoted
himself henceforth to caring for the poor
in his community, serving with extreme

self-abnegation and humility those whom
he had formerly persecuted.

Many people who led strictly religious and law-abiding lives were assumed to be Mahdawis, and, depending on the prevailing political situation, sometimes persecuted as such.

The persecution of the Mahdawis began at the beginning of the sixteenth century and reached its zenith during the Suri interregnum, when Humayun was in exile in Persia. The *shaykh al-islam* Makhdum ul-Mulk, who had been appointed by Humayun, became a devoted servant of the Suri ruler during his absence, and 'girded his loins with his strenuous efforts to exterminate these men of god'. The leader of the Mahdawis, Niyazi, a Pashtun from Bayana, was tortured, and eventually reverted to orthodox Islam. However his disciple Shaykh ʿAlaʾi was flogged to death in the Deccan in 1550, 'and it is said that during the night so many flowers were scattered over the *Shaykh*'s corpse that he was completely buried by them...'.

Shaykh Mubarak, who had held a very important position in Akbar's court, defended the two Mahdawis, with the result that he himself was later denounced as a Mahdawi. Badaʾuni, whose own orthodoxy was unquestionable, speaks with great veneration of both Mahdawi leaders, whose piety he greatly admired. Although he did not like Shaykh Mubarak in other respects, he praises him for his efforts 'to save the life of Shaykh ʿAlaʾi.

After the fall of the Suri regime, the persecution of the Mahdawis continued in a few provinces of the Mughal empire, especially in Gujarat, where Akbar's foster brother Mirza ʿAziz Koka persecuted them, whereas the *khankhanan* ʿAbduʾr Rahim left them in peace. Aurangzeb also attacked the small remaining groups of Mahdawis; however, splinter groups have survived to this day, especially in the Deccan and in Sind.

The general influence of the Mahdawis and their ideals on literature and politics in the early Mughal period merits closer study. Malik Muhammad Ja'isi, who was one of the earliest poets in Purabi, the dialect of the region, is said to have been a student of one of the leading Mahdawis of the time, Burhanuddin of Kalpi (died 1562-63). At about the same time, the first known religious poet in Sind, Qadi Qadan of Sehwan (died 1551) composed his brief *doha*, and according to a few sources, he too was a Mahdawi. However, it is not certain that his use of the term *da'ira* in his verses does constitute proof of this.

## THE RAUSHANIYYA

There was another religious sect that also seems to have arisen during Akbar's reign amidst the general speculation aroused by the beginning not only of a new century, but also of a new millennium. This was the Raushaniyya, named after Bayezid Ansari, the *pir-i raushan*, 'The Resplendent or Illustrious Master'. However, his opponents called him *pir-i tarik*, 'Master of Darkness', and the sect he called into being began its existence in the most desolate corner of the Mughal Empire, in the Afghanistan border region.

Bayezid came from Waziristan, and he began exhorting people to follow him at the significant age of forty. There are various theories as to the origin of his ideas. A few experts see them as a form of Pashtun national consciousness (and it was probably this political dynamite that alarmed Akbar). Others considered the Raushaniyya to be a movement with its roots in Sufism, for there have been incidents of politically and even militarily active movements developing out of this mystical tradition, and as this was not long before the new millennium, military ideals might well

have become entwined with mysticism and folklore. The Raushaniyya might also have been influenced by the Isma'ilis, one of whose centres was northern Badakhshan, a narrow strip of mountains abutting on Chitral, which forms the pass from Afghanistan into the Tajikistan of today. The great mediaeval Isma'ili philosopher, poet and missionary Nasir-i Khusrau (died after 1072) lived there for many years and was buried there. Isma'il splinter groups may already have come into being in Hunza at that time.

In any case, the Way which *pir-i raushan* taught was similar to the Sufi Path from the start. It commences with the duty of following the *shari'a*, the law revealed by God, then *tariqat*, the 'Way', followed by *haqiqat*, the 'Truth', which in normal Sufism constitutes the final step, which for the Raushaniyya meant contemplation of God. The concept of *ma'rifat*, which in Sufism means 'intuitive knowledge, gnosis', was understood by the Raushaniyya to mean seeing God everywhere, whilst *qurbat*, 'nearness', means knowing and apprehending God. *Wuslat*, 'connection', is the renunciation of all worldly goods; *tauhid*, unity, does not mean consciousness of the oneness of God, as it does in orthodox Islam, but rather the unification of the self with God. The eighth step, unique to the Raushaniyyas, is *sukunat*, 'stillness', which means achieving the power to radiate godliness.

Bayezid maintained that he had been initiated on to the Path by Khidr, the mysterious holy prophet, and that he was the 'absolute master'. Like the Mahdawiyya, he led people in the practice of silent *dhikr*, and caring for the poor. Like the Sufis, his followers held forty-day retreats. Problems arose from the irresolvable tension between the mystical Islamic aspects of the movement and the tribal ethic emphasised by the Pashtuns. However the appeal of the Raushaniyya was very great, and Akbar sent his best general, Raja Man Singh, to battle in the threatened northwest border region. By 1575 Bayezid was dead; however, the fight with his followers continued. His son Jalala held sway over a large area in 1575, and it took until around 1600 before the Mughals were able finally to conquer this region. To this day, the treacherous rapids at the confluence of the Indus and Kabul rivers are still remembered as the place where the last few fighters are supposed to have drowned.

Although the Raushaniyya were defeated as a political movement, Bayezid's enduring legacy is his contribution to literature in the language of his homeland, Pashto.

One of Bayezid's grandsons became a Mughal *mansabdar*. Whilst he was on duty in the Deccan, he established an *ʿidgah*, a large site where the people of Burhanpur could hold prayer festivals.[1]

### THE NUQTAWIS

Until now, not much has been known about the Nuqtawis, although they came in for brief but harsh criticism from Badaʾuni.[1] They were founded by Mahmud Paskhwani (died 1428 in Iran), who rejected Islamic rituals and beliefs and maintained that there were many prophets. Like the aforementioned Sayyid Muhammad, he claimed to be the promised *mahdi*; and furthermore, that the hegemony of the Arabs and Arabic had come to an end after the first nine centuries, and that now the superiority of the Persians was quite apparent.

He taught that life on earth evolved with the constant flux of existence and extinction over the course of millennia, and that humanity came into being at a certain stage of evolution, *nuqta*. This idea is also in Jalaluddin Rumi's famous verse in the *Mathnawi* (ii, 3901 f.):

See, I died as a stone and am reborn as a
    plant . . .

The view that all beings have the same roots and that the world consists of beings with basically the same origins tends to give rise to a feeling of unity. As Jahangir's friend Sharif-i Amuli put it: 'Anyone who torments another torments himself'. These ideas might have had an influence on Akbar's *sulh-i kull*, 'peace with all'. In other respects the Nuqtawis' views appear to be equally close to those of the Sufis and the Shiʿi. However, their belief in the eternal existence of the world, and their rejection of belief in the day of the Last Judgment, are closer to the views of philosophers.

The Nuqtawis were persecuted in Iran under Shah Tahmasp, and in 1592 Shah ʿAbbas had them massacred. However, the leading Nuqtawi of his time, Sharif-i Amuli, fled to Akbar's court in 1576 and was awarded a *mansab* of 1,000 *zat*. His followers regarded him to as the *mujaddid*, the 'renewer of the century', and, in his case, of the millennium, for the year 1000 in the Islamic calendar was approaching. Akbar was clearly influenced by him, and Jahangir counted him as one of his faithful followers. After Jahangir ascended the throne, he even awarded him a *mansab* of 2,500 *zat*. However, afterwards the influence of the Nuqtawis appears to have ceased.

### SHIʿI SECTS

*The Ismaʿilis.* From the beginning of the second millennium of our calendar, the northwest of the subcontinent was primarily ruled by Sunni Turks and Pashtuns, although there were clearly also small groups of Shiʿi Muslims. Thirteenth- and fourteenth-century sources mention the *ibahatiyan*, the 'lapsed', who did not adhere to the official religious observances and were therefore persecuted. These might have been the

Isma'iliyya, whose missionaries reached Gujarat and Sind in the twelfth century. Afterwards, with the succession of the Fatimid Caliph al-Mustansir in Egypt (reigned 1030–1094), a schism developed. One group, the Nizaris, who later came to be called Khojas, and are today known as Aghakhanis (under the leadership of the Aga Khan), lived mainly in eastern Iran, and also in Sind and Kutch, whilst the other faction, who came to India by way of the Yemen, were known as the Bohras ('Merchants'). Up to the twentieth century, they maintained contact with small groups in the Yemen. Small splinter groups formed, among them the Satpanthis, who originated in Burhanpur in the early sixteenth century. They are of interest for the extent to which they blended Hindu and Islamic thoughts and concepts, in fact so much so that 'Ali, the first Imam of the Shi'a, is revered as the tenth *avatar* of Vishnu. There is also some literary evidence for a close connection between the Shi'a and the Sufis. Although there is little mention of the different Isma'ili groups in the official chronicles, their existence nevertheless appears to have been regarded as a threat to the pure teachings, especially in Aurangzeb's day. A decree sent by Aurangzeb to Gujarat bears this out:[1]

Order for the appointment of the eliminator of prohibited practices.

The responsible officials in the jewel of the provinces, Ahmedabad, are hereby informed, that now, according to this exalted order, the office for the 'elimination of prohibited practices' in the province by the name of YX is to be extended to XY. This office must fulfil its duties and responsibilities in this province in an upright and correct manner.

It must not let its vigilance and care lapse for a moment. It must act as harshly as necessary in eliminating forbidden forms of belief regarding the illustrious holy law. It must install an orthodox Imam and an orthodox prayer leader in the mosques erected by the Isma'ili sect. It must take care that prohibited objects and intoxicating beverages are not used. It must exact a guarantee from this sect that they will renounce their erroneous convictions.

The named appointment is hereby conferred on the above named person. He is now invested with the duties and traditional rights of this appointment. (Those concerned) should be aware that he will employ the severest means in fulfilling them.

Aurangzeb attempted, as has been seen, to oppose the Isma'ilis in Gujarat. In 1688–9, he summoned Sayyid Shahjee, a wealthy Isma'ili leader from Ahmedabad, to his court. However, Shahjee took his own life, which led to uprisings in the country, which were brutally put down by the governor.

The year 1857, not long before the collapse of the Mughal empire, was a turning point in the history of the Isma'ilis. The leader of the Nizari-Khoja Isma'ilis, who was known as the Aga Khan, left Iran in 1839 and settled in Bombay. A court judgment acknowledged him as the legitimate leader of the Isma'ilis. It was his grandson, the famous Sultan Muhammad III Aga Khan (died 1959), who began to reform his community into a modern society.

*The Nurbakhshis.* The Nurbakhis in Kashmir were another group of Shi'i origins. Their founder came from the Sufi tradition of Sayyid 'Ali Hamadani (died 1385) who had been effectively active in Kashmir. Sayyid Muhammad Nurbakhsh (died 1464) declared himself to be the Caliph of the

Muslims. This and other political claims led to his imprisonment by the Timurid Shah Rukh. Nurbakhsh maintained that the *Imam*, the leader of the community, must not only be a descendant of ᶜAli and Fatima, but also a *wali*, a friend of Allah.

In 1484, twenty years after the death of their founder, the Nurbakhshis reached Kashmir, where they were joined by many members of the Chak clan. This led to clashes between them and the Hanafi *sayyids*, the Muslim elite in Kashmir.

The Timurid Prince Mirza Haydar Dughlat, one of Babur's cousins, who conquered Kashmir in 1541, regarded the Nurbakhshis as arch heretics, and their holy book, *al-Fiqh al-ahwat*, 'the all-encompassing religious law', as an embodiment of unbelief and heresy. Mirza Haydar, a strictly orthodox Sunni, put these views into action:

> Many of those in Kashmir who clung to this heresy were delivered by me to the true faith, whether willingly or unwillingly, and many of them I killed. A few sought refuge in Sufism; however, they are not true Sufis.

A few small groups of Nurbakhshis are said to be still living in Kashmir today, however they appear to have played no further role in Mughal history.

*The Twelver Shiᶜa*. The Twelver Shiᶜa began to play a greater role in India after the Safawid Shah Ismaᶜil established Shiᶜism as the state religion in Iran in 1501. In the Deccan kingdom, strong Shiᶜi groups were formed from the mid-fifteenth century, thanks to the efforts of the grandson of the Sufi master Shah Niᶜmatullah Kirmani, and a series of Shiᶜi scholars who had migrated there. Later rulers of Bijapur and Golconda were at least to some extent Shiᶜi, which increased the tensions between the predominantly Sunni north and the Deccan states. Humayun's religious convictions have never been fully clarified. During his sojourn in Iran he is supposed to have adopted the Shiᶜi form of Islam in order to please Shah Tahmasp, and he paid visits to the most important Shiᶜi shrines. The Persian poets and artists who streamed into India played a major role in the dissemination of Shiᶜi ideas in the Mughal empire.

At the very beginning of the Mughal era, the most important political leader was a Shiᶜi. This was Bayram Khan, thanks to whose efforts Humayan was able to reconquer his Indian empire. However Bayram Khan appears to have overplayed his hand – Badaᵓuni relates that he unfurled the banner of the *Imams* during a military march. There was always some doubt among his contemporaries as to the religious convictions of his son, the *khankhanan* ᶜAbduᵓr Rahim.

Akbar's appointment of the learned Shiᶜi Nurullah Shushtari as the chief *qadi* of Lahore was unprecedented. However, even Badaᵓuni, with his abhorrence for everything not strictly Sunni, praised the pious *qadi*, who was the author of a number of interesting works. Particularly important is his *Majalis al-muᵓminin*, which contains biographies of all the known authors and poets of Iran and the neighbouring countries. He regarded them collectively as Shiᶜa, who for pragmatic reasons practiced *taqiya*, 'concealment of the faith', as they feared persecution, living as they did in the midst of Sunnis. This has not been borne out by history. However, tragically Shushtari himself was accused of *taqiya*, for which Jahangir had him flogged to death in 1610, despite the lack of valid evidence. Shushtari thereby became the 'third martyr' of Shiᶜism.

A year later the attitude of the ruler towards the Shiᶜa softened somewhat, as Nur Jahan, his new Persian queen, was, perhaps naturally, on the side of the Shiᶜa. Perhaps that strengthened the opposition to the regime among the Naqshbandis. Decades later, during the internecine rivalry over the succession to the throne among Jahangir's grandsons, Dara Shikoh was supported primarily by the Shiʿa, and Aurangzeb by the Sunnis, who regarded him as a staunch ally.

By now, tensions between the Sunnis and the Shiʿa, which were longstanding in the Deccan kingdoms, were also increasing in the Mughal empire. The Turani and the Irani factions stood respectively for the Sunni nobility of primarily Central Asian and Turkish extraction, and for the Shiʿite nobility, which was gaining steadily in strength. These tensions, heightened by ethnic differences, later undermined the very structure of the Mughal empire.

They also played a role in the time of the weak leadership after Aurangzeb's death, and led to catastrophe when Nadir Shah marched on Delhi. The largely Shiʿite royal house of Awadh then established itself in the capital city Faizabad, later Lucknow. The Shiʿite nawabs, who had been kings of Awadh since 1819, developed a markedly Shiʿite culture. They offered refuge to numerous Shiʿite poets and scholars, whilst Delhi, despite being the official seat of the Mughal rulers, largely abdicated its cultural role. In Awadh and other partly Shiʿite provinces splendid buildings were built, such as the Imambaras, used for the Muharram festivities. Lucknow saw the development of the art of *marthiyya*, dirges for the death of Husayn, the grandson of the Prophet. Even the birthdays of the twelve *Imams* were celebrated with all due pomp.

The Muharram processions, which Aurangzeb banned in 1698, but which can still today be seen in many towns in the subcontinent, often gave rise to tensions within communities. In Hyderabad in the Deccan they resembled a kind of carnival. The combined celebration of the first ten days of the Muharram with *marthiyya* recitals and prayers has been retained to this day by Indian and Pakistani Muslims wherever they live, and is even celebrated in London and New York.

## SUFISM

Pictures from the time of the Mughals often show wandering dervishes leading a lion or a bear on a lead, sometimes dressed in an animal skin and strange headwear, and often wearing earrings and iron armbands. They sometimes have round brand marks on their arms from their initiation rituals. They usually carry a begging bowl and a forked stick, for use either when sitting or standing. Other pictures depict elderly men in long costumes, respectable in their turbans. In some pictures they are seated like *yogis*, with a shawl wrapped around their backs and calves to ease the strain on their knees. In others they are seen whirling ecstatically, their long sleeves flapping rhythmically at their cowls.

There had been Sufis of all kinds among the first Muslim groups to migrate to India. Not long after 900 the Baghdad mystic al-Hallaj travelled through Gujarat and Sind – probably along the Silk Route towards Central Asia. His name (in fact usually his father's name, 'Mansur') is still heard today in the subcontinent in Sufi folk songs, for 'Mansur' was the 'Martyr for the Love of God', who was put to death in Baghdad in 922. In Indo-Muslim literature he has been immortalised as a dashing lover, murdered by the heartless law abiding *mullahs*.[1]

In the middle of the eleventh century Sufis reached the part of northwest India under Ghaznavid control. The first important handbook of Sufism in Persian was written by Hujwiri Jullabi, who came from east Iran and was driven on to Lahore, where he is known as Data Ganj

43. Attributed to Shiva Lal, 'A Muharram Procession', *c.* 1615–20, pigment and gold on paper.

Bakhsh. His grave is honoured in Lahore to this day. For centuries Sufis coming from the north-west of the subcontinent used to 'request permission' at his mausoleum to continue on into the country.

The following centuries saw the arrival of many men of God belonging to different brother-hoods or following different 'Ways'. There were the Chishtis, lovers of music and poetry, whose centre, Ajmer, became very important for the Mughals. There were also the sober Suhra-wardiyya, who were initially concentrated in Sind, the Punjab and Bengal. ʿAli-yi Hamadani led the

Kubrawiyya into Kashmir. There was an active branch of this group, the Firdausiyya, in Bihar and Bengal. Babur visited Hamadani's grave in Khuttalan during his military campaigns. For a time the Shattariyya played an important role in central India, while the Central Asian Naqshbandiyya, who were averse to music and dancing, were increasingly important to the Mughals in the subcontinent. In addition there were numerous smaller groups, venerators of particular holy men, hybrids with elements from Hindu *bhakti* groups and so on. When Babur and his associates came to India there was

44. 'The hermit Shaykh
Salim Chisti in a hermitage
with his tame lion', *c.* 1700,
drawing with wash on
paper.

a dazzling array of different mystical paths. The theosophy of the Andalusian Ibn ʿArabi (died 1240)[2] was spreading in India at more or less the same time. Before this theosophy came to be generally accepted, there were lengthy disputes between the different masters. Their belief in the 'oneness of being', often designated as either pantheism or monism, coloured the poetry of all the languages of the subcontinent, and inspired mystically inclined scholars to compose numerous commentaries and original works. A textbook written by the strait-laced Badaʾuni, *Najat ar-rashid*, reveals the surprising fact that he too was a follower of the 'great master'.[3] The most famous of the teachers in India was Muhibbullah of Allahabad, who followed Ibn-ʿArabi, and who was venerated by Prince Dara Shikoh. However, not everyone took to his ideas, and Aurangzeb had a book by one of his students burned as heretical.

Babur's family had a long standing connection with the Naqshbandis, going back to Bahaʾuddin Naqshband, who died in Bukhara in 1389. His most important successor, Khwaja Ahrar (died 1490), was one of the most powerful men in Central Asia at the time, and Babur's father was a follower of his. Members of his family came with him to India and some of them married into the Mughal family.[4] Babur had Khwaja Ahrar's *Risala yi-walidiyya* translated into Turkish, convinced that this pious work would bring about a cure for his illness. He wrote the following verses:

> Though I be not related to the Dervishes,
> Yet I am their follower in heart and soul.
> Do not say that the rank of a king is remote
>     from the Dervishes –
> I am a king, but yet a slave of the Dervishes!

Babur's son Humayan was a great venerator of holy men. He visited the shrine of the leader of the Chishtis, ʿAbduʾl Quddus Gangohi (died 1538), and during his wanderings in exile in Iran, he visited all the accessible mausoleums, including the shrine of ʿAbduʾllah-i Ansari (died 1089) in Gazurgah, near Herat. A valuable transcript of the famous prayers of this holy man later came into the possession of the Mughals. Humayun visited the Kubrawi holy man ᶜAla ad-daula as-Simnani (died 1336), and also the mausoleum of Ahmad-i Jam (died 1141), who was related to his young wife Hamida. When Humayun had established himself in Kandahar, he began donating alms to the Sufis (1554). The Sufi with the greatest influence on the emperor was Shah Phul or Buhlul, who claimed to be descended from the great Persian mystical poet Fariduddin ᶜAttar, and who was renowned for his exorcisms. He knew the power of the names of God, and taught that it was even possible to influence the stars by means of them.

Humayan was his devotee in his youth, and learned from him methods for choosing auspicious days, the symbolism of colours, and much more. Shah Phul was killed by Humayun's brother Hindal, who feared his great influence over Humayun. However, there appear to have been other motives as well, which his daughter Gulbadan hints at. Shah Phul's brother Muhammad Ghauth Gwaliari (died 1562) had an even greater influence on many Muslims, and the Shattari order which he represented remained active for many years, for example in Burhanpur. Muhammad Ghauth was even praised by Babur as a 'strong and powerful spiritual person'. Muhammad endured a twelve year-long retreat in a pit, after which he completed his work 'The Five Jewels', a tangled skein of mystical, cosmological and magical teachings, which can only be unravelled by the initiated. There are also Persian and Arabic versions of this work. The great theologian ᶜAli al-Muttaqi, the author of a *hadith* collection which remained in use for a century, issued a *fatwa* against Muhammad Ghauth. However, the theologian Wajihuddin Gujarati spoke in his defence.[5] Akbar does not appear to have shown any great interest in these powerful

religious figures – a somewhat astonishing fact, which is mentioned by both Badaᵓuni and Abuᵓl Fazl. However Tansen, Akbar's favourite musician, was a venerator of Muhammad Ghauth, who is buried in a beautiful mausoleum with elaborate *jalis*, filigree lattice windows of yellow marble. It could well have been Tansen who had this mausoleum constructed only a few paces away from his own modest grave, in the belief that music was the best way of bringing about mutual understanding between Hindus and Muslims.[6]

Akbar was said to have been very keen on having letters from the Bihari Sufi Sharafuddin Maneri (died 1380) read to him, as they taught a sensible, wise form of piety. He and all of his descendents also loved the poetry of Maulana Rumi. Rumi's mystical poetry had been known in India since the early fourteenth century, and by the end of the fifteenth century it also became popular with the Brahmins of Bengal, according to one Hindu writer.

Akbar, however, was most strongly drawn to the Chishtis. The rulers of the dynasties preceding the Mughals had also venerated the Chishti holy man Nizamuddin Auliya of Delhi (died 1325). His mausoleum was one of Delhi's greatest spiritual centres, which every official guest had to visit. During Humayun's brief period of government in Delhi, the Turkish admiral Seydi ᶜAli Reis was directed there.

Akbar once visited the mausoleum of Nizamuddin's master, Farid Ganj-i shakar in Pakpattan in the Punjab, and for many years he visited the shrine to Muᶜinuddin Chishti in Ajmer.[7] He went there for the first time in 1564, and then made annual visits from 1570 to 1579. His son Danyal, who was born in Ajmer in 1573, carried on this tradition. The arrival of the ruler was always the occasion for great festivities, and every day it was his custom to be entertained at the holy mausoleum by holy men, scholars, and upright men. There were dance performances, at which all the singers and musicians were virtuosi without peer, who could play on your heart strings then rend your soul with an agonising cry, and silver and gold coins were showered down on them like raindrops.

Akbar was entertained by Hindi verses sung by dervishes, and all the while presents were being brought to the sacred site, such as gigantic candle stands, and enormous vessels for preparing food for the pilgrims. Jahangir donated a vessel large enough to feed five thousand people, and still today, during the holy festival of ʿurs on the 6 Rajab of the lunar calendar, they try to spoon the last ear of corn out of it. As well as this vessel, Jahangir donated a silver balustrade, as he recorded in 1613. Shah Jahan's daughter Jahanara, who was recovering from severe burns, also gave valuable gifts. Akbar is depicted in a miniature in the golden yellow robes of the Chishtis, which is evidence of his close connection to this order, which became even closer after the birth of Jahangir.[8]

Akbar also paid visits to the graves of popular holy figures, such as the mausoleum of Salar Masʿud in Bahraich. This legendary youth was said to be a nephew of the conqueror Mahmud of Ghazna, who had been slain during a battle with the Hindus in 1033, on the very night when he was to consummate his marriage with Bibi Fatima. A cult formed around Bahraich which was, at least in some respects, very 'profane'. This was one of the reasons why pious, law-abiding Muslims banned such festivals, and also reproached Akbar for his leanings towards the Sufis, at least towards their more unorthodox aspects. The most promi-nent of his critics was Ahmad Sirhindi, who also frequently appears during Jahangir's time. He was a Naqshbandi, and like many members of this 'strait-laced' order, he began his theological career by writing an anti-Shiʿa tract. Akbar's tolerance and his syncretism were completely at odds with Ahmad's narrow conception of the true Islam.[9] Ahmad wrote 534 letters, some of them very lengthy, mostly in Persian but some in Arabic, in which he tried to warn the most prominent people at court of the dangers of such religious hybrids, and to exhort them to adhere strictly to the way of the Prophet. These letters were later used by reformers, who distributed them all over the Islamic world. They were translated into Turkish, and exerted a significant influence in the Ottoman Empire, and even in modern Turkey.

Ahmad Sirhindi considered himself to be the *mujaddid*, 'Renewer', who was prophesied to appear at the beginning of every century. Further-more, he was the *mujaddid-i alf-i thani*, the 'Renewer of the Second Millennium' of the Islamic calendar, which began at the end of 1591. He even audaciously used the *kabbala* to establish a spe-cious connection between himself and the Prophet, whereby 'Muhammad' was transmuted into 'Ahmad'. He evolved his own theories to counter those of the increasingly influential Ibn ʿArabi. Whereas this Great Master's followers proclaimed that *hama ust*, 'Everything is He', Ahmad Sirhindi's were to say of him that *hama az ust*, 'Everything is from Him'; instead of *wahdat al-wujud*, the 'Unicity of Being', he substituted *wahdat ash-shuhud*, 'Unicity of Contemplation'. His claims were unacceptably large, and Jahangir, upon learning of Ahmad's criticism of his father's reli-gious policies, had him brought before him:

It was reported to me at that time that a braggart by the name of Shaykh Ahmad was casting the net of deception and hypocrisy in Sirhind and had caught many of the supposed worshippers in it, and that he had sent many of his students to every country and to every town, claiming that he is the *khalifa* ('Successor'), and that he is especially skilled at decking out his shop (at deceit) and peddling religious knowledge and deception. He had also spun any number of foolish tales to his students and followers, which he compiled into a book with the title *maktubat* ('Letters'). This absurd collection contains a lot of useless twaddle written with the aim of leading people into unbelief and lack of piety . . .

I therefore commanded that he be brought to the court, which strives to maintain right-eousness. In accordance with my command, he came to show his respect. He could give no sensible answer to any question I put to him, yet he presented himself to me in all of his ignorance with the utmost pride and self-satisfaction. I considered that the best thing for him would be a period in the prison of correction, in order to cool down the heat of his temperament and the confusion of his mind, as well as the agitation of the people. He was therefore put in the care of Anira'i Singh-Dalan and incarcerated in the fortress of Gwalior.[10]

However, while locked up in Gwalior, Shaykh Ahmad had an experience of the mighty majesty of God. He was released after only a year, and treated quite well by Jahangir, who gave him two thousand rupees, after which he continued to write and preach until his death in 1624. Pious visitors still pay their respects at his grave in Sirhind, and even Iqbal, who was quite incensed by some of his ideas, went there in 1932.

Some of Sirhindi's contemporaries were always highly critical of him. One of these was ʿAbduʾl Haqq *muhaddith* from Delhi, a great authority on religious tradition, who had much in common with the Qadiriyyas, and who was the author of a series of important works of Islamic theology. He presented his biographies of holy men, *Akhbar al-akhyar*, to Jahangir the same year that Ahmad Sirhindi was imprisoned.

Of all Sirhindi's assertions, the one which ʿAbduʾl Haqq found most absurd was his claim that he and three of his successors were of the rank of *qayyum*, 'The Eternally Existing', which is actually one of the names of God (*Sura* 2:155) and cannot be applied to a mortal. In Sirhindi's view, however, it was the highest possible spiritual rank for a devout man, below that of the Prophet, yet higher than the rank of *qutb*, the 'axis' or 'pole' of worldly existence. Sirhindi even believed that the *qayyum* controlled the rotation of the earth.

By a strange coincidence, shortly after the death of the fourth and last *qayyum*, Pir Muhammad Zubayr, in 1739, Nadir Shah captured Delhi and plundered it mercilessly – as if the divine pro-tection of the *qayyum*s had really ceased. It is diffi-cult to establish what role the *qayyum*s, and hence the Naqshbandis, played between 1624 and 1739. The works of their followers, such as the still unpublished *Raudat al-qayyumiyya*, are hagiogra-phies rather than objective historical works. It is not certain whether Aurangzeb was a disciple of Pir Muhammad Maʿsum, Sirhindi's son, but it is a possibility. [11]

The role of the Naqshbandis in India increased in importance. A disciple of the last *qayyum*, Muhammad Nasir ʿAndalib in Delhi (died 1758), went on to found the Indian *tariqa muhammadiyya*, a mystical fundamentalist movement, which initially opposed the Sikh rulers of the Punjab, then later the British. This movement was run-ning parallel to other movements, also known as *tariqa muhammadiyya,* 'The Path of Muhammad', which emerged at the same time in the Near East and in Africa, such as the Sanusiyya and the Tijaniyya. All of them evolved from Sufi orders into communities of fighters struggling against ever strengthening colonial rule in large areas of the Islamic world.

Muhammad Nasir ʿAndalib's son, Mir Dard, became the first great mystical poet in Urdu. There were other Naqshbandiyya who were also active at that time in Delhi, the most prominent being Shah Waliullah, the son of a lawyer who had been involved in compiling the *Fatawa-yi ʿalamgiri.*[12] He was born in 1703, and had spent several years in Mecca. After his return to Delhi, he attempted to bring about a revival of Islam. He was ordained in four Sufi orders, and attempted to prove that they were all equal and that each stressed a particular aspect of spiritual experience, as did the four traditional schools of Islamic law. In his view, the cause of the miserable conditions of Indian Muslims was their ignorance of the religious foundations of their culture. He attempted to remedy this with a translation of the Qurʾan into Persian, the language of cultivated people. He was right in thinking that the numerous commentaries and commentaries upon commentaries written about the Qurʾan had muddied rather than clarified the meaning of the Qurʾan. Interestingly, Jahangir had already given a copy of the Qurʾan written by the famous calligrapher Yaqut to a Sufi in Gujarat, the great grandson of the great Shah ʿAlam, and asked him to translate the holy book into clear and simple Persian.[13]

Shah Waliullah's great Arabic work, *Hujjat Allah al-baligha,* attempted to account for the plight of Muslims in India, pointing to the mismanaged economy, financial problems, neglect of the agricultural regions and much more besides. It should be remembered that *hujjat Allah,* 'proof of God', is one of the titles for a *mahdi,* and Shah Waliullah had no hesitation in ascribing to himself the title usually associated with a *mahdi, qaʾim az-zaman.* He claimed that God had made him His 'Admonishing Deputy', which meant that he was to reprimand Muslims for all their sins and errors – and which he did most vociferously! Philosophers, 'who gnaw on two-thousand year old bones', were attacked in the same vein, as they had been by the mediaeval Sufis; soldiers were rebuked for their immorality, and the feudal lords for their indifference to all grievances; even the Sufis did not escape his censure. Like Mir Dard, he portrayed them as the 'Sufi Supersalesmen'. He spoke out vehemently again the practice of visiting the tombs of holy men, especially the mausoleum of Salar Masʿud, on the grounds that it was sheer idolatry, and stated that if he were able to find even *one* relevant passage in the Qurʾan, then he would prohibit this sort of practice. It is significant that the Delhi mystics had no wish to be called 'Sufis' – they wanted to emphasise the difference between themselves and the popular, and not altogether highly spiritual, Dervishes.

Many of Shah Waliullah's observations, for example regarding miracles, are evidence of a rationalistic standpoint, and he is supposed to have had his doubts about the traditional interpretation of lunar fissures (*Sura* 54:1), however, he was a traditionalist when it came to his rousing Arabic hymns to the Prophet.

The Mughal government did not communicate all that much with the great intellectuals, but they did expect their advice. Shah Waliullah suggested enlisting the help of the Sunnis in Afghanistan in opposing the Sikhs in the Punjab and the Marathas in the south. However, these 'helpers' wreaked more havoc than the enemy.

The most level-headed of the Naqshbandis in

Delhi, Mazhar Janjanan, was killed in 1781 by a Shi'i fanatic, because the old man had mocked a Muharram procession. However, the influence of the Naqshbandi reformer continued in India even after the collapse of the Mughal empire, and a branch of his Naqshbandis still survives in Delhi.

The Chishtiyya also continued to play a role. Alongside these somewhat mutually antagonistic brotherhoods, another community was gaining in importance, namely the Qadiriyya, the oldest Sufi Way.[14] It was named after the Hanbali preacher 'Abdu'l Qadir al-Gilani, who was from Caspian Iran. He had been a successful preacher in Baghdad, where he died in 1166. His followers spread his teachings to the east and the west, so that eventually there were Qadiriyya everywhere in the Islamic world. In India, they gained their first followers in the south (Tanjore is still an important centre). Later on in the Mughal era, in the fifteenth century, Qadiris settled in Sind and in the southern Punjab. The tariqas rose in significance in Jahangir's era; Mian Mir, who came from Sind, had settled in Lahore in Akbar's time. Jahangir was very impressed by this holy man,[15] who then came into contact with the young Dara Shikoh. Mian Mir died in 1635, and Dara Shikoh dedicated a biography to the master, which contained a chapter on Mian Mir's spiritual sister, Bibi Jamal Khatun. Mian Mir is depicted in many miniatures, usually with a shawl around his bent knees and a prayer band in his hands, which were crippled with arthritis. Dara Shikoh and his sister Jahanara became disciples of Mian Mir's successor, Mulla Shah Badakhshi. Tawakkul Beg, who was another faithful disciple of Mulla Shah, acted as a messenger between his master and Shah Jahan in Kashmir. Tawakkul Beg also wrote a number of interesting descriptions of Mulla Shah's life and teachings of his master, as well as his correspondence with the princess. He quotes a few of Mulla Shah's four-line verses in Persian:

> You are astonished when alchemy transmutes
>     dust into gold –
> Yet your own dust is transmuted by poverty
>     into God.
> Humanity thus falls into the ocean of truth –
>     what becomes of it then?
> What becomes of a drop of water that falls
>     into the vast sea?[16]

After Dara Shikoh's execution, the Qadiriyya retreated into the background somewhat. They later found a new mode of expression in mystical poetry in regional languages, especially Punjabi. Sind and Baluchistan were their regional centres, where 'Abdu'l Qadir's remembrance day was celebrated so lavishly that the whole month of Rabi' II, the fourth month of the lunar calendar, was often called 'eleven', gyarhan, because the festival took place on the eleventh of that month.

There were many mystical groups and currents during the Mughal time, but only one other merits a brief mention: the Rishis in Kashmir. Anyone who has visited Srinagar will have come across the grave of Baba Rishi in Gulmarg, in a fragrant pine forest near the source of the Jhelum River. It is a place of pilgrimage for many religious people, including Hindus, who tie pieces of cloth to the lattice window testifying to the vows they make there. Baba Rishi was one of the Muslim Rishis who were even in contact with Akbar. Nuruddin is regarded as the founder of the Rishis, introducing the new spiritual path in 1589. They lived strictly ascetic lives, practiced breath control, planted fruit trees, and cared for their fellow creatures in tranquillity and humility.

There are many unanswered questions concerning the mutual influence of Sufism and

45. *Dara Shikoh visiting a Sufi faqir, c.* 1640-50, drawing on paper.

Hinduism, in the realms of literature and philosophy (where the powerful influence of Ibn ᶜArabi's adherents is very much in evidence) no less than in popular religion, in which Hindu and Sufi ideas and ideals were often inextricably mingled, to the annoyance of reformers.

The love of women is paramount in a few Sufi scriptures from the Mughal period; however, it is not clear whether these contain traces of Kashmiri Tantrism.[17]

There is one remaining question, which has only been touched on so far: how strong an influence was exerted on Indian Islam by the *ishraqi* teachings developed by Shihabuddin as-Suhrawardi, who was killed in Aleppo in 1191? The answer is uncertain; however, Badaᵓuni refers to these ideas, and much of Akbar's speculation about light seems to have been influenced by Suhrawardi's observation that 'Existence is all Light'.

What is certain is that Sufism permeated Indian Islam to a great extent, and right up to the end of the Mughal period the holy festival of ᶜurs, of Muᶜinuddin Chishti as well as of ᶜAbduᵓl Qadir al-Jilani, was celebrated in Delhi in the Lal Qila (Red Fort).

## RELIGIOUS CUSTOMS

In 1980 in Khuldabad, we saw a richly garbed little boy sitting near the tomb of Aurangzeb, and were informed that he was a *basmala ka dulha*, a 'Bridegroom of *basmala*', meaning that he was being introduced to the text of the Qurᵓan for the first time. This happens at the age of four years, four months and four days. A child is given a plate with the inscription 'In the Name of the God the Most Compassionate and All Merciful', written on it, often in honey, which he has to lick

to help him learn the text of the Qurᵓan. This custom was practiced in the time of the Mughals. Akbar had the ceremony performed for his son Salim Jahangir, who in turn arranged it for his own son.

Akbar had his three sons circumcised on 22 October 1573, although Abu'l Fazl commented that 'It is rather odd to insist on circumcising infants, when they are not burdened with any other religious duties.'[1]

The great religious festivals, such as breaking the fast at the end of *Ramadan*, and the sacrificial rite during pilgrimages, were evidently celebrated with great pomp. The latter festival was often a source of conflict in India, for the slaughter of any kind of animal was strictly prohibited by the Jains, and although the Hindus were not in general opposed to the festival, they were averse to the sacrifice of cows.

The pilgrimage to Mecca was the paramount duty of a Muslim. However the number of pilgrims was limited by the hazards of travelling. The journey to Mecca involved either a sea voyage across the Indian Ocean, which was largely controlled by the Portuguese, or the land route across Iran, through, a region ruled by the Shiᶜa since 1501, which very pious Sunnis felt uneasy about. A few *mansabdars*, like *khankhanan* ᶜAbduᵓr Rahim, built special ships for the use of pilgrims.

A 'pilgrimage' to Mecca was sometimes used as a form of exile, a way of getting rid of an official who had fallen out of favour with the emperor. The first person to be subjected to this punishment was Babur's son Kamran, who was banished by his brother Humayun. Many more were to follow, among them the two highest religious officials of the empire under Akbar, the *sadr as-sudur* ᶜAbduᵓn Nabi and the *shaykh ul-Islam* Makhdum ul-Mulk, who could not stand each other. Sometimes a pious man or woman would decide to retire to Mecca in old age, or to withdraw there for a period to escape the intrigue-laden atmosphere at court. Furthermore Mecca was the place to meet all the learned people of the world, and hear all the news about religious movements in the east and west. The chronicles give detailed reports of the pilgrimages undertaken in 1575 by a number of the women of the Mughal household. Princess Gulbadan and Akbar's consort Salima, along with many other noblewomen, apparently greatly enjoyed their sojourn in the holy city. The number of visitors was beginning to overwhelm the Ottoman authorities, who had jurisdiction over the holy city after 1516. They even asked Akbar to cease donating alms in Mecca; Akbar had recently given 600,000 rupees to the leader of a caravan of pilgrims, as well as 12,000 sets of clothing to be distributed to the deserving. The women experienced all kinds of hardship on the return journey, however they managed to convey a famous stone with the footprint of the Prophet to Akbar. Despite Akbar's supposed antipathy towards Muslim traditions, he treated the relic with great respect, according to the astonished Bada'uni.

The month of fasting and pilgrimage to Mecca were firmly based on the Qur'an, unlike the festival which was celebrated during the night of the full moon of the eighth month, Sha'ban. This was the shab-i barat, an ancient New Year festival from the time of the pre-Islamic solar calendar, which was supposed to determine the course of the New Year. There is not much mention of this night (laylat ul-bara'a, nisf sha'ban) in Arab regions, and the most recent reference to it in Persian regions is in the poetry by Sana'i (died 1131) in praise of it. The night was – and still is – celebrated with illuminations and fireworks. Jahangir described having the small lake at Ajmer illuminated on one of these occasions. Special sweets were also prepared and enjoyed at this festival. However, pious people concentrated on the prayer and religious devotions for the most part. For many religious people the shab-i barat was just as important as the laylat ul-qadr, when the Qur'an was revealed for the first time.[2]

The birthday of the Prophet, on 12th Rabi' I, the third lunar month, was apparently not celebrated lavishly, as this day was regarded, with historical accuracy, as the anniversary of the death of Muhammad, as it still is in a number of regions of Indo-Pakistan. Bada'uni writes that food and money were given to the poor in the name of the soul of the Prophet, which is the custom when commemorating a death. However, over time this date came to be regarded as the birthday of the beloved Prophet, as it had been for centuries in the Near East, and to be celebrated with illuminations and singing.

Since at least the sixth century, a vast amount of poetry, especially in regional languages, has been written on the subject of miracles performed by the Prophet.

Although, according to Bada'uni, Akbar did not want to hear the name of the Prophet, his poet laureate Faizi composed a number of magnificent hymns in honour of the Prophet. Popular poets, especially those who composed in Sindhi, sang little maulud, 'birthday hymns', for the Prophet, praising him as the beloved bridegroom of their souls, and pining for his last resting place in Medina.[3]

Relics of the Prophet were collected, such as the stone with the imprint of the Prophet's foot, which the ladies brought back from Arabia. There were similar stones, known as qadam rasul, in other provinces of India, such as East Bengal. Shi'i regions prided themselves on possessing a footprint of 'Ali (for instance in Maulali, Hyderabad, Deccan). So far as I am aware, there is no mention

46. 'Princess Zeb un-nisa, daughter of Aurangzeb, at the *shab-i barat* festival, Faizabad', early 18th century, gouache on paper.

in historical sources of the relic most highly venerated today, i.e., a hair of the Prophet, even though numerous shrines dating back to the sixteenth century, in Bijapur as well as in Rohri in Sind, are adorned with reliquaries containing a hair carefully preserved in a small glass bottle wrapped in scented silk cloth, which neither unbelievers nor women are permitted to see.

The construction of mosques was an important religious activity, second only to making copies of the Qurᵓan. The following words ascribed to the Prophet have been well known in India from ancient times: 'For whosoever builds a mosque, even if it be it as small as the nest of the *qata* (a desert bird), God will build for him a house in paradise!'[4]

Astrologers, who were usually Hindus, played an important role in the life of the Mughals. After Aurangzeb ascended the throne, he replaced the Hindu astrologers with Muslim ones, but other than that, nothing was changed, and it was still believed that the destiny of a prince was determined by the stars at the time of his birth. In fact, every step of his life was astrologically preordained, such the precise time to attack a city or to begin a construction project. Every historical work contains the horoscopes of the princes. At the end of the Mughal period, Mirza Ghalib added his own horoscope to a great poem of praise in Persian in honour of the Imam ᶜAli.[5] Shah Jahan was known as *sahib qiran*, the 'Lord of Auspicious Conjunction', i.e., Jupiter and Venus. He was the second holder of this title, the first being his distant ancestor Timur. Interpretations of predictions by astrological experts are found in all the chronicles and poems, and many verses make no sense at all without some knowledge of astrological terminology. For example, 'the Moon in Scorpio' means great misfortune, so when a poet writes of his beloved's radiantly beautiful face framed by scorpion-like black locks, he means that he is in danger from this love.

Books of omens, *Falnama*, were well known in Mughal times,[6] as were those dealing with the interpretation of dreams. Dreams were taken as seriously in the Mughal period as they are today in the Islamic world, and they could be used to determine a course of action; for example, when Jahangir dreamed that his father asked him to pardon Mirza ʿAziz Koka, who was imprisoned in Gwalior,[7] he immediately released Koka. The *Falnama*s were illustrated, and these pictures – often featuring figures and scenes from the life of the Prophet – were also taken into account in interpretations. For instance, a scene of a man being attacked by a camel and about to spring into a well full of dragons would definitely be taken as an inauspicious omen.

Humayun was obsessed by omens. Because the three knights accompanying him in 1552 were called *Saʿadat*, 'fortune', *Murad*, 'will, goal', and *Daulat*, 'wealth, luck', he was convinced that he would be successful in reconquering India.[8] The Mughal court even followed the ancient Mongolian custom of divining the future from the shoulder-blades of sheep or gazelles which had been placed in a fire. Humayun lived his entire life according to precise rules, with a particular day and prescribed hour for each and every job and activity, which was not unusual at

that time. Devout men and women observed the Friday Sabbath, so Jahangir never drank on Friday night. One of his amirs apparently used to donate a thousand pieces of gold for sweets in the name of ʿAbduʾl Qadir al-Jilani every Friday. Wednesday was associated with the last Wednesday in the life of the Prophet, so Bayram Khan never failed to take a ritual bath each Wednesday, nor to shave himself 'with the intention of achieving martyrdom', as he wished to prepare himself for death in battle, for anyone who dies in a holy war is considered to be a martyr.[9] It is clear from a book written by the pious Shaykh ʿAbduʾl Haqq Dihlawi (died 1642) that the custom of allocating particular days for particular activities was in fact ubiquitous in the Islamic world.[10]

Humayan's visitors had to take care not only to keep to the prescribed time: anyone who carelessly entered left foot first would be dismissed forthwith. He kept to this rule himself and always entered right foot first, which is also a general Islamic custom. Furthermore, the pious emperor would never utter any of the names of God when he was not in a state of ritual purity. Humayun's house was organised entirely according to astrological precepts, being divided into twelve sections, within which the courtiers had to sit according to their astrological signs. Everything down to the carpets was arranged according to the stars. Needless to say, particular rituals had to be carried out during a solar eclipse; alms would be distributed to the poor, and the ruler had himself weighed to determine the amount to be given.

Certain books were used as a source of omens; even the Mughal emperors consulted the *Diwan* by Hafiz in an attempt to foretell the future. One copy of the *Diwan*, which is kept in Patna-Bankipore, contains notes in its margins by Humayun and Jahangir, e.g. that this or that verse had proved to be true or had guided them in their lives. When Humayan set out on his return to India, he could hardly have found a more appropriate verse than the following:

Seek success in rulership from the imperial, *humayun*, bird and its shadow,
For crows and ravens lack the wings of high endeavour! [11]

The shadow of the wings of the *huma* was said to confer the right to rule on anyone on whom it fell – and in Humayan's case, the fact that he had the same name made the oracle's injunction especially appropriate.

The custom of 'breathing on' someone or something was also very common. When Humayun caught sight of the new moon after crossing the Indus, he breathed upon little Akbar.[12] It is still customary today to say a little prayer and to look upon a beautiful person or upon gold at the moment when the sickle moon first comes into view. The practice of first breathing upon water and then drinking it (*Sura* 112), is referred to by Aurangzeb as a form of medication.[13]

Another of the magical–religious practices of the Mughal court was the magical circle. Akbar walked three times around the sickbed of his son Humayan in order to take the crown prince's sickness upon himself. Not long afterwards he fell ill and died, whilst his son recovered. Jahangir's son Parwez carried out the same ritual almost a century later, in 1621.[14]

Asaf Khan's attempt to render some magic harmless is especially interesting (and also rather amusing). He was afraid that Mirza ᶜAziz Koka (who hated Nur Jahan's family) and his friends in Gwalior prison were going to use black magic against him.[15] In order for magic to be effective, it was essential to abstain from sex and meat-eating during the preparations, so Asaf Khan made sure that the illustrious prisoners in Gwalior were served with chicken and partridge every day.

Abu'l Fazl, who viewed Akbar as the most elevated of human beings, evidently believed that he had supernatural powers, such as the ability to bring rain or to heal wounds.

The Mughal court was steeped in such superstition, which imbued the magnificent empire with its peculiar atmosphere, and was in turn reflected in its literature and fine arts.

نور جهان

47. Nur Jahan, *c.* 1740–50,
gouache on paper.

FIVE

# Women at Court

I have handed the business of government over to Nur Jahan; I require
nothing beyond a *ser* of wine and half a *ser* of meat.
Jahangir [1]

For many people the Taj Mahal, the lily-white mausoleum built by Shah Jahan for his wife Mumtaz Mahal in Agra, symbolises Mughal India, in fact the whole of India. He was inconsolable after her death, and Mumtaz, 'the elect of the palace', became the ideal of a beloved wife – an image quite at odds with the apparent role of women in the harem or in the Islamic world today.

However, Mumtaz Mahal is far from being a unique case in Indo-Islamic history. The chronicles contain a wealth of documentation on women in the imperial household, who were often as powerful as their husbands; acting as patrons of architecture, art and science; sometimes playing a role in government; having the right to issue edicts, intervene on behalf of prisoners; and much more besides.

This was also the case with the dynasties which preceded the Mughals or were contemporaneous with them – Sultan Iltutmish of Delhi (reigned 1206–1236) chose his daughter Razia Sultana as his successor, and she ruled the kingdom for four years. Under Shah Jahan there were a number of very dynamic noblewomen, who took an active part in politics.[2] The brave Chand Bibi of Ahmednagar was especially famous. She took part in the defence of the fortress during a savage attack by the Mughals, spurring her soldiers on to greater efforts, until she fell victim to jealousy on the part of her own officers.

Just as the rulers were awarded honorary titles during their lifetimes and after their deaths, so were the ladies: Hamida, Akbar's mother, received the title *Maryam Makani*, 'occupying the place of the Virgin Mary'; her daughter-in-law, Manmati, a Rajput from the Amber family, who was to become Jahangir's mother, was *Maryam-i zamani*, 'Mary of her time', whilst Shah Jahan's mother Jodh Bai, likewise a Rajput, bore the title *Bilqis makani*. To some extent she also acquired the rank of Bilqis, the Queen of Sheba, which is appropriate in view of the numerous comparisons of Shah Jahan with Solomon. Mumtaz Mahal, whose real name was Arjumand Begum

Banu, also bore the title *malika-i jahan*, 'Queen of the World', as well as *mahd-i 'ulya*, 'Most Elevated Cradle', whilst her daughter Jahanara, 'Jewel of the World', bore the title *sahibat az-zamani*, 'Mistress of Time', but was usually called Begum Sahib (a title which was later also awarded to her niece Zinat un-nisa).

In order to understand the prominent role of women at the Mughal court, it has to be borne in mind that women in the Central Asian regions, from which the 'House of Timur' originated, enjoyed considerably more freedom and were more active than those in the Central Islamic regions. Alanquwa, the mythical female ancestor of Chingiz Khan, played an important role in the prehistory of the Mughals, and the mythological connection between Alanquwa and light was transferred to Akbar's birth by Abu'l Fazl. The chief wife of Timur, the founding father of the Mughal dynasty, was also a highly independent person. (Timur had a special garden laid out for each of his favourite wives.) In more recent history there was Babur's maternal grandmother, Isan Daulat Begum (died 1505), the wife of Yunus Khan Mughal, who after the death of Babur's father managed everything for her grandson, took over the administration of his Andijan territories and dealt with conspirators.

When it comes to tactics and strategy, there
    were few
Women like my grandmother Isan Daulat
    Begum.
She was intelligent and a good organizer.
Most arrangements were made according to
    her stipulations.

Furthermore, Babur's mother, Qutlugh Nigar Begum (died 1505) was the daughter of that very energetic lady, the chief wife of ʿUmar Shaykh Mirza, and she accompanied her son Babur on many of his campaigns.

The long lists of names, confusing though they may be for the reader, show how closely related the different branches of the Timurid and Chingizkhanid families were. Babur's daughter Gulbadan provides a very interesting description of the 'mystical festival' of her half-brother Humayun on 19 December 1531. On this occasion the young Humayun, who had been the ruler for only a year, had invited a number of aunts who lived within easy reach, a few first and second cousins and a number of other unidentifiable noblewomen, so that on his right side no fewer than 87 ladies were seated, and probably about the same number on his left, all dressed in their best and no doubt wearing their elegant high Turkish hats – you can almost hear them gossiping during the banquet!

Gulbadan, the author of the vivid description of this scene, was Babur's daughter by Dildar Begum, who also bore him Prince Hindal, who was very close to Gulbadan. She was about eight years old when her father died in 1530. However, the events of the crucial early years left such a strong impression on the child's mind, that decades later, when her nephew Akbar asked her to write about his father Humayun, she was able to produce a vivid picture of his turbulent life, up to the blinding of her half-brother Kamran, at which point the manuscript comes to an abrupt end.

From Gulbadan's account we learn that childless wives of the ruler, or those whose children had died, often adopted their nieces or nephews, which rendered the already complex kinship ties still more unfathomable, at least in the case of those born after such adoptions.

Babur gave all three of his daughters by Dildar Begum a name connected with *gul*, 'Rose', so it is not always easy to distinguish between Gulrang,

'Rose Coloured', Gulchihra, 'Rose Face', and the 'Roses' of subsequent generations. However, Gulbadan, 'Rose Body', who was married to a rather insignificant man, Khizr Khan, stands head and shoulders above them. It was she who later accompanied her niece Salima, one of her nephew Akbar's wives, on a pilgrimage to Mecca in 1575, together with a group of other Timurid ladies.[3] Not until 17 February 1603, when she was more than eighty years old, did she 'cover her face with the veil of annihilation'.

All of Babur's daughters and a few of his granddaughters played a role in life at court, even if only in keeping the family together. One interesting example is the life of Ruqaiya, the daughter of Gulbadan's brother Hindal, who became Akbar's first wife. She remained childless, but assumed primary responsibility for the upbringing of Akbar's grandson Khurram, the future Shah Jahan.

The importance of politically motivated marriages is demonstrated by Babur's marriage to Mubarika, a woman from the Pashtun clan of Yusufzay, which was later to be a source of problems for the Mughals. He married the Pashtun woman in 1519 (the same year in which Hindal was born to Dildar Begum), which improved his standing in the eyes of the Afghan highlanders. However, Mubarika remained childless. Rumour had it that some of the other wives, being jealous of Babur's great love for her, had administered drugs to her to prevent her from presenting him with an heir. Such accounts are not uncommon. Black magic and secret methods, it was often claimed, were used to prevent the birth of a child who might be a future claimant to the throne. It was Mubarika who in the end conveyed Babur's corpse to its final resting place in Kabul.

Babur's favourite wife, however, was Maham, whose ancestral relatives included the Persian holy man Ahmad-i Jam (died 1141). Babur married her in 1506, at the age of 22. Two years later she presented him with Humayun, who was to become his favourite son and heir. In 1529 she went to Delhi, where she was allowed to sit next to the ruler on the throne. When Humayun was enthroned two years later, she held a magnificent celebration for him. Since her other four children had died at a young age, she treated Gulbadan and Hindal as her own children.

Babur's oldest sister, Khanzada Begum, who bore the title Padshah Begum (1478–1545), was really the First Lady of the empire. On many occasions she intervened during political difficulties between her relatives, for example between Humayun and Kamran in 1541, and four years later, shortly before her death, between Humayun and ᶜAskari.

The ladies of the imperial harem always constituted a formidable lobby. In 1606, when Prince Khusrau, on the advice of Mirza ᶜAziz Koka, rebelled against his father, Jahangir, Salima sent a message to Jahangir:

> Majesty, all the ladies have assembled in the women's quarters for the purpose of pledging their support for Mirza ᶜAziz Koka. It would be better if you were to come here – if not, they will come to you![4]

There are other accounts of similar threats.

Humayun, who was surrounded by innumerable aunts and cousins, was not at all averse to the fair sex. His wives were from the most varied of family backgrounds. His first wife, Hajji Begum, was supposed to have taken care of the young Akbar when his own parents were taking flight in Iran. It was she who constructed Humayun's mausoleum in Delhi, near Nizamuddin, or at least supervised the building work.

Humayun's wife Gulbarg, 'Rose Petal', who came from the Turkmen clan of Barlas, had previously been married to the Sindhi ruler Husayn Shah Arghun. She accompanied Humayun in his flight to Sind, during which time he became acquainted with the young Hamida, whose family, like the Mahams, was extremely proud of its descent from the great Sufi master Ahmad-i Jam, known as *Zindapil*, 'the living elephant'. There are differing accounts about the marriage between the refugee ruler and the initially reluctant Hamida.[5] The marriage was arranged by Babur's widow Dildar Begum, against the wishes of her son Hindal, and possibly against her own inclinations as well. It is hardly surprising that the young girl, barely fifteen years of age, was not exactly thrilled at the prospect of marrying a penniless emperor with no empire, who already had a number of wives, and was an opium addict to boot. Nevertheless, in 1541 the marriage took place, and on 15 October 1542, after exhausting travels in desolate regions, the young girl gave birth to a son, who would became famous as Akbar. A small memorial plaque in Umarkot, Sind, commemorates the event.

Humayan continued to take flight, followed by his young wife. When the situation appeared hopeless, she left the baby behind in the care of Humayun's oldest wife, and accompanied her husband tirelessly on all of his travels through Iran. Together they visited the mausoleum of her ancestor Ahmad-i Jam, as well as the Shiʿite shrine of Ardabil in the northwest of Iran, the place of origin of the ruling Safavid dynasty. All in all, she proved herself to be an excellent travelling companion. In 1544, whilst they were still in flight, she bore a daughter. Not until 1545 did she see her little son again, in Kandahar. The scene where the three-year-old Akbar recognised his own mother among a group of women is one of the favourite themes for the illustrators of Akbar's biography.[6] For a while, Humayun left Hamida behind in the fortress of Kandahar. It was very hurtful for her that after his return to Kabul, the prince married Mahchuchak (actually, *mah chichak*, 'Moon Flower'), who was to suffer a sad fate. Her son, Mirza Muhammad Hakim – Akbar's younger half-brother – took possession of Kabul after Bayram Khan's fall. In 1563, he was attacked, unsuccessfully, by the *generalissimo* Munʿim Khan. Abuʾl-Maʿali, formerly one of Humayun's favourites, escaped from prison in Lahore, married Mahchuchak's daughter, and murdered his mother-in-law in 1564.[7]

Like most of the ladies of the Mughal household, Akbar's mother remained in Kabul, whilst Humayun gradually recaptured the Indian territories. One year after he had met his end, Hamida Banu went to Delhi, where she lived for most of the time afterwards, exerting a considerable influence on her son and grandson until her death in 1604. At her death, Akbar shaved his head and chin and gave up wearing jewellery.

The veneration of the mother was an important feature of the Mughals' culture. Jahangir gives many accounts of going to visit his mother, approaching her and bowing deeply before her, in order to honour her 'according to the custom of Chingiz Khan and Timur'. When Gulrukh Miranshahi, one of his mothers-in-law, fell ill in 1614, she gave the emperor a robe of honour, which he accepted 'out of respect for the custom (*töre*)', whereas in fact as the emperor he ought not to accept anything like that sort of robe of honour. This extreme expression of honour for the mother is of course reflected in the injunction, rooted in Islam, to honour one's mother above all other people.

In Akbar's youth he also had an extremely close relationship with Maham anaga, his *amah*.[8] In

Islamic law, foster children and genetic children are treated as equals, and they are not permitted to marry each other. For this reason a newborn prince had to be nursed for a time by a number of different noblewomen during the first few weeks and months of his life, as the children of these *amahs* were considered thereafter to be siblings. In this way a tight web of relationships and dependencies was created. As Akbar commented, when he was being urged to punish his foster brother (*koka*) Mirza ᶜAziz: 'there is a river of milk running between us which I cannot cross'. Mirza ᶜAziz Koka's mother was Jiji anaga, the wife of Shamsuddin Atga, whom Akbar also loved very much. In his early childhood, Maham anaga attemped to use magic to ensure that the infant Akbar would not drink Jiji's milk, and the eight-month-old Akbar is supposed to have comforted her at the time (another of the 'proofs' in the hagiographies for Akbar's supernatural perception).

Zayn Khan Koka, whose father had at one time accompanied Maryam makani whilst fleeing through Iran, was also the son of one of Akbar's *amahs*. His granddaughter later married Jahangir and presented him with his son Parwez.

The honour of nursing a prince was often awarded to a particularly trustworthy lady with strong connections to the family, which is why the mausoleums of famous *amahs* are to be found everywhere in the Indo-Muslim regions (there are particularly beautiful examples in Lahore and Mandu). Akbar himself carried the bier of his *amah* to her burial.

Of all the Mughal *amahs*, Maham anaga is the most famous. She was the wife of Nadim Koka. The younger of her two sons, Adham Khan, grew up with Akbar. Maham anaga had one of the first Mughal mosques constructed in Delhi – the *khayr al-manazil*, opposite Purana Qila, the 'Old Fort'. She is said to have managed everything in the empire, even though Munᶜim Khan was the actual *wakil*, Minister. She naturally used her position of authority to the benefit of Adham, who nevertheless managed to make himself so unpopular that Akbar singlehandedly threw him from a balcony and caused his death. Forty days later, Maham anaga followed her son into the hereafter. Akbar mourned her according to custom, and soon afterwards married Salima, the daughter of Babur's daughter Gulru (died 1613). She had been widowed as a result of the intrigues against Bayram Khan instigated by Maham anaga, which culminated in his murder.

Matrimonial politics in the Mughal era were largely based on power struggles, as can be seen from the following quotation:

> Because his honourable wife had suckled Aurangzeb, his sons were promoted to the appropriate ranks.

Furthermore, when someone married Nur Jahan's sister, 'the doors of power were immediately opened for him'.[9] Such comments frequently occur.

Even women who did not belong directly to the court played a not inconsiderable role there. Another *amah*, Fatima anaga, served as an ambassador, so as to be able to discuss possible marriages with Haram Begum, the daughter of the Timurid Mir Wayz Beg and wife of Humayun's cousin Sulayman Mirza, who was effectively ruling in Badakhshan, the northernmost point of Afghanistan. In 1529 she assisted Humayun during his expedition to Balkh, and visited him in Kabul in 1551, both to console him over the death of his brother Hindal, and also to win Kabul for her husband. She was the *de facto* administrator of the country, and had the right to order punishment to be inflicted.

Badakhshan had once before been ruled by a woman: Shah Begum, the wife of Babur's uncle Yunus Khan Chaghatay (died 1487), left the Mongol region for family reasons, and after wandering for a long time she met her step grandson Babur in Kabul in 1505. Although she had instigated a rebellion against Babur for the benefit of her grandson Mirza Khan, Babur treated her generously and even made her the ruler of Badakhshan. However, she was captured by robbers in Kashgar and died around 1507.

After Akbar's half-brother Mirza Muhammad Hakim's brief period as regent in Kabul, Bakht un-nisa Begum, who was the daughter of Humayun and Mahchuchak, also the ruler's half-sister, was put in charge of the administration of the region. Another woman, Sarwqad, 'Cypress-stature', also deserves a mention. Gulbadan relates that she sang one night by the light of the moon, and later married the *wakil* Mun'im Khan, after which she attempted to mediate between him and other politicians.

Like the Mughals, the Arghuns of Sind also came from the Afghanistan region, from the Herat district, so a number of family connections were established between them and the first and second generations of Mughals in India.[10] An Arghun woman first married Babur's foster brother, Qasim Koka, then one of her relatives, Shah Hasan Arghun of Sind. A daughter from this union married Babur's son Kamran, and stayed with him as his faithful companion after he had been blinded and banished to Mecca.

Many ladies of the first and second generation played an important role in Akbar's time, attempting to mediate between the generations. Hamida even left the fort and entreated her grandson Jahangir, 'who had spent a long time in Ajmer indulging in lust and debauchery in bad company', to honour his father and show contri-

tion for his rebellion, and to go to Bengal as he had been commanded.[11]

Abu'l Fazl relates that after the ruler's lengthy periods of fasting, the first food he took was brought to him from his mother's house.

One of the most influential women was the Rajput Manmati, who as Jahangir's mother was honoured with the title *Maryam-i zamani*. She founded the Begum Shahi Mosque in Lahore (1611–14) and constructed a cascading fountain near the *'idgah* in Bayana (1612). When she died in 1623, she was buried in Sikandra, the final resting place of her husband Akbar.

When Jahangir was in Allahabad during his rebellion against his father, he was accompanied by his women. Shah Begum, the Rajput mother of his son Khusrau, committed suicide in 1605 because of her distress at the disloyal behaviour of her brother and the disobedience of Khusrau, and was buried in Khusrau Bagh in Allahabad. Jahangir was so distraught at her death, he apparently ate nothing for four days, and Akbar sent him a robe of honour and his own turban by way of consolation. Jahangir's sister, Sultan Nithar Begum, was also buried in Allahabad after her death in 1622.

In Jahangir's time it was the women who encouraged the design and building of mosques, whereas the ruler himself did not instigate any large projects of this kind.

A number of legends have been woven around the story of Jahangir's rumoured love affair with a girl called Anarkali. In 1599 he was said to have exchanged adoring looks with the young lady whilst in the presence of his father, whereupon Akbar had the young lady arrested and walled up. In 1615 Jahangir had an octagonal tower erected in a garden. A cenotaph bearing the Ninety-Nine Names of God was placed in the tower, which gave its name to a district of Lahore. Today the building is used as an archive. There is no mention of this story in the official chronicles of Akbar's time, although it appears frequently in folklore as well as modern dramaturgy.

In 1611, when he was already the father of many children by different wives, Jahangir married a Persian woman called Mihr un-nisa. At that time she was known as Nur Mahal, 'Light of the Palace', but she eventually became famous as Nur Jahan, 'Light of the World'.[12] She was born in Kandahar while her family was migrating from Iran. Her father, Ghiyath Beg, would later on, as I'timad ad-daula, play a leading role in the empire. She married the officer Shir Afkan, 'Lion Beater', who was fatally wounded in Bengal in the course of killing one of Jahangir's foster brothers – rumour had it that Jahangir had something to do with this, as he had already seen the lady and fallen in love with her. The widow, who was already nearly 34 years old, lived at first in the house of Akbar's first wife, the childless Ruqaiya Begum, who was Khurram Shah Jahan's foster mother. Nur Jahan was undoubtedly the most dynamic woman in the history of the Mughals. Ineffectual aesthetes were no match for this cunning and energetic woman, who exploited their weakness for drugs and alcohol. Eventually the government was practically in the hands of her father I'timad ad-daula and her brother Asaf Khan. The ruler accepted this state of affairs because Nur Jahan was not only clever, but also a first class rider, polo player and hunter. Her father died in 1622, four months after the death of his wife. Nur Jahan inherited his entire estate, and erected a wonderful *pietra dura* mausoleum at Agra, of white marble inlaid with rare stones, so that the cenotaph it encloses resembles a treasure chest. She also built a number of gardens, such as the Nurafshan Garden on the north bank of the Jumna, and at the castle of Nur Mahal (1618–20).

The princess was a great landowner, who bestowed a number of fiefs and cared for orphaned girls. She was the *de facto* regent, and had coins minted in her own name. She was allowed to beat the ceremonial drum in Jahangir's presence. She also engaged in trade, with her brother Asaf Khan acting as the chief agent in the administration of her ships, which she used to transport indigo and other goods from Bayana to international ports on India's west coast. Nur Jahan was particularly interested in European goods, especially English embroidery. She became an expert in Indian textiles, and also designed jewellery and goldsmiths work. Since she received a vast income from customs duties, it is hardly surprising that during the celebrations for Jahangir's convalescence, the reception she held for his official weighing, and the presents, jewels and robes of honour which she gave, were by far the most impressive.

Nur Jahan's only daughter from her first marriage was married to Jahangir's son Parwez, and so found herself in a difficult situation during the conflicts over the succession: she was seen as 'the leaven of confusion'.[13] She turned Jahangir against his favourite son Khurram Shah Jahan, for which she is harshly criticised by some historians, whilst others blame her brother Asaf Khan for his support of Shah Jahan. Before Nur Jahan died, seventeen years after Jahangir, she had a beautiful mausoleum built for him in his beloved Lahore. Like her father's mausoleum, it was laid out in a garden. Her own simple grave lies on the other side of the Ravi, and is now separated from her brother Asaf Khan's tomb by a railway line. It is a modest plot, of which she herself is supposed to have written the following verse:

On mine, the outsider's grave,
No candle and no light,

48. Jahangir's tomb,
Lahore, 1627.

No burnt moth wings,
Nor nightingale song . . .

In a characteristic trope the soul is likened to a moth which flies too close to the candle and is consumed in God.

In 1614, not long after her marriage to Jahangir, Nur Jahan made sure that her niece Arjumand Banu Begum, Asaf Khan's daughter, married the designated successor to the throne, Khurram Shah Jahan.

Mumtaz Mahal, as Arjumand Banu Begum was by now known, accompanied her husband on his later wanderings through Telangana and Bengal, before he ascended the throne in 1628 after struggles over the succession. Immediately after his enthronement, the imperial seal was entrusted to her, so that she could read and seal all documents. She bore a child almost every year, and two girls and four boys survived out of a total of fourteen. In June 1631 she died whilst giving birth to her fourteenth child and 'responded to the call to "return" (*Sura* 89:27) with the open ears of submission and peace, and was united with the mercy of God'.

When the political situation required the ruler to be in the northern Deccan, Mumtaz Mahal was with him, and the pavilion in Burhanpur in which she lived for so long is still there to this day. There is a small lake on which she was sometimes rowed, and an open pavilion in which she was initially buried, before the plot for the planned mausoleum in Agra had been acquired from its owner, Raja Jai Singh of Amber. The chronogram of her death is 'The Place of Mumtaz Mahal is Paradise' = 1040/1631.

The world is a paradise full of delights,
Yet also a rose bush filled with thorns;
He who picks the rose of happiness
Has his heart pierced by a thorn . . .[14]

These lines were recited at the death of the empress. The loss of his dearly beloved wife was such a shock for the ruler that his beard turned grey. He could not stop weeping for two years, so that his eyes grew weak and he needed to wear glasses for a time. He wore mourning clothes all the time at first, then later on, every Wednesday, the day of her death, and also throughout the month of *Dhu'l Qa'da*, the month of her death.

Her oldest daughter Jahanara, barely eighteen years old at the time, was at her side during her last hours, and fulfilled all her filial duties lovingly. She then became the first lady of the empire, and occupied this important position with grace and dignity. Jahanara shared an interest in mysticism with her brother Dara Shikoh, who was a year younger than her. She was initiated into the Qadiriyya order by Mian Mir's successor, Mulla Shah, with the help of Tawakkul Beg and her brother. She wrote a detailed account of her introduction to the Sufi path:[15]

> Through the intermediary of my brother, Prince Dara Shikoh, I announced my true beliefs [to Mulla Shah] and asked him to be my spiritual leader, and he performed my initiation according to the noble rules of his brotherhood. The first time I set eyes on the venerable figure of the master, from the cabinet in which I was hiding, when he paid a visit to my father the emperor when he was staying in Kashmir, and when I heard the pearls of wisdom falling from his mouth, my belief in him grew a thousand times stronger than before, and heavenly ecstasy seized my very being. The next morning, with the master's permission, my brother initiated me into the mystical exercises, which consisted of reciting the litany of the Qadiri Dervishes and the order of Mulla Shah.
>
> In order to complete this pious endeavour, I went to the prayer room of my palace and remained seated there until midnight, whereupon I said the night prayers then returned to my quarters. I then sat down in a corner facing Mecca, and concentrated my mind on the picture of the master, whilst at the same time keeping a description of our holy Prophet before my eyes. Whilst occupied with this contemplation, I reached a spiritual state in which I was neither asleep nor awake. I saw the holy community of the Prophet and his first disciples with the other holy ones; the Prophet and his four companions [Abu Bakr, 'Umar, 'Uthman and 'Ali] were sitting together, surrounded by a number of important associates. I also noticed Mulla Shah. He was sitting near the Prophet, his head resting on His foot, whilst the Prophet said to him, 'Oh, Mulla Shah, for what reason have you enlightened this Timurid girl?'
>
> When I came to my senses again, my heart opened out like a rose bud under the impact of this sign of God's grace. Full of immense gratitude, I threw myself down before the throne of the Absolute. I was filled with unspeakable happiness, but had no idea how to give expression to all of the joy in my heart. I made a vow of blind obedience to the master, saying to myself: 'Oh what exceptional good fortune, what unheard of happiness he has vouchsafed to me, a weak and unworthy woman! I bring thanks and endless praise to the Almighty, the unfathomable God, who, when my life seemed all set to be wasted, allowed me to devote myself to the quest for Him, who granted me my longed-for goal of unification with Him, and who has immersed me in the ocean of truth and the spring of mystical knowledge!'
>
> I nurtured the hope that God would allow me to tread this path, which is comparable to the *sirat*, with firm steps and invincible courage. God be praised for allowing my soul to experience the greatest pleasure of all, that of being able to think of Him. God be praised for giving me, a poor woman, through the

special attention of the holy master, the gift of full apprehension of the Absolute, as I have always wished with all my heart. For anyone who does not possess knowledge of the Absolute is not a full human being, he is one of those of whom it is said: 'They are as the animals, in fact even more ignorant' (*Sura* 7:178).

Every human being who has achieved this highest form of happiness, will, solely by virtue of this fact, become the highest and noblest of beings. His individual existence will merge into the Absolute, he will become a drop in the ocean, a mote in the sun, a particle of the whole. Achieving this state, he is beyond death, beyond future tribulations, beyond heaven and hell. Whether man or woman, he is always the perfect being. That is the grace of God, 'which He gives, to whom He will' (*Sura* 5:54).

The poet ᶜAttar said of Rabiᶜa:

She was not a woman, far more so a man
From head to toe immersed in sorrow.

The princess certainly received her own share of 'sorrow' on 5 April, when she suffered a terrible accident. She brushed against a burning candle and

as her consecrated clothing had been saturated with perfume and scented oil, the fire engulfed it completely in the winking of an eye; the flames shot up high, and in a flash the source of happiness and purity became like a moth in a flame.[16]

Four servant girls threw themselves on top of her. Two of them did not survive their burns. Shah Jahan was inconsolable, and donated more and more alms so that the recipients would pray for the princess's recovery. Every time she seemed to be recovering, he donated a thousand rupees a day, and set prisoners free. He even assisted in caring for his beloved himself. Jahanara's burns kept her bedridden for four months, until finally an Iranian doctor found a way to heal them, and after eight months and eight days she was able to get up and walk unassisted. The doctor was royally rewarded, and given a *mansab* of 1500/200. At the celebrations for the recovery of 'the angelic one', Shah Jahan gave out 80,000 rupees in charitable donations. He gave his daughter 139 unpierced pearls and a large diamond, as well as the harbour dues at Surat, through which the majority of imports entered the country. Jahanara, who was a follower of the Chishtiyya, the traditional Mughal Sufi order, as well as the Qadiriyya, then went on a pilgrimage to Ajmer to offer up sacrifices in thanks for her recovery, as her ancestors had always done.

Jahanara – who was usually called Begum Sahib or Padshah Begum – had benefited from an excellent education. One of her teachers was Satti Khanum, the former lady-in-waiting of her mother, and the sister of Jahangir's poet laureate Talib-i Amuli, to whom the poet had dedicated a heartfelt poem. She gave the princess instruction in classical Persian and the Qur'an. When the teacher died in 1637, she was buried in an octagonal mausoleum near the Taj Mahal, like other women closely associated with the Mughal household; her adoptive daughter was married to Amanat Khan, the calligrapher, who provided the Taj Mahal with its exquisite inscriptions.

Jahanara shared her father's passion for building. In Shahjahanabad, a part of Delhi founded by Shah Jahan, she arranged for the construction of the Chandni Chowk – which is still an important commercial district today – as well as a palace, a bathhouse and a number of gardens.

Between 1634 and 1640 she was occupied with alterations to a garden in Kashmir, then in 1648 she donated a mosque made of red sandstone with white marble to Agra.

Jahanara was immensely wealthy. She had inherited half of her mother's fortune, but also traded with the Dutch, who had been in competition with the Portuguese and also the British since Jahangir's time. The princess was a good letter writer, and she corresponded with the princes of the Deccan. She also saw to it that the widows of *mansabdars* were well provided for.

Jahanara made a notable contribution to the arts and to learning. Thanks to her, a series of works on Islamic mysticism was compiled, including numerous commentaries on Rumi's *Mathnawi*, the most popular mystical work of Indian Muslims.[17] Having spent eight years of her life with her deposed father in the palace at Agra, Jahanara tried her best to prevent Aurangzeb from fighting against Dara Shikoh. She suggested that the empire be divided between them so that each brother would receive a share. Jahanara remained unmarried, as there was no suitable man who was her equal, which made her the subject of much gossip. Her close relationship with Dara Shikoh was sometimes wrongly interpreted, even though the crown prince loved his wife Nadira Begum, the daughter of his uncle Parwez, above all others. During the years she spent under house arrest with her father in the fort at Agra there were even rumours of incest. Bernier relates that a young man who was visiting Shah Jahan was discovered with her, so he quickly leaped into a large vessel. The emperor had caught sight of him, and so he advised his daughter to take a hot bath. He had a fire lit under the vessel, but Jahanara did not give the game away by so much as a facial expression or gesture. The same story is told by Jahanara's niece Zib un-nisa, and a few years ago it was dramatised in a moving Swedish television film.[18]

For all her piety and erudition, Jahanara was not averse to the lighter side of life. Manucci reports that she drank her own wine mixed with rose water, and she offered her guests alcohol served by Portuguese maids.

When she died in 1681, at her request she was buried in Delhi, where her grave, with its marble tombstone adorned with elegant *nasta<sup>c</sup>liq* script, is set among simple graves in the small courtyard of the mausoleum of the great Chishti holy man Nizamuddin Auliya.

Whereas Jahanara supported her brother Dara Shikoh, her sister Raushanara, who was three and a half years her junior, took the side of their brother Aurangzeb, who was the closest in age to Raushanara. During the crisis sparked by Shah Jahan's illness, Raushanara apparently appropriated Aurangzeb's seal to ensure that his seal was on all decrees, to establish him as his father's legitimate successor. However, the future ruler did not appreciate this meddling in his affairs.

If Manucci's salacious stories about her are to be believed, she used to hide young men in her house, and even disguised them in women's clothing and went riding with them on an elephant with a gilded *howdah*. After Aurangzeb's enthronement, she withdrew from the court until her death in 1671, when she was buried in the garden of the fort at Delhi.

Aurangzeb's daughter Zib un-nisa, who was born in 1639, was particularly close to her aunt Jahanara. She was primarily a spiritual person rather than a practical and assertive one. She devoted herself to poetry and mysticism, and like her aunt remained unmarried.

Although there is some doubt as to whether she was really the author of poems written under the pseudonym *Makhfi* ('Hidden'), these tender, melancholy verses attributed to her do have the ring of authenticity.

Oh waterfall, whom do you lament?
What worries crease your brow?
What pain drives you, like me, the whole
    night long
To cry and beat your head against the stones?

She might well have lamented in this fashion in the Shalimar Gardens in Lahore, which were laid out during her childhood; perhaps even in the Garden of Zib un-nisa, named after her, of which there are only a few sad remains in Lahore.[19] Her loneliness is also expressed in the following lines:

Were an artist to choose me for his model –
How could he draw the form of a sigh? [20]

Like Jahanara, Zib un-nisa was a patron of poets and writers. She gave 1,000 rupees and everything he needed for a pilgrimage to Mecca to Muhammad Safi Qazwini, the author of a commentary on the Qur'an with the title *Zib at-tafasir*. On his return in 1676, he dedicated a book to her, *Anis al-hujjaj*, 'The Pilgrims' Confidant'. Zib un-nisa's teacher, Muhammad Saʿid Ashraf, composed a poetical *diwan* and a *mathnawi*; and other scholars in her service made copies of important works at her request.[21] Zib un-nisa and her sister Zinat un-nisa (both names mean 'Jewel among Women') distinguished themselves as overseers of building projects. Although hardly anything remains of Zib un-nisa's gardens in Lahore, visitors can still admire the Zinat al-masajid, 'Jewel of Mosques', which Princess Zinat had constructed in *c.* 1700 by the riverside wall of the Red Fort in Delhi. In later decades the poets of Delhi would gather there to discuss the nascent Urdu poetry and its rules. Aurangzeb's daughters were benefactors to the devout, and provided dwellings for Sufis, such as Muhammad Nasir ʿAndalib and his son Mir Dard. Zinat un-nisa was also an advocate for incarcerated Maratha noblewomen.

Many other women closely connected to the Mughal household were able to put their position to good use for pious works, such as Shah Jahan's *amah* Dai anaga (died 1671), who had the beautiful tomb of Gulabi Bagh constructed, which can still to this day be admired in Lahore.

Sahibjee, the daughter of ʿAli Mardan Khan, the governor of Kabul, and his wife Amir Khan, was very competent in both political and financial matters. She managed to conceal the death of her husband until Aurangzeb's son Shah ʿAlam had been chosen as his successor, for which she was very highly honoured by Aurangzeb. She had no children of her own, so she took the children of her husband's concubines under her wing. She spent the last years of her life in Mecca. [22]

During the declining years of the Mughals there are numerous stories of dancing girls and other remarkable 'ladies' who captivated the rulers, Jahandar Shah's affairs being a typical example. Koki Jiu, the supposed foster sister of Muhammad Shah, was so influential that for a time she even had the imperial seal at her disposal. Her influence was no doubt also due to her friendship with Muhammad Shah's favourite, Qudsiyya Begum (the former dancer Udham Bai). The astute Qudsiyya Begum managed to ensure that her adoptive son became the ruler, under the name of Ahmad Shah, in 1748. She then enjoyed all the privileges of rank, while the 'genuine' widows of the deceased ruler lived out their lives in poverty.[23] Although she enjoyed the support of the eunuchs in maintaining her position of power, before too long she was put to death by strangulation.

There were also brave and determined women in the provinces, for example Munni Begum, the wife of the *nawab* Mir Jaʿfar in Bengal, who managed her husband's entire household and was the motive force behind the construction of one of the most important mosques in Murshidabad.[24]

In the Punjab at the same time there was the dynamic Mughalani Begum,[25] also the noblewoman Sharaf un-nisa, who became famous in the eighteenth century for her stand against the Sikhs. Her small mausoleum in the form of a tower still stands in Lahore, adorned with cypress motifs. Iqbal praised this brave woman, who relied only on the 'Qur'an and sword', in his *Javidnama*, in which she appears as one of the denizens of paradise.

There were also impressive women among the Hindu princesses, such as Tulsi Bai, a Maratha who led a mighty army into battle, or Rani Durgawati of Gondwana, famous for her courage and cleverness. The widow of the Raja of Srinagar, who ruled with a rod of iron in Shah Jahan's day, was particularly fond of ordering the noses to be cut off men who were judged to be guilty.[26]

What were the lives of women actually like at that time? Mirza ʿAziz Koka, 'who did not control his tongue', is supposed to have maintained that

> Every man should have four wives: a Persian, with whom he can converse; a woman from Khurasan for the housework; a Hindu woman to raise the children, and one from Transoxiana, whom he can beat as a warning to the others.

Although this was never adopted as a principle, the private quarters – *zanana*s – of princes and nobles contained representatives of many tribes and races. There were a vast number of women in the entourage of the Mughal rulers. According to Abu'l Fazl,[27] more than five thousand women lived in the women's quarters in Fatehpur Sikri, each with her own apartment. The concubines each had their own houses, the names of which indicated the days when the ruler could visit them. In addition there were the prostitutes, for whom Akbar constructed an entire city district called Shaytanpura, 'City of Satan', with strict regulations for its enjoyment.

The palaces and private quarters – the *zanana* – of the women were 'gilded cages', which were extremely luxurious, at least for the high-ranking women. Jahanara's rooms, which were close to those of her father, were decorated with murals of flying angels, and the marble or tiled floors were covered with valuable carpets. Many rooms had running water, and fine screens let in fresh air. Illustrations of life at court show that the women's quarters were surrounded by gardens, which were situated beside a watercourse and divided into regular beds planted with fragrant plants, cypresses or small orange trees.[28]

The princesses received a sizable allowance (between 1,028 and 1,610 rupees, according to Abu'l Fazl), which was precisely accounted for. As already mentioned, they could also conduct trade on their own account, and could own land. In addition, they were provided with food and other necessities of life. The cash they received was referred to as *barg baha* – '(betel) leaf money'. In addition, the women possessed vast quantities of jewels. Half of their income was in the form of cash from the treasury, the rest from their landed property.

Babur is supposed to have been the first ruler to provide his women with land. Jahangir raised the allowances of the women considerably as soon as he came to power. The princesses also received gifts from external sources, especially, in the case of those who engaged in trade, from merchants who wished to win their favour. Sir Thomas Roe and other Europeans – traders and diplomats – brought presents for all members of the court, including Nur Jahan and the other ladies.

In later times, as the Mughal household became steadily more impoverished, the women retained a share of the market and conducted trade; however, at times the situation was so bad that the ladies of the harem all threatened to throw themselves into the Jumna if they did not receive their allowances![29]

The leading woman in the harem – the *mahaldar* – enjoyed very high status and influence. Aqa aqayan, who was the same age as Akbar, became the *mahaldar* of the *zanana* after Jahangir's wedding. When she invited Jahangir to her house in Delhi, where she spent her declining years, he issued an order:

the governor should ensure that no dust of any kind be allowed to settle on the hem of her contentment.[30]

Aurangzeb treated his son's *mahaldar*s with great respect. When A°zam Shah did not take his *mahaldar*s with him on a journey to Ahmedabad, he reproached him in a letter and fined him 50,000 rupees for his foolish behaviour, to be paid into the state treasury.[31]

It was not only the most prominent ladies of the *zanana* who had an important role to play – the women were protected by respectable armed female guards, often of Abyssinian or Uzbek extraction. (In fact, the ruler himself also had female bodyguards, with archers in the front line.) There were Georgians and Portuguese among the employees in the women's palace. According to Bernier, the women 'were guarded by innumerable old crones and beardless eunuchs'. In fact miniatures often show fat eunuchs, mostly black, standing or squatting in front of the women's quarters, and at a distance, trustworthy Rajput soldiers, such as the guards of the *ahadi*s, standing at their posts.

At the end of the sixteenth century, there was one *mansabdar* who kept 1,200 women in his harem, and every time he left to go to court, he sealed the fastenings of their trousers. But he seems to have been a unique case, and his women soon sealed his fate with poison.[32]

The female guards had to report to the *nazir*, 'overseer'. When visitors called, they had to obtain a permit. The *mahaldar* held the position of greatest responsibility, and had to report anything at all unusual to the ruler. There were also secretaries working for the ladies, and when the ruler went to the women's quarters at midday, or, more usually, in the evenings, they presented the women's reports and requests to him.

The ladies had the right to approve appointments. Nur Jahan was even permitted to sign the *farman*, the ruler's own decrees. A few decrees issued by other princesses have survived, including one which is not particularly important, but is fairly typical, which grants Hamida Banu Begum's permission for a Brahman to graze his cows in a particular area. What is more significant is the fact that the princesses were able to seal the rulers' *farman*s, for the *uzuk*, the round seal, was kept in the harem.[33]

It seems incredible now that the Mughals took their women with them on to the battlefield, at least in the early days, as we learn from Babur's memoirs; they sat on elephants behind the army and watched the battle, which sometimes resulted in casualties among them. During Humayun's battle against Sher Khan Suri at Chausa, several of the women were killed or 'went missing', possibly having drowned in the Ganges. Gulbadan's descriptions of her half-brother's mediocre career contain a few scenes about the women's participation in his field campaigns.

Even without such adventures, the princesses' lives were far from monotonous. Like women

49. Mir Kalan Khan, 'Queen Udham Bai and her ladies being entertained by actors in Portuguese costumes', album leaf, 1742, gouache and gold on paper.

on the subcontinent today, they loved arranging festivities, especially weddings. Weddings were often celebrated in the palace of the ruler's mother, who would then indulge her grandchildren or nephews. The wedding preparations were very thorough, and were usually carried out either by the mother of the bridegroom, or in Dara Shikoh's case, by his older sister. The birth of a baby, especially a prince, was another occasion for a celebration, and pictures of these events are an excellent source of information about life in the

zanana.[34] In one, the prince's mother can be seen lying in a magnificent bed; a dignified elderly woman is seated next to her, almost certainly the proud grandmother; the baby is wrapped in swaddling bands, as is customary in the East, and the ladies of the family are standing outside the birth chamber. A large number of women are playing music and dancing. The astrologers are sitting in the courtyard, and a woman is telling them the exact time of the birth so that they can prepare the infant's horoscope according to both

Indian and Islamic astrology. Beggars are waiting at the entrance to the castle for their share of the alms to be given out as thanks offerings.

Artists have painted many moving scenes of mothers nursing their infants, and the many Mughal pictures of the Virgin Mary with the infant Jesus appear to have been influenced not only by European examples, but also Hindu pictures of the infant Krishna at his foster-mother's breast.[35]

Women were allowed to have abortions. One mother who had given birth only to daughters, and whose husband was threatening to throw her out, asked Hamida Banu Begum if she could get rid of the child she was carrying. Akbar, who was still a child himself at the time, is said to have talked her out of it, and in fact she brought the longed-for son into the world.[36]

Young boys were circumcised according to the *sunna*. When Akbar was circumcised in 1546 at the age of three and a half, all of the Begums of the Mughal household took part in the festivities, which were described by his aunt Gulbadan. The ritual weighing of the prince began at the end of his second year.

From time to time the ladies would organise a mini-bazaar in the palace grounds, at which they would sell their own handicrafts, luxurious fabrics, jewels and other items, attempting to obtain the highest prices from their customers, who were the ruler and his retinue. This custom appears to have originated in Akbar's time. Women in Indo-Pakistani society still enjoy organizing such bazaars.

During quiet periods, the ladies played games together. Many pictures show women playing board games (chess and *chaupasi*). They also enjoyed listening to music, and some of them went in for weaving, drawing and painting. However, in the entire Mughal history there was only one notable female artist, Sahifa Banu,

50. Sahifa Banu, A portrait of Shah Tahmasp, early 17th century, gouache on paper.

around 1620.[37] There is a fine drawing from the time of Shah Jahan, which depicts a female artist among the other women, capturing her surroundings on a drawing block.[38] However, it was more customary for women to devote themselves to calligraphy. Jahangir was given a copy of the Qur'an that had been written by a great-granddaughter of Timur, Shah Mulk Khanum, in fine *rihani* script.[39]

Miniature painters took great care when depicting women's clothing, which was for the most part much the same as it is today: the popular *shalwar qamis*, consisting of long trousers worn with a blouse-like over-garment, the length of which fluctuated according to changing fashion. Many of the miniatures depict transparent top garments made

51. 'Baz Bahadur and Rupmati on horseback', *c.* 1740, gouache on an album leaf.

of extremely delicate fabric revealing a slim figure beneath. Shah Jahan is said to have criticized his daughter on one occasion for her indecent costume; her response was to show him that she was in fact wearing seven layers of gossamer-fine fabric! Such fabrics, which usually came from Bengal, were aptly described as 'woven air'. Clothing was usually worn just once (which was also until quite recently the custom with noble women on the subcontinent). In the early Mughal period, the noble women almost always wore tall Turkish hats, often with small veils attached to them. Later on, they wore extremely fine veils which permitted a suggestive glimpse of their hair.

It must be borne in mind that artists were never allowed to enter the inner regions of the women's quarters, so that their portrayals of girls and women are based on contemporary ideals –

although it was generally known what the aristocratic Mughals looked like. Some portraits seem true to life. There is one colourful portrayal of a beloved older lady, gazing at a visitor with a maternal, somewhat ironic but warm-hearted expression. Her curved hat feather reveals her to be a high Mughal lady. This and some others are likely to be genuine portrayals of their subjects.[40]

As well as playing games together, the ladies spent time playing with their cats and birds. However, their chief occupation was adorning themselves. The elaborate bath facilities in Agra, Delhi and the fortress at Lahore, with hot and cold running water, demonstrate that their bathing culture was highly advanced. There are a few miniatures which depict women in transparent clothing enjoying themselves splashing about in ponds or bathtubs.[41]

52. Attributed to Govardhan, 'Jahangir with (?)Nur Jahan at a game of *Holi*', *c.* 1615–20, pigment and gold on paper.

After bathing, they were massaged with scented lotions. Particular attention was paid to the feet, which were rubbed with an earthenware foot rasp or a loofah. There is a famous story about an artist being handsomely rewarded by the *khankhanan* ᶜAbduʾr Rahim for his miniature of a beautiful lady, in which he has captured to perfection the delighted facial expression of someone having the soles of their feet rubbed with a foot rasp.[42]

Henna was often applied to the skin, and reddened hands and soles of the feet were common. The 'henna night' before a wedding was a highly enjoyable celebration, then as now. The bride's hands and feet were painted with delicate patterns (books of examples of such patterns can still be bought), giving the appearance of gloves or lace stockings, and the young women also threw the henna at each other, leaving permanent marks on their clothing. Also, when women started to go grey, they would henna their hair along the parting.

Women oiled their hair to make it smooth and shining, and their long plaits were braided with a silk band, gold threads or fresh flowers. Collyrium (*kohl*) was used as eyeliner to emphasize their eyes, and in later times, to elongate them. Many women also used *masy* (dentifrice) to blacken their teeth, something quite incomprehensible today. Heavy perfumes were always applied, especially attar of roses, the invention of which is attributed to Nur Jahan's mother.

Although most women devoted themselves primarily to their appearance and adornment, they did also engage in intellectual pursuits. Akbar took an interest in the education of women and established a school for girls in Fatehpur Sikri, so women did sometimes receive a literary education. Seal imprints in a variety of fine Persian scripts indicate that a few princesses, such as Akbar's wife Salima, had their own libraries. The

53. Gold forehead ornament, set with rubies, diamonds and emeralds, strung with pearls, with pearl and ruby pendants; probably 17th century.

women of the harem received instruction , at least for a time, in reciting the Qurʾan and in religious duties, and, most important of all, Persian, especially classical poetry. Many of the women became active patrons of *literati* who wrote in Persian, and some actually wrote poetry themselves, for example Zib un-nisa. The Royal Asiatic Society has a charming drawing of a group of Mughal women reading and writing under the guidance of a

54. 'A lady holding a bottle and
a cup', *c.* 1630–40, gouache
with gold on paper, from a
Dara Shikoh Album.

bearded, bespectacled *mulla*, and glancing out of the window at the garden from time to time.[43]

The women also took part in sports on occasion. Nur Jahan was an expert polo player, which she played with other women in the garden. Women also sometimes took part in hunting expeditions, and here once again it was Nur Jahan who distinguished herself with her accurate aim.

Sometimes the women went out on excursions. Gulbadan wrote an amusing account of an early trip to Afghanistan by Humayun's women, during which they visited a particularly beautiful waterfall. The women were determined to see the *rawaj* (a kind of rhubarb with long stems of pink flowers) in bloom in the meadows near Kabul. They were so insistent that they even annoyed the easy-going Humayun. The most beautiful miniature of Humayun shows him going on one of these trips into the countryside, with the colourfully dressed women in the background.[44]

Jahangir also describes an enjoyable excursion to Mandu with his women, and also a boat trip to a melon field near Ajmer, where he shared his love of nature with them.

When the women were travelling away from home, they were either carried by eight men in a sedan chair covered by red fabric – red satin in the case of imperial ladies; or in a *chaudoli*, a kind of sedan chair similar to those in use in Europe at the time, which could be carried by two servants, and were painted in bright colours and adorned with all kinds of silk decorations. Sometimes larger sedan chairs were carried between two elephants or two camels, but they were uncomfortable to ride in unless the animals walked exactly in step with one other.

Usually the imperial ladies sat in richly decorated *howdah*s carried by elephants – female ones only! – in full ceremonial regalia. When women

55. Abu'l Hasan, 'Nur Jahan Begum with a gun', from a Jahangir Album.

visited one another, they used a one-person carriage, apparently a sort of rickshaw, which had to be pulled by ladies in waiting, because, as Tavernier pointed out, male sedan chair carriers were not allowed into the harem. Nur Jahan was given an English carriage by Sir Thomas Roe, which she greatly enjoyed using.

There are a number of descriptions of these excursions by Europeans, from which we learn that eunuchs acted as messengers for the ladies, who acknowledged receipt with some betel to be taken back to the sender.

On longer journeys, such as to Kashmir, the women set off last but arrived first, as they travelled by a shorter route so that they could be there to congratulate the ruler on his safe arrival.

Needless to say, not all the women in the palace lived in luxurious conditions. Children from poor families, especially orphans, were often taken in, with the intention of helping them to lead a 'normal' life eventually. The court ladies provided a dowry for the girls, dowries still being customary in traditional families. Jahangir once told Hajji Koki, his father's foster sister, to bring all the women who had no land or money to him, in other words primarily the widows of serving officers or employees. He then established a sort of widows' benevolent fund for them. In times of famine or natural disaster, the ladies would help out with the relief efforts, for example by distributing food.

There was one absolutely inescapable fact of life in the palace, which was the total lack of privacy. When a lady went to bed, several female servants kept watch the whole night while she slept. Even when couples made love, a pair of female servants would be present to keep watch and to look after them.[45]

It is an interesting question whether any lesbian relationships developed. It was extremely rare for any man to enter the sanctity of the women's quarters, so many of the women must have been frustrated. However, historical sources are silent on this subject,[46] although some miniatures do give a hint of it.

The wealth of information about the life of the princesses and aristocratic ladies is matched by the paucity of information about the women of the middle and lower classes. Even so, there is a wealth of documentation about the *madad-i maʿash* sometimes given to women from respectable families, especially from the educated classes. This was a form of stipend, either in cash or else in the form of land, so that they could live off the income from it.

In devout Muslim families, girls received religious instruction. They might be taught how to recite the Qurʾan, as well as domestic science, and they were permitted a certain amount of play as they learned their duties as future housewives and mothers. However, education for girls was rare, and even if schools had existed, attendance would have been impossible for girls due to the very early age of marriage. According to tradition, a girl should be married straight after the menarche. Weddings were celebrated with great festivities, so it can be imagined that they must have plunged as many families into debt as they do today.

When middle-class girls left the house, they had to cover their heads. The *burqa*ᶜ, the tent-like costume covering the entire body with only a small grille for the eyes, was in use at the time of the Mughals. An instructive miniature from the time of Akbar depicts a group of women wrapped in *burqa*ᶜs, queueing in the bazaar to consult an astrologer.[47] When Muslim women had an opportunity to leave the house, they frequently sought solace at the tombs of holy men, just as Hindu women are depicted in miniatures visiting *gurus* or *yogis*.

There is little mention in Mughal sources of Hindu women, with the exception of the wives of the rulers. We know that in the sixteenth and seventeenth centuries there was a series of Hindu women who wrote mystical love poetry in Hindi, Rajasthani, Braj and Gujarati in the *bhakti* tradition. Religious themes especially popular with women were the veneration of Krishna, Krishna's romantic dalliances with the *gopis*, and his love for Radha.

56. 'Ladies visiting
a female ascetic',
*c.* 1760, gouache
with gold on an
album leaf.

Even though Akbar tried to abolish the burning of widows, the custom survived. It is on record that when his chief associate, Man Singh, died in 1614, no few than sixty women committed *sati*. A town or fort that was about to be conquered would be burned to the ground, so that the women inside were all immolated. This custom, which was known as *jauhar*, was practiced in Akbar's time, for instance during the conquest of Chitor.

The lives of poor women in both religious communities hardly differed. When they went out, they carried their smallest child on their left hip as they do today. Some miniatures depict scenes of poor women at work, hauling stones, dressed in long loose trousers topped by an abbreviated blouse, looking much the same as they do on building sites today, carrying mortar, stones and clay while wearing their entire wealth in the form of innumerable bracelets. Some pictures, especially illustrations in the margins of albums, show them carrying pitchers, bowls and flowerpots on their heads, as if the march of time had stood still.

Akbar viewed women carrying water as a symbol for the human heart:

> Hindu women carry water from rivers,
> cisterns or wells; many of them carry several
> pots on their heads, one on top of the other,
> while talking and gossiping with their
> companions, and making their way over
> uneven ground. If the heart could maintain
> the balance of its vessels in the same way,
> it would not be affected by suffering. Why
> should one be more lowly than these women
> in one's relationship to the Almighty?[48]

SIX

# The Imperial Household and Housekeeping

TEXTILES

'All the glory of Hindustan / Arrayed for you in wool and silk' was Goethe's wish for his beloved in the *West–Eastern Divan*. India was an important, if not the most important centre for the art of textiles, and the British coveted the extremely fine woven wool fabrics, feather-light Kashmir shawls, luxurious velvet brocade, and sumptuous knotted carpets. Miniatures give some idea of the magnificence of the country's fabrics and clothing. Abuʾl Fazl relates that Akbar received a thousand suits of clothing each year, of which a great number would certainly have been presented to the nobles at court, to ambassadors and even to artists as robes of honour. A robe of honour had to be worn by the ruler himself, if only for a moment, in order to imbue it with his power before it was given to the recipient. Such transfers of power created a ritual connection between the bestower and the recipient, so that Akbar warned:

Anyone who presents his clothing to ignoble people, such as rope dancers and clowns – it is as if he were to take part in their activities himself![1]

It was also customary for the bestower to place his own turban on the head of the honoured recipient. In times of bereavement, white clothing was worn, and it was customary for the ruler to present great *mansabdars* with a special robe of honour at the end of a period of mourning.

The *Mir Saman* was in charge of the wardrobe, where textiles were organised according to the date when they were received and stored.

The clothing worn in court circles changed very little during the Mughal era. For men, it consisted of the *payjama*, a long garment worn on the legs, reaching down to the feet, and the *jama*, a long tunic, the length of which varied according to fashion. There were various possible permutations of fabric and colour, and the length of the tunic, the cut of the collar and the shape of the sleeves changed with the fashion of the time.

Babur is shown in a few miniatures wearing a *jama* fastened in the middle with buttons and bows. The *jama* could also have a diagonal fastening, being buttoned under the right shoulder for Muslims, and on the left side for Hindus. In Jahangir's time they began adding decorative bands to this diagonal front opening. The bands could be either long or short, according to the taste of the wearer, and were often made of very costly material. The *jama* could be knee-length, or almost down to the ankles. It was usually made of such fine fabric that the colour of the leg garment, which was made of sturdier material, could be seen through it. Sometimes the *payjamas* were narrowed at the calf so that they fell in a row of elegant diagonal folds.

The *jama*s of the nobility were usually made of very fine muslin, with all kinds of woven or embroidered patterns. A prince might wear a *jama* with a motif of butterflies, or of animals in combat. The *jama* might have a pattern of radiant poppies, or golden tulips on a delicate lilac background, or iris-like flowers on a golden background. Shah Jahan appeared once in a *jama* with a woven pattern of countless little blossoms, paired with pale green trousers.[2]

Sometimes the two parts of the costume were of the same colour, but they were usually different. The *payjama* was naturally made of heavy material such as shimmering silk either with delicate stripes or worked with gold threads. Humayun, being a great believer in astrology, used to select the colours he wore according to the colour of the star which ruled that day. On Saturday, the day of Saturn, he wore black, then golden yellow on Sunday, white or green on Monday, red on Tuesday, which was ruled by Mars, pale blue on Wednesday, ochre on Thursday, and white or green again on Friday.

*Jama*s initially had a smooth, round neckline, but in Shah Jahan's time they were more likely to have a rather high, pointed collar.

Sometimes a kind of waistcoat was worn over the *jama*. Shah Jahan is shown wearing a gold brocade waistcoat over a brown *jama* flecked with gold. Another miniature (from the *Baburnama*) shows Babur wearing a waistcoat with pictures of animals on it over a red *jama*.

There was also another kind of long overgarment called a *qaba*. Jahangir once presented his son Khurram Shah Jahan with a *qaba* made of gold brocade with a pattern of blossoms made of jewels, fastened with pearls. Khurram Shah Jahan was particularly fond of the *kimkhwab*, a kind of velvet brocade from Ahmadabad, that only he was allowed to use, and which was otherwise sold only for export.[3]

In cold weather they wore long coats, sometimes gilded or made of brocade, which sometimes had fur collars, or narrow lapels. They were often sleeveless, and buttoned only at the top, so that one could glimpse the different coloured lining. A fashionable effect could be created by hitching up the coat and tucking a corner of it into the belt, revealing the lining. Jahangir refers with pride to an overgarment known as a *nadiri*, which was buttoned from the waist down to the feet. He presented one to his son Khurram, and also wore one himself when he was in Ajmer praying for a victorious conquest of the Deccan. At a later time he mentions a *nadiri* with pearl buttons.[4]

Even these costly garments were usually worn once only, even if the weavers, tailors and needle-workers had laboured for months to produce one.

The *patka* was a rather more durable item of clothing. This was a broad sash which was wrapped twice or three times around the waist. It was sometimes held in place by a narrow, less valuable belt, the ends of which were often richly decorated with gold embroidery or flower patterns, or produced by means of a complicated method of weaving. They could have a white or gold background, or else be made of colourful silk brocade. *Patka*s were signs of distinction, and not everyone was allowed to wear them. Jahangir is even depicted wearing a tie-dyed *patka*. This method of producing complex patterns by tying the fabric in small knots then immersing it in different coloured dyes is still common in Rajasthan today.[5]

57. A Mughal boy's coat, early 18th century.

Sometimes a tassel is seen hanging from the sash, producing the effect of a sort of golden flower at the end, and sometimes the sashes are decorated with pearls.

The ceremonial dagger, which was part of the equipment of every noble officer, could be tucked into the sash and hung from large buttons made of enamel or encrusted with precious stones. If the bearer was carrying a sword on his left side, the strap holding it in place would also be made of some costly material.

Miniatures from the time of Akbar and also the early days of Jahangir's time depict an unusual form of dress: instead of the *jama* being finished with a normal straight hem at the bottom, it ended in a sort of zigzag, with from four to six points, which were often tucked into the shawl or the belt of the wearer to allow freedom of movement when out hunting or during other such activities. These items of clothing are depicted not only in outdoor scenes, but also in palace settings, being worn by both men and women. Many illustrations in literary works from the time of Akbar depict this sort of dress, which appears to have gone out of fashion in the seventeenth century, perhaps because it was an 'absurd style', at least according to Bada'uni in 983/1572. The style was probably derived from the *takauchiah* of the Rajputs, which impressed Akbar as a typical Indian form of clothing, and was evidently then imported from the Deccan.

Clothing became ever more luxurious under Jahangir and Shah Jahan. However, the more ascetic Aurangzeb wore simple clothing, and always observed the religious prohibition on the wearing of gold and silver by men.

In the northern regions of the Mughal empire, warmer clothing was of course a necessity. Jahangir once had some warm clothing delivered to the Kashmiris. However, there are also reports that when he sent winter robes of honour to twenty-one *amir*s in the Deccan, the courier demanded '10,000 rupees from the recipients as tokens of thanks for the clothing'![6]

Sometimes fur or fur-lined coats were presented, and there is a reference to a sheepskin, and also sable pelts, which had been a highly desirable import item from Central Asia and Russia since the Middle Ages.[7]

Akbar took a great interest in the production of shawls, which were usually worn in the winter. Akbar called the finest shawls *parmnarm*, 'very soft'. The finest quality shawls, then as now, were the *shahtus*, made from the soft wool from the underbellies of mountain goats, which was collected from bunches of thorns which the animals had run over. Initially patterns were woven onto the edges, then later they came to be embroidered with the finest thread as well. The *buta* motif, a pattern of buds which is still seen today on shawls and carpets, was also common at the time of the Mughals. The finest wool was dyed white, black, or red. Wool and silk were often woven together.

In Kashmir at the time there were far more shawl weavers than there are today, and more than a thousand in Lahore, which is far from excessive considering it takes eight months to produce one *shahtus* shawl.

Akbar introduced a new way of wearing these wonderful shawls – thrown over the shoulders, either folded double, or loose. There are many references to a *parmnarm* being among the presents given by the Mughal rulers to their loyal servants. Jahangir once gave a high-ranking officer 'a shawl, which I have worn around my waist' as a token of his forgiveness.

There is a picture of a certain Hakim ul-mulk, whose name reveals him to be a doctor, wearing the typical clothing of the nobility at the time of Shah Jahan. He is wearing an almost knee-length golden yellow *jama*, and over it an equally long violet coat with a small gold pattern, with an orange lining. The wearer has draped the coat over himself, with the very long sleeves hanging down, and the red and pale yellow striped *payjama* visible beneath it. His shoes are coloured brick red and green, and he has a gold-embroidered *patka* hanging from a white belt. To complete the ensemble, Hakim has draped a magnificent broad red Kashmir shawl over his shoulders and part of his chest.[8]

Abu'l Fazl describes how these valuable shawls were stored. Upon receipt, they were first sorted according to weight, the finest material being more valuable than the heavier varieties. Then they were sorted according to colour, beginning with the natural hues, off-white, red-gold and so on, to blues and lilacs, and last of all dove grey.

To go with the clothing described above, people wore flat slippers, the backs of which were trodden flat so that the heels were usually open. Only rarely did they come to a high, curved, spur-like point at the heel. They were made either of leather or velvet and were often very colourful – red, yellow, or in contrasting colours. The finest slippers were decorated with gold thread or pearls. On certain occasions, such as hunting expeditions, they wore boots, which were often made of pale leather and sometimes embroidered. There are pictures showing ordinary people wearing a kind of leggings and strap sandals. Ordinary people wore minimal clothing - Hindus are depicted wearing *dhotis*, whilst Muslims usually wore a kind of knee-length baggy breeches (according to *shari'a* law, the body has to be covered up between the navel and the knee).

Whereas the combination of *payjama*s and *jama*s was the typical form of dress for people at court and for *mansabdar*s, learned men and theologians wore their own traditional long costume, which was usually white, often with a long dress or coat on top. One portrait of a *mullah* shows him in a pink coat and a turquoise turban.[9] The clothing of members or leaders of Sufi orders was usually in the colour of their order. The Chishtis wore shades from ochre yellow to cinnamon, the Qadiris wore green, and the Naqshbandis wore mostly white.

The servants at court each had their own livery. The *mahout*s, the elephant handlers, often appear in red jackets. In later periods the ruler's sedan chair carriers appear wearing white clothing with long red jackets.

The usual form of headwear for men was the turban, which was fairly flat, although its exact shape varied over the course of time. The end of the turban cloth was deftly held in place according to the Central Asian tradition. Another method, especially in the time of Shah Jahan, was to hold it in place with a different coloured band of cloth, perhaps with a long feather at the back. The turban ornaments of princes were generally very valuable, the most luxurious being adorned with fringes of pearls. The turbans of princes and courtiers were fairly small and flat, whilst those of learned men were large and round – the expression 'to swell one's turban' means 'to give oneself airs and graces, to brag'.[10]

In the earlier Mughal era, the emperor Humayun sported a strange form of headdress called a *taj-i 'izzati*. This was a high pointed cap with a sort of brim, slashed with V-shaped slits, so that it rather resembled the unfurling petals of a flower. At the same time women wore high Turkish hats, sometimes with a small veil attached. Noblewomen of Turkish extraction sometimes adorned their headdresses with a crest or a feather. Sufis are often depicted wearing hat-like items of headdress, and sometimes in high caps which curved backwards. Ordinary people are usually shown wearing close fitting caps with a small brim, and servants are sometimes seen in pointed caps.

Babies wore the same sort of close-fitting cap that was very common in Europe at the time. European hats were among the curiosities which Jahangir received from England. Muqarrab Khan, the superintendent of Surat, arranged their shipment on behalf of his master.[11]

Surat was the principle port for the loading, unloading and shipment of goods of all kinds, especially for textiles. Although India was the richest source of textiles, there was also great demand in India for the woven wool fabric produced in Turkey, England and Portugal. Iran was a source of sumptuous brocade, those produced by the master weavers of Ghiyath being especially prized at Akbar's court. Nevertheless, the most luxurious silks and woven wool fabrics were produced domestically. Benares was famous for its Banarsi saris made of silk shot with gold, and the Bengal towns of Satgaon and Sonargaon were also centres for the finest weaving. Gujarat was known for its velvet, as was Lahore, whilst Surat was known as the 'source of luxurious and rare items', since all imported goods passed through it.

Muhammad Salih Kanboh's description of the preparations for Dara Shikoh's wedding in 1633 provides a wealth of information on such matters. It appears from his account that the old Turkish custom of dividing gifts up into groups of nine was still practiced at the time of Dara Shikoh, since he mentions *toquz parcha*, 'ninefold' brocades.

Impressive though the mighty Mughal palaces in Agra, Delhi, Lahore and Fatehpur Sikri undoubtedly still are, they seem somewhat lifeless, rather like unfinished stage sets. It is hard to imagine how splendidly they would have been decked out on occasions such as the wedding of Dara Shikoh. In fact, the magnificent effect created by these great buildings was largely due to the carpets and fabrics with which they were everywhere adorned, as is clear from the chronicles, the reports of foreign ambassadors, from poetry and above all from miniature pictures in historical and literary manuscripts. The imperial tents were also full of hangings and cushions, and on special festive occasions even the streets of Fatehpur Sikri were laid with carpets. When Asaf Khan's brother-in-law Jahangir paid him a visit, he had the road from the imperial residence to his tent completely covered with velvet runners. In 1617, the daughter of the *khankhanan* ʿAbduʾr Rahim had the parched lawns in her father's 'Victory Garden', Fathbagh in Ahmedabad, covered over with green velvet, and the bare trees adorned with green silk!

The miniatures reveal that all the ruler's visitors had to walk barefoot on the carpets. Valuable carpets were also hung over the window breast-walls, especially over the *jharoka* window, where the ruler sat whilst permitting his subjects a view of himself.

All carpets, tents and curtains were stored in the *farrashkhana*, where a large number of officials were responsible for organising them. It was a catastrophic loss when the *farrashkhana* in Fatehpur Sikri was destroyed by fire in 1578, not only for the emperor Akbar, but also for the history of art in the Islamic world. All of the woven fabrics and knotted carpets for the interior of the palace were kept there, including curtains of gold brocade and of European velvet, of wool and damask, also many other materials, together with carpets from Iran and Central Asia, and felt coverings.

Whilst the best carpets by far were imported from Iran, during the Mughal era factories were established in Lahore, Agra, and Fatehpur Sikri. Lahore and Ahmedabad were famous for the production of velvet as well as carpets.

Mughal carpets were very popular in Europe. The East India Company began to export large Lahore carpets in 1615. However, these were difficult to come by, because the emperor, understandably, reserved the best examples for his own use. In England, these large carpets were primarily in demand for use as coverings for large tables at official functions. Holbein's paintings show Turkish carpets being used as table coverings elsewhere in Europe too.

The trade in carpets was organised and supported by the government. However because of the enormous demand in England, the private sector developed to have carpets produced to order, and the coat of arms of the customer could be woven into the pattern. As well as carpets, dyed and printed wool fabrics and chintz from Sarkhej and Burhanpur were also exported to Europe.

The few surviving fragments of carpets from Akbar's time reveal that they were extraordinarily imaginatively designed. Apparently many of the original designs which the weavers worked from had been created by artists, so that some of the earlier carpets resembled enlarged album pages. There are occasional examples of medallion carpets such as those found in Iran. In general, elaborate fantasy scenes were favoured, such as an elephant with his *mahout*, crocodiles, dragons, a camel fight and winged four-legged creatures, together with cheetahs, combining to create the effect of a magical forest.[12] Sometimes there are strange animal masks. Some classical Persian carpets display row upon row of arabesques. Animals might be sprouting from the jaws of other creatures, or from buds. Cheetahs are swallowing fish and birds. One particularly grotesque example is the large carpet in the Museum of Fine Arts, Boston, Massachusetts. The eye-catching centrepiece is an animal with the head of a lion and the body of an elephant, surrounded by seven small elephants somehow attached to its body.[13]

The Mughal fascination for depictions of animals or hunting scenes is everywhere apparent, especially on carpets from the latter period of Akbar's time, which sometimes have strange additional features – one such carpet depicts small cheetahs running all around the border.[14]

From time to time the artists also produced carpets with naturalistic landscape scenes, such as those held in Vienna today, with realistic depictions of trees and magnificent birds. In other specimens, such as the long Mughal runners, there are simple or multiple repetitions of the central motif.[15]

The preference in Akbar's time for sometimes quite grotesque carpets did apparently diminish somewhat, as evidenced by surviving fragments and miniature paintings. Patterns gradually became more subdued, and the carpets seen in pictures sometimes have small flowers on a black or dark blue background. Jahangir's painter Mansur was an expert at painting flowers, and his superb flower paintings might have provided the inspiration for a few carpet makers. Also, along with the Jesuits, European botanists began arriving in India at that time. Their drawings had an influence on paintings in the margins of picture albums, and might also have influenced some carpet producers. Nur Jahan's great interest in English needlework might also have inspired the carpet artists to develop new patterns. Floral carpets appear to have been especially popular under Shah Jahan, as well as naturalistic floral decoration of all kinds, for example in crystal vessels, *pietra dura* work, and jewellery.

Carpets from the middle of the seventeenth century often had a pattern of fine trelliswork covered with flowers. Under Aurangzeb, *mille-fleur* patterns, whether indented or not, were very popular.

Sumptuous ornamental carpets were certainly essential items, and Shah Jahan's poet laureate Kalim was quite right in wishing his ruler thus:

May the joys of life never flee from your
threshold,
But resemble a tightly woven pattern in a
carpet![16]

As has already been mentioned, many carpets
were extremely long. Abu'l Fazl mentions one
which was twenty *gaz* (cubits) long and six *gaz*
wide (about 16 m.). The most beautiful Mughal
carpet in the Metropolitan Museum in New York
measures 8.33 by 2.9 metres, and is patterned with
imaginary animals, birds and trees on a dark red
background. Some carpets were round, and they
could also be woven or knotted into any other
shape to fit a particular space exactly. There are
pictures of carpets which were produced specifically to surround the imperial throne, the most
beautiful example being a cherry-red, horseshoe-
shaped carpet, 3.47 metres wide. It is covered with
a floral pattern arranged so that the flowers appear
to be growing outwards from the throne.[17]

The warp of Mughal carpets was cotton, and
the weft was wool. Whereas in Iran, silk was the
material of choice for the knots of luxury carpets,
in Mughal India *pashmina*, the delicate Kashmir
wool, was considered to be the ideal material for
this purpose. The *pashmina* was dyed in the most
exquisite shades. There were a number of court
workshops in Kashmir producing knotted carpets, and as Lahore was the nearest large town to
Kashmir, a significant carpet industry developed
there, especially during its years as the ruler's seat.

Coarser wool blankets, however, came from
Kabul and Iran.

Simple floor coverings were made of cotton,
such as the kelims which are still in use today. Even
chintz was used to make floor coverings – a piece
almost 7 metres long and 4.6 metres wide was
donated to a Sufi centre in the seventeenth century.[18] Chintz was sometimes used for the walls of
tents (*qanat, saraparda*), in which case the dyed and
printed cotton was glazed, reinforced and then
ironed or pressed to give a shiny, waterproof
surface. The most popular chintz in England was
produced in Burhanpur, and coverings of all kinds
were made from this light, colourful material.[19]
Miniatures often show cushion covers with pictures of people, animals and flowers, sometimes
also dancing girls, noblemen, cockatoos, and blossom trees. In fact, more colourful versions of the
sort of illustrations found in books and flowers
were simply transferred onto fabrics. Such motifs
also appear on clothing, particularly for the legs, in
which case heavy silk rather than chintz would
usually be used. However, the artists were clearly
capable of embellishing every kind of material
with woven, painted or gilded scenes of every
description. The great halls and tents, festooned
with colourful, figurative hangings, must certainly
have made a tremendous impression on visitors.

## JEWELLERY

Numerous miniature pictures of Mughal princes
and ladies, and exhibits in the great museums of
the world, give the impression that life in the
Mughal court and for the nobility was one of
unimaginable luxury, and this impression is
confirmed by reports from European ambassadors, merchants, and artists.

Since it was hoped that Babur's son Humayun
would inherit the Indian crown jewels, a masterpiece made of precious stones was created for him
whilst his father was still alive.[1]

The love of precious stones has a long history
in the Islamic world, as can be seen from the
numerous classical Arabic treatises on stones and
also from mediaeval Arabian inventories of royal
gifts.

During the time of Harun ar-Rashid (reigned 786-809), an unusually large and flawless pearl was acquired for not less than 70,000 dinars.[2] Pearls played an especially important role during the time of the Mughals, and double and triple strands of pearls were symbols of nobility by the time of Akbar at the latest. In early portraits, Babur and Humayan are portrayed wearing little or no jewellery;[3] however, an alluring string of pearls round the neck of the current ruler appears with ever greater frequency over the decades, particularly in pictures from the latter part of Akbar's rule and the early Jahangir era. When a visitor or ambassador presented the ruler with an especially beautiful, large or regular pearl, the gift would be accepted with pleasure and, as was the custom, entered into the records by the secretary in charge of gifts.

Pearls were obtained from the Gulf for the most part, however they sometimes also came from the waters around Sri Lanka.

A miniature from about 1619, depicting Shah Jahan, who was the Crown Prince at the time, with one of his young sons, shows the great pleasure the Mughals took in jewellery.[4] The boy must be either Dara Shikoh, who would have been about five years old at the time, or the somewhat younger Shah Shuja, whom his father was particularly attached to. He is shown rummaging in a bowl full of jewels, and wearing such a quantity of jewels himself that it looks as if he might snap one of his pearl necklaces whilst playing. There are two fairly close fitting strands of large pearls around his neck, also a longer pearl necklace with emeralds and rubies, and finally two more long pearl necklaces! A dainty dagger with a gold handle is tucked into his gold-embroidered sash. His turban, like his father's, has strings of pearls wrapped around it, and is adorned with a crest with a long feather curling backwards. Shah Jahan's turban also has a few large rows of pearls. If such pictures are to be believed, even tiny babies wore pearl necklaces – at least to have their portrait painted – as did nursing mothers. Aurangzeb is seen in one picture wearing a few thick ropes of pearls over a green costume, which renders him all but invisible in the wooded landscape. These depictions were probably not exaggerations, nor a case of artistic licence, since Jahangir related that on one occasion queen Nur Jahan lost a ruby worth around ten thousand rupees whilst out hunting (which fortunately was recovered two days later).[5] Noble ladies and gentlemen were never seen without their pearl necklaces, whether flirting on the terrace of the harem, or even asleep in bed. It is therefore hardly surprising that they also used rosaries, *tasbih*, made of pearls and rubies worth tens of thousands of rupees.

Even servants, court ladies and singers were never portrayed without pearl jewellery, however it is doubtful whether this was an accurate reflection of reality, and it may have been an artistic convention to denote the importance of the person depicted.

Pearls and precious stones were used to make earrings, which came in various forms, from large plain pearl studs for the earlobe, to complicated pendants. Women are often depicted with their entire ears covered by flower-shaped earrings. Earrings or studs for men appear to have come into fashion under Jahangir, since in 1615, in token of thanks for his recovery, which he believed he owed to the holy man Muʿinuddin Chishti, he had pearl earrings made for himself, which signified that he was a 'slave' of Muʿinuddin - the Persian expression *halqa be-gush*, 'ring in the ear', means 'slave'. Jahangir's gesture was then imitated, becoming customary among nobles and courtiers.

Large pearls were used as buttons for luxurious *kaftan*s, and not only at court, as the use of such

58. Pair of gold earplugs, set with rubies, diamonds and emeralds, with pearl and ruby pendants; early 17th century.

buttons was also recommended for the true gentleman.[6] Sometimes decorative strands of pearls are seen hanging from the belt of a nobleman, and they were probably a standard accessory to a particular type of robe of honour.

In order to fasten the strands of pearls which were occasionally wrapped around turbans, either the *sarpati* was used, an oval fastening made of a precious stone, or the *sarpech*, which came in many forms. Not everyone at court was permitted to wear precious stones. A picture of Akbar handing his son Jahangir a *sarpech* is intended to signify his acknowledgment of him as the legitimate ruler.[7]

The *sarpech* could also be made of feathers, usually from the Himalayan pheasant, which are shimmering blue-green and very long, curving backwards over the turban. The string of pearls which was wrapped around the turban might also be interspersed with rubies. It was sometimes held in place by an emerald brooch with a large feather hanging from it, with another emerald at the back of the turban, as can be seen in one portrait of Shah Jahan.

The *jigha*, a turban ornament of bejewelled gold made in imitation of the feather decoration, was especially popular in the time of Jahangir and

59. Gold and enamel turban ornament, set with emeralds and diamonds; probably second half of the 17th century.

60. Gold and enamel
necklace, set with rubies,
diamonds and emeralds;
c. 1620–40.

Shah Jahan.[8] They were often made with pearls
and emeralds as well. In the case of less costly
crests, a rock crystal with a green foil underlay was
used as an imitation emerald. The most beautiful
crest known, along with so many other luxury
items, was among the vast booty which Nadir
Shah brought back with him from Delhi to Iran in
1739, from which in 1741 he gave 29 diamonds, 47
rubies, 39 emeralds, a garnet and three rock crystals as a present to the Russian Tsarina Elizabeth.

Miniatures provide an excellent illustration of
the kind of jewellery worn by the ladies: strings of
pearls, rings, upper arm bangles, and frequently
also anklets can be seen, although of course the
artists themselves were not allowed to enter the
women's quarters. Manucci, who, being a doctor,

was allowed direct access to the princesses and their entourage, was able to provide a description of the fabulous jewellery which the women proudly displayed to him. Among the many different kinds of jewellery popular at the time was the *kundan*, still popular to this day, which is a chain of gilded stones, usually crystal, whether rock or glass.[9]

The best description of the Mughal household's jewellery is provided by the diligent Abu'l Fazl in the *A'in-i akbari* (III), where he relates in great detail how jewels were sorted and stored according to their size and value. Pearls were evidently strung according to their worth, the number of fine threads used corresponding to the estimated value of the pearls, which enabled the right size to be found immediately. The most valuable grouping consisted of one thread with twenty large and absolutely flawless pearls, every one of which was worth at least thirty gold pieces. Each string of pearls carried the imperial seal, which guaranteed its origin. When the ruler came into possession of a new costly pearl or a neckband, it was classified according to its worth. Abu'l Fazl gives not only the value of the pearls, but also reports how much it cost to pierce each size category.

Diamonds were found in Golconda in the Deccan, and sometimes also in Bihar. The youthful Amrullah, the son of the *khankhanan* 'Abdu'r Rahim, was richly rewarded for his conquest of an important diamond mine in Golconda. The diamond wealth of the Deccan was the primary motivation for Mughals' desire to conquer the kingdom, as the mines appeared to be inexhaustible, and prospecting for the diamonds was easy. Golconda was not only a source of diamonds as clear as water, but also of delicate green ones (such as the 40.7 carat diamond in the Green Vault in Dresden), delicate pink, sapphire blue, aquamarine, and yellowish hue. Jahangir even mentions a violet diamond, which quite amazed him.

The Kohinoor (*kuh-i nur*, 'Mountain of Light'), which in its natural state weighed 787.5 carats, was given to Shah Jahan in 1656 by Mir Jumla, when this Persian dealer, 'who counted his diamonds by the sackful', was leaving his employer, the Qutbshahi ruler of Golconda. Mir Jumla, formerly a penniless groom in Gilan, then transferred his allegiance to the Mughals and his career advanced under them. The Kohinoor was among the booty which Nadir Shah brought back from Iran; it passed into the hands of his successor Ahmad Shah Abdali, and was then inherited by the Afghan ruler Shah Shuja[c]. He fled to Kashmir before the superior might of the Sikhs, and then had to hand over the Kohinoor to secure his release from them. When the Sikhs were finally defeated by the British in 1849, the stone went to England.[10]

In India diamonds were cut so that as much as possible of their mass remained, which meant that they did not achieve the brilliance which had been the speciality of the European technique since around 1600.

In general, rubies were more highly regarded than diamonds, and they too were cut as cabochon. During Akbar's time, Maulana Ibrahim, a court engraver, engraved the words *la'l-i jalali*, 'Ruby belonging to Jalaladdin[Akbar]' onto every ruby.

There are in fact two distinct stones which tend to be translated without differentiation as 'ruby'. *La'l* is a transparent red spinel, whereas the genuine ruby is *yaqut*, a corundum, a member of the same family as sapphire and topaz. The *la'l* was a stone from Badakhshan, the most highly prized being the colour of pigeon's blood. It was widely known in Europe, being referred to by Dante as Balascio. This stone was highly valued in the

61. Inscribed royal spinel ('balas ruby'), with inscriptions of the Timurid, Safawid, Mughal and Durrani periods, including those for Jahangir, Shah Jahan and Aurangzeb.

Orient, as it had a stronger lustre than the ruby; also, with a density of 7, it was softer than the *yaqut* (density of 9) and was therefore easier to engrave. Many rubies were passed down the Mughal family line by inheritance. There was one such stone, shown above, a *laʿl* of 249.3 carats, which originally belonged to Timur, and had the name of the Timurid Ulugh Beg engraved on it. This passed by a convoluted route to the Iranian ruler Shah ʿAbbas, and finally to Jahangir, who had his own name engraved on it.[11] Another Mughal *laʿl*, similar to the Kohinoor diamond, was transferred from the Sikhs into British hands. The 123-carat stone has the names of Jahangir, Shah Jahan and Aurangzeb engraved on it. Rubies, or rather spinels, appear very often in pieces of jewellery. Jahangir mentions one particular ring made from a single ruby with particular enthusiasm. He was also delighted by a dagger with a 'yellow ruby' (i.e. topaz) half the size of a hen's egg on the pommel.

Emeralds, which were exported from Colombia from 1519, were highly valued and popular. The Mughal treasury contained one of the best known emeralds, which was prized not only on account of its lustrous colour and purity, but also because of the exquisite design engraved on it.[12] Since emeralds are hexagonal crystals, if they are cut diagonally, it is relatively easy to produce hexagonal sections which can then be engraved with diamond splinters. One such emerald of 233.45 carats, 5.7 cm wide, was decorated with a pattern of grasses and flowers during Akbar's time. There are many fine examples of this type of stone. Possibly the most beautiful example of stone engraving from the time of Shah Jahan is a hexagonal 73.2-carat emerald engraved in the finest script with the throne verse from the Qur'an (*Sura* 2:255), which served for a long time as a protective amulet. The script is flawless, even though the longest letter, the *alif*, is barely 1.75 mm in height. The reverse side is decorated with engravings of foliage. It was worn in an upper armband as an amulet. However, in our age, the throne verse failed to protect the priceless piece – it vanished from the Kuwait National Museum during the invasion of that country in 1990.

Not only purely decorative pieces were so richly decorated, but also objects for practical use, for example the thumb rings which were worn on the right thumb to assist with drawing the string of a bow. They were sometimes worn as belt ornaments, and often regarded as purely ornamental, since the rings were inlaid with so many different precious stones that they could hardly withstand the strain of pulling on the bowstring. In any case, the Mughals increasingly used guns rather than bows and arrows. Such thumb rings were often made of nephrite, and also agate, carnelian, rock crystal, even emerald.

62. Gold pendant, set with rubies, diamonds and emeralds, with emerald pendant; probably first half of the 17th century.

Jahangir took particular pleasure in a thumb ring made from walrus tusk, as the grained walrus horn was unusual and extremely difficult to come by, also because it was regarded as an antidote to poison, and was supposed to have healing properties.[13] Shah Jahan possessed a few particularly valuable thumb rings, which were enamelled on the inside, and in some cases had his title *sahib qiran-i thani* inlaid on the inner surface of the ring in flawless calligraphy with minute rubies

63. Inscribed emerald, with inscription of the 'Throne Verse' from the Qurʾan (*Sura* 2:225); 17th century.

throne verse, as well as Shiʿite texts: invocations to the twelve Imams, or the Shiʿi prayer *nadi* ʿ*Aliyyan*, 'Call on ʿAli, who shows wondrous . . . ', which was frequently used, especially on weapons. The magic square *buduh*, believed to offer protection, is also found on nephrite tablets. The numerical value of *buduh* is 2-4-6-8, a square which is found in India on the entrance gates of forts and other buildings in need of heavenly protection. Every style of Arabian script was used for such inscriptions.

It is often difficult to distinguish between decorative objects and those put to practical use. Just

which had been ground flat.[14] No wonder the superintendent of goldsmiths bore the title *Bebadal Khan*, 'Sir Incomparable'.

Semi-precious stones also played in important role during the time of the Mughals. Jahangir particularly liked a rosary made of Yemeni carnelian, which was considered to be an especially lucky stone. He asked Shah ʿAbbas for some turquoise, which however failed to live up to his expectations. Turquoise is still today considered to offer protection against the evil eye.

The jade, or rather nephrite, which was most often used usually came from Khotan and the southern border of Xinjiang, and was sometimes also sent by the ruler of Kashgar. White or greenish coloured nephrite jewellery was often worked in slices which could be handled easily, and were then sometimes adorned with rubies, or more often decorated with religious inscriptions. Such tablets often bear Qurʾanic inscriptions, such as the already mentioned

64. Gold finger-ring, set with rubies, emeralds and turquoises; probably first quarter of the 17th century.

65. Miniature illuminated manuscript of the Qur'an, bound in nephrite jade, inlaid with gold, set with rubies and emeralds, dated AH 1085 (1674–5), with gold and enamel pendant case set with diamonds, rubies and emeralds (case probably late 17th century).

as thumb rings were often regarded as ornaments and status symbols, this was even more the case with daggers. Daggers were often among the imperial gifts given to persons of high rank, for weapons were symbols of honour, comparable to our Orders of Chivalry, so pictures from the Mughal era display a vast array of different types of daggers. When which dagger was to be lent or carried was determined by protocol.

Daggers were subdivided into three different categories: the *katar* was a thrusting dagger with a long triangular blade with a dual cutting edge; it was held by two longish metal bands with two diagonal clasps, and tucked into the belt. The metal bands and diagonal clasps could be adorned with precious stones or gilded. The *kard* was a straight knife with a single cutting edge; it had a triangular profile, and a length of 35 to 40 cm. The most important – and effective – weapon was the *khanjar*, a flexible curved dagger. In addition to the dagger of honour, a scimitar often appears hanging by a valuable cord on the

66. Engraved gold box, set with rubies, diamonds and emeralds; 18th/19th century.

left side of the wearer. Sometimes a ruler or prince is portrayed leaning on a long straight sword.

The blades of these weapons were made from carbon steel. It took about a month to forge a blade with the characteristic watered pattern. Sometimes the steel of the blade was gold damascened, often with religious inscriptions, prayers for victory and blessings.

The sheaths of the weapons were made of leather or coloured velvet, or even wood padded with fabric. However, the most magnificent sheaths, especially for daggers, were sometimes set with hundreds of precious stones.

A dagger sheath which was finished in 1619 may well be the most extravagantly luxurious ever produced. It is plated with gold, and set with no fewer than 2,400 worked precious stones and numerous rubies, these being cabochons held in place by tiny emerald fragments and adorned with barely visible diamond splinters.[15]

The hilt of a dagger was even more important than the sheath. The imaginations of the craftsmen were clearly given free rein during their production. There are hilts made of white jade set with spinels, emeralds and diamonds, which open out downwards rather like the calyx of a flower. There are others with hilts of rock crystal and silver in the shape of flowers and leaves, all richly encrusted with precious stones. The hilts could also take the form of living creatures – there are examples of handles shaped like the head of a nilgay or a sheep with dainty little locks of wool. There are even human figures or heads. There are horse heads made of nephrite with the eyes and bridle made of rubies, also hybrids with a long necked horse head on one side, and a compact *makara*, a kind of crocodile's head, on the reverse side.[16] Shah Jahan's poet laureate composed the following verse:

The handle of his dagger is in the form of
  a horse,
For victory to ride on the day of battle.[17]

Jahangir describes with great enthusiasm a handmade grained walrus tusk dagger, decorated with a floral and leaf motif in seven lustrous colours.[18] No wonder he rewarded the engraver and cutter who had produced this fabulous masterpiece – one of the master craftsmen received the honorary title ʿajaʾib-dast, 'Wonder Hand', the other received an elephant, a robe of honour, and a gold armband.

Even objects for practical purposes, such as powder horns or small powder bottles, could become works of art in the hands of the court craftsmen. There are examples of powder horns of ivory in the form of a frog or a gazelle, and oth-ers made of carved nautilus shell. Many were luxuriously set, or gilded. An elegant surviving powder horn is in the form of a toad made of grey-green jade, 11 cm. long. The stone has been carved into a superfine shell, and has been decorated with a delicate floral pattern on the back. The animal itself appears completely lifelike.[19]

To protect the head and ears on the battlefield, there were domed turban-helmets, which were often gilded and engraved. The arm plates were even more magnificent – one particularly splendid example is made of gilded silver with gold inlay, with no fewer than 550 emeralds and rubies in cabochon form, with tiny diamonds glittering in between them. The plates are padded with velvet.[20]

Such weapons were far too fine for the rigours of battle, and other objects were likewise too luxurious to be put to use – in fact all Mughal household objects were exquisitely beautiful, being made of nephrite, jade, crystal, precious metal and enamel. Who could bring himself to use a jade inkwell inlaid with rubies for its ostensible purpose? Among the masterpieces in Jahangir's possession were a dark green, round jade inkwell with an inscription in Persian,[21] as well as a white jade pen-box inlaid with ruby flowers and emerald petals with strands of gold, which also contained an inkwell and a penknife. A pen-box made of gold or precious stones was a highly prized gift.

Another one of Jahangir's treasures is a small jade cup in the form of a poppy flower, from which he took his opium mixture.[22] Wine bowls and cups were often made of pale jade in the form of leaves or flowers, with the curved stalk serving as the handle. Sometimes Persian verses extolling the virtues of wine were engraved on the stone, or inlaid in gold. One of the most beautiful objects of this kind is a wine cup made of translucent nephrite, which appears to be almost organic. The body is in the form of a fruit resembling a half gourd, 14 cm. wide, from which a goat's head is growing like a tendril. The animal has the most doleful facial expression, as if it were giving vent to all the suffering of the world with an inaudible cry of pain. One year after this bowl was made, Shah Jahan was deposed and incarcerated.²³

Jahangir sent a wine flask in the form of a cockerel as a gift to Shah ᶜAbbas. He also loved vessels set with precious stones in the form of fish. There are examples of mirrors made of rock crystal backed with silver, and others backed with jade engraved with flowers and tendrils, or inlaid with rubies. An especially beautiful mirror from the end of Akbar's reign is backed with delicate green jade with a gold trellis pattern.²⁴

Rock crystal vessels were quite common, such as cups deeply engraved with floral patterns of Turk's-cap or lilies. Such floral decorations were especially popular under Shah Jahan, during whose reign naturalistic flowers were ubiquitous in all art forms.

There must have been an inordinate number of bottles and jugs at court. Jahangir was delighted at receiving a jug of white jade with the name of the Timurid Ulugh Beg and the date of its manufacture engraved in large *riqa*ᶜ script; he then added his own and his father's name in a contrasting style of script. Almost every miniature depicts a few narrow, or, more rarely, rotund bottles made of all kinds of precious materials. They are often seen in alcoves in the walls, where they were usually kept. Many were set all over with precious stones. Qatiᶜi, the poet from Herat who lived at the courts of both Akbar and then Jahangir, wrote:

> Shah Jahangir commanded a bottle to be
>   made,
> Set all over with *balas* rubies.
> Its every pearl is absolutely pure,
>   incomparable,
> One precious pearl is worth the entire tax
>   revenue of Oman!

67. Carved rock crystal cup, inlaid with gold and set with rubies and emeralds; late 16th/early 17th century.

Its turquoises are more colourful than
   emeralds,
And every corundum on it shines like the
   stars . . .[25]

Although the use of gold vessels was prohibited by religious law (which led in the earlier
centuries of Islamic history to the development of
lustre-decorated ceramics with a beautiful golden
sheen), in the Mughal era there were golden flasks,
as seen in miniatures, which were used with small
matching cups for wine or anack – which were of
course forbidden. Whenever the ruler was over-
come with feelings of penitence, he would have
these beautiful vessels smashed.

There are examples of richly decorated, long-
necked silver bottles, and the *gulpash*, a long-
necked flask from which rose water was sprinkled,
which is still in use to this day. Such vessels, usually
from 26 to 30 cm. in height, might be set with
cabochon emeralds and spinels, or decorated with
golden flowers. All vessels, of whatever kind and
of whatever material, were often set with rubies in
floral patterns. This was also the case with the
small silver flasks, around 9 cm. in height, sometimes in the form of sprigs of blossoms, made to
contain antimony, which the ladies used to blacken
their eyes.

In Jahangir's time, gold and silver vessels were
also occasionally imported from Europe, and the
Chief Superintendent of the harbour at Surat
proved himself to be very adept at acquiring valuable objects for his ruler.[26]

Enamel work became highly prized in the
Mughal period.[27] The combination of gold and
precious metal with enamel was the height of
fashion under Jahangir, and Shah Jahan also loved
this work. All kinds of vessels could be decorated
in this way, including bottles and dishes of all
sizes, of which there is an especially good selection in the Hermitage in St Petersburg. Whether
round or square, large or small, many trays are
radiant examples of white, green and red enamel-
work. Transparent green enamel, with its silken
sheen and contrasting red floral patterns, often on
a white or gold-coloured enamel background, was
very popular. Spherical censers for incense, small
boxes or *pandans* for the betel ceremony, the
highly elegant enamelled spittoons – everything
shimmered and shone. Even buttons on ceremonial garments were works of art: a button scarcely
4 cm in diameter was inlaid with rubies and flat
emeralds, with a poppy of red and green enamel
on the reverse side. Such buttons were worn on
the belt sash to hold the dagger in place.
Enamelled jewellery came into fashion at a later
date. In about 1740 Jaipur became a centre for this
art, which is still popular in India to this day.

From the time of Jahangir, the technique of
*cloisonné* was incorporated into enamel work,
most notably *bidri*ware, which was produced in
the Deccan, in Bidar. An alloy of zinc, copper, lead
and tin was blackened with sal ammoniac then
chloride, followed by silver, and sometimes brass
too was hammered into shallow depressions. The
radiant pattern on the silver, whether of flowers,
or, less commonly, geometrical design, covered
most of the surface of the vessel. From the seventeenth century onwards, silver vases, bowls, and
bottles were often produced using the incompara-
bly beautiful *bidri* technique.

Water-pipes, *huqqa*, became increasingly popular from the early Jahangir period onwards. The
vessels containing the water for these pipes were
often of *bidri*ware, but were sometimes made of
glass. Long necked glass decanters had long been
produced in India. Glass vessels were often decorated with delicate colours. The colourful glass
bracelets which are still popular with women
today were found during the time of the Mughals.

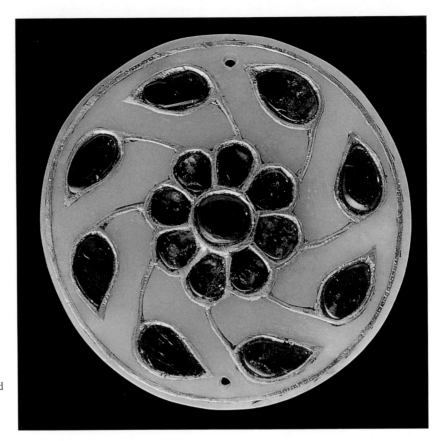

68. Nephrite jade dagger sash-cord ornament, inlaid with gold and set with rubies and emeralds; 17th century.

Especially valuable small objects were often kept in wooden cabinets with drawers inside, which were decorated with ivory or inlaid with delicate arabesques of mother of pearl. Such cabinets were sometimes inlaid with inscriptions in differing styles of script and subject matter, whether Qurʾanic verses, or Arabic or Persian poetry. Such small cupboards or chests were primarily produced in Gujarat. Akbar had experts in the art of inlay brought to Fatehpur Sikri, and the wooden cenotaph for his Sufi master Salim Chishti was carved by such artists.

A chapter on the luxury of the Mughal rulers would not be complete without a description of the object which came to symbolise the splendour of court life: the Peacock Throne, which was inaugurated by Shah Jahan in 1636, after his artists had worked on it for seven years. Tavernier, who was himself a jeweller, describes 'Aurangzeb's throne',[28] i.e. the Peacock Throne, which he inherited from his father. It was from four to six feet large (around 1.20 to 1.80 m), and was adorned with 108 large *balas* spinels, the smallest of which weighed 100 carats. It was also decorated with 116 emeralds, from 30 to 60 carats in weight. It was surrounded by twelve golden columns wrapped round with strings of pearls, each single one weighing from six to ten carats. Most important of all, however, is the golden peacock, its raised tail made of blue sapphires and other colourful

69. *Akbar II with his servant Nazir, c.* 1830, gouache with gold on paper; from an album of miniature portraits.

stones, with a large ruby in the middle of its breast, from which hung a pear-shaped ruby of around 50 carats . . .

Pictures of Shah Jahan sitting on the Peacock Throne do not correspond exactly to Tavernier's description; however, they give an idea of the most magnificent throne of all time, which would later on be dismantled in Iran.

## KITCHENS AND CELLARS

Anyone with some familiarity of contemporary oriental hospitality will not be too surprised by descriptions of Mughal feasts, nor by the realistic portrayals of picnics by Mughal artists, in which firewood carriers can be seen scurrying about their business, huge pots on top of the fire being fanned by a wicker fan, and a man kneading dough for bread or something similar. Two cooks are seen turning an enormous *shish kebab* spit over the fire and wearing white masks – both texts and pictures verify that they had to cover their mouths and chins so that their breath would not come into contact with the food.[1]

According to pictures, servants wore knee length breeches and a small turban or cap on such occasions.

An embroidered white tablecloth was spread out on the carpet on which the guests were to sit crosslegged, as often happens today. The pots, filled with duck, lamb, rice, and whatever else was being provided, were placed upon the tablecloth, covered up at first. Then they were uncovered. The huge pot filled with rice was carried in on a pole by two strong men. Often a number of small bowls were placed in front of each guest so that they could easily serve themselves.[2]

Feasts were usually arranged more or less in this way. People ate with the first three fingers of their right hands, and only drank at the end of the meal, according to the tradition handed down by the Prophet. This ritual is sometimes still followed to this day, for example in gatherings of dervishes.

Abu'l Fazl, who was famous for his huge appetite, has provided particularly detailed information about Akbar's kitchen,[3] and much of what he wrote about the customs at court in his time would also apply to some extent to those of his followers, as evidenced by Jahangir's *Tuzuk*.

There were extremely complicated ritualistic kitchen procedures that had to be followed, and it is important to bear in mind that the office of Superintendent of the Imperial Kitchen was one of the highest ranks to which a *mansabdar* could aspire. The position was held for many years by the famous doctor Wazir Khan (died 1641), who later became the governor of the Punjab. The positions of kitchen overseer and head cook, *Mir bakawal* and *bakawalbegi* respectively, were also held by high ranking, trustworthy men, and in fact only men with impeccable reputations were employed in any capacity in the kitchens. The emperor's food was always tasted first, for the possibility that someone might attempt to poison him was a constant fear. Babur almost fell victim to an attempted poisoning when a kitchen servant, acting on the orders of a Lodi prince who had been captured by Babur, sprinkled poison on the meat. Fortunately Babur vomited immediately, before the poison could take effect. However, the food taster, as Babur recorded with some satisfaction, was hacked to pieces, the cook was flayed, and two women who were also under suspicion were thrown in front of the elephants. It is quite likely that Babur's final illness was also caused by poisoning.

The bowls for the imperial table, or rather for the tablecloth spread out on the ground, were made of gold and silver in Akbar's time, and also for some time afterwards. The use of golden vessels was actually prohibited by religious law, so whenever the rulers were assailed by feelings of repentance, they used to hurl these vessels violently or break them, as proof of their vow to live righteously for a time. Everyday crockery in the imperial kitchen was made of copper and was 'tinned' twice a month, according to Abu'l Fazl. If one of these pots was damaged it would be melted down and refashioned. In Akbar's time this kind of metalwork was also produced in Lahore.

The large, beautifully made basins of copper or bronze, such as the tall pots used as hand basins, were often decorated with the finest arabesque work or inlaid decorations. Many of these vessels bore inscriptions, and the best examples of this form of art are from Golconda. There are also examples of bowls in the form of boats, *kashkul*, which were used to hold snacks for nibbling.

Also in daily use was Chinese porcelain, as recorded as early as Babur's time. Miniatures show porcelain vessels with blue and white decoration, which as a rule were displayed in wall alcoves, as was other porcelain or glassware. Everyday utensils made of Chinese porcelain had long been in use, and the Chinese even produced porcelain with pseudo-Arabic inscriptions for export to the Islamic world.

Akbar used to eat alone, at whatever time suited him, so the kitchen had to be able to place any dish he desired in front of him within an hour. Metal bowls were kept wrapped in red cloth – the colour red was in fact reserved for the emperor's exclusive use – and porcelain vessels were wrapped in white cloth, which was sealed by the Head Chef. A scribe recorded everything that was brought into the dining room. Whilst the sealed bowls were being taken to the ruler, men wielding clubs walked in front of and behind the carriers, and no unauthorised persons were allowed to watch. Waiters remained standing in front of Akbar throughout the meal. After a portion of the food had been set aside for the dervishes, the monarch began to eat. In later times, food for banquets was placed in covered bowls, which the servants carried on trays resting on their lower left arms. A little way off, servants stood with ewers and basins, ready to rinse the guests' hands. On special occasions, such as when Mirza Sulayman came to Fatehpur Sikri from Badakhshan, a magnificent feast was served in the *diwan-i ʿamm*.

The kitchen budget was prepared annually. At every single meal, care was taken to ensure that only the freshest and best produce was brought from the garden and the field to the table. Before poultry could be prepared for the table, the bird would have to be fed a special diet for at least a month. The ever curious Jahangir once commanded servants to cut open the crop of a bird which had been served to him, and he was so disgusted with its contents that, quite understandably, he would never again eat such a bird.[4]

Akbar often fasted, which only means that he refrained from eating meat, a practice known as *sufiyana*, living 'the Sufi way'. He did this on particular days, and sometimes for an entire month, as he considered it to be improper for humans to use their stomachs as a grave for animals. From his childhood, Akbar felt little inclination to eat meat, and according to Abu'l Fazl, he once remarked that butchers, fishermen and the like, who had no other occupation than taking the lives of other beings, should live in a particular area of the city, and it should be a punishable offence to associate with them. His decree of abstinence did not apply to all of his subjects (although vegetarianism has always played an important role in India); how-ever, it was his wish that people should refrain from eating meat during the month in which he came to the throne as a gesture of thanks to the Almighty, so that the year would be an auspicious one.

When Akbar reached the end of a period of *sufiyana*-life, the first meat he ate would be brought to him from his mother's house, then other dishes were brought from the residences of the other court ladies and the nobility.

Aurangzeb was likewise very puritanical and often fasted, as Tavernier reported. However, if portraits of his plump successors are anything to go by, they did not accord all that much importance to dietary asceticism.

The *abdar khanah* was a very important part of the palace. This was where drinks such as delicious fruit juices were stored under the supervision of a *sharbatji*. Akbar used to drink water from the Ganges, which was brought to the court after it had been filtered in sealed jars. To keep drinks cool, initially they used saltpetre, which had to be handled in a particular way. However, after 1587 they used snow or ice for cooling purposes, as had long been the custom in the Near East. In Akbar's time, a four-man boat delivered snow and ice from the mountains every day, and there were ten such boats. Ice was also brought to the court by fast runners.[5]

Although Akbar attached little importance to food, Abu'l Fazl provides the reader with a comprehensive list of dishes which were prepared at court, many of which are still popular today in the subcontinent. There were *sanbusa (samosa)*, pastries filled with meat or vegetables; and *sag*, a tasty spinach dish, prepared with 10 *ser* of spinach and fenugreek, 1.5 *ser* of *ghee* (clarified butter), an onion, some fresh ginger and a hint of cardamom and clove. There were all kinds of meat dishes, such as *harisa*, made from meat, cracked wheat, *ghee* and cinnamon, and *halim*, the same dish with vegetables and pulses added. The recipe for *bughra*, a dish that Humayun mentions being served at an enjoyable party in Kabul, sounds especially interesting: ten *ser* of meat and 3 *ser* of flour were mixed together with 1.5 *ser* of ghee and chickpeas, some sugar, onion, root vegetables, spinach, fenugreek and ginger, then spiced with saffron, cloves, cardamoms, caraway and peppercorns. *Yakhni*, a still-popular meat stew, is recorded, as well as many different types of kebab. Whole lambs were often roasted – the Mughals loved a fat lamb! Beef eating was apparently scorned – Humayan once reproached his half-brother Kamran in Kabul for offering his half-sister Ruqaiya nothing better than beef to eat.[6]

After a hunting expedition, game such as partridges and quail, as well as hares, deer and gazelles, was prepared in the kitchen, as mentioned by both Babur and Jahangir. The nilgay was also apparently a very popular dish. Once, when Jahangir caught sight of one of these animals when out hunting near Ajmer, he vowed to donate it to the Dervishes at the mausoleum of Muᶜinuddin Chishti, if he succeeded in bringing it down – and sure enough, his bullet hit its mark.[7] He had his cooks prepare a *dupiyaza* of nilgay calf, a rich *ragoût* with onions, garlic and other spices, which he especially enjoyed.

In addition to the imperial recipes, there are also Persian manuals containing regulations for Mughal noblemen, whose diet was supposed to consist primarily of pilau dishes. *Kabuli* with chickpeas was recommended for them, this being a pilaf dish with rice, meat, *ghee*, onions, ginger and caraway, which, according to the manual, made the fingers very greasy. Rice and split pulses also played a very important role in the diet. Jahangir considered *khichri* – a mixture of lentils and rice – prepared in Ahmedabad to be especially delicious, because it was made with millet and peas. However, he did not like thick stews, even if prepared from these ingredients. For gentlemen of the seventeenth century, a barley soup prepared with lemon juice, rose water, sugar and herbs was recommended, and also *sarpacha*, 'head and feet' of a sheep, which was prepared with vinegar, mint and lemon juice. The importance of *dal*, made with split lentils, can be appreciated from the following anecdote: when Aurangzeb had imprisoned his father Shah Jahan, he made him the generous offer of allowing him to eat his favourite dish every day for the rest of his life; the canny prison cook advised him not to choose a complicated, costly dish, but to ask for *dal*, for, he assured him, he could make a different dish out of that every day of the year.

Jahangir considered the best fish of all to be the *rohu*, a large river fish which is still popular in India and Pakistan. Otherwise, there is little mention of fish. Only Abu'l Fazl mentions it as one of the main dishes in Sind, praising the *palla* fish in particular (despite its many bones).

Lettuce, green coriander and mint made up the favourite salad, and *achar*, a sharp-tasting pickle, was as popular then as it is today. Very little radish was eaten – 'radish eater' was an insult, meaning idiot. The true gentleman should 'regard leeks and radishes as enemies of God because of the flatulence resulting from eating radishes, which was worse and more uncomfortable for the spirit than the sound of gunfire or the smell of gunpowder'.[8]

There were many different types of bread, including *chapatis*, still eaten today. Jahangir was amazed to find out that the Kashmiris ate no bread.

Sweets were as highly popular then as they are today, especially *faluda*, a delicious pudding which was very sweet and also very soft, hence the following verses:

When luck is on your side,
Your teeth can crack an anvil;
When the stars are inauspicious,
A pudding can crack your teeth![9]

*Firni* was a milk-based rice pudding served in small clay bowls. According to the *Mirzanama*, this tended to make people lazy. However, following is the imperial recipe for *zarda*, 'golden rice': 10 *ser* of rice, 5 *ser* of sugar, 3.5 *ser* of ghee, together with 1.5 *ser* of almonds, raisins and pistachios, a pinch of salt, a little fresh ginger, a very little saffron and a hint of cinnamon. These quantities are enough for four people. There were various other kinds of sweets as well as these. The Central Asian author Mutribi, who spent some time at court during the last year of Jahangir's life, mentions an enormous block of sugar being carried on to the table.

There was a fruit store at the court where a great variety of different domestic and imported fruits were stored. Melons, which came from the northwest of the empire, were especially popular. According to the *Mirzanama*, it would be blasphemous to consider the mango superior to the melon. However, the mango was considered important by writers in later generations, starting with Abu'l Fazl. Aurangzeb was especially fond of them. Grapes and other kinds of fruit were carried from Kabul and the surrounding area by runners in baskets carried on their backs. They were taken to Agra or Lahore, and thence to the emperor, wherever he happened to be. Whilst Jahangir was staying in Ahmedabad, he received oranges from Bengal, which had not spoiled. There the emperor had his first taste of freshly-picked figs. He was especially taken with a particular kind of cherry whilst he was in Kabul, and could eat as many as 150 in a day![10]

Pomegranates were very popular, especially the juice. There are references to the aromatic guava, as well as quinces, also custard apples, which are full of pips but have a very juicy flesh.

The margins of early seventeenth-century Mughal albums are often illustrated with very realistic depictions of fruitsellers.

Jahangir shook his head in dismay at the generally very poor diet of the Kashmiris, who, he discovered, nourished themselves with cold cooked rice, and dressed their vegetables with walnut oil. One European, Tavernier, who was filled with admiration for the patience and accomplishments of the ordinary soldiers in the Mughal army in the second half of the seventeenth century, was very concerned to discover that their daily rations consisted merely of flour, which they mixed with water and molasses into

70. 'A Fruitseller', *c.* 1605–28, gouache on paper.

a ball, and also *khichri*, a dish of split lentils and boiled rice. Before eating they dipped their fingers in *ghee* to make the food somewhat more tasty and nourishing. Perhaps their meat rations were restricted to sacrificial animals slaughtered in festivals, as in many regions of the Islamic world.

After the official part of the meal had been concluded, and perhaps also at other times of the day, they drank *qahwa,* coffee, which had been introduced to India by the Portuguese from south Arabia. The following Persian verse is attributed to Akbar:

I'll drink no coffee, bring me wine!
I'll play no harp – bring me my flute![11]

Whilst Jahangir's guest Qatiᶜi praised coffee thus:

Coffee is pleasing to princes –
The water of *Khidr* is concealed within:
In the gloomy kitchen filled with its smoke,
The coffeepot seems like the source of life![12]

They evidently drank their coffee black, as Terry describes the coffee in Jahangir's time as being 'a beneficial rather than pleasant liquid made from black kernels boiled in water'. Tavernier also mentions the usage of coffee a few times.

From Humayun's time, it was customary to chew betel, *pan*, after eating, as it still is today. One poet wrote that 'the red juice appears to Indians to be like the blood of lovers'. Giving betel was a sign of friendship. Occasionally it would be wrapped in flimsy pieces of gold or silver leaf, as is the case with sweets today. The beautiful *pandan*s, the artistically made little containers in which the ingredients were kept (green leaves, finely chopped arecanuts, chalk paste etc.) show how widespread the use of betel was – there were said to have been 3,000 betel shops in Kanauj alone! Since betel colours the teeth and the saliva red, there were spittoons everywhere, often made of precious metal. The *Mirzanama* warns people to cover themselves when in the presence of a talkative betel chewer lest his spittle stain the garments of his illustrious partner in conversation. It seems to have been primarily women who had a taste for betel.

Tobacco, like coffee, was introduced to India by the Portuguese, and was apparently first used in the Deccan. In 1604, Akbar's ambassador Asad Beg wrote:

In Bijapur I came across some tobacco . . .
I brought some with me and made a good
pipe decorated with jewels. Its neck was three
cubits long; it was dried and dyed, and both
ends were decorated with precious stones and
enamel work . . . The mouthpiece was an oval
Yemeni carnelian. A golden burner was used
to light it.[13]

Asad Beg filled a betel box with tobacco (he appears to have brought larger quantities of it) and improvised a silver bar to hold the pipe. The entire equipment was covered with velvet. Akbar was amazed, and attempted to smoke, however his doctors were aghast when they saw this unfamiliar stuff. Asad assured them that it was even used in Mecca and Medina. Akbar had them fetch a cleric, who testified that there was nothing poisonous nor unusual about it. Even though the doctors refused to be convinced that tobacco was innocuous, smoking soon became fashionable among the nobility, so fashionable in fact that as early as 1617 Jahangir issued a decree prohibiting smoking because the smoke, especially the smell

of it, was so irritating to those present. At the same time, Shah ᶜAbbas I banned smoking in Iran. Unfortunately Khan ᶜAlam, the Mughal ambassador at the Iranian court, was a chain smoker, so Shah ᶜAbbas made an exception in his case and wrote the following:

The ambassador of our friend
Is so fond of smoking –
I shall light up the tobacco market
With the candle of my friendship!

Whereupon Khan ᶜAlam of course replied by means of an appropriate verse.[14]

Towards the end of the seventeenth century, the Urdu poet Zatalli sang the following:

Smoking tobacco is a pleasant occupation,
Which banishes worry and sorrow,
It is a companion in times of loneliness,
And a cure for indigestion.[15]

Soon people took to using water-pipes, which were painstakingly decorated by artists. The water container, which was usually spherical and made of coloured glass or overlaid with colourful molten enamel, or sometimes of *bidri*work, was placed on a stand of richly decorated rings. Many miniatures reveal that women were equally fond of the water-pipe.

One of the proclivities of the Mughal court was not officially permitted: Jahangir wrote that when he became the ruler, he prohibited the production of wine and spirits – a rather futile act, considering the bad example which he himself set. The consumption of wine and drugs was apparently just as widespread in his time as before, if not more so.

## DRUGS AND ALCOHOL

Two of the most interesting works of art from the Mughal era provide evidence of one very negative aspect of life at the time, especially in aristocratic circles, namely the problem of drug abuse and alcoholism. One of these is Jahangir's opium cup, the other is the picture of Inayat Khan as he lay dying.

The small cup is made of white nephrite in the form of a poppy flower, 8 cm in diameter, with tiny emerald leaves. The bowl is an example of perfect beauty as well as the artistry of the palace craftsmen. Jahangir used to eat a mixture of strongly spiced wine and opium, often with some brandy added to it, from such pots. He himself was quite open about his repeated unsuccessful attempts to give up this habit and to wean himself off the enjoyment of such substances. Even Nur Jahan's efforts to help were in vain. Jahangir's gradually deteriorating health, his instability and frequent mood swings were all attributed to his enjoyment of wine and drugs.

One of Jahangir's senior officers in fact presented him with a perfect example of the detrimental effects of opium and wine. ʿInayat Khan, who is seen in one miniature as a good looking young man, ruined himself completely through his drug addiction. However, instead of regarding this human wreck as a warning, Jahangir was fascinated by the appearance of the dying man, and ordered his artists to paint him. He wrote (*Tuzuk*, II, p. 43):

News of Inayat Khan's death came today. He was one of my closest confidants. Since he was an opium addict and also extremely fond of drinking wine whenever he had the chance, his mind was gradually destroyed. He was not a robust man, and he drank more

than he could tolerate; he was afflicted by dysentery, and two or three times he fainted whilst in this state. On my instructions, Hakim Rukna prescribed medication; however, nothing he could do provided any relief. At the same time, he was overwhelmed by a huge appetite, and although the doctor tried very hard [to convince him] not to eat more than once every 24 hours, he was unable to control himself. He threw himself like a madman into water and onto fire, until his body was in a wretched state. In the end he became addicted to water, and totally weak and emaciated. A few days previously, he had asked for permission to go to Agra. He was laid in a sedan chair and brought to me. He appeared so weak and wretched, that I was amazed – he was nothing but skin stretched over bones, in fact even his bones were disintegrating.

As this was a quite exceptional case, I instructed artists to paint his portrait. Really, I found his alteration quite remarkable . . .

Jahangir advised the sick man to think of God, and since he had lamented his poverty, he gave him 2,000 rupees. He had clearly wasted all of his fortune on drugs. He died the next day, liver cancer possibly being the actual cause of death.

There are two versions of the portrait in existence. One of them, which is in the Bodleian Library in Oxford, is a terrifying depiction of a man lying on a bed; the other, in the Museum of Fine Arts in Boston, is a colourfully executed picture of the same scene, which depicts the dying man in an olive-green jacket lying on a red cushion; there are numerous long-necked bottles in an alcove in the wall behind him.[1]

The use of opium had long been customary, and in Jahangir's time there were reports of women taking their own lives with an overdose of opium. Not only courtiers, but also many subjects were drug addicts, and Bada'uni wrote of one young man: 'May God give him relief from his opium addiction, his pride and his deceit and bragging!'

In Malwa, according to Abu'l Fazl, people gave opium to small children to keep them quiet (which is still customary in the orient). In Babur's memoirs there are frequent references to his and his officers' enjoyment of *ma'jun*, 'electuary'. This drug, which is still known today, is made by pressing dried fruits such as plums, tamarinds, apricots, sometimes also sesame, and mixing the extract with a small amount of opium. *Ma'jun* was easy to carry during military campaigns and on journeys, and was sometimes consumed in large quantities at parties. Babur's son Humayun had a taste for this substance, which, in addition to its medical use as a painkiller, was a socially acceptable recreational drug. In a poem by Shah Jahan's poet laureate Kalim, he asks for some *kif*, which is another stimulant (*mufarrih*).[2] Despite its widespread use in the subcontinent today, *bhang*, cannabis, is not mentioned in the classical sources. Perhaps then, as now, it was primarily used by dervishes, musicians and ordinary people, for there is a miniature from a seventeenth century picture which shows a large number of dervishes and ordinary people occupied with small pots, bowls and pipes[3] – a procedure which can be observed today in many locations (such as the mausoleum of the Punjabi poet Bullhe Shah in Kasur). Although the picture's caption reads: 'The production, preparation and enjoyment of opium', they are in fact using *bhang*. Bada'uni, who renounced all more or less illegal pleasures during Akbar's time, condemned the use of both *bhang* and opium.[4]

Opium is especially dangerous when used in combination with wine, as Babur himself warned.

However, the Timurids were extremely fond of wine. Babur related that his uncle Sultan Ahmad Mirza would sometimes drink for three weeks on end, sometimes with his wife. He would then remain sober for a while. Baysunghur Mirza of Herat 'was too much enamoured of the wine glass' – however, when he did not imbibe, he performed his devotions'. (The Qur'an in fact says: 'Approach not prayer with a mind befogged until you can understand all that you say', *Sura* 4:43).

In Kafiristan, the young conqueror noticed with amazement that every Kafiri carried a leather wine pouch around his neck. Three centuries later, the German missionary Ernst Trumpp also commented on the alcoholism of the Kafiris, and described the Kafiri wine as 'somewhat disgusting'.[5]

When he was about twenty years of age, Babur described quite innocently his introduction to wine. At a banquet at the court of his cousin Muzaffar Mirza, near Herat, his relatives drew him into their circle and offered him something to drink:

> At that time I had not yet committed the sin
> of drinking wine, and had no experience of
> drunkenness nor real intoxication, otherwise
> I would gladly have drunk some, and my
> heart urged me to leap across this valley. As I
> was only small, I had no longing to do so, and
> did not know the pleasures of wine; when my
> father had offered me wine, I excused myself
> and committed no sin. After the death of my
> father, I was pious, and followed in the
> blessed footsteps of Khwaja Qadi. How could
> I, who avoided anything dubious, commit
> such a sin? Then, when I felt the stirring of a
> nascent inclination to drink wine, no one
> offered me any . . .

At this same banquet he declined to drink wine

because it would have been impolite to drink in the house of a younger relative when he had refused to in the house of an older one.

However, this was apparently his last resolute attempt at abstinence. Unfortunately there is a nine-year gap in the *Baburnama* which makes it impossible to ascertain when he first experienced intoxication, however, later on, in his reports on his military campaigns in Afghanistan and northwest India, the following observations recur frequently: 'And in the evening we imbibed', or: 'We drank in the morning...'. There are also references to the fact that during the period from 1526 when Babur and his followers were gradually conquering India as far as Agra, camel caravans conveyed excellent wines from Ghazna for the enjoyment of all of his followers.[6] Furthermore, in one of the most famous scenes from the *Baburnama*, which is also illustrated, the prince relates with no hint of remorse that he was so drunk one night that he was quite unaware of what he was doing, that he mounted his horse, holding a lantern in one hand, and rode off more or less in the direction of his tent – fortunately the horse was apparently sober enough to find the tent.[7]

Before the decisive battle against Rana Sangha, Babur did abstain from wine and had the goblets broken in order to dedicate himself to the struggle in a state of obedience to God. However, he found this very difficult; he related that he cried when eating nothing but melons, and:

I am befuddled since renouncing wine
I know not what to do – I'm going crazy.
People repent, then they give up wine –
I gave it up, and now I am repenting!

Three thousand soldiers joined him in his repentance, and the remaining wine had salt added to it to make it undrinkable.

Akbar drank occasionally; however he was not as addicted to alcohol and drugs as were his father Humayun or his sons. His second son, Murad, died in 1599 in a state of *delirium tremens*. Perhaps Murad's constant opposition to his father, and his refusal to cooperate with other officers during military campaigns, was caused by his consumption of alcohol and drugs. The third prince, Danyal, who worked with the *khankhanan* ʿAbduʾr Rahim in the Deccan, and was married to one of his daughters,

died at the age of thirty-three. His death occurred in a strange way. He loved guns, and hunting with guns. He had named one of his muskets *yaka u janaza*, 'exactly like a bier' . . . When his consumption of wine became excessive, and his father had been informed of this state of affairs, a *farman* was sent to the *khankhanan*. Naturally he forbade him to drink wine, and employed a number of conscientious people to try and keep him in line. Now that his access to wine was completely blocked, he started to cry, and put pressure on one of his servants to 'find a way of bringing me some wine!' He said to Murshid Quli Khan, a musketeer who was directly beneath him in rank: 'Pour some wine into this *yaka u janaza* and then bring it to me.' This wretched fellow did as he was told in the hope of getting a reward. He poured double distilled spirit into the flint gun, which had for a long time contained gunpowder and its fumes, then brought it to him. The rust on the iron was dissolved by the alcohol and mixed into it, and the prince had scarcely drunk from it when he fell down dead.[8]

This was Jahangir's report on the death of his brother on 11 March 1605. The *khankhanan* blamed himself for the death of his son-in-law, which, alas, did not bring Danyal back to life.

The emperor himself was also an abuser of alcohol and drugs, and as a young man had been imprisoned by his father for a while for that reason. Sir Thomas Roe described his encounter with the ruler in January 1616:

> Jahangir sat cross-legged on a small throne, entirely clad in diamonds, pearls and rubies . . . ; around him were his nobles in their best attire, whom he commanded to drink to their hearts' content, whilst different varieties of wine were being placed before them in large flasks.

A gift of red wine, which was brought by the British ambassador, was therefore most welcome. Jahangir did, however, abstain from wine on Thursday evenings, as Friday, the holy day, commenced at dusk.

Shah Jahan was very different, if this account by Muhammad Salih Kanboh is to be believed:

> his majesty the emperor had the good fortune both early on in his youth and in the full bloom of his maturity to have no inclination to indulge in wine or any other intoxicating substances, and he received the support of heaven as protection from them, so that from the time when he first developed powers of discrimination, until the age of 24, he had experienced absolutely no desire to imbibe wine, and was most certainly not addicted to it.

Jahangir, according to the chronicler, forced him to drink. However, as a general rule he only drank on festive occasions, and 'not from inclination'.[9] When he was hoping to subjugate the Deccan, he recalled Akbar's oath before his battle against Rana Sangha and gave up wine, at least for a time. He also renounced the use of gold and silver vessels, which were prohibited by law. Aurangzeb abstained from alcohol as a law-abiding Muslim; however, later Mughal rulers, such as Muhammad Shah Rangela, were more than a little fond of forbidden pleasures.

The ladies of Shah Jahan's court seem to have been extremely liberal in their consumption of wine, according to eyewitnesses such as Manucci, whose reports often amounted to a *chronique scandaleuse*. Apparently even Princess Jahanara served female visitors with wine or spirits. In miniatures there are many depictions of merry women with golden bottles and bejewelled goblets who are either serving wine or about to imbibe themselves.

The chronicles testify to the widespread consumption of alcohol among the nobility. The *Mirzanama* expresses the view that the *mirza* should not indulge too frequently in alcohol, and then never in full sunlight, but only 'when the sky is clouded over and when there is light drizzle'.

It would be interesting to know more about the proof of spirits. Abu'l Fazl mentions it, primarily referring to the fermented juice of sugar cane. If this were distilled three times strictly in accordance with certain instructions, then a high proof arrack was produced, which was also mixed with wine, as can be seen from notes in the margins, with lethal results! This was also the case with palm toddy.

From time to time we get a glimpse of the diet of the *mansabdars*, who lived fairly simple lives. One of them had a curry prepared from *one* roast partridge, whilst another is supposed to have consumed the incredible quantity of one thousand mangoes each day – which is quite impossible merely from the point of view of time![10] Some of them lived quite moderately themselves, but had to feed thousands of paupers each day, whereas others like Asaf Khan were used to luxury at table. There are some very interesting accounts which reveal that the alcoholic excesses of the nobility were not condoned. One Amir invited a number of his colleagues in Kabul to a meal of roast pork (pork being absolutely forbidden). When Jahangir reproached him, he replied: 'Wine is just as strictly forbidden as pork, but apparently the court only takes heed of the prohibition on pork . . .'.[11]

## RECREATION AND ENTERTAINMENT

In *A'in* I, no. 29, Abu'l Fazl describes the leisure activities of the Mughal aristocracy, and other sources provide more details to complete the picture. The Central Asian author Mutribi, who was quite elderly at the time, visited the Mughal court during the last year of Jahangir's reign, and wrote a vivid account of his time there. Apparently the ruler was a connoisseur of Central Asian music, and he once held a 'white party' by the light of the full moon, to which all the guests had to dress in white.[1] Jahangir himself relates that whilst he was making his way towards Kashmir, in the region of Ghakkar (not far from present day Islamabad), he commanded his fellow travellers to take off their turbans and to wear bunches of flowers instead, so that they resembled a 'wonderful flowerbed'.[2]

There were plenty of pretexts for parties in the daily round of life. Circumcisions were celebrated – Akbar had his three sons circumcised on 22 January 1573 amidst great festivities with lavish musical entertainment, as was the custom in the courts of oriental princes, for instance in Mamluk Egypt or Ottoman Turkey. The commencement of education was also cause for celebration, with the *basmala* ceremony being part of the ritual. The ritual weighing of a prince when he reached the age of two years was an especially important event. He was initially weighed against one item, and every subsequent year another 'counter-weight' would be added. The ruler would be weighed twice, on his birthday according to both the lunar calendar and the solar calendar. In the lunar year he would be weighed against eight different items, whilst in the solar year he would be weighed against twelve – gold, silver, precious stones, coins, plus iron, rice, and salt. The gold or other valuable objects would then be distributed to the needy. Sometimes the ruler would also be weighed during a solar or lunar eclipse, so as to avert its baleful influence by his consequent generosity to the poor. Aurangzeb made no secret of his scorn for this custom; however, he did not abolish it since 'it was a boon for the poor'.[3]

There is a miniature depicting the sixteenth birthday celebrations of Prince Khurram, the future Shah Jahan, which gives by far the best impression of the splendour of the weighing ceremony. The prince is shown standing on golden scales held by his father, the highest ranking military officers of the empire, and *khankhanan* ᶜAbdu'r Rahim, whilst the highest dignitaries – Jahangir's father-in-law Iᶜtimad ad-daula, his brother-in-law Asaf Khan, next to him Mahabat Khan, and Khan Jahan Lodi – watch the proceedings. There are all kinds of valuable objects in the foreground, and the entire hall is glittering with gold and jewels.[4]

These festivities often took place in the house of the emperor's mother.

The New Year Festival, *nauruz*, was celebrated with great pomp in the palace, and as in Iran it went on for thirteen days.

The palace was decked out like the canopy of heaven with patterned carpets and beautifully

71. Bhola, 'The Weighing of Shah Jahan on his 42nd Lunar Birthday [23 October 1632]', c. 1635, gouache on paper; an illustration from Shah Jahan's *Padshahnama* ('Chronicle of the King of the World').

coloured cloths, and was transformed into a duplicate of the Chinese artists' legendary studio.

wrote Muhammad Salih Kanboh at the time of Shah Jahan, for in Persian literature, the skill of Chinese artists was legendary. Akbar's religion paid homage to light and to the sun, so the appearance of the sun in the constellation of Aries in the spring was celebrated especially lavishly. Slaves were set free, and presents given out. Aurangzeb did not hold with this 'heathen' festival, to the regret of his son Mu'azzam, who used to enjoy the celebrations.

Weddings were celebrated especially lavishly in the royal household, as these have always been an excellent opportunity to display the wealth of empires. The illustrations in the *Padshahnama* give an idea of the quantity of gifts which were showered upon Prince Dara Shikoh at his wedding to Nadira, the daughter of his uncle Parwez: they show numerous porters carrying dishes heaped with treasures upon their heads. Musical bands and singers are seated upon richly ornamented elephants, and a dazzling firework display can be seen above the garden and the river. Everything had been planned down to the last detail by Dara Shikoh's sister Jahanara. The chroniclers used the most elaborate metaphors in their descriptions of the events, for it seemed to them that:

> The legendary creations of Mani (the founder of Manichaeism) and the Chinese and Frankish painters, and even the chameleon-like iridescent and radiantly enamelled heavens themselves, would not bear comparison with the magnificence of this dazzling festival . . . which would put their own paltry works to shame.[5]

Every prince received a *sehra* made of pearls as a present from their father. A *sehra* was normally a garland of flowers, but in this case it was a veil of pearls which held a picture of the bridegroom's face.[6]

Fireworks were perhaps the most conspicuous element of any celebration. They were set off along the pathways and riverbanks, and bamboo frameworks of all shapes and sizes were specially constructed to hold them. Akbar is said to have had a bamboo framework made in the shape of his vanquished enemy Hemu. One Mughal drawing shows a firework handler in the process of fashioning a gigantic bamboo firework frame in the form of an elephant.[7]

Outside in the garden there were all kinds of entertainments for the enjoyment of the guests. There was a juggler from Karnataka who could juggle with ten balls. Acrobats, clowns and dancers performed in animal costumes with rabbits' ears or with animals' horns to amuse the people,[8] who might well have sung Rumi's verse:

> Today is the day of the rose, now is the rose's year . . .[9]

Sometimes small seats were placed in shady tree-tops. These were primarily for the observation of hunts, however, such 'tree terraces' were also provided in gardens, as somewhere for people to indulge in drinking and other pleasures, as can be seen in the illustrations to romantic texts.[10]

There were excursions, not only month-long expeditions to Kashmir, but also sightseeing trips in the surrounding countryside, as described by Gulbadan. Sometimes the ladies were taken along as well. In 1558, when Akbar was a youth of sixteen, he was taken to Delhi in a lavishly decorated boat. Jahangir wrote many accounts of his excursions and short boat trips, especially in Mandu. He once went on a trip by sea from Sarkhej. Even his former tutor, the *khankhanan* 'Abdu'r Rahim, risked putting out to sea in an open boat after his conquest of Sind. Evidently even the *generalissimo* was made somewhat anxious by the mighty swell of the waves – could it have been arranged by his vanquished opponent to bring about his overthrow?[11]

The most important excursion was the hunting expedition. Although Akbar expressed his disapproval of excessive enthusiasm for hunting – especially after his own enlightenment whilst out hunting in 1578 – his successors followed the

72. 'Salim [Jahangir] spearing a lioness', *c.* 1600–05, colour and gold on paper.

Mughal tradition and were excellent hunters. Jahangir used to keep an exact count of the number of animals he had shot during the course of his hunting career spanning almost fifty years. The final count amounted to 23,948 animals, from tigers to hares and all kinds of birds.[12] One of their favourite hunting grounds was at Palam near Delhi – today the site of the Indian capital's enormous airport.

Many pictures reveal that their favourite method of hunting was one which appears very unsporting to us. They hunted within a *qamargah*, which was a fenced off area several kilometres in area. The boundary fence was gradually moved inwards, trapping hundreds of animals within it, until they came within shooting range. In that way they could easily be shot by the emperor, who was usually on horseback, but sometimes seated on his elephant. Swift cheetahs were used to bring down

gazelles and stags. Ilahwardi used a huge net to surround a *qamargah* for Jahangir. It was 10,000 cubits long, 6 cubits high, and so heavy that it had to be transported by eighty camels.[13] Unauthorised persons were strictly prohibited from entering the hunting grounds. If anyone, whether native or traveller, had the misfortune to wander into the corral, he would be taken and sold into slavery, or slain just like one of the wild animals. This could even happen to members of the hunting party themselves, for instance if one of the beaters or servants accidentally scared off a wild animal or put the ruler off his shot.

A few of the women at court actually took part in the hunt themselves, and Nur Jahan distinguished herself as a markswoman – but then it was hardly a great achievement to sit in a sedan chair on the back of an elephant and bag four tigers with six shots!

They also hunted with falcons. Falconers' gloves, with their broad, richly embroidered cuffs, were as elegant as other works from the period, and there are exquisitely beautiful pictures of these noble birds of prey in Mughal albums.

As has been mentioned, Nur Jahan was an excellent polo player. Just as today, polo was considered to be the supreme sport, despite the risk of accidents. It was played in teams of four – one miniature depicts Jahangir with his sons Parwez and Khurram and his brother-in-law Asaf Khan, and pictures of the women's teams show a similar composition. A *chukker* generally lasted twenty minutes. Akbar even had luminous polo balls made so that games could be played at night.

Animal fights were popular spectator sports – even gazelles were pitted against each other. Cockfights were also common, and although betting was against religious law, they apparently used to bet on animal fights.

As well as animal fights, wrestling was perennially popular. Babur often mentions wrestling matches taking place in his encampment, and Jahangir once asked Sultan Ibrahim ᶜAdil Shah of Bijapur to send him a good fighter from the Deccan. He describes with great enthusiasm the man's skill in overcoming his opponent. The victor was rewarded with 1,000 rupees, a robe of honour, and an elephant.[14] (Wrestlers were also drafted into the army.)

If a man had one son who became a wrestler, and another who became a pigeon fancier, then he was fortunate indeed. Akbar loved both kinds of sport – when he was barely three years old, he beat his cousin in a childish game of wrestling, and flying pigeons was one of the favourite occupations of the Mughals. Traditional families today still enjoy keeping these graceful birds.

There were training courses and instructors for the different types of sport. The fencing master

73. *Akbar and his son Prince Jahangir*, late 17th-century copy after an Awadh school original of *c.* 1605–12, gouache on paper.

was once honoured with the title *Warzish Khan*, 'Sir Sport'.

Of all the other forms of recreation which were enjoyed at court and by the populace at large, the most important was music.[15] The names of musicians are often mentioned, and musicians frequently received their weight in silver, gold, or coins. One of them once notched up 6,300 rupees on the scales. No musician was more famous and popular than Tansen, who came to Akbar's court from Gwalior in 1562. When he died on 26 April 1589, a chronogram was composed in commemoration: 'The Disappearance of Melody'. Tansen was buried in a relatively modest grave in Gwalior, near the great mausoleum of his spiritual master Muhammad Ghauth Gwaliari.[16] Indian folk legends still recount the miracles which his songs

74, 75. Basawan,
with Asi, brother
of Miskina (left
panel) and Tara
the Elder (right
panel), The
Emperor Akbar
watching a fight
between two
bands of Hindu
devotees at
Thaneshwar,
Punjab, 1597–8,
gouache and gold
on paper, from a
manuscript of the
*Akbarnama*.

are said to have caused, and musicians often go to pay their respects at his mausoleum.

Pictures often show musicians playing the *ektara*, a simple, elongated string instrument. A sort of bulbous lute is also seen, especially at large festivals. Flautists were usually female, as were tambourine players. For dancing, Chaghatay- or Indian-style costume was worn, and a form of castanet was used. Large drums are depicted being supported on small stands. Drummers are depicted playing a double drum, which is such an essential a part of Indian music, supported on the back of a kneeling man. The female entertainers wear anklets, as they do today. A sword dance is shown being performed by a strong man at Babur's court in Afghanistan. Chagatay dancing girls are recognisable by their high pointed hats. Pictures of these festivities, which give such a marvellous impression of Mughal music and dances, often illustrate collections of poetry and historical epics.

There are also some individual portraits of especially famous musicians, most notably, of course, of Kalawant Tansen. ʿAli Khan, the *karori* (finance officer), who was neither particularly slim nor elegant, is also depicted carrying his *vina*, a double-bodied stringed instrument. Although his official rank was in finance, Ali Khan was one of the most famous *vina* players. In 1607 he was made *Naubat Khan*, Chief Military Bandmaster.[17]

In Jahangir's time, there are references to a lute player by the name of Shauqi, who was awarded the title *Anand Khan*, 'Sir Rapture', in recognition of his distinguished rendition of Hindi and Persian songs. A man of Armenian descent by the name of Zulqarnayn-i Firangi was also praised as a composer and singer of Hindi songs.

Akbar was clearly partial to Sindhi music. Badaʾuni was furious when a Brahman called Birbal, who was a musician from Kalpi, was award-

76. Kalawant Tansen, (?)late 1580s, gouache on paper.

ed a high position in the *mansabdar* hierarchy at Akbar's court, and was correspondingly pleased when the hated *raja* 'fell into the maws of the hounds of hell' after his military incompetence and obstinacy led to catastrophe for the Mughal army during the battle with the Yusufzai Pashtuns, at which 8,000 Mughal soldiers died.

Pure Indian classical music such as the *dhrupad*, was apparently extremely popular at court. One *dhrupad* singer, Bakhtar Khan, who was closely related to the music lover Sultan Ibrahim ʿAdil Shah II of Bijapur, was especially popular.

The fastidious Jahangir was, however, far from enthusiastic about Kashmiri music, especially their choral singing.

The palaces and gardens must have been alive with the sound of music – whenever a palace scene is shown in a painting, there is always a pair of musicians to entertain the noble gentlemen and/or ladies, and many *mansabdar*s employed their own household musicians. There was also folk music in the villages, as can be seen in one particular vivid portrait of a couple of folk musicians, which perfectly captures the atmosphere one late afternoon in the countryside.[18] Artists must have been particularly inspired by the ecstatic dance of the whirling dervishes, judging by the numerous depictions of festivals at Sufi shrines.

Educated men were advised not to risk making fools of themselves by singing!

Artists often painted strangely garbed Sufi musicians, who wandered the land carrying a musical instrument on their shoulders. On a more intellectual level, there are any number of tracts from the Mughal era devoted to the theory and practice of music, including treatises by great mystics such as Nasir Muhammad ʿAndalib.

The evening was the time for storytelling: 'story' and 'sleep' are traditionally closely associated in the Orient (this connection most likely being behind the main storyline of 'One Thousand and One Tales of the Arabian Nights'). Akbar liked to be read to in bed, and Jahangir commanded that the work of the lamplighters and storytellers should commence with a verse which he himself had composed:

So long as the sun in heaven may shine
Let its reflection not stray from the ruler's
    parasol![19]

Akbar was known to be fascinated by historical sagas such as the imaginative *Hamzanama*, and Jahangir once rewarded an accomplished story-teller with his own weight in gold – unfortunately, since the master was extremely thin, that amounted to only 4,400 rupees' worth. However, he also received a robe of honour, an elephant and even a small *mansab* of 220-*zat*/20-*suwar*.

When the gentlemen were not listening to music or stories, or watching sport of some kind, they liked to play chess. Chess had been popular in India from time immemorial, and there are many treatises on the subject. The Royal Asiatic Society in London has a chess manual with 64 (somewhat damaged) pictures. It was usually played by one man against another, but women also occasionally played against each other.[20]

*Nard*, backgammon, was played, as well as *chaupar*, a game played by four players, each with four counters, which was widespread in India. According to Abu'l Fazl, Akbar invented a board game called *chandal mandal*, for sixteen players with four counters each.[21] Babur and Humayun both played *ganjifa*, a card game in which the cards were divided into four suits of twelve. *Ganjifa* was also known in the Middle East, where there are some Egyptian cards surviving from Mamluk times, whereas the oldest surviving *ganjifa* cards from the Mughal Empire only date back to 1674.

As well as the aforementioned somewhat innocuous pastimes, many people went in for other, rather more sensuous pursuits.

Persian poetry – including the verses of Babur and his successors – were full of praise for charming beardless youths, and pederasty was widespread. Akbar, however, as we know from Badaʾuni's accounts, 'found the company of boys highly repulsive', and Babur was very critical of the homosexual theme of the Persian romance 'The Shah and the Beggar', composed at the Timurid

77. Dancing dervishes, late 16th century, gouache on paper.

78. 'The murder of Qubad in his pavilion', an illustration from the *Hamzanama*, *c.* 1562–77, painting on cotton.

court at Herat. Akbar was particularly opposed to open love affairs between officers, and he punished the men concerned – in the case of the 'beardless boy', he locked him up. Nevertheless, the tendency was very much in evidence, and many men 'developed a particular interest in unbearded youths . . . who shaved their eyebrows and dressed themselves in elegant attire'. Interestingly, there are reports of a few Mughal and Deccan rulers and officers who were particularly interested in eunuchs. The ruler of Bijapur, ᶜAli ᶜAdil Shah (reigned 1557–80), was stabbed by a handsome eunuch.

## PERFUMES

No account of the pleasures of Mughal court life would be complete without a consideration of the

role of perfumes. The perfumes of Arabia had been well known for centuries, and the Prophet Muhammad had expressly recommended their use – people should be pleasantly scented as they made their way to say their prayers.

Scent compounds –with musk and ambergris as the basis – were popular gifts in mediaeval Islamic courts, and still are today in oriental cultures. This was especially true of the Mughal court. Abu'l Fazl devotes a whole chapter of his *A'in-i akbari* (no. 30) to perfumes, as Akbar loved them, and was said to have developed a few concoctions himself. The palace was often permeated with the aroma of incense, which was always burned in silver censers.

The two basic ingredients of perfumes, musk and ambergris, were both highly prized. The blackish musk was derived from the musk gland of the Central Asian musk deer, and ambergris was obtained from the sea, the highest quality of all being white. In hot climates, cooling snow-white camphor was used, and the scent of the civet cat also appears in Abu'l Fazl's list of ingredients. As well as incense they burned ͨud, aloe wood, which was obtained from eastern India, and had been highly prized since the Middle Ages. As today, flower oils were used on the body, especially jasmine. The most popular perfume of all

79. Attributed to Govardhan, 'The poet Hafiz, holding a book, in a garden', from a dispersed manuscript of Hafiz, *c.* 1580, pigment and gold on paper

80. Late 18th-century Mughal playing-cards.

was *attar* of roses, and Nur Jahan's mother was said to have invented a special method for distilling it.

All perfumes were very oily, and miniatures often depict dark patches under the arms of both men and women, which were caused by their heavy perfumes. However, since clothes were usually worn only once, it did not matter if they had scent marks which could not be removed.

## MEDICINE

> Yesterday said death, as he was about to take
> the life of a sick man:
> Everywhere I go, he has been there before
> me![1]

This verse was written about a doctor at the Mughal court, who was known as *sayf al-hukama*, 'The Sword of Doctors', for instead of healing his patients, he 'helped them on their way to the other side'. The story is even more amusing given the fact that the doctor in question was also a poet, whose *nom de plume* was Dawaʾi, from *dawa*, 'healing remedy'.

This doctor was certainly not unique – satires on incompetent doctors are a popular theme in Islamic literature, reaching their apogee during the decline of the Mughal dynasty in the great Urdu satire by Sauda (died 1781), with the sobriquet 'Dr Ghauth' (i.e. 'Help').[2]

There were clearly other, more competent doctors, who were awarded flattering honorary names, such as *masih ad-din, masih ul-mulk*, or *masih az-zaman*, 'Messiah of the Faith, of the empire, or of the age', for *al-masih* is Jesus, who is praised as a great healer in the Qurʾan (*Sura* 5:110). A good doctor could also be dubbed *jalinus az-zaman*, 'The Galen of His Age', in reference to the great Roman physician.

There was a series of doctors associated with the Mughal court who not only dedicated themselves to medical practice, but also wrote medical and pharmacological treatises, beginning with commentaries on the work of Avicenna, which was considered for centuries to be the standard work in both Europe and the East. An overview of medical terminology was dedicated to Avicenna in Babur's time. When Babur was ill (which was often depicted in manuscript illustrations), Yusufi-yi Herati wrote a textbook, 'On the Maintenance of Health'. The same Yusufi also compiled a work for Humayun, *Riyad al-adwiya*, 'Gardens of Medicines' (1539).

One generation later, in 1595, a rhyming tract on pharmacology was dedicated to Akbar, to which the ruler himself gave the title *fawaʾid al-insan*, 'Things Useful to Humanity'. Another work with the same title also appeared at the time of Akbar and Jahangir. Although the second work was supposedly written by another doctor named Ruhullah Bharuchi (*ruh Allah*, 'Spirit of God', is another name by which Jesus is known), the two works may in fact be one and the same. As a reward for healing Nur Jahan, Ruhullah received a fiefdom in Broach, and also his weight in silver.

The former chief doctor at the court of Shah ʿAbbas, who had the fitting sobriquet of Shifaʾi (from *shifa*, 'healing'), had also served Akbar. Abuʾl-Fath-i Gilani, who was a distinguished patron of Persian poets, and who corresponded with the most prominent men of the empire, played an especially important role. In 1602, Ruknuddin Masih appeared at court, and was active there until the time of Shah Jahan. As well as becoming Shah Jahan's favourite doctor, he also composed mystical verse.[3] The pharmacologist Nuruddin-i Shirazi, who was a nephew of Akbar's trusted friends Fayzi and Abuʾl Fazl, also appeared at the time of Shah Jahan. He wrote many works on pharmacology for the ruler and the crown prince, and he also composed mystical works. There is a three-volume Persian manuscript treatise in large format, now in the possession of the Royal Asiatic Society in London, with the title *Muᶜalajat-i Dara Shikohi*, written by Hakim Mir Muhammad Abdallah, which covers topics from the creation of Adam and the universal intellect to dietary advice and sexual hygiene.[4]

Aurangzeb certainly had his own doctors. There were also European court doctors at that time, men such as Manucci and Bernier, who enjoyed the confidence of the ruler and so were able to observe court life at close quarters, even the life of the court ladies.

Historical sources provide some information on epidemics, also the ailments from which the rulers suffered. The autobiographies of Babur and Jahangir are important sources of information on the way the Mughals treated their own illnesses. Babur describes a time when he suffered from intermittent fever for 25 days. He had also fallen ill during his childhood, and miniatures in the *Baburnama* show one servant crushing drugs in a mortar, and another one administering them to him. Elsewhere he writes about some medication derived from barley flour, which was mixed with other medicine, and that the resulting concoction 'tasted quite disgusting'.[5] The treatment of abscesses was also rather unpleasant – pepper was boiled with water in a clay pot, then the afflicted person held the abscess above the steam and bathed it in the hot water. When the ruler was cured, everyone would come to offer their congratulations, after which he would go to the 'convalescence bath', as was the custom.

Jahangir described being bled from his left arm, and how he was laid low with a headache and fever, from which no doctor could give him any relief – only his beloved wife Nur Jahan knew of an effective remedy for him. He ascribed his cure to the spiritual power of Muᶜinuddin Chishti, to whom he had prayed for help - after all, his great grandfather Babur had once transposed a religious treatise, the *Risala-yi walidiyya* by the Naqshbandi Sufi ᶜUbaydullah Ahrar, into Turkish verse during a period of illness, and had been cured.

People could also be cured by prayer to the Prophet, as had happened to Busiri in Egypt, or else by the power of friends of Allah;[6] alternatively, there was an ancient ritual which involved someone walking three times around the sick bed and taking the ailment upon himself, as Babur had done during Humayun's illness. Jahangir's son Parwez also ritually circumambulated his father's sick bed (which his father clearly disapproved of).

Jahangir once suffered from a bout of diarrhoea after eating too many mangoes. He also frequently suffered because of the climate, for instance in Agra, but especially in Gujarat, where he was plagued by fever and vomiting, and his doctors naturally advised him to reduce his consumption of wine and opium. Jahangir apparently also suffered from asthma attacks. Once again, the doctors were ineffective, but his clever wife was able to treat him successfully.[7]

Jahangir carefully recorded bouts of illness and unusual occurrences, and he observed that people living on the border between Kashmir and India proper developed a goitrous swelling at their throats, which was caused by a deficiency of iodine, which often occurs in mountainous regions.

There are many references to the plague, which erupted in 1616 in the Punjab, then two years later in Agra. The ruler was intrigued by the fact that the young daughter of his brother-in-law Asaf Khan had noticed a rat just before the plague broke out.

Jahangir did not want to see any cripples or invalids when he appeared at the festivities on the day of *Nauruz*, as they offended his aesthetic sensibilities. However, he related with some amusement a story about a man who was so fat that he was absolutely incapable of doing anything – when he tried to put on the robe of honour which had been presented to him, he died from sheer exertion![8]

The chronicles only mention a few of the frequently occurring illnesses. A satirical poem from the end of the sixteenth century describes an unpleasant individual who was frequently afflicted by ailments:

> Fever, colic, haemorrhoids, consumption, dropsy, measles, tapeworms, epilepsy and delirium.

The biographies of many officers and scholars reveal just how widespread colic and diarrhoea were. Sufferers were comforted with a saying attributed to the Prophet: 'He that is afflicted with the colic is a martyr', which was quoted at the death of Mian Mir, the great holy man of Lahore, in 1635.

There are many references to haemorrhoids, which were particularly unpleasant because the resulting bleeding prevented participation in ritual prayers (during prayers, no stains are permitted on clothing). When the suffering became so intolerable that sitting was no longer possible, an operation was attempted – which must surely have proved fatal.

The poet Kalim, who wrote a poem on 'Itching and Pustules', was undoubtedly not the only one to suffer from these afflictions.[9]

Interestingly, alopecia, complete loss of hair, is mentioned in connection with two young members of the Mughal family. Another one of Jahangir's afflictions was the retention of urine. Dropsy was a not infrequent occurrence, as witness the verse quoted above. One amir, whose trouser waistband measured an immense 1.6

metres, was fully cured following a holy vision.

There are many indications of cancer; however, leprosy was almost unknown among the upper classes.

Pictures and poems show the use of spectacles from the late sixteenth century, but there was no record of the use of an artificial eye made of crystal until the early eighteenth century.[10]

It took an expert to diagnose the multifarious symptoms of illnesses and ailments afflicting the upper classes –one doctor himself died of 'punctured lungs'. However, despite the many attacks of asthma and the frequent bouts of indigestion, the most common cause of death among the nobility was their excessive consumption of drugs and alcohol.

## THE ROLE OF ANIMALS

> While approaching a sheet of water near Kabul, we saw a wonderful thing – something as red as the rise of the dawn kept showing and vanishing between the sky and the water . . . When we got quite close we learned that the cause was flocks of geese, geese innumerable which, when the mass of birds flapped their wings in flight, sometimes showed red feathers, sometimes not.

This was the twenty-year-old Babur's description of something he experienced not far from Kabul. Although all translations until now have called the birds 'geese', they were in fact clearly a species of flamingo, *qaz-i husayni*, 'Humayun's Goose', a few of which still survive in the region of Afghanistan referred to by Babur.[1]

This passage is an example of the young prince's powers of observation as a naturalist. His autobiography contains a large number of important

81. A corpulent prince
(perhaps Khusrau), *c.* 1670,
tinted drawing by
a Deccani artist after a
Mughal original

descriptions of the flora and fauna of Afghanistan and especially northwest India, where he saw many strange creatures, which he describes with a mixture of amazement and disparagement. Babur's great-grandson Jahangir inherited his interest in all aspects of nature, and his painters produced a remarkable pictorial record of all the animals shown to the ruler, from grasshoppers to yaks.

Babur was most of all impressed by the elephants he saw in India (though they had long been exported to Persia via Central Asia), and he devoted a lengthy section of the *Baburnama* to them. Indian painters depicted them realistically, albeit sometimes too large in proportion to their riders.

In the period when the Mughal empire was being stabilised under Akbar's rule, elephants assumed a role of the utmost importance and prestige at court, as can be seen from the enormous elephant staircase which was reserved for the use of the state elephants; Abu'l Fazl also wrote far more about the ruler's elephants than any other animal (*A'in,* 41–48).

Miniatures depict elephants playing in their natural state, and also elephant hunts, during which men climbed trees to fasten ropes that were then used to lassoo the beasts. Often a whole herd would be captured in this way. Only the best would be kept, and the rest were driven back into the jungle.[2]

The animals were trained at court, and proved themselves to be especially quick learners. As the astonished chroniclers noted, they could learn melodies and keep time, which was important during parades. When the ruler held a reception, elephants standing in front of the throne or the *jharoka* window would bow and raise their trunks up high (as can often be seen in miniatures); or else they would kneel on command. During the ceremonial weighing of the ruler, Sir Thomas Roe was amazed to witness an elephant laying its trunk on the ground then lifting it up over its head a few times in succession, trumpeting three times as it did so – he was under the impression that the animal was actually performing the *taslim*, which the emperor was required to perform.

Such descriptions lend credence to a report of an event at the court of Awadh: at the court of King Ghaziuddin Haydar (reigned 1819–1826), who was an exemplary Shiʿi, there was an elephant which was said to have been trained to trumpet loudly on the tenth of Muharram, at the festival of mourning commemorating the death of Husayn, the grandson of the Prophet, in Kerbela. The trumpeting was interpreted as *Waaaaah Hussaynaaaah waaaah Hussaynaaaa.*[3]

Abuʾl Fazl reports that the animals learned to hold bows and guns in their trunks, and to pick up objects which had been dropped and give them to their keepers. From time to time a sabre or spear would even be tied to their trunks.

The imperial elephants were divided into four groups according to their shape and colour, the shape of their heads and length of their trunks, and other characteristics. Of all the groups, the white (actually pink) albino was the most highly prized. In Shah Jahan's time, in 1630, one of these elephants was brought to the court from Pegu. At first he seemed to be quite unremarkable, however, he developed into a marvellous animal, about which Shah Jahan's poet laureate wrote:

> Your white elephant – do not allow it to come
>   to any harm!
> For he who gazes on it, raises his face in
>   wonderment!
> And when Shah Jahan, the master of the
>   world, mounts it,
> It is as if the sun were rising out of the white
>   dawn light![4]

The artist Bichitr painted a portrait of the crown prince Dara Shikoh on this noble animal.

Elephants were also classified according to their temperament. It was believed that calm elephants would be long-lived, and that proud, greedy, or lazy ones might become wild and dangerous. They learnt to breed from specimens of the desired type. It was assumed that elephants could live to the age of 120, so they were divided into seven age groups, and fed an appropriate amount for their age group and size. The ruler's private elephants were of course the best fed – Akbar's favourite elephant received 500 rupees' worth of food each month (the monthly salary of a regular soldier was 2 rupees!) A special tax, the *khurak-i filan-i halqa*, was even levied to pay for the food of the imperial elephants. In 1577, in Akbar's time, the inhabitants of the northern Deccan were exempted from this tax on the grounds of their poverty.[5] The daily diet of the imperial elephants included 5 *ser* (approx. 4 kg) of sugar, *ghee*, and rice with cloves and pepper. A few elephants were also fed milk and corn. In the sugar cane season, which lasted two months, each of the state elephants was given 300 canes of sugar.[6] Mahabat Khan fed his favourite elephant lotus rice and Persian melons. Apparently some elephants were even fed meat and wine from time to time. Asad Beg, Akbar's special ambassador to Bijapur (1604–05) reported that an elephant which Ibrahim ᶜAdil Shah sent to Akbar needed two *man* (about 40 litres) of wine a day, and 'I was forced to satisfy the animals' needs with cases of expensive port wine'.[7] No wonder elephants in Mughal miniatures often appear to be smiling!

Every elephant had several servants to look after it, according to its rank: the highest class, a *mast* – a young, temperamental, strong animal – had five and a half (!) servants, namely the driver (*mahout*) and another servant sitting behind him, and other men of both higher and lower ranks to feed, saddle and deck him out. Even the smallest imperial elephant had two servants, and the largest female elephants had four.

A few pictures show the mahouts wearing a special costume consisting of a tight red suit. They all carried an *ankus*, or elephant goad, which was sometimes decorated with gold and silver. Any number of people were employed to train the animals in small or large groups. An *ahadi* had to submit a daily report on the health of the animals, and to report if any animal was sick or injured. In case of any injury resulting from carelessness on the part of a servant, the guilty man would be harshly punished. If an animal was drugged, i.e. if the supervisor mixed drugs into its feed, and the animal consequently became ill or even died, the guilty man might be executed or sold into slavery. Jahangir recorded a case of rabies resulting from a dog bite.

There were a number of methods of calming or frightening unruly or disobedient elephants. One method of subduing them was to drill a hole in the middle of a bamboo cane then fill it with gunpowder and set light to it.

Good elephants were expensive. In one portrait of a wonderful specimen of an elephant and a plump calf, the price of the elephant is given as 100,000 rupees! Perhaps this was Gajraj, described by Jahangir as the 'chief of my special elephants'. The same amount was paid for Dara Shikoh's parade elephant.

These valuable animals were naturally extremely well looked after. Each had its own blanket of wool and cotton, as well as a goad. The animals were caparisoned in red velvet embroidered with gold or of gold brocade, and adorned with silver chains and cords, often ornamented with precious stones and, most importantly, different size bells. A net of brocade was sometimes draped on their foreheads, and yak tails[8] were often tied onto their tusks, foreheads and necks, 'like enormous moustaches'. Their tusks were often cut off, but they gradually grew back. The shortened tusks bore metal caps and rings for reinforcement as well as decoration.

In dangerous situations, such as battles, the elephants' heads and bodies were protected with steel armour or armoured plates which were lined with fabric. A few pictures show their protective red face masks fitted with long, upright ears like those of hares, giving the mighty animals a rather demonic appearance. At the battle of Panipat in 1556, the animals were an important means of intimidating the enemy. An especially strong animal could also have an iron plate fixed to its forehead and heavy chains hung from its tusks, so that it could be used as a battering ram.

When the material used for the elephants 'clothing' was worn out, it was given to the handlers so that they could make something useful with it.

There were immense displays of pomp, especially at state receptions – when Akbar's relative

Mirza Sulayman arrived in Fatehpur Sikri from Badakhshan, Bada'uni reported that Akbar had no fewer than 5,000 elephants on display. On other occasions, a lavishly adorned cheetah would be placed upon every other equally richly decorated elephant. Their foreheads, tusks and ears were occasionally painted red.

If conquered princes or foreign ambassadors brought elephants as gifts, the animals were usually renamed, for example, when Akbar was in Ajmer, near the mausoleum of Mu'inuddin Chishti, he changed the name of an elephant called *Ram Prasad*, 'Gracious Gift from Rama', to *Pir Prasad*, 'Pleasing Present from Pir'. People were fond of giving appealing names to these noble animals, for example *Nainsukh*, 'Pleasing to the Eye', *Subhdam*, 'Morning Breeze', *Faujsangar*, 'Ruler's Jewel', *Bakhtbuland*, 'Great Luck' (the latter animal, whose estimated value was 80,000 rupees, was said to have been led to the court at *Nauruz* in a golden bridle and chains).[9]

Akbar was famous, or notorious, for fearlessly riding the wildest of elephants. One oft-repeated story concerned an incident when the nineteen-year-old was riding his *mast* elephant Hawa'i, and chased another elephant on to a pontoon bridge over the Jumna River. Many painters, among them Basawan, portrayed this dramatic scene; the subsequent relief of the onlookers, their hands raised in prayer, can very well be imagined! Even in later years, Akbar did not allow the fears of his household to deprive him of such pleasures. Abu'l Fazl reported that the ruler regarded such foolhardy undertakings as opportunities for a judgment by God.[10]

The ruler was, however, more frequently seen riding upon a richly adorned state elephant, with a towering structure a bit like an elegant beach basket fastened on its back, which, according to the chronicler, could serve as a 'mobile dormitory'.

Behind the ruler and somewhat lower down sat a servant with a flywhisk. An elephant decked out in this way was kept always at the ready. When the ruler made use of his elephants, the stable servants received an addition to their salaries.

On festive occasions, the animals were covered with ornaments, and a small square platform might be fastened to their backs as a stage for singers and musicians of all kinds to entertain the spectators.[11]

In cases of emergency, the animals were transported into battle on large barges, for instance around 1574 en route to Jaunpur. These barges were themselves sometimes shaped like the front of an elephant.[12] However, this was not an easy method of transport, and there was always the risk that an elephant might 'fall into the whirlpool of annihilation'.

Akbar took good care of his elephants, but his son Jahangir clearly doted on his – he noted in his diary that it pained him that the animals had to be washed in cold water in the winter, so he ordered his servants to heat the bathwater, which was kept in large leather bags near the animals, before washing them!

Elephant fights were one of the ruler's favourite entertainments. The men watched from a distance as the mighty animals fought one another on the bank of the Ravi beneath the fortress of Lahore, and the ladies of the royal household watched the fight from their quarters. Deciding on the outcome of an elephant fight was the prerogative of the emperor, and a dispute over an elephant fight was said to have brought Akbar's life to a speedy conclusion.

Elephants also served as executioners, as being trampled to death by them was a commonly used form of execution.[13]

The emperor's love of elephants was not restricted to real ones, as enormous statues of the animals were erected next to many public buildings. In Akbar's time, two poets were richly rewarded for composing lengthy poems in Persian about 'the waves of the ocean of calamity', in other words, the fearsome elephants. These were Haydari Tabrizi, who died in 1593, who received 2,000 rupees and a horse as a reward for his ode, and the versatile, humourous Qasim-i Kahi (died 1580), who received no less than 500 rupees for a poem with every possible meaning of the rhyming word *fil*, 'elephant', running through it (including 'bishop' in chess) – however, he was not given an actual elephant, although these were often granted as a reward.[14] The fine arts made frequent use of elephants – ornamental ivory carvings were very popular, and the calligraphers of the later Mughal period created the figure of an elephant from the text of *Sura* 105 of the Qur'an.

One noteworthy speciality of Mughal artists was combining a variety of pictures – such as of humans, animals, birds or demons – to form composite elephants.[15]

The horses in the royal stables also played an important role: Akbar was said to own 12,000 steeds. The best horses bred in India came from Kutch, as they had some Arab blood, but best of all were those from Iraq, the thoroughbred Arabians. Strong, swift post horses came from the Turcoman steppe – in fact, more than 75 percent of Mughal horses were imported, by far the majority from Central Asia. They were given romantic names such as *Sumer*, 'Gold Colour', *La'l-i bi-baha*, 'Priceless Rubies', *Sabaraftar*, 'Runs Like Zephyr', *Khushkharam*, 'Prancing Beautifully', and *Padishahpasand*, 'Pleasing to the Ruler'.

In Akbar's time there a special area of the capital city for the horse dealers, so that they could be watched to ensure that they treated the animals well. The best dealers were awarded the honorary title *Tijarat Khan*, 'Sir Dealer'. Akbar's private stables were supposed to have six stalls with forty horses in each. Like the elephants, these were fed according to their worth, and their feed included everything from cooked peas, grass or hay and legumes, to sugar, *ghee*, molasses and corn. Just as there was the 'Chief' among the imperial elephants, Jahangir refers to a *dun*, which was supreme among his horses.

A veterinary doctor tended to the health of the animals - handbooks of equine medicine were in existence by the early middle ages in Europe and the Islamic world. The Wellcome Museum in London has an abundantly illustrated manuscript from the seventeenth century on horses and equine medicine, which was translated from Sanskrit and Arabic sources into Persian. There was a superintendent in charge of each stall, and a finance official responsible for payment and punishment. The Master of the Imperial Horses, *atbegi*, was one of the highest nobles. The condition of the animals was inspected regularly. There was a whole class of servants who were responsible for the saddles and bridles (*akhtaji*), and an *ahadi* to measure the speed of the horses. Horse races were held from time to time, with young Rajputs as jockeys. Palfreys were also among the valuable breeds. There were lowly stable boys whose job it was to muck out the stalls. Just how valuable the horses were can be seen from the fact that *sipand*, wild rue, was burned at the entrance to the stables to ward off the evil eye.

Every six months the horses were given new tack, which was allocated according to the value of each animal, as was the case of the elephants. Each one had its own saddlecloth of padded chintz as well as a *yalpust*, a mane covering, which was flocked on festive occasions. Particularly noble horses sometimes wore ornamental headgear. Their festive caparisons were often embroidered with gold, or made of embroidered leather. The horses sometimes had bell-shaped metal rings placed around their fetlocks, and their legs, even their whole lower bodies, might be hennaed. In battle, the horses, at least the leader, wore chamfrons and harnesses, as can be seen in many miniatures, particularly in the *Baburnama*.

On arrival in the stable, a new horse had its price branded on its left cheek. The cavalry *mansabdar*s also had to brand their horses to prevent any deception. As the climate in Bengal was so unhealthy for horses, the cavalry stationed there received a higher salary to enable them take good care of their animals, which represented the bulk of their wealth.

Each of the imperial princes had his own stable, and two personal horses as well as three courier horses were always at their disposal. It is not known whether it is at all significant that a series of paintings depict the ruler or a prince mounted on a piebald horse, or in a few cases on a dapple grey.

Not only high-bred horses were used; pack ponies and mules were used to carry pack saddles and bells, and they were provided with a saddle cloth and a feed bag. Their standard equipment also included washing and grooming implements.

Mules were often imported from Iraq and Persia, then also from the north of Rawalpindi, and some which had been bred in the Shiwalik mountains, near Islamabad today.

Camels especially trained for riding were of course also kept, the best specimens coming from Sind, especially the Thatta region. They were often used for the transport of heavy goods such as logs of wood. Sometimes two-humped Bactrian camels were also used for this purpose.

Riding camels, like other riding animals, were heavily ornamented. Their girths and breast bands were set with shells or metal bells, and their caparisons were made of fine, colourful material – no fabric or jewellery was too valuable for the best

camels. The animals were groomed with pumice stone and rubbed with sesame oil, sometimes also with buttermilk. Their saddles and other tack were replaced every three years.

Rulers were just as fond of camel fights as of elephant fights. The most vivid known depiction from the Mughal era of a camel fight[16] is a miniature by the elderly ʿAbduʾs Samad, which shows two camels going for each other, foaming at the mouth and with their coats streaked with dust; their humps are covered with colourfully embroidered cloth, and the two grooms are holding onto fine cords attached to the forelegs of the animals.

Jahangir once tried camel milk and found that it did not taste too bad. However, usually the Mughals drank the milk of cows and buffalos.

Buffalos were often used to carry burdens and haul heavy loads. Miniatures depict them with perfectly formed half-moon shaped horns, carrying heavy burdens, especially gun carriages. Sometimes they are shown laden with building materials and firewood, or else patiently turning the winch at a well, perhaps harnessed together with a mule.

Four of the best class of buffalo were placed under the care of one man, and they were fed with, among other things, wheat flour, molasses and grain. As well as the beautiful, mostly silver-grey buffalos, which were always popular subjects for painters, there are also pictures of black and white speckled cows, usually in idyllic settings. One picture by Basawan of a cow with her suckling calf in an idealised landscape resembles a European genre painting.[17] Just as today, milk and dairy products (yoghurt, *lassi* (buttermilk), butter and *ghee*) were highly prized. Buffalo fights were another popular court entertainment, and there are some very realistic paintings of these dangerous combats.[18]

A Tibetan yak was once presented to the court as a gift, but the poor animal soon expired in the heat of India. However, Jahangir was delighted that Nadir az-zaman had already painted the animal's portrait. (Exactly the same thing once happened in the case of a Tibetan Musk Deer.)[19]

Cheetahs were among the 'domestic' animals kept by Akbar and his successors and had become thoroughly acclimatised, especially in Gujarat. These animals, roughly the size of a leopard, golden in colour with black spots, and extremely slender, were caught in the jungle, usually in pits, and then transported blindfold, in wicker-covered carts, to the stables for training. Their training usually lasted around three months; however, as Abu'l Fazl relates with admiration, thanks to Akbar's humane and skilful handling, this could be reduced to eighteen days, as the emperor himself helped to train the animals within the palace.[20] Akbar was said to have kept no fewer than a thousand cheetahs, which, however, never mated, Jahangir recorded. Two hundred keepers looked after the animals

According to early Persian historical sources, cheetahs lived on cheese[21] – if so, perhaps the animals were put on this diet to keep them hungry and all the more effective as hunters. But according to Abu'l Fazl, the best class of cheetahs were fed five *ser* (around 4.5 kg) of meat a day, and the eighth and lowest group received 2.75 *ser*.

The cheetah would be blindfolded, usually in red, on the way to a hunt, just as falcons have hoods put over their heads. The elegant creature was covered with a colourful blanket, sometimes of brocade, and transported in a light two-wheeled cart to the hunting grounds, where it was released. Sometimes the cheetah sat sideways behind the rider on the back of his horse; however, an especially valuable animal would be carried in a kind of sedan chair between two horses. As soon as they sighted the gazelles or other game,

the blindfold was taken off the cheetah, which then sprang after the animal with mighty leaps, which Qasim-i Kahi at Akbar's court described in the following verse:

> When chasing a gazelle, the whole body of
> the king's cheetah
> Turns into eyes, the better to see it.[22]

In other words, its black spots appeared to have turned into eyes. During one hunt, when one of these cheetahs managed to catch a gazelle which seemed to be out of reach by making an incredible leap, Akbar was so delighted that he 'raised the rank of the cheetah and made him the leader of the cheetahs, and he commanded that a drum should be beaten in front of this cheetah', as was the custom with high officials.

One wonders what sort of expression would have been on the face of this recently dubbed Chief Cheetah on this occasion – perhaps it was beaming with pride, like the paternal cheetah in a picture by Basawan, which is gazing at its mate and their four tiny playful cubs with the contentment of a satisfied tomcat.[23]

Light, swift greyhounds were also used for hunting, as can be seen in many pictures, especially by the painter Manohar, who depicts them lying placidly at the feet of the ruler or the princes. Bloodhounds were introduced by the Portuguese, and Jahangir requested Sir Thomas Roe to procure a number of different breeds of dog for him in England. Clearly, there was a complete menagerie at court.

Ram fights were also held, primarily between strong longhaired rams. Surely no one who witnessed these animals butting each other, like two tanks ramming into each other, would be able to derive much enjoyment from this sport – nor, indeed, from any of the other animal fights?[24] The

82. A hunting cheetah, *c.* 1610, tinted drawing with gold, album leaf.

princes also pitted different species of animals in fights against each other, for instance a tiger and a buffalo, and Jahangir describes with some amusement that on one such occasion a tiger sprang at a *yogi*, not aggressively, but 'as if the poor man were its mate . . .'.

Even gazelles, or long-horned antelopes, were used in animal fights. Akbar once sustained an injury to his scrotum when he was gored by the sharp horn of an animal, and the doctors had great difficulty healing him.

Gazelles were popular pets in the palace, as can be seen from the story about the memorial built by Jahangir to his dearly beloved gazelle, 'the alpha female among the special gazelles'. The memorial was a small fort-like edifice called

the Hiran Minar. It was set in an artificial lake in Shaykhupura, about 30 kilometres from Lahore, with a pavilion, where musical evening entertainments were held. The emperor also had a gravestone constructed for her in the shape of an antelope, which unfortunately is no longer in existence.

Jahangir had a large number of captured gazelles brought to Fatehpur, where they were released; eighty-four of them were fitted with silver nose rings. He sometimes had prayer mats made for pious Sufis from the pelts of gazelles which had been killed during hunts.

Painters liked to capture these graceful animals in motion; the Berlin Museum of Islamic Art has a portrait of a colourful gazelle against a rosy background, which puts one in mind of late afternoons near Hiran Minar.[25]

There were other animals surrounding the ruler and his women. Abu'l Fazl does not list any cats in his inventory of domestic animals, but there are numerous pictures of long haired, flat-nosed Persian cats – mostly in scenes of the harem, or in the company of eminent scholars and devout men, for 'the love of cats is an article of faith'. However, there was one unfortunate incident when an imperial cat managed to catch a hunting falcon . . .

Doves were particularly popular in the palace. Bets were placed on races, and people also enjoyed their acrobatics, which Akbar compared to the ecstatic whirling of dervishes. The ruler named the doves' dances ʿishqbazi, 'love play', and he himself bred especially beautifully coloured ones, of which there were said to be more then 20,000 at court.[26] Gifts of valuable doves are mentioned in court correspondence, and there are many pictures of these inimitably elegant birds. Jahangir had them trained as mail carriers during his stay in Mandu, when he needed to be able to communicate rapidly with his headquarters in Burhanpur.

Humayun, three generations earlier, had kept a white cockerel, which he fed on raisins. The animal lived in one of the rooms where porcelains were stored, and according to Aftabji, it used to wake the servants up for their morning prayers.

Apparently there were also other birds in the palace, as evidenced by luxurious birdcages. An amazing amount of effort and artistry went into the construction of these cages, some of which were made of ivory, with geometrical and floral patterns.[27] The admiration of the prince and his artists for the beauty of birds can also be seen in the wonderful portraits of them by the master painters at Jahangir's court. Peacocks, the birds of the Hindu goddess Saraswati, were regarded as typical 'Indian' birds. Never have they been more beautifully or luminously portrayed than in Mansur's picture of a pair of peacocks. Akbar once issued a decree forbidding the killing of peacocks.[28]

During his last visit to Kashmir, Jahangir had a so-called *huma* bird brought to him, and carried out an experiment to see if it was true that they fed on bones, as legend had it. Splinters of bone were indeed found in its stomach, and the noble creature, 'which would harm no living thing', was rightly admired.

Jahangir had an insatiable interest in natural history, and an immense love of painting. He had a picture painted of every interesting animal he encountered and every strange plant he saw. He was once shown a strange animal which looked as if it had been painted with stripes. This was a zebra,[29] which he later gave to Shah ʿAbbas of Iran as an extremely valuable gift. The enormous turkey, a species which had recently been introduced via Goa into Islamic India, was also an extremely impressive bird, and its bright red throat and comb must surely have delighted all the painters![30] Jahangir carried out experiments, for instance successfully crossing a cheetah with a tiger. He was delighted to be able to report on his successful attempt to mate a markhor (a spiral-horned goat) with a barbary goat, which produced some charming kids. They also produced pheasants, placing their eggs under domestic hens for hatching. He found the mating habits of sarus cranes very interesting, and described them in great detail in the *Tuzuk*.

Perhaps the most beautiful of all the Mughal animal paintings is an autumnal landscape in Kashmir. Dozens of squirrels are shown gambolling in an enormous plane tree with golden autumn leaves; a hunter wearing a fur-brimmed cap is climbing stealthily up the trunk, unnoticed by the young creatures. One can almost hear the mute exchange between the two tiny baby squirrels in a hole in the tree trunk and their mother, who appears to be explaining something to her children about the wide world beyond the tree.[31]

In addition to their numerous depictions of animals, artists from the Mughal era also perfected the illustration of fairy tales and legends, whether of Noah's Ark,[32] or the animal empire of the prophet-king Solomon, who was able to speak the language of the birds, or the traditional animal fables of India. The Mughals displayed a genuine interest in the animal kingdom, as can be seen not only from Babur's observations and Jahangir's curiosity, but also from the fact that in Akbar's time, a classic mediaeval zoological handbook, the *Hayat al-hayawan al-kubra*, 'The Great Life of the Animals', by Damiri (died 1405), was translated from Arabic into Persian.

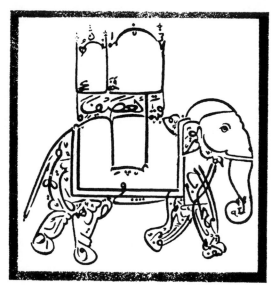

83. 'The Elephant', *Sura* 105, from the Qur'an, written calligraphically in the shape of an elephant.

84. 'An elderly official with an inscribed tablet', *c.* 1670, pigment and gold on paper.

# SEVEN

# The Life of a *Mirza*

Our knowledge of the daily routine of the rulers, their duties and also their pleasures, is quite comprehensive. In addition, two works in Persian describing the ideals of the nobility have fortuitously been preserved. Below the nobility was a relatively broad class of *mansabdars*, who held quite important offices at court and in the provinces, and there was also a notable middle class of theologians and scholars of all kinds. Then there were the merchants, some of whom were extremely wealthy, yet concealed their wealth in order to avoid being bled dry by taxes.

The *mirza*, as described in both of the seventeenth-century Persian *Mirzanama* by ᶜAziz Ahmad, was a nobleman who moved in court circles – in these works the title '*mirza*' is not applied exclusively to members of the Timurid household, but is also used in the sense of 'Sir' or 'Baron'.

What were the distinguishing qualities of a *mirza*? He had to come from a good family, and have sufficient wealth to be able to live appropriately. He ought also preferably to be a *mansabdar* of 1,000 *zat* or more, but if he had no *mansabdar*, then he had to be an accomplished merchant. His basic capital should consist of 10,000 *tuman*. However, the acquisition of wealth or personal advancement should not be his goals, for such desires were unbecoming to a *mirza*, whose worth was not measured by the fact that he adorned his turban with flowers, strolled through gardens, and wore a green turban (which is the insignia of the *sayyids*, the descendants of the Prophet); on the contrary, a genuine *mirza* had to concentrate on his education, to study ethics every day, also to know the classics, such as Saᶜdi's *Gulistan* and *Bustan*. He should recite the Qurʾan regularly, and also have some knowledge of the law, however he should not enter into discussions about such weighty problems as 'free will and predetermination'. He ought naturally to take an interest in poetry, which was *de rigueur* for all educated persons. It appears to have been considered important for him to know Persian, Arabic and at least some Hindi and a little Turkish. The *mirza* also had to be a good letter writer – there was no shortage of books containing specimen letters – and he should make no spelling mistakes. He was also supposed to write in *shikasta*, the 'broken' script, which was standard in seventeenth-century India and Iran, rather than *nastaᶜliq*, the classical script for Persian. However, he had to use the *naskh* script when making copies of the Qurʾan or other religious writings.

As a nobleman, he had to know the characteristics of a good horse and a good hunting bird, and also the different weapons, though he ought not to actually use a weapon, as the smell of gunpowder was so bad. However, he should be courageous in battle.

It was not seemly for him to haggle when making purchases.

The author also gives the useful recommendation that the *mirza* should be concise and to the point in speech; however, if someone else were talking to him at great length, he should act as if he were listening attentively, whilst thinking of something else . . .

If a *mirza* were to fall into financial difficulties, he should go to a Hindu moneylender, because the Hindus (who were traditionally the financial specialists in the subcontinent) did not charge such a high rate of interest, and were more polite than their Muslim counterparts.

The *mirza* should take an interest in music, yet not sing himself, for if he could not sing well, it would irritate his listeners. If he were to invite a small musical group to play, there should be a *qanun*, harp, *daʾira* and *tanbur* as well as a *rabab* and *vina* (as can be seen in many miniatures). The author of the *Mirzanama* also gives precise instructions as to the kinds of songs, harmonies and melodies to which the *mirza* should listen, as well as those which he should try to avoid.

If the *mirza* liked to drink wine, he should do so with care. His wine should be scented, and when drinking in company, he should have a bottle for himself, not only one bottle for everyone. Wine should ideally be avoided because it can cause stomach ache, and abstinence from tobacco is also recommended because of its unpleasant smell. Suitable times for drinking were also stipulated. The wine should be poured by a bearded attendant, not by a seductive youth (so that no unseemly incidents should ensue).

When the *mirza* held a party, he should use a gold embroidered tablecloth, fine drinking vessels and a decanter set with precious stones, if at all possible. Pistachio nuts should accompany the wine, but not kebabs, because these make the fingers oily. After the meal, the air should be perfumed. Finally, the guests should smoke a water pipe and listen to some music together.

For normal meals the *mirza* should use a colourful chintz tablecloth, if he does not possess a gold embroidered one, or alternatively a white linen one, which must always be freshly laundered. The servants, like the wine pourer, should not be too attractive. The crockery should preferably be all the same colour, ideally of Chinese porcelain or Mashhad pottery. Fruit juice should be offered before the meal, followed by seasoned rice for the main course. The author gives all kinds of suggestions as to what should be eaten, whilst stressing that the most important element of a successful meal is the cleanliness of the cook and the kitchen. He recommends eating only a little, and not to eat until one feels full. A *mirza* should definitely not eat with a glutton, or anyone lacking table manners, who passes wind frequently, for example.

Betel should be offered at the end of the meal.

In winter, aromatic substances such as incense or aloe wood should be added to the coal fire burning in a bowl. In summer, there should be lightly scented, cooling curtains of *khas* grass, plus partitions, light mats on the floor, and vases filled with seasonal flowers in the house.

The *mirza's* house (as is usually the case with the houses of the well-to-do in the orient) should have at least one garden, with a fountain (as people usually enjoyed sitting by a pond or a spring) surrounded by flower pots, so that guests could enjoy the plants and birdsong. However, if the

85. An embroidered
hunting coat, *c.* 1605–27,
silk on satin.

*mirza* had a *mansab* of less than 500-*zat*, then he had better not invite any guests at all.

When the *mirza* left his house, he should ideally do so in a sedan chair, for if he rode on an elephant or a horse, he risked the indignity of falling off. However, if it was raining, then an elephant was recommended, because one could get wet and dirty in a sedan chair. When going to see gardens and flowers, he should ideally ride a dappled horse; for he must of course have a variety of horses in his stable.

There were also precise instructions regarding hunting. When following a falcon, the *mirza* ought not to gallop as he might fall off his horse, or his turban might slip down. On the way back from the hunt, the *mirza* should sit under a tree by a brook to rest, and a white cloth should be laid out on the ground so that his clothes did not get dirty. Coffee should be drunk, then the spoils of the hunt should be divided up between his companions. Kebabs should be made from venison, whilst any game bird should be carried past all the soldiers so that they could all see it.

The *mirza* should be a lover of flowers; however only on very exceptional occasions should he place in his turban a rose he had picked himself.

When bathing, he should use one brush for his body and another for his feet, and his attendant should not have a beard (so that no hairs fall upon him).

The *mirza* should wear rings of rubies, emeralds, turquoise and carnelian, as each of these stones has its own characteristics; however rubies, according to the second *Mirzanama*, are to be preferred above all other stones.

In case of illness, the *mirza* should remunerate his doctor extremely well, for good health is far more important than wealth.

Anyone at all familiar with the way of life of the large, ancient families of the subcontinent will recognise a great deal in the foregoing descriptions, for the traditions remained very much alive until well into the twentieth century, and have only fairly recently begun to change.

86. 'Dara Shikoh attending a debate between Mian Mir and Mulla Shah', 1650–60, album leaf with gold.

# EIGHT

# Languages and Literature

Under the Mughals, all forms of literature flourished, from poetry and popular Sufi verses to learned prose and historiography. Sixteenth- and early seventeenth-century literature in the Persian language is relatively well-known, and the historical works of that period have long since been studied; however, there has been a tendency to overlook the fact there was literature in languages other than Persian, much of which was first written down in Akbar's time. Arabic has always played an important role, being the language of the Qurʾan, of theology and philosophy. Elegant prose and poetry were also composed in Arabic, not only in southern India, but also in the north. The Turkish language, or rather Chaghatay-Turkish, Babur's mother tongue, also played an important role. Until the early nineteenth century it was still spoken to some extent in the ruler's palace, and also by many of the nobility. In the sixteenth century, regional languages appeared for the first time in literature, then mystical writings, followed by secular ones. Sindhi, Punjabi and Pashto came into prominence during this time, and Bengali and Kashmiri, which had long been literary languages, are also noteworthy. Hindi – including the various dialects spoken in northern India, such as Braj and Purabi – played an important role, and,

thanks to the translation project initiated by Akbar and his great-grandson Dara Shikoh, Sanskrit also became an important literary language in the Muslim world. Finally, towards the end of Aurangzeb's era, Urdu became the quintessential literary language of Indian Muslims. What follows is a brief overview of all of these languages, in order to give some idea of the multiplicity of the literary life of the Mughals.

In general, poetical forms which had been developed in classical Arabic literature, and to an even greater extent those in Persian literature, were transposed into Perso-Turkic Urdu poetry during the Mughal era. They follow the same strict rules with regard to metre, and include the *ghazal* (lyric) form, which is a short lyrical poem with a single rhyme at the end of each line, usually expressing sacred or profane love. The first two half-verses rhyme, setting the tone, or the mood. Alternatively, it commences with a *qitʿa*, a 'bridge', which was popular in the case of descriptive and topical verses (prayers, chronograms, etc.). The *qasida* (ode), which had the same rhyming pattern but which was longer and also more strongly orchestrated, was usually employed in panegyrical poems, whether religious or profane. The *mathnawi* (narrative) is an epic or romantic poem in rhyming

229

couplets, which can run to thousands of lines; a fairly short *mathnawi*, which often commences with a plea for pardon, but which can be used to treat any theme, is called a *saqinama*. The *ruba'i* (quatrain) with the rhyming pattern *aaba*, was often used. Over time, the juxtaposition of other forms became popular, for instance a number of *ghazals* would be connected by means of interim verses, which either changed or remained the same strophic poem (*tarji'band, tarkib band*). This led to the development of poems with five- or six-line stanzas at most, each with its own rhyme, which could then be concluded by a line with a different rhyme. Verses with all kinds of themes were composed in this form, for instance *sarapa*, 'from head to foot', which were usually for descriptions of beauty; and *shahrashub*, 'to excite the city people', which might describe 'heart-rendingly' beautiful people, or else cruel ones; or it could deal with the themes of artisans and their work, or politics.

In the last lines of *ghazals* and *qasidas*, the poet would refer to himself by his *nom de plume*, which could either be given to him by his teacher, or might be derived from his father's occupation (*Hafiz*, 'he who knows the Qur'an by heart', *Urfi*, 'he whose father was a knight who rode out in defence of law and order', *urf*. Often, especially in the earlier periods, the names were of a highly elevated kind, such as *Fayzi*, 'touched by the grace of God'. However, over the course of the Mughal era, these became increasingly pessimistic and melancholy, such as *Bedil*, 'heartless, dull', *Bikas*, 'friendless, miserable'. Sometimes the entire history of a poet's family, or a chain of events, could be traced from these names: the poet *Gul*, 'Rose', named his pupil *Gulshan*, 'Rose Garden'; his pupil was *'Andalib*, 'Nightingale', and his son was called *Dard*, 'Pain' (as felt by the nightingale when deprived of the rose); and Dard's brother was called *Athar*, 'Trace, Effect'.

Poetry in regional languages followed the traditional forms of its place of origin. In Hindi and in early Sindhi, the two-line *doha* or *sorath* form was often used. In Pashto, the *tappa* or *landey* forms were often used, rhymed distichs of 9 + 13 syllables, which had been introduced from Persian. There were also hybrid forms, especially in Sind and in the Punjab: *siharfi*, 'thirty-letter poems', are a kind of 'Golden Alphabet'; *barahmasa*, 'twelve-month poems', express the longing of a lover for her beloved in a different way for each month of the year. Both types are found in varying long or short forms. Popular poetry, which was written down at a relatively late stage, was almost always intended to be sung, hence the frequent repetitions and the alliterations, of which singers are so fond.

ARABIC

Arabic has been the language of Islam from its very beginnings, and a vast number of works on theology and jurisprudence have been written in Arabic from the time Muslims first arrived on the subcontinent. *Hadith* literature – the sayings of the Prophet and traditions of his life – flourished, and India has remained a thriving centre for *hadith* studies. The same was true for Sufi works, and for the Arabic grammars used by the students at *madrasas*; the Arabic textbooks were often rhyming, and the students had to learn them by rote. The great works of al-Ghazali (died 1111), and the introduction to Sufi ethics, *Adab al-muridin*, by Abu Najib as-Suhrawardi (died 1165), were in circulation at the time. During the course of the fifteenth century, the writings of the great theosophist Ibn 'Arabi (died 1240), especially the *Fusus al-hikam*, 'Ring stones of words of wisdom' achieved great popularity in India. The most important Sufi work written in Mughal India was

'The Five Jewels' by Muhammad Ghauth Gwaliari, a Sufi primarily associated with Humayun. His complex work, which weaves together elements such as astrology, *kabbalah* and name invocations, had a great influence on popular Islam in India. There are still copies in existence today, in both Arabic and Persian.

Less influential albeit far more remarkable was the *Sawati al-ilham* by Akbar's poet laureate Fayzi (died 1595). This commentary on the Qurʾan is an immensely difficult work, because it is written in Arabic entirely without dots, which are normally essential to differentiate most of the consonants, which otherwise look exactly the same. If they are omitted, many verb forms cannot be distinguished, giving rise to innumerable possible misreadings of the text. Fayzi's commentary was dismissed as an 'utterly irrelevant work'. However, his purpose was to demonstrate his absolute mastery of the Arabic language, and, as he pointed out, the declaration of faith, *la ilaha illaʾ llah Muhammad rasul Allah,* also consists of nothing but undotted letters. Badaʾuni countered that Fayzi must have written the commentary whilst in a state of ritual impurity, and thereby committed a grave sin.[1]

Despite Akbar's attempts to limit the scope of the language of the Qurʾan, theologians continued to compose works in Arabic. In fact, the important *hadith* collection of ʿAli al-Muttaqi from Burhanpur, titled *Kanz al-ummal,* which remained in circulation for centuries, was firmly rooted in the Mughal tradition. A letter sent by Ahmad Sirhindi to the Mughal nobles was also partly written in Arabic. Furthermore, the writings of his contemporary ʿAbduʾl Hazz Dihlawi (died 1642) were written partly in Arabic and partly in Persian. Great works in Arabic started to appear once more in Aurangzeb's time, when the ruler began taking an interest in reviving traditional Islamic education, which was neither mystical nor syncretistic in orientation. The writings of Mulla Jiwan (died 1717) are relevant in this connection. Jiwan and the ruler read together Ghazzali's groundbreaking work *Ihyaʾ ʿulum ad-din,* 'Revivification of the Sciences of Religion'. His contemporary Muhibbullah Bihari (died 1707), the Chief *Qadi,* was a distinguished writer in Arabic, whose *Musallam ath-thubut* (Chronogram AH 1109 = 1697) is considered to be one of the most important of the later textbooks on *usul al-fiqh,* the 'laws of jurisprudence', whilst his *Sullam al-ʿulum,* 'Scientific Manual', is regarded as the best work on logic ever written in India. Also noteworthy is the great collection of legal precedents, *Fatawa-yi ʿalamgiri,* which was compiled for Aurangzeb, and which provides an important insight into Muslim law at the end of the seventeenth century. Many new Arabic commentaries on the Qurʾan, and works on Qurʾanic recitation, appeared in Aurangzeb's time, also Arabic prayer books, as well as an index to the Qurʾan, *Nujum al-furqan* (1691).[2]

Arabic theological literature flourished in the eighteenth century. The pre-eminent work from this period was the *Hujjat Allah al-baligha,* 'Conclusive Proof of the Eloquence of God', by Shah Waliullah of Delhi (1703-1762), which dealt with Islamic problems and possible solutions. In spite of its idiosyncratic Arabic style, the book is still studied at al-Azhar University in Cairo. Waliullah's numerous Arabic and Persian works draw on his great breadth of knowledge, which was derived both from his family traditions (his father was among the people who worked on the *Fatawa-yi ʿalamgiri*) and also his experiences in Mecca at the very time when new 'fundamentalist' movements were arising there. In his Arabic poems in praise of the Prophet, he made use of the full range of classical Arabic vocabulary to great effect, as did some of his learned contemporaries. One of these, ʿAbduʾl ʿAziz Bilgrami (died 1726), who worked as an official in various provinces of the Mughal empire, wrote eulogies of Muhammad, whilst ᶜAbduᵓl ᶜAziz's nephew, Azad Bilgrami (died 1785 in Aurangabad) composed a work which merits careful study, titled *Subhat al-marjan*, 'The Coral Rosary'. In this book he attempted to present India as the true homeland of the Prophet, to find connections between Arabic and Sanskrit poetry, and to show that many good Muslims, especially Sufis, came from India.

Like Shah Waliullah, Azad had made a pilgrimage to Mecca. Somewhat later, Sayyid Murtaza, a pupil of Shah Waliullah's also went to Mecca. Sayyid Murtaza was later called az-Zabidi after the city of Zabid in the Yemen, which for centuries had served as a halting place for Indian pilgrims, and was also an important centre for theologians and scholars in its own right. Sayyid Murtaza, whose Indian origins are often overlooked, was the author of the great Arabic dictionary, *Taj al-ᶜarus*, 'The Bride's Crown', and also an indispensable ten-volume commentary on Ghazzali's *Ihyaᵓ ᶜulum ad-din*. He never returned to India, but died in Cairo in 1798.

The relationship between the Deccan states, especially Golconda, and the Arabic world culminated in a gathering of Arabic poets and writers at the court of Golconda in the seventeenth century. As Delhi declined with the gradual weakening of the empire towards the end of the eighteenth century, the court of Awadh became a cultural centre. During this period, an Arab aesthete staying at Awadh by the name of Ahmad ibn Muhammad al-Yamani ash-Shirwani composed a work in Arabic in the style of the famous 'Maqamat of al-Hariri', the acme of classical Arabic, which has been extensively imitated on the subcontinent ever since the medieval ages, and studied by every advanced student in India. His *Manaqib al-haydariyya*, dedicated to the ruler Ghaziuddin Haydar of Lucknow, was the first work to be printed on an Arabic printing press with moveable type, which had been imported by the ruler. The importance of this work was twofold: it was evidence of Muslim India's continuing interest in Arabic, and it was also the product of the first printing press on the subcontinent with Arabic type – not, however, of the first printing press, since the Portuguese had brought one to Goa during Akbar's time.

Every Muslim is supposed to have at least a rudimentary knowledge of Arabic, and so it is no wonder that Arabic verses, flowery phrases, clauses, even whole sentences, should appear in popular poetry in regional languages, as well as Persian and Urdu literature. When Pakistan was founded, it was even suggested that Arabic should be the national language of the new Islamic state.

## TURKISH

The role of Turkish not only in the literature, but also in the life of the Mughals, is especially interesting. For not only did Babur write his autobiography in Chaghatay-Turkish, but the language of his Central Asian forefathers remained in use for an astonishingly long time. Turkish had been spoken in India long before the Mughal era, in fact numerous leading families, especially Sufis, had their roots in Central Asia, primarily the region known today as Uzbekistan; for example the Sayyids, who came from Bukhara, and still today play an important role in the politics of the subcontinent. Even though such families only spoke their mother tongue at home, and used Persian or Arabic at other times, the substratum of the language remained. Amir Khusrau (died 1325) made the following lament in a Persian verse:

*zaban-i yar-i man turki u man turki namidanam . . .*

The tongue of my friend is *Turkish*,
And I know no *Turkish* –

Amir Khusrau's own father was of Turkish extraction, and the great mystical guru in Delhi, Nizamuddin Auliya, affectionately called the poet *Turki Allah*, 'God's Turk'. However, the word Turk was traditionally also used to mean a beautiful, fair-complexioned, lively, sometimes also cruel beloved, compared to which the miserable lover felt himself to be but a lowly, humble, swarthy Hindu slave. The literary counterpoint *turk-hindu*, which can also mean 'white-black', was in use for centuries in Persian literature, and had had its counterpart in reality on the subcontinent since the days of the Sultan Mahmud of Ghazna. Mahmud was of Turkic lineage, and he invaded India no fewer than seventeen times between 999 and 1030. As a result the Turks were established as a military force, and they also formed the ruling class, under whose auspices the theologians and lawyers thenceforth had to work.

At the time when Babur laid the foundation for the rule of the 'House of Timur' in India by his victory at Panipat in 1526, the use of Turkic terms was widespread. Military and hunting jargon was Turkish, as were the terms for family relationships and titles. Turkish words also gradually infiltrated the Hindustani language, so that even the universally accepted name for it, *Urdu*, is itself a Turkish word, meaning the language of the *urdu-yi mu<sup>c</sup>alla*, the 'illustrious army encampment' (the English word 'horde' is derived from the word *ordu*, meaning army encampment).

Many Turkish words designating family relationships, such as *apa*, 'elder sister', *ata*, 'father', *koka*, 'foster brother', *yanga*, 'sister-in-law', also *beg*, *bey*, 'master / mister', and *khan*, 'Sir', and words derived from them, including the feminine forms *begum, khanum*, are still in use today. First names are often also Turkish, including Babur, meaning 'tiger', and that of the founder of the line, Timur, from *temur*, 'Iron', and also conjunctions such as *tanriberdi*, 'God given', or good omens such as *qutlugh*, 'fortunate'.

There are many Turkish names for animals: *qaraquyruq*, 'black-tailed gazelle', *turna*, 'crane', *tuygan*, 'white falcon', *qatir*, mule, among others. When people went to the *ilaq*, the 'summer meadow', they might be accompanied by a *kumukju*, an 'assistant', and certainly a *qushbegi*, 'Chief Falconer'.

The clothing and equipment of the early Mughal period displayed many Turkish features. The first generation of Mughal women can be recognised in miniatures from their high Turkish hats. Princes and officials in Mughal India wound their turbans fairly flat on their heads, a style which originated in Central Asia, whereas scholars wore large turbans. Gifts were *toquz*, 'nine', because they were given out nine at a time, according to the Turkish custom.

Even before the Mughal era, the word *turk* was used to mean 'Muslim' in India, as is especially evident in the literature of its regional languages.

Chaghatay developed into the main language of high literature among Babur's Central Asian ancestors. The court in Herat of Babur's relative Sultan Husayn Bayqara (died 1506), was a centre for Chaghatay literature, which was cultivated by the prince himself as well as by his minister and friend Mir <sup>c</sup>Alishir Nava<sup>ɔ</sup>i. The *Khamsa*, 'Quintet', by Nawa<sup>ɔ</sup>i, which is an imitation of Nizami's 'Five Romances', is in Turkish. This work, which the emperor Jahangir greatly admired, was illustrated with miniatures by the greatest masters of the Mughal court, such as Govardhan and Manohar. The greatest calligraphers at the court of Herat made copies of these works, which the Mughals were proud to have in their possession. A copy of the Turkish *Divan* by Sultan Husayn Bayqara, in the

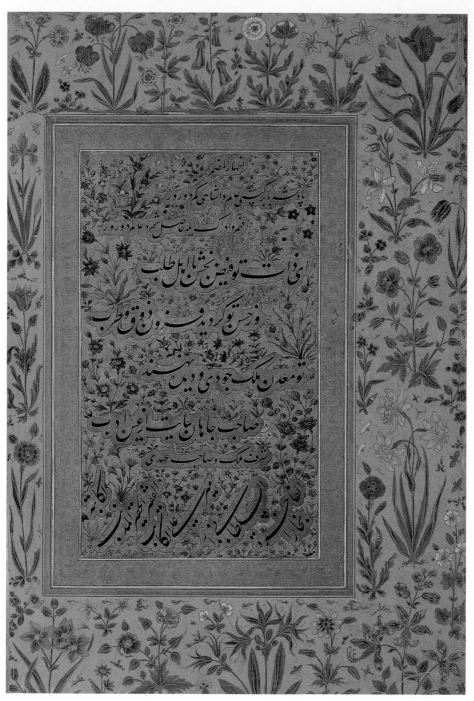

87. Dowlat, border and floral illuminations to a piece of remounted calligraphy by Mir ᶜAli of verses in Persian and Turkish, *c.* 1520s, gouache on paper.

calligraphy of the Herat master, Sultan ᶜAli Meshedi, was kept in Shah Jahan's library, later to be inherited by Dara Shikoh.[1]

At the beginning of the sixteenth century, the Iranian ruler, Shah Ismaᶜil, a Safawid, and the Mamluk Sultan of Egypt, Qansuh al-Ghauri, both composed poetry in Turkish, as did the Uzbek Shaybanids, who took over the Timurid Central Asian empire. Turkish verses have even been attributed to the spouse of Shaybani Khan, Mughal Khanum.[2]

It was therefore quite natural that Babur should be fluent in the language of his kin, and he wrote not only his vivid autobiography in Chaghatay, but also many poems, among them 52 *muᶜamma*, riddles – the leading specialist in riddles of the time, Shihabuddin Muᶜammaʾi, was his close friend. Furthermore, in his *Risala-i ᶜaruz*, the 'Treatise on Prosody', Babur employed the most varied types of Turkish poetical forms as well as those of classical Persian, thus providing the modern reader with an overview of Turkish verse forms, such as *tarkhani*, *qoshuq*, and the much loved *tuyugh*. Babur was the author of a discourse on the Hanafi legal system (which is used by all Turkic peoples), and even dared to compose his own version of the *Risala-yi walidiyya*, a theological work by the great Central Asian Naqshbandi master ᶜUbaydullah Ahrar (died 1490), in 243 lines of simple Turkish verse. He worked on this project in November 1529, in the hope of finding favour with God, so that he would be granted a full recovery from a stomach complaint.

Babur's son Humayun wrote in Persian; another son, Kamran Mirza (who was finally blinded and banished to Mecca because of his incessant political intrigues, and who died there in 1557), was an excellent poet in Turkish, and even his foster brothers were said to be poetically gifted. Kamran was married to the daughter of the Arghun prince, Husayn of Sind. Turkish was spoken at the Arghun court in Thatta, Sind, for the Arghuns originated from the Central Asian region of Afghanistan, as did the Tarkhans who succeeded them in Sind. A few anthologies were compiled at their court of the works of Fakhri Harawi, who wrote about poetic princes (*Raudat as-salatin*) and female poets (*Jawahir al-ajaʾib*). These anthologies demonstrate the popularity of Chaghatay in Sind during the early Mughal period. The Turkish language was particularly popular among the army, which was mostly made up of men from Turkish families. The military leader Bayram Khan composed an excellent *Diwan* in Turkish and Persian, 'and his verses are on every tongue', as Badaʾuni remarked.[3] It was Bayram's son, the *khankhanan* ᶜAbduʾr Rahim, who translated an early Turkish translation of Babur's memoirs into Persian. He also composed a few rather modest Turkish poems of his own.[4]

Abuʾl Fazl reported that Humayun spoke Turkish to one of his servants, and this was corroborated by his valet.[5] The language of their ancestors was kept alive at court, although interest in Turkish waned somewhat under Akbar, who was more drawn towards the Indian world. However, his son Jahangir stated with pride: 'Although I was raised in Hindustan, yet I am not ignorant of Turkish', and he completed a manuscript of Babur's memoirs in Turkish. William Handlin, an English merchant who went to India in 1610 and who could speak Turkish, was one of Jahangir's drinking companions for a time. He was apparently delighted to see one of his friends wearing a typical Central Asian turban.

Jahangir's granddaughter was also supposed to have been fluent in the language of her forefathers.

The ties between the Mughal empire and Ottoman Turkey meant that educated people of both empires took an interest in each other's literary traditions. Many Ottoman-Turkish commentaries were composed in Istanbul on the Persian poetry of Urfi, the leading poet during Akbar's time (died 1591). Furthermore, an Ottoman poet, Nef'i, compiled a *qasida* in honour of Jahangir, an additional testament to their mutual interest.

Although Akbar entrusted his son Murad to the Jesuits so that he could learn some Portuguese, he encouraged his grandson Khusrau to pursue Indian studies, whilst Khurram, who later became Shah Jahan, studied Turkish under Tatar Khan.[6] During the reign of Shah Jahan, a close friend of his who was in Iraq buying horses was able to make himself understood in Turkish with the Ottoman Sultan Murad IV.[7]

Turkish was important not only in Sind and Delhi, but also in the Deccan, where the Adilshahis of Bijapur, as well as the Qutbshahis of Golconda, prided themselves on their Turkish origins. However, Turkish was not a literary language for them, as far as can be seen.

In Delhi, the Sunni Turanis, who were of Turkish extraction, were increasingly coming into contact with the Iranian Shi'i majority faction. Perhaps for this reason, Aurangzeb, who had been brought up strictly Sunni, began to take a great interest in his Turkish heritage, and a series of Turkish grammars were completed at his instigation, as well as a *Lughatnama-i turki*, a Turkish dictionary, followed by a number of similar books. Renowned scholars then embarked on the task of compiling Turkish-Persian-Arabic-Hindi dictionaries – in some cases, even attempting to do so in verse! Many such works appeared during the course of the eighteenth century. Before the sack of Delhi by Nadir Shah's troops in 1739, the Mughal ruler Muhammad Shah and the conqueror, as well as the prime minister, Nizam ul-mulk, attempted to negotiate a treaty through the medium of the Turkish language.[8]

Urdu was at this time the pre-eminent literary language. However, many poets who wrote in Urdu also composed a few Turkish riddles, and even occasionally some quite good Turkish verses, for instance Sa'adat Yar Khan Rangin (died 1835), who was of Turkish descent.

There was one poet whose accomplishments went beyond just playing with language merely to demonstrate his own versatility. This was Azfari Gurgani,[9] a member of the Mughal household whose nickname, Gurgani, testifies to his descent from Timur Gurgan. He was born in 1758 in the Red Fort in Delhi, which was swarming with idle princes and lesser royals at that time. He fled from there and took up residence for a time at the court of Awadh in Lucknow, where he composed a *Lughat-i turki ya farhang-i azfari*, a Turkish lexicon which is now in the possession of the India Office in London. Afterwards, the restless prince continued on eastwards to Azimabad (Patna), where, at the request of a Hindu, he completed another work in Turkic, a grammar, which begins with the words *khaliq bari* in imitation of a didactic poem attributed to the Amir Khusrau.[10] Azfari finally settled in Madras, where he completed a work which established the grammatical rules of the Turkish language (*nizam-i turki*). His treatment of the poetic form in the *'Aruzzada*, 'Son of the Prosody', is especially interesting. He based this on Babur's treatise on prosody, which had been kept in the palace at Delhi since the time of Jahangir, and which had clearly been read by many a Mughal prince, either out of intellectual curiosity or perhaps merely boredom. Azfari earned his living in Madras by teaching Turkish. Khan 'Alam Bahadur Faruq, the ruler of Mysore (1792–1854) learned enough Turkish from him to be able to compose a few Turkish verses, as well as English ones.

Azfari, who died in 1819, left behind a riveting autobiography in Persian. He was the last Mughal prince with a thorough command of the language of his Central Asian ancestors. The task of deciphering his handwriting on a number of manuscripts kept in Madras still awaits the attentions of a patient and experienced Turkologist.

## SANSKRIT-HINDI

In addition to their perennially strong interest in the Turkish language, the Mughal household took an increasing interest in Hindi and the related new languages of India. After the first Hindi epics, for example *Lor Chanda*, by Maulana Da'ud, had been composed in the fourteenth century, the famous epic *Padmavat* was composed by Malik Muhammad Ja'isi, in Babur's time. Akbar not only loved Persian poetry but also enjoyed Hindi songs, such as the ones sung by Sufis at the mausoleum of Mu'inuddin Chishti in Ajmer. He is supposed to have been able to speak some Hindi, and Jahangir once commented that a certain Lal Kalawant had taught him everything he knew about Hindi. Historical sources refer to a number of Hindi poets who composed for the Mughal rulers, and Bada'uni relates that Burhanuddin, a Mahdawi from Kalpi, recited his beautiful mystical Hindi poetry in Chunar in 1559.

A year later, Surdas *mahakavi*, 'the great poet', paid a visit to Akbar, and whole families of Hindi poets prided themselves on being under the patronage of the Mughal ruler. One of these poets was proud of the fact that his grandfather had been under the patronage of Akbar, his father under Jahangir's, and he himself under Shah Jahan's patronage. The latter also had a distinguished poet laureate, *mahakaviray*, by the name of Sundardas, who wrote in Hindi, and was on a par with his colleagues who composed in Persian.[1]

The most famous Hindi poet from the time of Akbar and Jahangir was Tulsi Das (died 1623).[2] He was very close to the great personages at court – the Hindu general Man Singh as well as the *khankhanan* 'Abdu'r Rahim were good friends of his. The *khankhanan* is known to this day as the author of some especially beautiful and tender Hindi poems, which are still highly regarded. He was a patron not only of Persian poets, but also numerous Hindu ones, who sang verses in his praise.[3] Akbar's youngest son, Prince Danyal, loved Hindi poetry, and composed a few verses himself in this language. There was also a Muslim poetess, Taj, who is said to have composed Hindi poems. A number of amirs in the sixteenth and seventeenth centuries professed to love the Hindi language, among them the Sufi poet Khub Muhammed Chishti, who lived in Gujarat in Akbar's time, and was the author of a number of important writings in Gujarati and Hindi.

The interest in Hindi poetry lasted throughout the time of Shah Jahan. One poet, Maniram Kavi, sang to commemorate the newly constructed capital city of Shahjahanabad-Delhi. When another Hindi poet, Pandit Rasagangadhar, was named as Shah Jahan's *mahakaviray*, poet laureate, he received his weight in silver.[4]

Since Hindus played an important role as astrologers, a number of works on astrological themes were written in Hindi.

There was already a long-standing interest in Sanskrit writings – the *Amrtakunda* had long ago been transliterated into Arabic as *Bahr al-hayat*, 'Sea of Life'. However, it was during Akbar's time that the holy language of the Hindus came in for special attention from the government, and a number of original works in Sanskrit were produced by Hindu and Jain authors at the court. A Jain scholar, Samayasmidarjee appeared in Lahore in 1592 to present his Sanskrit work to Akbar, and received in recognition the title *upadhyaya*. Birbal, whose *nom de plume* was

Brahman, was an entertainer who was elevated to the status of *raja* at Akbar's court, and honoured with the title *kaviray*. He became a member of the emperor's innermost circle, the *nauratan*, the 'nine jewels'.

There are numerous instances of Jain poets who wrote in praise of Akbar – one of them did so in no fewer than 128 Sanskrit verses! A generation later, Rudra Kavi sang his songs of praise in Sanskrit for the *khankhanan* ᶜAbduʾr Rahim, as well as for Akbar's son Danyal and Jahangir's son Khurram, who later became Shah Jahan. He too was later honoured with poems of praise in Sanskrit composed by a Pandit from Benares, primarily in the hope of convincing the emperor to repeal the pilgrimage tax, which had always been a bone of contention with Hindus.

Astronomical, astrological, and medical works were composed in Sanskrit. Akbar received instruction in Hindu legal problems from Sanskrit scholars. The finance minister, Todar Mal, compiled an entire encyclopædia on Sanskrit, its literature and cultural role.

As time went on, there was increasing awareness of the necessity for a better knowledge of the grammar of the different languages spoken in the empire. In the mid-seventeenth century, an attempt was made to produce a grammar and a handbook of Turkish, and then a Sanskrit grammar was written under Aurangzeb.[5] A Persian-Arabic-Sanskrit Dictionary had already been produced in 1643, during the time of Shah Jahan, by a certain Vadangaraya, which concentrated on astronomical terminology.

The *Amrtakunda* was translated quite early on into Bengali, and there was another translation in the possession of the followers of the great Sufi Muhammad Ghauth Gwaliari. A certain Nizam Panipati, assisted by two Pandits, completed an abridged translation of the *Yoga vasishta*, which he dedicated to the crown prince Salim (Jahangir). There is a copy of this work, illustrated with depictions of various yoga postures, in the Chester Beatty Library.

Various translations of collections of Sanskrit fairy tales, which were translated in the sixteenth century, have long since reached the West from the Islamic world, for instance the *Pancatantra* and the *Hitopadesa*. The former appeared as *Mufarrih al-qulub*, 'The Heart's Electuary', and was dedicated to Humayun. The *Tutinama*, 'The Chronicle of the Parrot', became known in India in its Persian version, after Ziaʾuddin Nakhshabi (died 1350) had recited it in this language. This collection was especially popular in Akbar's time, as can be seen from manuscripts illustrated with miniatures.[6] It was also well received in Turkey and Europe. This was also the case with the fables of the *Panchatantra*, which had been translated into Arabic as early as the end of the eighth century, under the title *Kalila wa Dimna*. At Akbar's instigation, Abuʾl Fazl translated it into Persian under the title *Ayar-i danish*, as an earlier version, *Anwar-i suhayli*, 'The Lights of Canopus', which had been completed at the court of Husayn Bayqara of Herat, was too complicated for Akbar. There are many illustrated versions of this work in the Islamic world.

Akbar had still more translation projects in mind. First of all, he wanted his Islamic subjects to be acquainted with the Hindu epic, the *Mahabharata*, so he had that translated, under the title *Razmnama*. Badaʾuni, who took part in this project, resented having to work on translating a book 'full of irrelevant absurdities', the stories of which were like the dreams of a fevered mind, according to another disheartened collaborator. In all cases, learned Brahmans first translated the Sanskrit text into Persian or Hindi, then the Muslim 'translators' transposed it into elegant Persian.

88. 'Khujasta and her parrot', from the *Tutinama*, *c.* 1580, pigment and gold on paper.

89. 'Krishna and
Satyabhama arrive on
Garuda to kill the demon
Narakasura', leaf from a
dispersed manuscript of
the *Harivamsa* ('Genealogy
of Vishnu'), *c.* 1590,
gouache and gold on
paper.

Akbar reproached Bada'uni many times for his aversion to the Hindu fables and pantheon of 'deities', which were anathema to pious Muslims. Bada'uni was given more translations to work on, and the ruler even had him read Indian legends to him at night.

The translation of Valmiki's *Ramayana* elicited yet more protests from Bada'uni. The *Ramayana* was illustrated in the *khankhanan's* studio, and then presented to Akbar.[7]

These translations from the Sanskrit in fact inspired Akbar's artists to produce their finest works – the Hindu painters must certainly have enjoyed portraying the colourful legends of their own tradition as finely as possibly. The wonderful scene from the *Harivamsa*, of Krishna raising Mount Govardhan, is an inspired portrayal of the Indian legend, and the artists have managed to capture the ineffable religious mood inspired by this miracle.[8]

## PERSIAN

Since the conquest of the northwest of the subcontinent by Mahmud of Ghazna at the beginning of the eleventh century, Persian became the language of literature for Indian Muslims, and not long afterwards of administration as well. The first Persian poets appeared in the capital, Lahore, in the middle of the eleventh century. Hujwiri Jullabi, who is still honoured to this day in Lahore as Data Ganj, wrote in the Persian language about Sufism. The poetry of Masud ibn Sa'd-i Salman was recited in northwest India down through the centuries, as was that of Abu'l-Faraj Runi, although to a lesser extent. Mas'ud's poems about imprisonment became a model for the – all-too-frequent – poems written in gaol, which to this day appear in Indo-Muslim poetry, for instance by Faiz Ahmad Faiz.

90. Leaf from the *Farhang-i Jahangari* (Persian dictionary) of Jamal ud-din Husayn Inju, 1607–8.

Historical and literary works in prose as well as biographies of poets appeared during the twelfth and thirteenth centuries in northwest India. The greatest of all Persian language literary authors in the subcontinent was the versatile Amir Khusrau (1256–1325), who was the son of a Turkish father and an Indian mother. He was a disciple of the

91. 'The poet Saʿdi (c. 1184–1292) being given a drink', from Saʿdi's *Gulistan*, 1628–9, pigment and gold on paper.

great Chishti master of Delhi, Nizamuddin Auliya (died 1325). Khusrau distinguished himself not only by his soulful love poems, (although his style was sometimes disparaged as 'cosmetic'), he also wrote romances in traditional style (in imitation of the *Khamsa*, 'Five Romances', by Nizami) as well as lyric poems on contemporary events, thereby initiating a new genre. He also authored an interesting although difficult work on epistolography. As further testament to the breadth of his range – and contribution to Indo-Muslim culture – it is even maintained that if he did not actually invent the sitar, the most important stringed instrument in Indian music, then at the very least he improved it. He is also said to be the actual founder of the Hindustani musical tradition. The fact that the most famous Persian lyricist, Hafiz, copied Amir Khusrau's 'Khamsa', is further proof of his greatness.[1]

Amir Khusrau remained the pre-eminent model for all those lyricists of the following cen-turies who were not oriented towards the great Iranian masters, such as Hafiz and Saʿdi. There were a great many poets who wrote in Persian living in the subcontinent during the Mughal period; however, none of them achieved more than marginal renown.

More noteworthy are the many collections of letters, mostly compiled by Sufis, also the *malfuzat* genre, the sayings of learned Sufis and accounts of their daily lives.

When Babur founded the empire of 'Timur's family' in India in 1526, there were no great Persian language poets in the country. In addition to his Turkish verses, Babur composed some moderately good minor Persian verse himself, and the poems of his son Humayun and the writings of his daughter Gulbadan reveal that the Persian tradition was still alive.[2]

The situation changed with Humayun's flight to Iran and his subsequent return to India. It was a fortunate coincidence for Mughal culture, that this was the very time when Shah Tahmasp was in the throes of 'sincere repentance'. This led to the decline of panegyric and secular poetry in Iran, as there were now neither generous patrons nor appreciative audiences for lyrical and somewhat frivolous poetry – religious and ethical themes were the order of the day. However, Humayun presented an unanticipated opportunity for Persian writers, as he engaged a number of painters and poets during his sojourn in Kandahar and Kabul, setting in train a flow of migrant artists during the course of the following decades. Under Akbar, the Mughal empire became a land of plenty for writers of all kinds, and they came in droves – not only to the imperial court (even though Abu'l Fazl refers to the 'thousands of poets'), but also to work for the nobility, such as Akbar's court doctor and his chief military general, the *khankhanan* ʿAbduʾr Rahim. All of them surrounded themselves with poets, who were glad to sing the praises of their patrons. The *khankhanan* played a special role in this – during his lifetime no fewer than 104 Persian language poets were said to have come under his patronage.[3] India was a goldmine for poets from Iran, who were able to escape from penury and obscurity by moving there. Talib-i Amuli (died 1617) used the phrase 'black fortune' as a play on words, meaning 'misfortune', and also alluding to the traditional designation of Hindus as 'black', in the following verses:

No one brought a single Hindu to India –
Go, Talib, and leave your 'black luck' in Iran![4]

Among the first poets to move from Iran and be mentioned in historical sources was one Maulana Qasim-i Kahi, the dates of whose life are not quite certain. He became famous for his epigrams, in which he mingled colloquial expressions with classical imagery, thereby initiating a trend which subsequently developed in the so-called *sabk-i hindi*, or 'Indian style' of poetry.[5]

The reflection of your cheeks
Fills the mirror with roses –
So a parrot reflected in it
Would at once become a nightingale.

The verse plays on the traditional association of parrots with mirrors, which were supposed to help it learn how to speak. The love of nightingales for roses is one of the most common allusions in Persian–Turkish poetry, and the comparison between cheeks and roses recurs thousands of times in oriental poetry.

Akbar created the position of poet laureate, the first incumbent being Ghazali Meshedi, who was succeeded by Fayzi, the son of Mubarak.

In Hermann Ethé's work on 'Indian' Mughal poetry, he aptly described the 'Indian style' as being 'the Indian summer of Persian poetry', even though this expression is actually an allusion to the colourful autumnal New England woods, for the colours of poetry altered over time, becoming gradually stranger, seeming to reflect the melancholy autumn at the end of the Mughal period, or, as Percival Spear called it, 'the twilight of the Mughals'.

Imitations of classical works, whether epic, lyrical or panegyric poetry, became more and more common. Poets were admired for writing poetry with the same *zamin*, 'basis', namely metre and rhyme scheme, as well-known works. In this way they could show off their art to best effect, for there was no demand for the poetical expression of personal experience – what was wanted and expected was ever more refined expressions of existing forms and images, somewhat comparable to variations in European music. With the passage of time, the more nostalgic people became, the greater their interest in Persian classical works of the eleventh to fifteenth centuries, and the greater their desire for contemporary versions – it was the task of poets to find 'universal underlying themes' in them, according to Naziri (died 1612), one of the greatest Mughal poets.

Classical Persian poetry was renowned for its harmony. Images were supposed to be elegantly linked, and even though the uninitiated would find it difficult to discern the underlying structure of a verse, a Persian would grasp it immediately, realising why the poet had utilised a particular juxtaposition of imagery and words. The Indian style is less harmonious, and mixed metaphors and strange juxtapositions of words occur, not altogether pleasingly, to our taste at any rate. Consequently, the 'poetical' translation of an Indo-Persian poem can be more difficult to comprehend than a classical *ghazal*. Classical imagery was brought up to date with the introduction of contemporary objects, such as 'glasses', which were also beginning to appear in miniature pictures of the time – the first pictures portraying a painter or scholar wearing a pince-nez appeared in the second half of the sixteenth century, and not long afterwards poets such as Qasim-i Kahi and Fayzi started using this somewhat unpoetical word. For example, Kalim used the far-fetched metaphor of the sun and the moon as the glasses of the sky, by means of which the fine arabesques on the binding of a book by Shah Jahan could be studied.[6]

'Hourglass' became a modish word after Jahangir's court painter depicted him enthroned upon a giant hourglass. His grandson Aurangzeb mused:

> The world's sorrow is so vast –
> I have but one beating heart –
> How can the whole desert's sand
> Fit into just one hourglass?[7]

Other poets maintained that religion and worldly ambition were incompatible, for was not one half of the hourglass always empty? In a long poem about the terrible famine in the Deccan, Kalim even dared to write that the earth was like an hourglass, with one side emptied of the living, the other side full of the dead.

Seventeenth- and eighteenth-century poets also made allegorical use of other objects depicted in paintings.[8] Just as earlier Persian poets had spoken of the *shisha-i halabi*, the 'bottle' or 'glass of Aleppo' (Syria had earlier been famous for its fine glassware), poets now began referring to porcelain vessels. Celadon had long been imported from China, but poets, at least, were particularly fond of crackleware. Comparisons, whether innocent or tasteless, were made between the hairline cracks in the porcelain and the pigtails of Chinamen, and especially the hair of the Chinese emperor, often resulting in grotesque caricatures.

Velvet also appeared in poetry: when the nap of the finest velvet, such as is produced in Lahore and Gujarat, is lying quite flat, the Persian expression for this is 'it is napping', so that poets could write that the costly fabric, on hearing the world's cries of pain, wakes up from its nap, ruffles itself, and looks at the poet with its thousand terrified eyes.

Another favourite word of the poets (in early Urdu as well) is 'footprint' – the poet gets lost in his own footprints, or else he is trampled underfoot by people and events, until he is obliterated and vanishes.

The theme of ever-moving sand dunes deceiving travellers occurs during the same period – the whole world is seen as a desert in which no one can find a firm footing, or any reality.

The unpoetic word *abla*, 'pustule, foot blister', whilst rarely used by classical poets, recurs repeatedly – to the dismay of translators – in the Indian style of poetry, where the poet suffers constantly from blisters on his feet as he trudges on in his hopeless quest. Stars were even seen as pustules on the face of heaven!

Translators were even more dispirited by the word *khamyaza*, which really means 'yawn', but which in the Mughals' time signified ceaseless longing. It came to prominence for the first time in a poem by Urfi, who sings in his great hymn about the oneness of God: 'He pulled the bowstring into a "yawn" . . . '. In other words, the bowstring is pulled out as far as possible so that it has sufficient force to shoot the arrow. Yawning could also signify the endless longing of the shore to become one with the ocean.

Another favourite word of the Mughal poets was *shikast*, 'broken'. To be broken was seen as a cure for all suffering:

My heart, in the grip of folly,
Cannot without pain be opened –
For a lock that is rusted up
There's only one key: to be broken (Nasir ᶜAli)

It seems significant that this word came into ever more frequent usage as the Mughal empire itself was breaking up – not from without (its territory was in fact still expanding, especially after Aurangzeb's conquest of the Deccan), but from within, as the administration and social structures were slowly collapsing, which became all too evident immediately after the death of Aurangzeb.

Allegories were also based on the Sufi ideal of the breaking of the individual ego, and the precept that treasure can only be found by searching amongst the ruins. According to one pronouncement by God, which is not in the Qurʾan: 'I am with those whose hearts are broken on my account.'

At just the time as the word *shikast* was becoming a favourite of poets, a style of calligraphy was developing which is known as *shikasta*, 'broken'. This style, which is especially difficult to decipher, is a variant of the *nastaᶜliq* script, which became very popular from the seventeenth century on, and has long been used in Iran and India for writing Persian texts.

Another intriguing artistic device was the *habsi firangi*, the 'Frankish (i.e. European) prison', which was often used to symbolise the entire colourful material world. The European presence into the Indian subcontinent began in 1498 with the Portuguese, and became more and more conspicuous during the time of the Mughals with the subsequent arrival of the British and the Dutch. For poets, the colourful European pictures came to symbolise their imprisonment in the polychrome mundane world, which they contrasted with the monochrome realm of God.

Many poetical utterances of the time appear to us to be rather masochistic. Persian imagery is known for a certain cruelty (see Goethe's comments on this subject in his *Notes and Essays on the West-Eastern Divan*), but this element was intensified in the Indian style and in also adopted in Urdu poetry, which developed alongside Persian poetry, so that in the end roses, wounds, fire, blood and wine were inextricably linked.

In addition to strange imagery and unusual juxtapositions, there were also grammatical peculiarities, such as the use of plural infinitives. Tortuous literary language was often interwoven with colloquial speech, as in the case of Urdu also. Mirza Ghalib, the last classical author in Persian and Urdu, who died in Delhi twelve years after the collapse of the Mughal empire, was a master of such rhetorical formulations.

For European readers, many aspects of this poetry are unpleasing – the ever more refined use of particular themes and formulations really appeals only to connoisseurs. Just as Mughal craftsmen bored grains of rice, and adorned tiny precious stones with meaningful texts, and embroidered gossamer-fine woven fabric, the poets also produced astonishingly exacting little pieces of art, such as the chronogram. This ubiquitous art form was especially common in the Islamic world. Since every Arabic letter has a numerical equivalent (according to the old order of the letters of the Semitic alphabet), names and numbers could easily be linked: In the name Ahmad, for instance, a=1, h=8, m=40, d=4, totalling 53. (Since the short vowels in Arabic writing are not written down, they have no numerical significance.)

The art of chronograms enjoyed great popularity during the time of the Mughals. A skilful poet could express his true opinion on the character of a deceased contemporary, couched in a chronogram with multiple meanings. Following is one of a number which were composed on the death of the dog-loving poet laureate Fayzi: *che sagparasti murd* – 'What a dog worshipper has died!' (1004/1595).

Numerous chronograms were composed as Jahangir came to the throne, some of which were even engraved on coins. This one commemorated the enthronment of his grandfather Humayun: *khayr ul-muluk*, 'The best of kings' (937/1530). This one was composed on his death: *Humayun Padshah az bam uftad*, 'Emperor Humayun has fallen off the roof' (963/1556).[9]

The extensive Persian work *Haft qulzum*, 'The Seven Oceans', printed at the end of the Mughal era by King Ghaziuddin Haydar of Awadh, contains dozens of examples of this form of art. The first hemistich of one poem gives the date of Akbar's enthronment (AH 963/1556), whilst the second half verse gives the birth date of his son Salim Jahangir (AH 977/1569). One of the most artistic examples of this art form is the *qadisa* composed by Agha Tahmaspquli Wahmi on the occasion of Dara Shikoh's wedding (AH 1043/1633). Every hemistich of its nineteen verses gives the date in question, whilst every dotted letter of that hemistich also denotes the same date, as do all the undotted letters. The initial letter of each half verse is an acrostic, which also contains four chronograms, so that the poem consists of no fewer than eighty chronograms. It must have been this particular poem which earned the poet the rich reward he received from the ruler – he most certainly deserved it![10]

However, even this achievement was overshadowed by that of a poet who undertook 'the atrocious labour' (as Friedrich Rückert, the German translator, aptly described it) of commemorating the enthronement of Aurangzeb in the year AH 1068/1659 with a *qasida* of no fewer than 4512 chronograms, which people blithely tend to regard as just a normal poem.

Another form of literary art which was very popular at the Mughal court was the *mu*c*amma*, the riddle, whereby one had to hunt for first names concealed in the midst of an innocuous seeming line or observation, which required a great deal of ingenuity on the part of the poet. The art of *mu*c*amma* had been very popular in Timurid Iran, and it was also practiced in India at the beginning of the Mughal era. The most famous master of riddles, Shihabi, was a friend of Babur, and Babur himself composed a series of such riddles.[11] Special studies of this 'system of spinning webs', as Rückert aptly described it, were also dedicated to later rulers. Following is a simple (?) example:

My rival and the dog keep on playing together!
Open your eyes and study their repetitious
    game!

'Game' is *bazi*; the 'eyes' refer to the letter c*ayn*, which also means eye; this letter should be 'opened', i.e.

pronounced with a short *a*, and in the 'repetitious game' – *bazi bazi* – can be found *zi zi*: so the concealed name is ᶜ*azizi*...[12]

It is impossible to mention all of the great and not so great poets in Mughal India, even just in passing. At Akbar's court, there was rivalry between Fayzi, the brother of the court chronicler Abuʾl Fazl, and the young Shiraz poet Urfi, who distinguished himself with his splendid *qasidas*. His poetry is steeped in deep melancholy, which seems, to me at any rate, to be quite genuine, even though the Shirazi poet was considered by his contemporaries to be intolerably arrogant. Fayzi, whose poetry is perhaps somewhat flatter, was also a good poet. Nevertheless, Badaʾuni's view of him was extremely negative:

> He could construct the skeleton of a verse, but there was no marrow in the bones, and the salt of his poetry had absolutely no taste.

Over the course of centuries, comparisons have been made between Fayzi and Urfi. Ottoman Turks as well as Indian critics have wondered who was the greater poet of the two. In my opinion, Urfi's great *qasida* with repeated rhyming variations of *raftam*, 'I went', is one of the most moving poems in Indo-Persian literature:

> From my friend's gate – how can I describe
> The manner in which I went,
> How full of longing I came,
> Yet how embittered I went!
> How I beat my head on the wall
> In that narrow alleyway...
> In ecstatic intoxication I came
> In troubled silence I went.
> My faith, heart, reason, tongue
> All of these, to me please return,
> So that I can say: 'I had *something*

> As away from my friend I went!'
> A song on my open lips
> Of hope, so I came...despondent,
> Biting my teeth together
> In my heart – thus I went.
> In the morning I came, like shoots
> On the twigs of the rose bush at Lent...
> In the evening: like a choir mourning
> The dust of martyrs, I went...
> The winter night of my life
> Says to the twilight: 'Oh woe,
> Uselessly, vapidly chattering,
> To the end of my days, I go!'
> I am a withered shoot,
> Exposed to the autumn wind,
> The smile snarling on my lips,
> My head quite hidden, and gone...

Urfi died in 1591, when he was barely sixty-three years old, in Lahore, which was Akbar's residence at that time. His corpse was later transferred to Najaf, which was one of the holiest of Shiᶜite Islamic sites.

There was a constant stream of Persian poets arriving in India, and the *khankhanan* ᶜAbduʾr Rahim, who had been a patron of Urfi in his last decade, continued to welcome new poets into his sphere of influence. Among them was Naziri, who came from Nishapur. In his poetry, the Indian style became even more complex and cerebral than in Urfi's verses, which were passionate in spite of their rhetorical artistry. The following beautiful lines by Naziri are the most frequently quoted:

> The spring wind should be thanked,
> For ravishing your garden –
> For in your hand the rose
> Is fresher than on the twig.

After Naziri's return from his pilgrimage, which had been financed by the *khankhanan*, as had the pilgrimages of many other poets, he returned to Gujarat, where he is said to have worked as a goldsmith. Jahangir once extended an invitation to him, and rewarded him with a robe of honour, a horse, and a thousand rupees. The poet died one year later, in 1612.

Some time later, in 1617, Talib-i Amuli, from the Caspian Sea region, was named as the *malik ash-shu*ᶜ*ara*. For some time afterwards he lived with Mirza Ghazi Tarkhan in Sind. He went to the Mughal court in 1611, where he composed poems of praise, not only in honour of Jahangir, but also to his father-in-law Iᶜtimad ad-daula, and to Nur Jahan. One of his verses has almost become a byword, for he gave very moving expression to his discretion – the most important duty of a lover!

> I have sealed my lips so tight to keep in
>     speech -
> They'll become, one would think, the scar of
>     a wound.

A large number of comprehensive Persian dictionaries were compiled during this time.[13]

The Mughal ruler's beloved gardens were in Kashmir, and many poets spent at least part of each year there, especially during Shah Jahan's rule. One such poet, Qudsi, composed poems in praise of the Prophet Muhammad, which are still recited today. He also wrote beautiful aphorisms:

> It is no good to have one's wishes granted –
> The page once fully written is turned over.

Qudsi, who died in 1646, was a friend of the author of the most accessible poetry for modern readers, namely Abu Talib Kalim, who probably came from Hamadan, and who distinguished himself at the Mughal court with his descriptive verse, among other accomplishments. Thanks to his poetry, we know what his contemporaries might have been thinking as they gazed upon the Peacock Throne, or how a privileged courtier might have reacted to the sight of an album of miniatures and calligraphy, and what people thought of Kashmir, not only when the flowers were in bloom, but also during the muddy rainy season, when the beautiful country was far from being a paradise.

Abu Talib Kalim's most notable poem is the already mentioned lengthy one about the famine in the Deccan. However, there are also some individual verses within his longer poems which are especially impressive. (The tendency of compilers of anthologies and biographies of poets to quote only the best verses of a poem, and hardly ever the full poem, is quite understandable!) Kalim's concise, apt observations are just as moving to modern Western readers:

> Not only the laughing buds
> Are always fleeing from me;
> No, even the desert thorns
> Draw their pricks away from me.
> Their relationship to me
> Is like that of the beach to the sea:
> Always coming towards me,
> Then ever fleeing from me!

> Life's tragedy lasts but two days.
> I'll tell you what these two are for:
> *One* day, to attach the heart to this and that;
> *One* day, to detach it again.

At this time, the crown prince Dara Shikoh was trying to express his ideals in somewhat dry verses. He commences, in the spirit of the mystic Ibn Arabi, as well as the *Vedanta*, with the plea:

In the name of that which has no name
And which reveals itself, whatever you call it . . .

The prince compiled anthologies of everything he liked in the classical Sufi tradition – passages from the works of Rumi, Aynu'l Qudat-i Hamadani, Ruzbihan-i Baqli, and anything else which was accessible to the Mughal court. It is difficult to establish the extent to which his poetical endeavours were influenced by his friend Sarmad, a Judeo-Persian convert to Islam. Sarmad is famous for being the best quatrainist in Persian literature. He was an eccentric, who once ran naked through the streets, then wrote the following to prince Dara Shikoh about the incident:

The one who did bestow his royal splendour (*shikoh*)
Has given us a way out of our confusion.
He gave clothing to one whose lack he saw;
He gave the immaculate one a robe for his nakedness.

The poetical talent of the Mughal family was also evident in Dara's niece Zeb un-nisa, who wrote under the pen name *Makhfi*, 'Concealed'.

Another noteworthy Persian author at Dara Shikoh's court was the Hindu Chandra Bhan, whose prose work *Char chaman*, 'Four Gardens', describes events at court, in the provinces and in the cities, as well as giving his thoughts on morality, and information about himself.[14]

There were a few noteworthy poets – and numerous nondescript ones – writing in Persian at the end of the seventeenth century and beginning of the eighteenth. Nasir ᶜAli Sirhindi (died 1697) is considered to be rather abstruse in his choice of vocabulary and imagery. However, the most complicated poet of the time was undoubtedly Bedil (died 1721), who was born into a family of Turkish extraction in Patna. He was strongly drawn to philosophy and mysticism, and wrote great works of prose, which have yet to be examined in the West. He also produced a *Diwan*, a poem consisting of around one thousand pages of large format Kabul print, which displays the peculiarities as well as the advantages of the Indian style. The reader (not only Western!) has to wade through this dense lyrical poem to find the occasional exquisitely beautiful and moving verse. The verses of this Indian philosopher-poet never really found favour with the Persians (and some of his poems have only recently been published for the first time in Iran), yet he is the favourite poet of Central Asian Muslims. In Afghanistan there are numerous groups studying Bedil, and his poetry is much admired in Tajikistan. He is one of the poets whom Muhammad Iqbal cites as a formative influence in the development of his own craft.[15]

The judgement of many critics was probably influenced by the Persian poet Hazin, a refugee from Iran who lived in India during a time of great political upheaval, and who was totally dismissive of Nasir ᶜAli and Bedil, dismissing their work as ridiculous.

Aurangzeb's death in 1707 did not bring about the demise of Indo-Persian literature, although Urdu has gradually been gaining ascendancy in the north of the subcontinent. All Delhi *literati* have continued to use Persian. Even though most of the great mystics and poets, such as Mir Dard and Sauda Mir, wrote primarily in Urdu, they also produced a significant amount of work in Persian. Mir Dard (died 1785) wrote a mystical autobiography (*ᶜIlm ul-kitab*), as well as his spiritual diaries (*Chahar risala*, 'Four Treatises') in beautiful classical Persian. The reputation of the last master of the Mughal era, Mirza Ghalib (died 1869), is based on his slim volume of Urdu poetry, even though he wrote far more poetry in Persian. In the twentieth century, Muhammad Iqbal helped to maintain the balance between the two 'Islamic' literary languages.

## PASHTO

Akbar, with the help of Man Singh, had succeeded in putting down and almost annihilating a religious-political movement called the Raushaniyya, which was mostly made up of Yusufzay Pathans. They were called the 'way of darkness' by their opponents, and they appeared to present a great threat to the security of the northwestern border regions. However, they are very interesting for a quite different reason to literary historians, as Bayezid Ansari, the *pir-i raushan*, composed his literary work in his mother tongue, Pashto. His *Khayr ul-bayan*, 'The Best Exposition', which is partly written in Pashto, is the first written work to appear in this language.

Pashto, or Pakhto, is an Indo-Iranian language, which for centuries was the colloquial language of the Pashtuns (Pathans) in the eastern region of what is today Afghanistan, and the region bordering the Indian subcontinent. As early as the end of the thirteenth century, the Delhi poet Amir Khusrau remarked that there were Pashtun groups living around Multan whose speech sounded as if they were rolling pebbles in their mouths – a remark which the Pashtuns of today still find very offensive.

Many of the pre-Mughal ruling dynasties of India were Pashtuns, such as the Lodis and the Khaljis. Tribes from the mountain regions had had a reputation as fearless warriors since time immemorial, which is why Akbar and his generals regarded the movement led by Bayezid Ansari as especially dangerous.

Bayezid was not only an impassioned preacher, he elevated his mother tongue to the level of a literary language and ensured its survival with his *Khayr ul-bayan*. The ancient oral tradition of attractive and popular folk songs, lullabies, and ballads, also the *landey* or *tappa*, a couplet of 9 + 13 syllables, which are sometimes reminiscent of *haikus*, also still survive to this today.

Bayezid Ansari was one of a series of mystical poets and preachers who used the vernacular language in order to convey the message of the love of God and humanity to ordinary people, which was also happening at the same time in the case of other Indo-Muslim languages. His work bore fruit – not only did his theological opponent, Akhund Darwaza (died 1631), compose his works in Pashto, but a whole series of Sufi balladeers emerged in the course of the following centuries, culminating in the wonderful poetry of Rahman Baba, who died in 1709 near Peshawar, some of whose songs are almost as beautiful as psalms.

However, the supreme master of the Pashto language was a man called Khushal Khan Khattak, who also played a decisive role in the history of the Mughals.

In 1645, Khushal was the leader of the Pashtuns from Khattak, south of Peshawar, who fought on Shah Jahan's side in the battle against Balkh and Badakhshan. However, almost twenty years later the Mughal governor of Kabul, in league with a number of his many relatives, sent Khushal to Peshawar, where he was imprisoned in the infamous fort at Gwalior, in central India. The poems he wrote in the 'Hindustani Hell' are good examples of his poetical skill. When he was allowed to return to his homeland in 1669, he supported the leader of the Afridi Pashtuns in his defeat of the Mughals at the Khyber Pass in 1672. He himself fought the Bangash Pashtuns, who were on the side of the Mughals, before relinquishing his role as leader to his son Ashraf in 1674. Like his father,

Ashraf was a poet, and was later also incarcerated by the Mughals. Khushal wandered around the Pashtuns' regions, calling them to unite against the Mughals, in the course of which he also had to fight against a few of his 49 sons. He lived in the inaccessible Tirah region, and died in 1689 in the Afrid region. No other poet of his time expressed his political goals, his hatred for the Mughals, and his passionate love for his homeland as dramatically as Khushal. He was buried far away from the great land route, so that even in death he would be out of earshot of the tramping of the Mughal horses' hooves. Some years ago an impressive monument was erected on the site of his modest grave.

Khushal is the real founder of Pashto poetry which is not primarily religious. His subject matter was apparently limitless: passionate love ballads to the beautiful Afrid girls among others, hunting with falcons, medical and political poems. His poems reveal the influence of classical Persian literature, especially the verses of Sa'di (his son transliterated the Persian classic Sa'di's *Gulistan* into Pashto), and make skilful use of traditional poetical forms, although the metre has been adapted somewhat for the Pashto language. Khushal was a master of the popular *ruba'i*, the quatrain form, and he expressed his sceptical world view in many of his *ruba'iyyats*. He was clearly very well versed in the Sufi tradition, however, his mastery is shown to best effect in his poems in honour of his homeland, such as his ode to the autumn and its pleasures. Aurangzeb had no harsher critic than this Pashtun prince, whose lamentations on Mughal tyranny continue to inspire freedom-loving Pashtuns forced to live under foreign rule.

## SINDHI

Sindhi poetry appeared in written form somewhat earlier than Pashto poetry. Sindhi, the language spoken in the lower Indus region, was one of the richest of all the Indian languages, with a centuries-old oral tradition of ballads, legends, proverbs and riddles. A Sindhi poet was supposed to have recited a poem in his mother tongue at the court of Baghdad; however, the Arabic version is indecipherable. The Isma'ili religious ballads, the *ginans*, may be the oldest surviving literature. In Sindhi, as in other new Indian languages, it is sometimes difficult to determine whether a poem on the theme of love and longing is of Muslim origins, or whether it was an expression of Hindu *bhakti*-mysticism, since the love of God and the longing of the soul (which was portrayed as feminine) were expressed in almost exactly the same terms in Sufi and Islamic poetry.

Throughout Humayun's years of wandering in Sind, during which his son Akbar was born in Umarkot, a *qadi* in Sehwan, on the Indus, was composing short mystical verses. Qadi Qadan, as he was called, is thought to have been a Mahdawi who had arrived in Sind from Gujarat around 1500.[1] There is little in Qadi Qadan's poems to link them specifically to the Mahdawiyya, as they express sentiments common to all mystics and all Sufis: love for the unknowable God, and trust in him. Until the mid-1970s, only seven *doha*, two-line verses in Indian metre, were known to exist, but subsequently about a hundred more religious texts of Hindu origin were found in a manuscript in Haryana. Although their authenticity is not recognised by all experts, the first *doha* from the traditional verses has been quoted hundreds of times and also imitated.

Leave grammar and syntax to others –
I just contemplate the beloved.

This is a long-standing theme of Sufism. Just as the Prophet Muhammad was *ummi* (Sura 7: 157–158), which is translated as 'ignorant of reading and writing', so the lover is not interested in knowledge which is written down, as he only desires to contemplate heavenly beauty, the beauty which, as Qadi Qadan put it in another verse, resembles a banyan tree, which is only one tree, yet it resembles an entire forest because of its many roots above the ground. This is compared with the unattainable oneness of God, and the multiplicity of forms in the material world (thoughts which developed out of the ideas of Ibn ᶜArabi).

In his verses, Qadi Qadan sometimes wrote about the poor people in the provinces, or compared the overwhelming experience of the love of God with the flooding of the Indus River into numerous canals. Qadi Qadan's verses paved the way for mystical poets in the following generations. His spiritual legacy also had an effect on the Mughal household, as his grandson Mian Mir introduced this Sufi tradition to Prince Dara Shikoh, who dedicated a comprehensive biography to Mian Mir.

Even though the *khankhanan* ᶜAbduʾr Rahim was very interested in mystical poetry, he probably had little familiarity with the verses of Qadi Qadan when he besieged Sehwan in 1590. However, Sindhi balladeers apparently went to the court of Akbar, who liked to listen to their words of wisdom. Mir Maᶜsum, an educated Sindhi who was a friend of the *khankhanan*, was not only a good storyteller and calligrapher (who wrote the inscription on the entrance gate at Fatehpur Sikri), but was also a doctor, whom Akbar sent as his ambassador to the Persian court.[2]

After Sind had been annexed to the Mughal empire in 1591, the province continued its isolated existence under a number of governors, whose activities are documented in a series of somewhat critical Persian chronicles from the seventeenth century.[3]

Innumerable Persian works were produced in Sind during the course of the seventeenth century, with many new adaptations of traditional material – for instance, the familiar Qurʾanic tale of Yusuf and Zulaykha fused with traditional Sindhi love stories.

Poetry in the vernacular gradually increased in importance. Shah ᶜAbduʾl Karim of Bulrri[4] composed some charming *doha*s, in which he appears to have adapted themes from popular tradition with allusions to the famous lovers of the Indus Valley and the Punjab. This process was developed beautifully in the work of his great grandson Shah ᶜAbduʾl Latif of Bhit (1689–1752).

These were terrible times for Sind and for the entire Mughal empire, for after the death of Aurangzeb, in fact during the last years of his life, the empire was collapsing, and both Delhi and the provinces were riven by internecine fighting amongst the various factions.

Those years also saw the rise of a Sufi militant, whom modern Sindhi intellectuals regard as a land reformer, and indeed as the first 'socialist'. This was Shah ᶜInayat of Jhok.[5] He had lived for a time in India, most likely in Burhanpur. This city was a centre of Sufism, where a large group of Sufis had lived since 1540, mostly producing the famous cotton, chintz and silk fabrics. After Shah ᶜInayat's return, he came in for persecution – all the errors which orthodox believers associated with 'pantheistic' mystics were attributed to him. Furthermore, since so may ordinary people were drawn to ᶜInayat's highly charismatic personality, the great landlords started claiming that he was enticing the agricultural labourers to follow him, and was distributing land to them. In Delhi he was accused of plotting the overthrow of the Mughal government, even though this would have been out of the question for such a small group of dervishes. After a lengthy siege, Shah ᶜInayat was overwhelmed by superior force, and executed in January 1717. A troop from Kalhora in the north of the province had taken part in the battle against him, and not long afterwards they took over as rulers.

There is no mention of these political struggles in the poetry of the great Sindhi poet Shah ᶜAbduʾl Latif, even though his family had property in Bulrri, the scene of the fiercest attacks against ᶜInayat. There is also no mention of the catastrophe which befell Sind and the entire weakened Mughal empire two decades later, i.e. the incursion of the Persian army under the ruler Nadir Shah, who marched through Afghanistan and reached the Indus Valley. In May 1739, his troops brutally sacked Delhi, killing tens of thousands of people. In Sind, the conqueror demanded a huge payment from the government, which they could not meet. However, the clever financial comptroller of the province, a Hindu, brought him a sack, claiming that it was full of the most valuable commodities which Sind could offer – the dust of holy men and the descendants of the Prophet . . .

Shah ᶜAbduʾl Latif lived in his own world, the world of the worship of God. As a young man, he went on a pilgrimage with a group of *yogis* to Hinglaj, the holy mountain cave in Makran. Then he settled in Bhit, near Hala – where the great Makhdum Nuh (died 1590) had lived for a time. Shah died in Bhit in 1752, and the prince of Kalhora had a charming mausoleum built for him there, the columns of which look as if they were made of pale blue blossoms.

Shah ᶜAbduʾl Latif's poems have been collected in a *Risalo*.[6] The most well-known edition consists of thirty chapters named after the musical form in which the verses were to be sung, whether Indian or Sindhi melodies, or ones composed by the poet himself. The *Risalo* contains some very mystical musings, but to some extent it is the sagas of the Indus Valley which form the basis for these stories told in verse, going right back to their very beginnings. Each story, almost every one of which features a heroine, is an allegory of the evolution of the soul, which, having strayed on to the wrong path, or fallen into the 'sleep of idleness', must be purified by all manner of suffering, before achieving the longed for unification with its beloved – namely with the beloved God. The heroine is always from a humble caste, the beloved from a higher caste. All of these female souls suffer in all manner of adverse circumstances until they are finally purified: Sassi, the water carrier, has to follow her abducted prince across deserts and mountains, without ever finding him, until she herself is quite transformed by love; Sohni – in a reversal of the Hero and Leander theme – is in danger of being drowned in the river; because of Lila's desire for a valuable necklace, she allows her servant to sleep with her husband one night, as a result of which he rejects her. Possibly the most beautiful story is the one about the village girl Marui, who is abducted by Prince Umar of Umarkot, but who refuses to submit to his will, and who pines for her own village. (In this story the poet often quotes Rumi's *Mathnawi*, which in India is second only to the Qurʾan in importance.) The speeches written for these women by Shah ᶜAbduʾl contain the most tender love poems and most passionate cries of pain ever known in Sind, and many of them have become bywords. There is one portrayal of *yogis* as genuine holy men, adrift in the world, driven along 'like pumpkins'; another chapter is about spinning, which is used as a symbol for the contemplation of God, *dhikr*. Shah ᶜAbduʾl Latif's powers of observation are used to good effect in *Sur Sarang*, the 'Rain Song', which contains a naturalistic depiction of the plight of peasants and fishermen hoping for rain – meaning not merely earthly rain, but also the rain of grace, which is manifest by the Prophet Muhammad as *rahmat li'l-ʿalamin*, 'mercy for the world' (*Sura* 21:107), and so the rain is called *rahmat*, 'compassion'.

At almost exactly the same time, other Sindhi poets began composing ballads in praise of the beauty and benevolence of the 'bridegroom Muhammad' with novel and sometimes realistic portrayals of the Prophet, and also of actual wedding customs such as rose chains and the scattering of small coins. Sometimes they sing of their yearning for Medina, the final resting place of the Prophet.[7]

Followers of the Naqshbandi order had become influential in Delhi by now, and a few of its leaders had begun to play an important role in Delhi politics, especially Shah Waliullah. The Naqshbandi order was also active in Sind at this time. Mian Abu'l-Hasan put in verse the introduction to Islamic ritual, the *Muqaddimat as-salat*, which had been popular for centuries, and now even Sindhi children could be given an introduction to the Qurʾan in their mother tongue thanks to the *tafsir-i Hashimi* by the pious Makhdum Muhammad Hashim (died 1763). Quite early on some passages of the Qurʾan were put into verse, and some initial attempts were made at translating the holy book.[8]

In 1774, the administration of the province of Sind was transferred from the Kalhora to their disciples, the Shiʿite Talpur, a Baluchi family. Afterwards, Sachal Sarmast, a Sufi with a formidable command of language, who came from Draza, not far from Rohri, continued to sing his songs in the northern part of the province. Shah ʿAbduʾl Latif is supposed to have said of him that he 'lifted the lid from the pot', in other words, he brought out into the open matters which were supposed to

remain concealed, and kept expressing his feelings about the all-pervading Oneness of Being in new verses in Sindhi, Siraiki, and Persian. His ballads in Siraiki, which is a dialect of Punjabi, are especially moving. He never ceased to assert that God was everything, that He was Moses, He was Pharaoh, He was the judge, that He was the mystic martyr Hallaj, and that He was He . . . [9]

A decade and a half after Sachal's death in 1826, the Talpurs lost Sind to the British in the battle of Miani in 1843.

## PUNJABI

When Akbar had his residence in Lahore, the city was also known as the seat of a popular holy man, Madhu Lal Husayn, an ecstatic poet. So far as is known, he began singing mystical verses in his mother tongue, Punjabi, giving voice to the love of God and mystical ecstasy in exuberant and sometimes paradoxical language. He was very closely connected with a Hindu disciple, Madhu Lal, whose name was subsequently appended to his own. Both of them were eventually buried in a modest mausoleum near the Shalimar garden, which was laid out half a century later. Today their memorial day at the beginning of spring is still celebrated joyfully as *mela chiraghan*, 'Fair of Lights'. Husayn is supposed to have been a wise man, who was visited by many of the great personages of Akbar's court. It is quite likely that the *khankhanan* ʿAbduʾr Rahim would have conversed with this venerable holy man before his departure for Sind – although probably not about the preparations for the military campaign, but about mystical verse in the vernacular, which both men loved. However, that is pure conjecture. What is certain is that Punjabi became a literary language thanks to Madhu Lal Husayn, just as Pashto has Bayezid to thank, and Sindhi has Qadi Qadan – and in each case, this occurred at the beginning of the Mughal era, shortly before the turn of the second millennium of the Islamic calendar.

It is possible that, like Mian Mir, Husayn was a member of the Qadiriyya, which founded a centre in Ucch on the Sutlej in the fifteenth century, and then spread out towards Sind and into the Punjab. They had great influence on Prince Dara Shikoh and his sister, which may be the reason why the Qadiris withdrew somewhat after the execution of the crown prince in 1659. Nevertheless, perhaps because they were not active in politics, they played an important role in the development of the mystical poetry of the Punjab. A century after Madhu Lal Husayn, one of the most famous mystical poets of the Mughal era, Sultan Bahu, was active in the Jhang District. His colourfully adorned little mausoleum is still today a centre for the devout in the southern Punjab. Like many other Sufis, he composed a large number of Persian theoretical writings on Sufi theosophy. However, his reputation rested on his *siharfi*, the thirty-letter-poem. This was a form which was very popular in regional dialects, in which every strophe begins with a letter of the alphabet – i.e. a 'golden alphabet'. In the Punjab, the Gurmukhi alphabet, which was used for the Punjabi language, was even used for *siharfis*, with the addition of its numerous extra letters.

In the poem by Sultan Bahu, every line ends with the call *hu*, 'He', which is the call to God of the dervishes, and this call gave the poet his name. The first strophe of the *siharfi* has become a byword:

A – Allah is a sprig of jasmine,
Which has been placed in my heart – *hu*!
With the water 'of none but Him'
Have I nurtured it – *hu*!
'Til its aroma fills my heart
And moulds my entire being – *hu*!

May my master live long,
Who nurtures and cares for the blossom – *hu*!

In other words, with the constant repetition of the assertion of faith *la ilaha illa ʾIlah,* 'there is no God but God (Allah)', the master nurtures the tender plant – the 'heart' – and the 'tree of God' grows in the heart of the seeker, finally permeating him through and through. This is one of the most beautiful expressions of the effect of contemplation of God, by means of which humanity can finally find God within its own heart. The other verses of the *siharfi* mostly contain simple ethical lessons.

As well as the *siharfi* genre, *bara masa,* 'twelve month poems', are found in both Sindhi as well as Punjabi. This is a form which originated in the Indian tradition, expressing a woman's longing in each of the twelve months of the year. This was originally intended only for the Hindu months, in which the rainy season plays a special role, but then *barahmasa* came to be sung for the Muslim months, during which the soul lives through the festivities and mourning periods of the Islamic calendar, and in the last month, the time of pilgrimage to Mecca, she experiences the longed for unification with her Godly beloved, or even with the beloved Prophet. In the nineteenth century, poems began to be composed for the Christian months, which had been introduced by the British.[1]

Two generations after Sultan Bahu, the most famous Punjabi Sufi poet appeared, Bullhe Shah[2] (died 1754) from Kasur, which is east of Lahore. He sang ecstatic verses about the oneness of being, with the constant repetition of: 'All cottonwool balls are uniformly white . . . ', for differences only appear during manufacture, just as the Absolutely Colourless One manifests itself in innumerable forms and colours.

There are also regional cotton spinning songs,[3] in the Deccan as well as in Sind, for cotton spinning was one of the most important industrial activities. Cotton spinning could be compared to the *dhikr*, the contemplation of God: just as the thread becomes ever finer by means of the steady spinning, so the human heart becomes ever purer by means of continuous contemplation of God, until finally God awards the highest prize, namely paradise, to the devout (compare *Sura* 9:111). The lazy girl, the indolent soul, however, will find herself naked and disgraced on the day of the wedding – i.e. death. Less attention tends to be paid to the fact that cotton in this spinning song is also an allusion to al-Hallaj, 'the Cotton Carder', the 'martyr for the love of God', who was executed in 922.

Bullhe Shah was also alluding to the Punjabi epic *Hir Ranjha*: the lover who loves Ranjha in defiance of convention and danger, who will be united with him in death. As she sang: 'Repeating Ranjha, Ranjha in my mind, I myself have become Ranjha!' Not long afterwards, Bullhe Shah's fellow countryman Warith Shah developed the legend of *Hir Ranjha* into an epic, which came to be regarded as the national poem of all Punjabis, whether Hindu, Muslim or Sikh.

Whilst the Sufis were singing their mystical ballads and becoming intoxicated with *bhang*, as they still do today in Kasur, the Sikhs were gradually taking control of the Punjab. After the collapse of the Mughals, they secured their position of power in their home province, and finally, with the help of the British, they installed their own administration. Ranjit Singh ruled for many years from his base at the Mughal fort in Lahore. Shah ʿAbduʾl ʿAziz, the son of Shah Waliullah, the reforming theologian from Delhi, tried to fight the Sikhs, assisted by the preacher Ismaʿil Shahid. Both men lost their lives in 1831, and the British took over the administration of the Punjab in 1849.

Whereas Sindhi became a thriving literary language for both Muslims and Hindus, Punjabi remained a literary language for the Sikhs alone, written in their *Gurmukhi* alphabet. Although there are Punjabi versions of great classical poems such as Rumi's *Mathnawi*, for the most part Urdu is the literary language of Muslims, although a Muslim Punjabi literature is beginning to emerge.

## URDU

The slow disintegration of the Mughal empire after Aurangzeb's death was reflected in the literature of the period. With the emergence of significant poetry in regional languages, mostly with mystical themes, the predominance of Persian was weakened – the highly complex literary conceits of the 'Indian Style' were evidently falling out of favour with audiences and readers alike. There was a need for new ideas and forms, and they started appearing from southern India.

Since the end of the fifteenth century, *Dakhni* ('southern') Urdu had been in sporadic use as a literary language in the Deccan, in Golconda and Bijapur and the surrounding region, alongside local languages such as Telugu and Tamil (as was the case with Gujarati in Gujarat). The first mystical writings appeared there somewhat earlier than in the comparable poetry of northwestern India. Secular poetry, for example with romantic themes, developed more rapidly in the Deccan than in the north. The melodic, cheerful verses of Muhammad Quli Qutbshah of Golconda (ruled 1580–1612) and his neighbour Ibrahim ʿAdil Shah II of Bijapur (ruled 1580–1627) are a refreshing contrast to the complex Persian poetry composed during the same time at the Mughal court. The crucial difference was that Urdu and various other Indian languages, especially Hindi, which is grammatically almost identical to Urdu, were in widespread everyday use in the north, not just for literature and administration.

Around 1700, a few writers began to take an interest in systematising the vernacular language of Hindustani (this being accomplished a later stage for Urdu and Hindi). Wali, who was the pre-eminent poet in the *Dakhni* Urdu language, left the south for Delhi, where he demonstrated to his colleagues the flexibility and versatility of his poetic language. Consequently a few of the Delhi poets began composing the *urdu-yi mu<sup>c</sup>alla*, the language of 'the illustrious army encampment' (i.e. the Mughal court). The language became *rekhta*, 'mixed', with the addition of Indian, some Turkish and many Persian elements. The first known Delhi *rekhta* poet was Ja<sup>c</sup>far Zatalli, a humourist, whose satirical verses led to his execution by the emperor Farrukhsiyar in 1713.

Whatever may have been the initial impetus for the use of *rekhta*, Urdu as a poetic medium, during the political turbulence after the death of Aurangzeb, and especially in the time of the hedonistic Muhammad Shah Rangila (ruled 1719–1748), a number of poets began leavening their native languages with elegant Persian. They discussed amongst themselves the application of Persian prose forms to Urdu, formulated models for pure rhymes, with Khan-i Arzu (died 1756) being chiefly responsible for establishing the 'rules' of the nascent literary tradition. The poets gathered together in a small mosque, the Zinat al-masjid in Delhi, which had been constructed under the auspices of Aurangzeb's daughter Zinat un-nisa, who unlike her sister Zib un-nisa, Aurangzeb's other daughter, did not compose Persian lyrics. However, the mosque she established played a vital role in the establishment of Urdu literature.

Literary historians describe the most influential poets of the eighteenth century as the 'four

pillars of Urdu'.[1] They are Mir Taqi Mir (died in 1810 at the age of nineteen), Khwaja Mir Dard (died 1785), Mirza Sauda (died 1781), and Mazhar Janjanan (died 1781). Today, however, Dard is primarily remembered as the leader of a branch of the Naqshbandi order, which is still active today. Mir Hasan (died 1786), whose *mathnawi*, the *Qissa-i benazir*, 'The Incomparable Story', is one of the finest romantic fairy-tales ever written, would now be more appropriately named as the fourth poet. His work is a blend of all kinds of stylistic artistry, and it contains many descriptive passages about gardens and palaces, clothing, and the customs of lovers, which make it an important cultural historical record.

Mir Taqi Mir is the greatest lyricist of the early Urdu poets. His verses sound like gentle sighs, mostly about love, nearly always unrequited. The poet makes elegant use of colloquial speech and typical everyday expressions, which render his verses as beautiful as they are untranslatable. He himself wrote:

Don't call me a poet! For I only collected
Sorrow and pain . . . and made them into a
  book!

The perennial theme of the transitory nature of beauty is the subject of one of his verses, in which the 'smile' of the bud signifies that it is opening, which is a premonition of decay:

How long is the life of the rose?
The bud just smiles.

For his prose work, Mir used Persian, and we have him to thank, not only for an account of contemporary poets writing in Persian and Urdu, but also for a shocking description of the sacking of Delhi in 1761 by its 'friends and helpers'.[2]

Khwaja Mir Dard is the most mystically inclined of the early Urdu poets. The Naqshbandi order, which is not generally known for its artistic endeavours, nevertheless produced a few of the best lyricists in Delhi, as had been the case four centuries earlier at the court of the Timurid Husayn Bayqara. Dard, 'Pain', was the son of Muhammad Nasir ʿAndalib (died 1758), who was inspired by a vision of the Prophet to found the *tariqa muhammadiyya,* a deeply mystical movement which adhered strictly to religious law. Dard spent his whole life attempting to express his total identification with his father and spiritual leader. Although he was the author of comprehensive autobiographical works in Persian, his reputation is largely based on a few hundred verses in Urdu recounting his mystical experiences. Although the ecstatic Deccan poet Siraj Aurangabadi was also composing overblown passionate mystical verses in Urdu at the same time, it is Dard's verses that became universally known. Everyone with any knowledge of Urdu knows the following lines by Dard:

Oh thou portal! When we die
To us shall be revealed:
All we saw was but a dream
All that we heard, a fable!

Although it was contrary to the ideals of the Naqshbandiyya, Dard, like his father, was a connoisseur and lover of music. He often used to hold concerts in his house in Delhi near the Turkoman Gate, which had been a present to his father from one of Aurangzeb's daughters. These concerts were even attended on occasion by the emperor ʿAlam II Aftab, who had composed a few volumes of poetry himself.

For modern Western readers, Mirza Sauda's verses are much easier to read than Dard's soulful poetry. Sauda was an Afghan and also a fervent Shiʿi and brilliant satirist, who portrayed the foibles of his age very dramatically in verse, without the use of too many rhetorical devices. He wrote a great poem, which is often quoted, about a starving nag, which is an allegory for the miserable situation of the vast number of starving soldiers during the disintegration of the Mughal empire. He lampooned quacks as well as money-grubbing merchants, and also, naturally, his own fellow poets, especially Mazhar Janjanan, whom he compared to the 'the washerman's dog', who feels out of place whether in the house or on the riverbank (where the washing was done). Sauda's skilful verses are rich depictions of the situation in the Delhi area, whereas Dard, like Shah ʿAbduʾl Latif, his senior contemporary in Sind, paid scant attention to external circumstances. Only Dard's lament that 'tears instead of rivers' were flowing in Delhi revealed the extent of his concern for the city he never left.

Sauda also composed a large number of Urdu *marthiyya*, which are dirges on the death of the grandson of the Prophet, Husayn ibn ʿAli, who was killed on 10 *Muharram* 680 in Kerbela, in Iraq, by the troops of the Umayyad Caliphs. The art of *marthiyya*, which was developed especially in Shiʿite Lucknow, is an important legacy of the Mughal empire, and also of the province of Awadh, and Hyderabad in the Deccan, which were gaining independence towards the end of the eighteenth century. The two great *marthiyya* poets in Awadh were Anis (died 1875) and Dabir (died 1874), both of whom wrote hundreds of long, extremely detailed meditations on the battle of Kerbela. For this purpose, they developed the *musaddas* form, which is a poem of six-line stanzas, with the rhyming scheme *aaaabb ccccdd,* and so on, which was used to expound religious or ethical concepts to the listener, hence its important role in later Urdu literature. Muslims who lived through the disintegration of

92. 'Bahadur Shah II enthroned at a *durbar*', *c.* 1839, miniature, pigment and gold on paper.

the Mughal empire and the transition to colonial rule compared their own sufferings under British rule to those of the descendants of the Prophet under the 'godless' Umayyads.

In 1800, the British established Fort William in their new capital of Calcutta. This was to be the locus for the development of Urdu as a language of everyday use, because complex, flowery Persian and literary Urdu were useless for the practical purposes of British officials, lawyers and officers working in India. And so, in the last decades of the moribund Mughal empire, Urdu, or, as it is usually called, Hindustani, began to be developed as a practical working language. However, in 1835, the Macaulay *Edict* led to the replacement of Persian by English as the language of administration.

Even the last days of the Mughal empire were a time of great literary output. In Lucknow, Urdu

reached new heights of elegance, and was used by many poets for charming, if also often rather frivolous verses. Anyone who enjoys humorous and witty turns of phrase will enjoy the language of the poets of Lucknow, which 'tingles on the tongue like champagne'.[3] Their poems also featured a sprinkling of Turkish and the first usage of English words such as 'glass' and 'bottle'.

In Delhi, a more traditional form of Urdu was flourishing; however the pre-eminent writer was Mirza Asadullah Ghalib (1797–1869), the range of whose Persian output vastly surpassed his small Urdu *diwan*.[4] As was the case with Mir Dard, it was Ghalib's 'colourless' Urdu verses, as he himself disparaged them, which today are universally known among Urdu-speaking Indians and Pakistanis. Ghalib made frequent use of the alternation between highly complex images and metaphors

93. Portraits of Dust Muhammad Khan (Amir of Afghanistan), emperor Bahadur Shah II and three Mughal court ladies, *c.* 1864, watercolour on ivory set in a gold bracelet set with emeralds.

and light colloquial speech, which is well known in the Indian style. This is still enjoyed today even by readers ignorant of the long historical tradition behind some of these phrases. Ghalib's letters in Urdu are praised as masterpieces for their vivid, lively style, whereas little remains of his Persian work. The book he was commissioned to write by the Mughal court on 'The History of the House of Timur', is not exactly easy to read, and his description of the uprising of 1857 is almost unreadable because of its archaic style. The poet called this portrayal 'Fragrant Bouquet', *Dastanbu*, a word used by the Persian poet Khaqani (died 1199) in a poem of praise to the spouse of his patron. It is also used in a booklet by Ghalib with reference to another woman, Queen Victoria, who from 1858 was the Empress of India.

This is only a single, but typical, example of the widespread and extensive use of classical models, of which Ghalib was a master. In his Persian *qasida*s he not only wrote highly complex poems in praise of the Prophet, and, good Shi'i that he was, to 'Ali, but also to British officials, and to the last Mughal ruler, Bahadur Shah Zafar. In Ghalib's poetry, Bahadur Shah Zafar's few remaining soldiers were depicted as mighty armies, like constellations of stars.

Bahadur Shah Zafar was a poet himself, like many of his ancestors: Babur, who wrote in

Turkish and also in Persian to some extent, his children Gulbadan and Humayun who wrote in Persian, Kamran Mirza who wrote in Turkish, Jahangir, his granddaughter Jahanara and his niece Zeb un-nisa who wrote in Persian. Aurangzeb also wrote powerful works of prose in Persian – not to mention the many occasional verses which the members of the Mughal household improvised. Shah 'Alam II was a poet in Urdu, as was his less well known son Shu'a. Bahadur Shah, however, was one of the best Urdu poets, whose lively ballads are still sung at concerts in India today. The most famous of all his verses was the last one he wrote whilst in exile in Rangoon, where he died in 1862 in wretched circumstances. It is one of the most moving poems in Urdu, the language which achieved its finest flowering after the demise of the Mughal empire, and which is today the literary language of Pakistan and much of north India. So, with the last sigh of the emperor, bowed down by old age and misery, the Mughal empire came to its end:

I am the light of no one's eye
The balm of no one's heart –
I am no use to anyone
A handful of dust, that's all.

I have no form nor colour now
My friend torn from my side
The springtime of a grove am I
By the autumn destroyed, that's all.

I am no longer a lover for you
Nor any rival am I
Annihilated joy of life,
A desolate landscape, that's all.

I am no song to gladden the heart,
For you to hear with joy –
Just the sound of utter pain
Of the tortured lamenter, that's all.

Who would pray on my behalf?
Or bring me a bunch of flowers?
Who would light a candle for me?
I am naught but a gloomy tomb.

94. The poet Hafiz (*c.* 1326–90), *c.* 1780, drawing on paper.

# NINE

# The Arts

## THE RULER'S LIBRARY

Bibliophily appears to have been hereditary in the Timur family line. Timur's otherwise highly critical biographer Ibn ᶜArabshah describes how Timur liked to be read to from historical works, and his descendant Sultan Husayn Bayqara of Herat (died 1506) was quite a passable poet, even though Babur was rather critical of his uncle's monotonous verses. During the last quarter of the fifteenth century, the most outstanding poet in Chaghatay, and also the masters of calligraphy and miniature painting, were all at the court at Herat. Babur wrote his autobiography in Chaghatay, not least as a way of legitimating his claim to be a descendant of Timur and Chingiz Khan, so it is hardly surprising that he also dabbled in the literary traditions of the line, which continued until the days of the last Mughal rulers.

Babur and his descendants all shared a great love of fine books. After the siege of Panipat in 1526, Babur gave the books he found in the castle of the vanquished Ibrahim Lodi to his sons Humayun and Kamran. Humayun apparently carried the books with him everywhere, for after one battle, when his encampment was looted, 'a few rare books went missing, which had been his

faithful companions'.[1] However, when Kabul was recaptured in 1552, they found two camels laden with chests of books, so he recovered at least some of his treasures. Humayun's son Akbar appears to have been illiterate, or perhaps dyslexic; however, he was taught scholarly subjects for a time, and despite his evident aversion to the written word, he displayed a great love of literature and had all the books which came into his possession read out to him from cover to cover. He must have had a formidable memory to be able not merely to take pleasure in classical Persian poetry, but also to be able to compose a few small verses from time to time:

What fall onto the rose are not dewdrops –
They are only the nightingale's teardrops.

Abu'l Fazl mentions that Akbar liked reciting the poems of Hafiz, which he studied regularly with a teacher. He also quoted the poetry of Jalaluddin Rumi.

Abu'l Fazl also provides a welcome account of Akbar's library. It contained the *Akhlaq-i nasiri*, a work of moral philosophy, part of which still survives in the form of an exceptionally beautifully illuminated manuscript.[2] There was also the 'Elixir of Happiness' by Imam Ghazzali, as well as the *Qabusnama* by the Persian Prince Qabus ibn Wushmgir (died 1012) on the correct demeanour of princes – a work in which Goethe took a great interest. Akbar's particular favourites were works of history, such as the *Jamiᶜat-tawarikh* by Rashiduddin (died 1317), especially, for obvious dynastic reasons, the sections on the Turkish-Mongolian rulers. The passages about Alanquwa, the mythological antecedent of the Mongols, and Abaqa, a descendant of Chingiz Khan, contain illustrations depicting these heroes in exotic costumes with enormous feather crowns.[3] Akbar's library also contained the 'History of the Barmecides', who played such an important role under Harun ar-Rashid, until their sudden fall from power. There was also the semi-historical *Darabnama*, bearing the seal of Akbar's wife Salima. The palace contained two versions of the *Kalila wa Dimna*, a traditional collection of educational books on Indian zoology – a translation completed in Herat, *Anwar-i suhayli* as well as Abu'l Fazl's version, ᶜ*Ayar-i danish*.[4]

The collection included the works of Saᶜdi (died 1292 in Shiraz); the *Gulistan* (Rose Garden) and *Bustan* (Garden) were among the classics studied by all Persian scholars for the elegance of their style and their sage observations on life. Akbar also had a splendid copy made of the *Gulistan* for the library in Fatehpur Sikri. The large format manuscript is illuminated with numerous naturalistic pictures of birds, and there are portraits of the calligrapher Zarrin Qalam and the painter Manohar at the end.[5]

The poetical works of the 'Indian Parrot', Amir Khusrau (died 1325) were partially illustrated in Akbar's studio. A romance of his dealing with a contemporary event (*Duval Rani Khidr Khan*), bears the seals of Salima, Shah Jahan and Aurangzeb. The *Tughluqnama* was completed two generations

95. The calligrapher Zarrin Qalam and the painter Manohar, c. 1582, gouache on paper; colophon to a manuscript of Saᶜdi's *Gulistan* from Fatehpur Sikri.

later, under Shah Jahan, for which the poet received his weight in gold from the ruler.[6] The other romances by Amir Khusrau were also a rich source of subject matter for miniature painters, as was the work which served as the model for the poet, the 'Five Romances', the *Khamsa*, by Nizami (died 1209). The manuscript of Nizami's *Khamsa* illustrated for Akbar, which is in the British Museum, is one of the finest examples of the Indo-Muslim arts of the book.[7]

It would have been very surprising if the imperial library did not contain manuscripts of the heroic Persian romance, the *Shahnama* by Firdawsi. An illuminated manuscript of this epic, which was produced in 1440 for Muhammad Juqi and then taken to Samarkand, bears the seal of all the Mughal rulers up to Aurangzeb, and Jahangir and Shah Jahan have added their comments in its margins. During the time of Jahangir and Shah Jahan, precious manuscripts of this work were sent to the court as gifts from provincial governors.[8]

Bada'uni describes an attempt to render this epic (consisting of more than 50,000 verses!) into prose in order to make it more comprehensible – which, according to the outraged chronicler, was like making sacks out of the finest linen.

The work of Jami (died 1492 in Herat) was illuminated at the Mughal court, and a valuable manuscript of his most popular romance, *Yusuf u Zulaykha* (the story of Joseph and Potiphar's wife, based on *Sura* 12 of the Qur'an) was in the possession of the unfortunate Prince Kamran, and the *Baharistan*, 'Spring Garden', was in Akbar's possession. In 1609, *khankhanan* 'Abdu'r Rahim gave Jahangir a beautiful manuscript of *Yusuf u Zulaykha*, written by the master calligrapher Mir 'Ali of Herat, complete with miniatures and a wonderful binding.[9]

Abu'l Fazl makes no mention of any romance by 'Attar (died 1221); however, his brother Fayzi clearly loved the mystical works of the Persian poet. After the death of their father, Mubarak, he wanted Abu'l Fazl to send him 'Attar's *Musibatnama* as a consolation, for

From 'Attar is derived the medicine for the
pain of love, for when his shop was destroyed,
he received holy solace.[10]

96. Shah Jahan's seal and signature of ownership on a manuscript of Firdawsi's *Shahnama* (copied *c.* 1440–45) with an autograph note by Shah Jahan recording the entry of the manuscript into his library in 1628, as well as seals of other owners (the Emperors Babur, Humayun, Jahangir and Aurangzeb).

As well as educational works by Arabic and Persian authors, Akbar's library also contained great panegyric works, for example by the very difficult Khaqani (died 1199), whose verses are still quoted, and the poetry of his senior and fellow countryman Anwari.

In 1589 a small manuscript copy of Anwari's *Diwan* was made on featherweight paper in the then capital city Lahore, and decorated with seventeen fine miniatures. Jahangir quoted from this work when he paid a visit to the Garden of Gulafshan:

'Tis a day for pleasure, for delight in the garden,
When roses and fragrant herbs await.
The dust is perfumed with musk and amber,
The seam of the zephyr is scenting the air . . .'[11]

The *Hamzanama* is an extremely important work, and the first sizeable testament to Akbar's enthusiasm for painting. This is a heroic tale of the adventures of Hamza, the uncle of the Prophet Muhammad, which Akbar had comprehensively illustrated. The *Hamzanama*[12] was written on fabric and illustrated with 1,400 pictures, measuring 56 x 65 cm. It was painted on one side, with the text on the reverse side in blocks of nineteen lines, so that the reader could recite them whilst holding the corresponding picture up for his audience to see. This enormous work was begun perhaps in 1558, and dozens of artists worked on it for fifteen years under the supervision of two of the Safawid Shah Tahmasp's principal painters, ʿAbduʾs Samad and Mir Sayyid ʿAli. Unfortunately, fewer than 200 folios of the *Hamzanama* have survived.

There were a number of important Sufi writings in Akbar's library. The ruler and many other devout people particularly liked reading the impressive and straightforward Persian letters by Sharafuddin Maneri of Bihar (died 1380–81).[13]

*Hadiqat al-haqiqat,* by Sanaʾi, was the first Persian mystical-didactic poem in couplets. Khan-i Aʿzam ʿAziz Koka brought it from Ghazna, where Sanaʾi was buried. It was later augmented in the court studio. There is one surviving manuscript, which was written and illuminated by the master calligrapher ʿAbduʾr Rahim.[14]

A particular favourite of Akbar's was the *Mathnawi* of Jalaluddin Rumi, which a century earlier had been extolled by Jami as the 'Persian language version of the Qurʾan'.[15] Babur's father had also rated this work very highly. Dara Shikoh copied extracts from it, and Aurangzeb was moved to tears during recitations. The nobility often held recitations of this work at their homes, and numerous commentaries and collections of selected excerpts were compiled, particularly under the auspices of Shah's Jahan daughter Jahanara.

The number of books in Akbar's library was constantly increasing, partly through legacies from friends,as for instance when he inherited 4,600 valuable manuscripts of Fayzi's, many of which were autobiographical works by the author. They were organised under three categories: 1. Poetry, Medicine, Astrology, Music; 2. Philosophy, Sufism, Astronomy, Geometry; 3. Qurʾanic Exegeses, *Hadith*, Islamic Law. The order of these categories led Badaʾuni to the conclusion that fundamental Islamic works were of little interest to the ruler.[16]

Jahangir and Shah Jahan always made scrupulous note of the date when any manuscript was submitted and added to their libraries, sometimes noting its purchase price as well. The seals of many surviving manuscripts reveal their ownership as well as the interests of princes from Timur to Nadir Shah – Nadir Shah took with him a large number of the 24,000 manuscripts remaining in the Mughal library.[17] Many display comments by princes in the texts.

Manuscripts were kept carefully wrapped in silk cloths. The bindings were often of richly decorated lacquer or of leather embossed with gilt, or with mother of pearl inlay. Miniatures often depict such books in the hands of illustrious readers.

97. Folio 441 from the *Sharhul kafiya*, dated AH 1050 (1640),
with manuscript notes by the Emperor Shah Jahan and his
prime minister.

tions on buildings, appeared in Ajmer and on the
Qutub Minar in Delhi. However, it was soon
supplanted by a variant of the cursive *thuluth*,
which appeared on buildings from the late thirteenth century in Delhi and elsewhere, and which
can be distinguished by its strokes, which are
thickened at the top. The bold inscriptions on the
Qutub Minar in Delhi are a good example. In
many regions of Bengal, a highly decorative form
of epigraphy for buildings was developed, which
reached its zenith around 1500.[18]

The two main calligraphic styles were the
rather stilted *naskh*, and the *Bihari*, which until the
nineteenth century was commonly used for making copies of the Qur'an. Like the North African
*Maghrib* style, the rather square and irregular *Bihari*
style does not adhere to the classical rules as stipulated by Ibn Muqla (died 940). Manuscripts in this
style, like those produced in Morocco, are often
wonderfully colourful.

The *ta'liq* style was developed in Iran for writing
Persian texts. This was a 'hanging' style, meaning
that the letters slanted from top right to bottom
left. Around 1400 this evolved into the *nasta'liq*
form, which followed the strict rules of Ibn Muqla
regarding 'hanging' letters. Gradually a style developed in which there was a clear distinction
between the 'hair' lines and the 'foundation lines'.
This elegant style came to be known as the 'Bride
among Styles'.

The undisputed masters of this style were
Sultan ʿAli Mashhadi (died 1519), acknowledged by
Babur as the best calligrapher, and the younger Mir
ʿAli Herawi, both of whom were working at the
court of Husayn Bayqara. Mir ʿAli was later taken
by the Uzbeks to Bukhara, where he had to write
ceaselessly. Sometimes he slipped a little unpoetic
verse of his own into his writing, lamenting that
'writing has become a shackle for my feet', for
whilst he was much admired abroad, he was never

The Mughals attached great importance not
only to the contents of books but also to fine calligraphy, and they were keen collectors of albums
of tablets, *lauha*, by the hands of great masters.
Few gifts pleased a ruler more than such a page or,
better still, an entire album written by a famous
calligrapher.

In Muslim India, a relatively simple form of
cursive writing was employed. The complicated
braided *kufic*, an interlacing, artistic form of lettering, which was used in the Islamic world during
the twelfth and thirteenth centuries for inscrip-

98. A folio from the *Risala-i-Khwaja ᶜAbduʾllah Ansari*, dated AH 921 (1521), with autographs of the Emperors Jahangir, Shah Jahan and ᶜAbduʾr Rahim *khankhanan*, plus seals of Shah Jahan and Aurangzeb.

99. Attributed to Mir ᶜAli Herawi (*fl.* late 15th–first half of the 16th century), *nastaᶜliq* calligraphy of a verse in Persian from an anthology of poetry, *Courtly Pastimes*; ink, gouache and gold on paper.

able to leave Bukhara. Mir ꜥAli became the favourite calligrapher of the Mughals. His son is said to have taken many of his father's works to India, among them a rhyming version of the introduction to Islam, *Muqaddimat as-salat* from 933/1526-7, which bears the seals of Jahangir, Shah Jahan and Aurangzeb.[19]

A large number of Persian texts from the time of Akbar were written in a somewhat harsh *naskh* style, for instance the Cleveland *Tutinama* and the *Darabnama*. However, Indian calligraphers soon mastered the elegant *nastaꜥliq* style, also the many flourishes of the *tughra* style, with its interlacing strokes. *Nastaꜥliq* was originally used for drafts and the official titles of decrees by the ruler, also for the first page of valuable manuscripts. At the beginning of Shah Jahan's album, his title was written in *tughra* and surrounded by an incredibly delicate gilt border pattern with all manner of arabesques, on a small area measuring only 39.1 x 26.7 cm. How this masterpiece was created, and how many months of ceaseless work it must have taken, remains a mystery.[20]

As time went on, Mughal artists, like their counterparts in Ottoman Turkey, developed new variations, formed pictures and figures out of words (e.g. from Qurꜣanic verses, and also used *gulzar*, letters filled in with floral patterns. In addition to all kinds of variations to the *tughra* style, they developed mirror writing and other techniques, which later were occasionally used to decorate buildings.

In a number of Mughal manuscripts, the colophon contains a portrait of court painters and calligraphers. Akbar's favourite calligrapher, Muhammad Husayn Kashmiri, who was known as *Zarrin Qalam*, 'Golden Pen' (died 1611), is depicted in a beautiful small portrait in the colophon of the *Gulistan* manuscript from Fatehpur Sikri. He is portrayed as a tall, bearded man, and he is in the company of a younger painter, Manohar, the son of Basawan. A precious manuscript of the *Akhlaq-i nasiri* also has portraits of several painters and calligraphers; men are seen in front of the studio busy with preparations for writing, such as smoothing their paper or polishing a picture. The artists themselves are seated on the ground, working with their papers resting on their raised left knees, just as artists had done for centuries.[21]

Perhaps the most moving picture of a calligrapher is one from Bichitr[22] depicting an old man with an exercise book in his hand, and below it another book, which he is copying, concentrating fully on this task. He shows the signs of a long life of toil; however, his gold-threaded *patka* also reveals that he has been awarded many a royal distinction, although whether he received an honorary title such as 'Golden Pen', 'Musk Pen', or 'Amber Pen', or whether, like Maulana Dauri in Akbar's time, he was dubbed 'Writer of the Kingdom', can never be known.

Artists and calligraphers were expected to produce ever more difficult works of art, which spurred them to great achievements. Badaꜣuni reports that Sharif-i Farisi, the son of the great painter ꜥAbduꜣs Samad, wrote the entire *Sura* 112 on one side of a poppy head, which sounds quite incredible, despite the brevity of this verse – however, since calligraphers still today write quite lengthy texts on grains of rice, then it might well have been possible. Badaꜣuni reports that one artist wrote a verse on the tip of a toothpick, and another drew a polo scene on a grain of rice. Nishani, a steel engraver, engraved a minute seal with the names of seven of Akbar's ancestors, going back to Timur, as well as Akbar's name and title – an equally astonishing accomplishment, and certainly more useful, which took him four months to complete.[23]

The Mughal emperors were not merely admirers of calligraphy, they were also practitioners. Babur was known for his calligraphy during his lifetime, although it was forgotten after his death.[24] Jahangir and Shah Jahan both wrote *nasta'liq* in a not particularly artistic style. An album compiled by Shah Jahan in his youth contains many writing exercises by the prince, which is understandable[25] in view of his father's love of calligraphy. Upon learning that Mir 'Imad, the best of all contemporary *nasta'liq* calligraphers in Iran, had been murdered – either on the orders of Shah 'Abbas, or at least with his connivance – he is said to have cried out: 'If only my brother 'Abbas had sent him to me – I would have given him his weight in pearls!' Rashida Daylami, a nephew of the murdered man, later came to the Mughal court to instruct Prince Dara Shikoh in writing. The prince was also taught by the supervisor of the imperial library, Mir Muhammad Salih Kashifi (died 1651), who was known as 'Musk Pen'. Although he mastered various styles of writing, most surviving documents by Dara Shikoh are written in a flowing *nasta'liq*, with a few surviving ornamental pages in *thuluth*. In many cases, there are patterns radiating out from Dara Shikoh's signature, or else painted over it, probably by members of Aurangzeb's entourage. Dara Shikoh was later executed as a heretic.

Aurangzeb excelled at writing *naskh*, and he especially liked copying out Qur'anic templates, a few of which still survive. He was also accomplished at writing *nasta'liq*.[26]

The Mughal household retained its love of calligraphy to the end, and fine handwriting was always regarded as a essential accomplishment for a nobleman. The last Mughal ruler, Bahadur Shah, liked transforming the texts of devout supplications and prayers into flowers and faces. Works on Mughal calligraphers and painters continued to be produced right up to the time of Shah 'Alam II,[27] as

were manuals to teach the finer points of calligraphy, which have yet to be put to use.

## PAINTING

There are many that hate painting; but such men I dislike. It appears to me, as if a painter had quite peculiar means of recognising God, for a painter in sketching anything that has life, and in devising the limbs one after another, must come to feel that he cannot bestow personality on his work, and is thus forced to think of God, the giver of life, and this increases his knowledge.

This was the view of Akbar, whose enlightened policy enabled Mughal painting to develop. Mughal painting came into being by chance, or rather because of an accident of history. In 1544, Humayun, who had been forced to flee, was staying with his Iranian neighbour Shah Tahmasp, and he admired the pictures he saw at the imperial court in Tabriz. Tahmasp loved painting, and was quite an accomplished practitioner.[1] The magnificent *Shahnama* manuscript was created for him. However, he was then undergoing 'sincere repentance', was abstaining from worldly pleasures, and no longer taking any interest in the fine arts. So Humayun, who was staying in Kandahar in 1546, was able to take at least two of the Tabriz artists away with him. One of them was Mir Sayyid 'Ali, the son of Mir Musawwir, a master of elegant arabesque lines; the other was 'Abdu's Samad, who later became famous as *Shirin qalam*, 'Sweet Pen'. The two of them followed Humayun to Kabul in 1549, and then on to Delhi in 1554, and continued to work under Akbar after Humayun's death. 'Abdu's Samad taught Akbar painting when he was a child. A portrait of the 'House of

Timur' painted on fabric is attributed to him. This picture depicting Timur's family laid the foundation for the dynasty, and later on it was expanded with additional family members.[2]

Akbar must have had some familiarity with traditional Indian painting. He would have had access to Jain and Hindu writings, and he attracted Hindu artists to his court to work with the master painters from Tabriz, a decisive move for the development of Mughal painting. The Mughal style developed from the interaction between the refined Persian style and the strong, lively vision of the Hindu artists in a relatively short period of time. The first work to be illustrated at that time was the *Tutinama*, with around 250 miniatures demonstrating the confluence of these two traditions in great detail. This was followed by the monumental *Hamzanama*, which was extremely realistic as well as highly imaginative. When this gigantic work was completed more than fifteen years later, *c.* 1570s, the Mughal style was born.

A few of the great masters are known not only from their signatures, but also from true to life portraits of them in the colophons, which show them at work, sitting on the floor, with their paper resting on one bent knee, like the calligraphers. Their brushes were bound together with the finest hairs from the whiskers of kittens or squirrels, so that the brush came to a point with a single hair. Next to them are the tiny bowls – often shells – containing their pigments, which were derived from mineral, vegetable or animal sources. For white, they used chalk and soapstone (they used white for corrections, since it was easy to paint over mistakes with it); ochre for red and yellow was obtained from different types of clay, red from hematite. Green was derived from malachite, blue from lapis lazuli and azurite (which is also found in malachite). Certain insects were used to made red lacquer, and yellow was derived

from the urine of cows fed on mango leaves, also from arsenic sulphide. For green tones they sometimes also used verdigris, a by-product of copper, which unfortunately eats into paper.

Gold and silver leaf were obtained by beating the metal into thin strips between pieces of leather, then grinding them up with salt, and finally letting the salt rinse away. For red-gold, some copper was added, and for lighter gold tones, silver was added. Many artists enhanced the gold by polishing it or by making fine puncture holes to create particular light effects.[3]

The stones and other ingredients were ground in a mortar until a uniform consistency was obtained. The stones were then selected according to their quality – the more valuable a picture was to be, the more care went into the selection of, for example, the darkest and richest lapis lazuli.

The production and use of different types of paper also required a great deal of expertise. They used paper made from rags, also from jute, cotton wool and silk. Paper was occasionally made from bamboo, or certain types of tree bark. In Akbar's time, artists favoured a stiff, cream-coloured paper, whereas in Shah Jahan's time they used a lighter grade of paper, which was often made from silk threads. Kashmir was always an important centre for paper production, but it was also produced in Lahore, Ahmedabad and Daulatabad. They were familiar with the art of marbling, and the most beautiful calligraphy was written on marbled paper. However the art of creating marbled figures was a speciality of artists in the Deccan. Not all pictures were coloured. There is a particularly elegant style called *nim qalam*, in which the scene is drawn with brownish lines, sometimes highlighted with gold or very delicate colours.

Great care was taken with the preparations for illustrations to manuscripts. The first sketch was

100. 'Hamza, killed in battle at Mount Uhud, is beheaded and mutilated by the Lady Pur', an illustration from the *Hamzanama*, *c.* 1562–77, gouache on cotton.

usually drawn by a master, then coloured in by another. There were artists who specialised, for example in faces. The artists' signatures revealed who had contributed to the work.

Occasionally, pictures – often figures drawn from life – were placed on extremely thin, transparent gazelle hides, and then both would be pierced with the finest needles all around the outline of the figure. Then fine charcoal could be rubbed over the pelt, so that a copy could be made on a piece of paper placed underneath. This pounce method was used particularly for portraits of courtiers, who appear so frequently in *durbar* scenes that they almost seem like old acquaintances. In many *durbar* scenes, the figures are not all the same size, because the original pelt stencils were of different sizes.

Once the picture was ready, it was turned over and placed upon a hard, flat surface and then rubbed with an agate to make the surface flat and even.

In Akbar's time, artists used to present their work to the ruler every week, and his great appreciation for art appears to have given them a lot of encouragement in their work.[4]

There were a number of artistic families among the Mughal painters: father and son, uncle and nephew, as well as brothers.[5] There was also a female painter, Nadira Banu, the daughter of a pupil of Aqa Riza, who made copies of Flemish etchings. Children grew up in the artistic tradition, and learnt the techniques of mixing colours and making brushes from a very early age. They also learnt the elements of drawing by copying simple examples, commencing with spirals or triangles, then progressing on to fish, flowers, architectural elements, and then progressing further to different types of horses, elephants, and then people. This method of instruction accounts for the uniformity of shapes and forms in miniatures.

The creation of a miniature required a great deal of patience – in the later Mughal period it used to take six months for an artist to produce one small picture.

For Akbar, painting was a means of bringing historical and romantic texts vividly to life, and also a way of getting to know his fellow human beings better. Studying the portraits of the officers and courtiers who were under his command enabled him to make judgements about them, such as whether they merited promotion; the pictures could sometimes even serve as warrants for their arrest.

There is a story about Akbar who, as a small child, was staying in Kabul, where he drew a figure with missing limbs. This may have been merely a childish drawing; however, when he was asked who it was, he said, 'Hemu!'. Years later, in 1556, when he faced Hemu in battle, he would not kill him himself, for he had already 'dismembered' him when he was a child.[6]

During Akbar's time a new element was introduced into Mughal tradition – the European works brought to the court by the Jesuits. Illustrations in the *Royal Polyglot Bible* and Flemish copper engravings apparently had a tremendous influence on Mughal artists, who not only adopted biblical themes, but also European techniques of perspective and so on.

One of the most interesting miniatures resulting from the initial encounter between Indo-Muslim and European art was an illustration for Nizami's *Khamsa*, the poetical 'Quintet', dating from around 1595.[7] It depicts Plato in front of a portable organ, which had been given to the delighted Akbar by the Portuguese. Surrounding the philosopher are all kinds of animals and birds in a state of ecstatic rapture – anyone who has seen a cat intoxicated by valerian (catnip) will appreciate the lifelike way the Mughal artists painted the lions, panthers and cheetahs lying around with raised paws in a blissful state. Beside the organ, which is decorated with all kinds of European-looking pictures, a man in European clothing wearing a hat can be glimpsed.

Although Akbar was a passionate lover of painting, Jahangir is considered to be the true connoisseur among the Mughals. Jahangir would certainly have been able to watch the artists at work in his father's studio during his childhood, and during his season in Allahabad in 1599 he surrounded himself with painters. One of these artists was Aqa Riza from Herat, whose son Abu'l-Hasan, born *c.* 1588, would later become one of the two most brilliant animal painters at Jahangir's court, and who truly merited the title *nadir az-zaman*, 'The Rarity of his Age'. After Akbar's death, Jahangir dismissed a number of painters who were not up to his exacting standards. This gave rise to the establishment of a number of provincial schools of painting, which further developed the existing style of painting, and also had some influence on the Rajput artists.

Jahangir prided himself on his powers of observation, which enabled him to recognise a painter from his style, and even when several painters had worked on the same picture, he could say straight away which of them had painted the eyes, who had selected the colours and so on.

Jahangir was interested in many aspects of painting. Like his father, he used paintings as a guide to physiognomy, to enable him to recognise and assess his nobles, which was important when engaging and promoting officials. According to a guest of his, Mutribi, Jahangir even had pictures of two Central Asian poets, whom he had never personally seen, improved according to Mutribi's descriptions of them.[8]

To some extent Jahangir regarded paintings as

scientific instruments by means of which he could study the world. He took a great interest in all kinds of animals and plants, and missed no opportunity to have a rare or strangely coloured or shaped creature painted – even the dying ʿInayat Khan. Nothing was too insignificant to merit his attention. There is a realistic depiction of a gecko, with its speckled skin and alert gaze; also one of a noble, mournful-looking nilgay. Magpies and water birds, mynah birds and plants, all were depicted by Mughal painters. The flora of Kashmir was especially thoroughly documented. The pre-eminent painters of the natural world were Abu'l-Hasan and Mansur, however Bishndas was regarded as the best portrait painter. Jahangir sent him to Iran with Khan ʿAlam to paint a number of portraits of 'his brother' Shah ʿAbbas I. Manohar and his father Basawan, two Hindu masters of soft, fluid form, who painted incisive portraits of holy men and *yogis*, were also very high in Jahangir's esteem.

Many different types of portraiture developed in Jahangir's time.[9] The most important kind was the standing portrait, thanks to which we are able to recognise not only a number of Mughal rulers, but also numerous members of the court, who are also depicted in groups at receptions and festivities. Painters did not write the names or ranks of people they painted in their pictures, either beside the figures or on their clothing. However Iʿtimad ad-daula is immediately recognisable by his fine aristocratic profile; Mirza Rustam Qandahari (a grandson of Shah Tahmasp), is recognisable by his blue eyes and pale face; and Mahabat Khan is easily identified by his pale, round face, somewhat flattened nose, small moustache, and cunning expression. The Deccan rulers Ibrahim ʿAdil Shah and Qutb ul-mulk both asked Jahangir for his portrait.[10]

As well as standing portraits, there were the so-called *jharoka* portraits, which depicted the ruler's head and shoulders, or down to his chest, as his subjects would have seen him when he appeared at his window.

The nobility are often portrayed on horseback or seated on a throne or high seat, or out hunting, emphasising their strength and skill. There are many pictures of the ruler and his household at a *durbar*. Family portraits are especially appealing, as they clearly show the princes' tender affection for their children. Rulers and princes are shown visiting holy sites or holy men. As well as the relatively large portrayals of the members of the court, there are also small pictures, about 2 x 2 cm, which were sometimes worn on turbans. These were occasionally carved as onyx cameos.

There was another development during the time of Jahangir, who loved allegorical pictures as well as realistic ones. This might have been partly due to the influence of the European prints taken to India by the Portuguese and the British. Jahangir became exceptionally interested in European painting, and his artists copied a portrait brought by Sir Thomas Roe so accurately that it could hardly be distinguished from the original. Sir Thomas then ordered a number of large English paintings for the court, which provided inspiration for the miniaturists.

These may have been the origin of the allegorical figures and strange forms from antiquity which are found on both outer and inner palace walls – curiously shaped plump *putti* or winged angels' heads appear in the most unlikely places, especially on portraits of Jahangir.

In one portrait, Jahangir is seen with his foot on a small globe, indicating the extent of his power, with the key to it on his belt. Small golden angels can be seen on the roof of his tent. In another picture he is again shown with his foot on a globe; however, in this case it is the head of the Deccan

101. Abu'l Hasan, 'Jahangir shooting the head of Malik Amber', from a Minto Album, *c.* 1616, pigment and gold on paper.

army leader Malik Amber, who was putting up a great fight against the Mughal army in the northern Deccan. Jahangir hoped eventually to be able to defeat him with the assistance of the magic power of portraiture.[11] In this state of wishful thinking, he is shown wearing a striped silk waistcoat with a high collar and a transparent floral patterned *jama*, as well as a strange high hat, all of which contribute to the grotesqueness of the scene. Carefully inspection of the background reveals innumerable tiny soldiers, which is typical for this kind of picture.

One of the most famous views of Jahangir was painted by Abu'l-Hasan. The emperor had a dream in which he embraced Shah ᶜAbbas of Iran, and the court artist painted a picture of his dream. The Iranian monarch is shown in a dark red costume threaded with gold, looking rather weak. He is allowing Jahangir, who is shown as large, radiant and bejewelled, to pull him towards his breast, and is to some extent bathing in his reflected glory. The globe which the two rulers are holding displays a scene of a lion lying down peacefully beside a lamb[12] – symbolic of the eventual state of peace which was a popular theme of poets. Aurangzeb attempted to bring this state of peace about by leading a tame lion and a goat through the streets of Delhi every day. In the picture of Jahangir's dream, the elegant lion is shown gently pushing his Iranian neighbour's shabby sheep into the Mediterranean, which adds greatly to the picture's appeal, even if unintentionally. It is not only the allegorical aspect of the picture which is important – Jahangir was a descendant of Babur, whose name means 'Tiger', whilst Shah ᶜAbbas belonged to line of the Turkoman Aqqoyunlu, the 'White Sheep', so the animals had dynastic as well as political significance.

Even more famous is a picture of Jahangir on an hourglass, which has been the subject of extensive study by Richard Ettinghausen: 'Jahangir setting a Shaykh against the power of the world'. The Shaykh, who is being handed a book by the ruler, and who is seated upon a gigantic hourglass, could well be a Chishti master. Next to him is an imaginary portrayal of an Ottoman sultan, and a portrait of the British King James I, copied from a European source. The painter Bichitr has also placed himself in the bottom left-hand corner of the picture, holding a picture in his hand. The tiny angels in this picture are little Europeanised rascals.[13]

Despite their imaginary embellishments, Jahangir's portraits are quite true to life, and the painters were not afraid to show the signs of aging,

whereas all but a few portraits of Akbar depict him as a vigorous ruler in the prime of life. Under Shah Jahan, the art of portraiture became more formalised, and pictures tended to be flattering. Akbar's son, like his grandson, preferred to be painted holding a flower or jewel rather than riding on a racing elephant, and their portraits are models of decorum. Jahangir had a portrait painted of himself holding a small picture of his father, undoubtedly as an assertion of his dynastic right to rule (his rebellion in 1599, which had so angered his father, had not been forgotten).

A feature common to all portraits, whether of the rulers or the nobles, is that they are three-quarters or full-length profiles, never face on, so the posture of the subject sometimes appears somewhat awkward. The position of the subjects' hands is quite significant – the holy man Mian Mir, for example, is typically depicted holding a rosary with fingers bent with arthritis.

Family portraits of the rulers and princes are particularly appealing. Prince Khurram and his son are shown playing together with jewels, as casually if they were just coloured stones.[14] There are numerous romantic portraits of Mughal princes with young women, especially of Shah Jahan's youngest son Murad, often on a terrace or beside a river or pools, in evening light, with elegant cushions. Servants are shown bringing wine and other refreshments, averting their gaze whilst the prince fondles the young lady's breasts.[15] There is even a small picture of Dara Shikoh dressed for bed. He and his beloved – undoubtedly his dearly loved wife Nadira Begum – are gazing deeply into each other's eyes; their servants' clothing is shimmering against the dark background, and the lamps are casting a golden light. It is an extremely atmospheric scene, which Balchand has captured with great delicacy. Balchand, like his brother Payag, loved dark tones and nocturnal scenes.

102. Attributed to Abu'l
Hasan, *Jahangir holding
a portrait of the Madonna,*
c. 1620, gold and ink on
paper.

After the fall of the empire following the death
of Aurangzeb (who was not all that interested in
painting), there was an increasing interest in intimate, in fact rather too intimate scenes. There is
a scene of Muhammad Shah Rangela, 'The
Dissolute', on a sedan chair, being carried by
young ladies into a garden,[16] There is even a picture of him making love which is reminiscent of
Hindu depictions of Krishna and Radha, and illustrations in the *Kama Sutra.*

Developments in landscape painting from the
latter part of Akbar's rule are an important aspect
of Mughal art. Painters had learnt the art of perspective from European prints, and they began

incorporating this, for aesthetic reasons rather
than in the interests of scientific accuracy. The
background of many miniatures, especially from
the time of Jahangir, almost resemble pencil drawings, with surprising additions, such as a railway
bridge and buildings which look like churches, or
else a Dutch church tower, even though the picture itself might be of people in Kashmir or Agra.

Figure drawing became much more realistic,
with Govardhan's half-naked *yogis* being good
examples of this artistic development.[17] The vast
number of people shown in the background, for
instance of hunting or *durbar* scenes, is very interesting – at first glance, there appears to be a

103. 'A European in an Indian landscape', *c.* 1610, gouache and gold on paper.

delicate grey net over the background; however, closer inspection reveals it to be a mass of people, and in the case of battles, even equipped with weapons. Individual figures can only be made out if the picture is greatly enlarged, for instance in a slide projection, which sometimes reveals them to be accurate characterisations. It is quite remarkable to see an entire regular 'forest' of lances depicted with the most delicate brushstrokes. The best example of the painters' skill in this respect is a picture of the battle of Samugarh in 1658, where Aurangzeb defeated his brother Dara Shikoh. The background of this decisive battle is a mass of tiny horses, elephants, tents and vehicles.[18] Sometimes artists added scenes from daily life to the background of their pictures, which are a source of information about the life of peasants working in the fields with their carts, or country people drawing water, which would not by themselves merit a larger portrayal.

The influence of the *Polyglot Bible*, and of European brush techniques, was not limited to technical aspects such as perspective. The incorporation of Christian themes is particularly interesting. There are pictures of the Madonna, also of legends about Christ, which were familiar to Muslims from the Qur'an and from religious, especially mystical, literature. One example is the familiar story in which Jesus happened upon a dead dog and admired the radiant beauty of its teeth, whereas his disciples were only aware of the stench of the cadaver.

European pictures were often 'Mughalised'. One especially beautiful example of this is the picture of a hermit, by Farrukh Beg, who worked at court from 1585. It is derived from a portrait of Marten de Vos;[19] however the Mughal artist has added a few cute kittens playing with milk bottles around the hermit, and the large tree with its stylised foliage is definitely oriental.

104. 'Virgin and Child with an angel and attendant', early 18th century, watercolour and gold on paper.

Another result of this East-West cross-fertilisation was a large number of portrayals of angels, in addition to the rather poor renderings of angel heads in allegorical paintings of Jahangir. Belief in angels is part of Islamic dogma, and they appear in many works, from angel scribes (*Sura* 80:15–16) to the angel of death, from guardian angels to Gabriel, the angel of revelation. The Mughals were clearly very interested in angels, which also appeared on the imperial robes worn by Jahangir, Shah Jahan and Jahanara, and probably on many other items now lost.[20] They are also frequently found in illustrations to classical works, such as the excellent portrayals of the Prophet Muhammad on his journey to heaven. The prophet king Solomon, to whom Shah Jahan felt a special affinity, is depicted in the company of angels, in this case rather plump ones.[21] There is an interesting example of the interaction between Christian and Muslim interpretations of a theme in the Musée Guimet in Paris, the so-called 'Angel of Tobias'. The angel is dressed in a luxurious gold brocade dress with a blue blouse and a red shawl, and a sort of floral crown in the style of European Mannerist painters. Its wings are bright blue, red, greenish and black, and it is holding a huge fish. The biblical story of Tobias is unknown in Islam, and the Mughal artist must have had a picture of the archangel Michael in mind, who, in popular mythology, distributes food to the world.

When pictures began to be collected in albums, people evidently felt the need to 'frame' them, often with a pretty border. The borders were initially floral or geometrical patterns, with arabesques, usually in half-tones or delicate gold. Gradually they became more colourful, with the addition of half-tone figures. Floral decorations gradually became more common, and, especially in Shah Jahan's time, more artistic. An album of Jahangir's, which is now in Berlin, displays the early stage of development.[22] Another album assembled by Jahangir and his son has highly artistic floral or geometrical borders. Whereas the miniatures themselves are often elegant, formal portrayals of the ruling class, the figures in the margins are full of life. They portray not only Christian themes, but also skilfully drawn everyday figures, such as fruit sellers, students, holy men, hunters with guns or bows and arrows, gardeners digging, women with pots and baskets of flowers on their heads, musicians, and many others, which provide a vivid, if only marginal, portrayal of daily life in the time of Jahangir. Only rarely did court paintings take scenes from the bazaar or from daily life as their central theme.[23] (A new edition of Hermann

Goetz's work, *Bilderatlas zur Kulturgeschichte der Moguls*, which was long out of print, is very welcome for its reproductions of many such drawings and miniatures.)

All Mughal rulers, from Babur onwards, were passionate collectors of books, and at the beginning of the seventeenth century a new form of book came into being, the album. Jahangir and his descendents had portraits, pictures of animals or allegorical scenes mounted together with pages of wonderful calligraphy, each illustrated page being backed by a page of writing. They were bound so that the written and illustrated pages faced each other, both sides having similar border decorations. A few albums had been compiled in earlier times, for instance under Shah Tahmasp, but the most luxurious examples were made in the time of Jahangir and his son. The son continued working on an album bequeathed to him by his father, and his poet laureate Abu Talib Kalim praised the work in two poems:

> It is a colourful copy from the 'rose bush of heaven', and it is not merely an album – no, the dipping 'pen' has created a mussel containing a priceless pearl: every written passage (*khatt*) is as enchanting as the region (*khatta*) of Kashmir; each round letter intoxicates the reader like a glass of wine; the courtesans of paradise can be found within, and the long locks of these beauties and the locks of the long letter *lam* (l) are harmoniously entwined; if only these beautiful figures were really able to take an elegant stroll in the garden of the pages of the album . . . [24]

The writer reveals his fantasies as well as his admiration for the painter and the calligrapher of the work which was held in such high esteem at court.

105. 'A Christian knight fighting a Saracen foot-soldier', c. 1630, gouache with gold on an album leaf.

A few miniatures in albums are surrounded by very elegant passages of text, which are revealed by close inspection to have nothing to do with the subject of the miniature. Almost certainly this was because the compilers were using up scraps, for these little verses – very rarely prose – have been cut out and pasted on. The size as well as the style of these fragments reveal that they have been taken from anthologies known as *safina*, 'boat'. These *safina* are often portrayed in miniatures, especially in scenes of someone reading in a garden, holding a slim volume in his hand. A *safina* was a kind of *vade mecum*, bound on its short side, which had been in use in Persian regions at least since the mid-fifteenth century, and which contained verses, usually in Persian. People compiled their own anthologies, or had them written by artists in the most exquisite miniscule lettering. *Safina*s could easily be carried in people's sleeves, which were often used to carry small objects, or in the folds of a turban, as a 'pocket book'. Many families which migrated to India from Iran and Afghanistan during the course of the sixteenth century appear to have taken such *safina*s with them, which gradually fell apart from frequent perusal.

Because people were reluctant to throw away the remaining pages with poems, or extracts of poems, written on them, a use was found for them in the studios, where they were cut up and stuck around pictures as decorations. The fragments of poems bordering the so-called 'Kevorkian Album', for example, are by a variety of authors. The name Shahi (died 1453), the favourite poet of readers of the fifteenth and sixteenth centuries, frequently appears, and his *Diwan* was adorned with very fine miniatures in Akbar's studio.[25] Even fragments of Chaghatay poetry by Sultan Husayn Bayqara of Herat, in the handwriting of Sultan ʿAli Meshedi, can be found as marginal decoration.

106. 'A composite elephant with prince and cup-bearer sitting in a howdah', 17th century, ink and pigment on paper.

These pretty marginal excerpts provide additional if only fragmentary information regarding the reading matter of the Mughal court. Turkish sources reveal that a similar cut and paste technique was practiced at the Ottoman court.

There is one more speciality of Mughal art which deserves a mention. They liked drawing or painting composite figures, for example an ele-

phant, or other animal, even a human being, made up of human, animal or demonic components. All manner of variations were created by Mughal painters; however they were not the first to use this technique, for there are earlier examples by Persian artists. The Mughal artists appear to have taken particular pleasure in fantastical themes, undoubtedly fostered by Hindu traditions.[26] Sometimes the figure of a slim woman would be made into a swing, or faces or figures would be created out of human forms. This form of art was also known in Europe, as can be seen from a picture by Willem Schellinks, with the title *Shah Jahan and his Sons*, which depicts the four imperial princes Dara Shikoh, Shah Shuja<sup>c</sup>, Aurangzeb and Murad riding horses composed of slim female bodies – the very embodiments of European fantasies of the sensuous orient.[27]

Europeans were familiar with Indian miniatures from the seventeenth century, and no less an artist than Rembrandt, who possessed a collection of miniatures from the time of Jahangir, made 21 copies of miniatures, including the famous drawing of four holy men sitting in an idyllic landscape. In 1656, some of his miniatures were sold at auction. Twenty years later, Friedrich Wilhelm of Brandenburg inherited an album with 57 Indian miniatures, worth 200 *talers* at the time. In 1728, more than 450 miniatures belonging to the Mayor of Amsterdam, Nicholaas Witsen, were auctioned. The collections held by European museums were for the most part acquired from these formerly private collections.[28]

There is an even larger collection in Schönbrunn, where in 1762 the Empress Maria Theresa had 260 miniatures created in the Millions Room, where they were used as a sort of wallpaper, cut up or assembled out of pieces.[29] Mughal miniatures were the first examples of Islamic art – in fact, of Islamic culture – to reach Europe. It was these small but wonderful pictures, as well as the reports of merchants and travellers, which inspired a jeweller in Dresden to create his famous work, 'Aurangzeb's Birthday Celebration'. Miniatures were a source of inspiration for European artists long before literary works from Muslim Indian were known to the West.

## BUILDINGS AND GARDENS

> I am quite certain that this building deserves to be counted among the wonders of the world far more than the pyramids of Egypt, those formless masses!
> Bernier on the Taj Mahal (1670)

The architecture of the Mughals is incredibly rich. As well as fortress-like palaces, it was above all burial places to which architects of the Mughal empire devoted their best efforts, with Humayun's mausoleum in Delhi serving as a model in this respect. Akbar's mausoleum in Sikandra, near Agra, is a remarkable conglomerate of different styles, and, like all mausoleums, is in a large garden, which is supposed to be modelled on the garden of paradise. His son Jahangir is said to have paid one and a half million rupees for it. It contains wonderful inlay work of white marble in red sandstone, typical of the period. There are supposed to have been murals on the inner and outer walls depicting, among other subjects, the Virgin Mary. However, according to Manucci, these were obliterated by Aurangzeb. Even more of the lavish fittings were lost in 1691 when the mausoleum was looted by the Jats.

Akbar's mausoleum is predominantly red sandstone, which at sunset seems to radiate light of its own. Red sandstone also predominates at Jahangir's mausoleum outside Lahore, which is level with the ground in a garden, shaped like the mausoleum of his father-in-law I<sup>c</sup>timad ad-daula, and encrusted with cheerful depictions of vases, jugs and goblets. In the following centuries, many of the beautiful mausoleums from the time of Jahangir and Shah Jahan have been stripped of their white marble casing, which has then been reused elsewhere. All that remains of the noble building erected by the *khankhanan* <sup>c</sup>Abdu'r Rahim

107. 'The Gateway of Akbar's tomb at Sikandra', *c*. 1820, watercolour on paper.

for his wife near Humayun's grave in Delhi is the red sandstone inner structure.

The Taj Mahal, which Shah Jahan had built for his beloved wife Mumtaz Mahal, is unquestionably the epitome of Indian architecture, the most photographed of all buildings in India. The Taj Mahal is so magnificently constructed that the visitor is quite taken aback on realising just how enormous the delicate looking structure actually is. It is built on a high platform, which makes it appear quite inaccessible.[1] Tavernier records that 20,000 men worked on its construction. The building is set in a traditional garden so that it is reflected in a central canal, which was also intended in the case of the above mentioned mausoleums, but was not so successfully achieved in their case. This layout follows the traditional nine-fold pattern, which reached its highest expression in Humayun's mausoleum. The size of the building is impressive enough, but the *rauza-i munawwar*, 'The Illustrious Tomb Garden' is even more astonishing. Numerous marble reliefs, mostly of flowers and blooms, decorate the outer walls, enhancing the general impression of delicacy, even transparency.

Experts are astounded at the enormous inscriptions around the entrance, which are of Qurᵓanic verses composed of flawlessly beautiful white marble lettering. The broad terrace at the rear looks out over the Jumna river, and towards the Red Fort in the distance. In addition there are many smaller buildings in the large complex, including a mosque, the mausoleums of a few women especially closely connected to the Mughal household, and houses for servants.

There has been a great deal of debate regarding the architects, whom it is assumed were working under French or Italian influence. Apparently the architect Ustad Ahmad Lahori, who was also known as *Nadir al-ᶜasr*, 'The Rarity of the Age', (died 1649) was chiefly responsible for the building. He also worked on the Red Fort in Shahjahanabad. Amanat Khan (died 1644) was the master calligrapher who created the inscriptions.

There is no better way of following the change in the artistic climate of India than by comparing the Taj Mahal with the burial place built by Aurangabad, the son of Shah Jahan and Mumtaz Mahal, for his wife Rabiᶜa Daurani. This building

108. Thomas Daniell, *The Great Gate leading to the Taj Mahal, Agra*, between 1786 and 1793, pencil and water-colour.

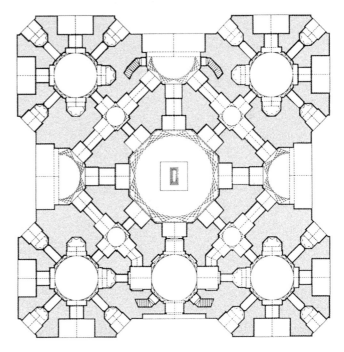

109. Floor-plan of the mausoleum of Humayun, Delhi.

was constructed in Aurangabad, in the Deccan, scarcely twenty years later, in 1660. Although this narrow fronted building is certainly attractive, it looks a bit like a stunted Taj Mahal. Instead of marble, shining *chuna* was used, a fine mortar which reflects like a mirror when polished.

The Mughals were accustomed to the uncertainty of life, and when Akbar first decided to found a large city, Fatehpur Sikri, the plans for the city only really began to take shape when Shah Jahan designed his new city in Delhi, which was built to a geometrical plan with wide, straight streets. It was initially called 'Shah-jahanabad', although it later became known simply as 'Delhi', even though it was quite some distance from the traditional districts of the city, such as Nizamuddin. Construction began on 12 May 1639, and the inaugural celebrations were held nine years later, on 19 April 1648. The fort was adorned with velvet brocade from Gujarat and a canopy measuring 70 x 45 royal cubits (*c.* 25 x 15 m.), with a height of 22 yards (*c.* 19 m.), which was supported on four silver pillars about 2.5 yards (2.20 m.) in length.

The Timurids were very familiar with the concept of a mobile palace, as were the Mughals, who put it into practice during their numerous travels and military campaigns. Early Mughal buildings in India developed out of the Timurid style found in Samarkand and Central Asia. The first two rulers of the 'House of Timur' had no time to devote to building. Babur built the fort in Agra, on the Jumna. Humayun spent too much time out of the country to be able to carry out much building work; however, his mausoleum, in which the nine-fold foundation plan was perfected, set a standard for subsequent Mughal buildings. It had a central area surrounded by eight smaller rooms, with al-coves and corners. This ground plan long remained the ideal for

Mughal buildings, just as the location of Humayun's grave at the far end of a garden is typical for most monuments from the following decades, even centuries. Almost all important Mughal buildings are situated by a river.[2]

Akbar had a number of palace fortresses built: Jaunpur (1566), Ajmer (1570), Lahore (renovated and remodelled before 1580), Attock (1581) and Allahabad (1583). The most important building from his time was the fort at Agra (1564–70). Abu'l Fazl records that it was comprised of more than five hundred buildings of all kinds. However here, as in all other buildings, there were three distinct areas for traditional purposes: the *diwan-i ᶜamm*, the public area, the *diwan-i khass*, accessible to dignitaries and special visitors only, and finally the private quarters of the ruler and the court ladies.

Fatehpur Sikri, Akbar's dream city, is the most surprising structure of all. According to many art historians, it symbolises an all-powerful monarchy, a microcosm, or even an *imago mundi*.[3] In 1571 Badaʾuni wrote:

> He laid the foundation for a new shrine (i.e. Salim Chishti's mausoleum) and a tall, spacious mosque, which was so large that it appeared to be part of a mountain. Scarcely anything like it can be seen anywhere in the inhabited world. The building was completed within five years, and he called the place Fatehpur, and built a bazaar and an entrance gate and baths, and the nobles built towers and tall palaces for themselves. According to the chronogram: 'There is nothing comparable to this anywhere else'.

The enormous 54-metre entrance gateway to Fatehpur Sikri, which can be seen from miles away when approaching the city, is undoubtedly unique. The inscription on it was written by Akbar and

110. Detail from a panorama of the fort at Agra, c. 1815, watercolour, inscribed in ink with identifications of the buildings.

111. The mosque of Shaykh Salim Chishti, Fatehpur Sikri, 1569–74.

Jahangir's loyal historian, calligrapher and diplomat Mir Maᶜsum Nami, from Bhakkar (Sind). It is dated 1603, by which time the city had long since ceased to be the residence of the court. There is a saying carved on it, attributed by Islam to Jesus, concerning the impermanence of all things: 'The world is a bridge, cross over it, but do not build a house on it!' There was a commercial route between Fatehpur Sikri and Agra.

Fatehpur Sikri has been the subject of extensive study by art historians, especially the red sandstone buildings, many of which display traditional Indian features, especially from Gujarat. From the descriptions provided by art historians it is possible to recognise the *diwan-i khass*, the upper room of which is supported by one single column, the appartments where the ladies and the nobility lived, and the area where the pool and the polo grounds would have been located. The delicate pearl-white mausoleum of Shaykh Salim is located on the far side of the broad courtyard. The ruler had his son Jahangir to thank for this small white jewel with wonderful carved *jalis* (latticework windows), and an exquisitely inlaid roof. From the holy mausoleum to the courtesans' quarters, everything had been carefully planned. However, even a visitor who spends hours strolling around the huge complex needs a lot of imagination to be able to visualise the rooms carpeted and filled with all manner of artists busy creating the first great masterpieces of Indo-Muslim painting, and Akbar himself in discussion with representatives of the different religious groups.

Under Shah Jahan, architecture became 'botanised' (according to Ebba Koch), and balustrade columns and arched roofs came into fashion.

Abu Talib Kalim's ode to the palace built by Shah Jahan in Delhi could also apply to many of the great edifices of the Mughal period:

How beautiful you are, palace, almost like fire!
Your radiance illuminates the world like the
glow of New Year!
Your roof is a mirror for the cheeks of heaven,
The stars receive their light from you.
Your building so high, so enormous your
throne –
The dust underfoot: the great Ctesiphon.
Your shade: God's grace upon the earth,
Beggars entering your door become princes!
No one who has gazed upon your entrance
arch
Could view with wonder the canopy of
heaven!
Within sits Shah Jahan, enthroned in all his
might –
What could be higher, or possessed of greater
pomp?[4]

There are a few more noteworthy features of Mughal palaces (and a few mausoleums); the rooms and corridors were shielded from the outside by *jalis*, which were sometimes constructed from a single block of stone. These latticework windows, which were often made of red or yellow sandstone, or, especially in Shah Jahan's time, of marble, display the great creativity of Mughal stonemasons. They used a stone tablet, which usually measured from 1 to 1.5 metres in height, and only a few centimetres in thickness, and carved out an interweaving geometrical pattern, or botanical patterns in which buds and blooms appeared to be growing naturally out of the stone. In some *jalis*, the stone looks as if it has been moulded like wax into bowed and curved shapes.

The *jalis* allowed the light entering the rooms to cast delicate shadow patterns onto the marble walls, and for the breeze to serve as air conditioning, which is most welcome on the pathways around mausoleums.

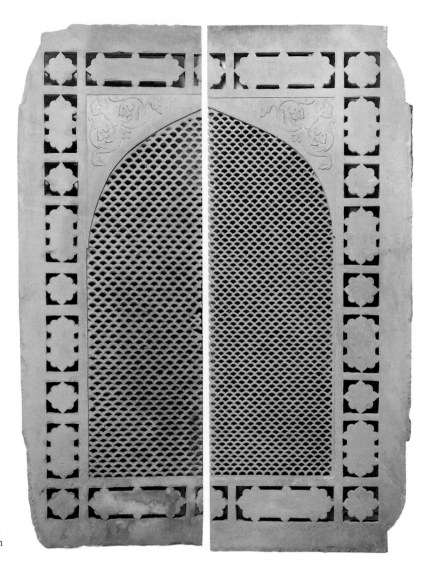

112. A carved sandstone *jali* window-lattice (17th or 18th century).

In the interior of the palaces, especially in Shah Jahan's time, there would often be a 'mirror room', *shish mahal*, the walls (and sometimes also ceilings) of which were covered with a mosaic of little mirror pieces in all kinds of patterns, which created a wonderful effect by candlelight in the evening, shimmering hypnotically. Other rooms, including bedchambers,

were sometimes also fitted out in this fashion. In Shah Jahan's private rooms in Shah Burj, Lahore, there were also pictures, which were whitewashed over for a long time, and only discovered a few decades ago.

Another kind of wall decoration which was popular at a much earlier period, and which can be seen in numerous miniatures, were numerous wall alcoves in which bottles, vases and glasses were kept.

Small waterways were often used to provide air conditioning in the central areas of the palace. Small waterfalls were constructed, with the water cascading down stairways or sloping surfaces, which were sometimes patterned – zig-zag patterns of different coloured marble made the water appear to be flowing very rapidly (such as in Lahore Fort, 1631–32).[5] In places the water also flowed over inlaid emeralds, so that it appeared to be emerald green in colour. When such waterfalls were constructed in gardens, they might flow in front of a *chinikhana*, a small wall with alcoves containing bouquets of flowers by day, and oil lamps by night, which sparkled through the water. In addition to mirror mosaics and alcoves, miniatures reveal another form of wall decoration in Mughal palaces whereby all kinds of pictures were painted on the marble or *chuna*, for instance a pair of larger than life-size hares facing each other, cheerful hunters, or European-looking allegorical figures.[6] British visitors to the Mughal court during the time of Jahangir reported that the walls of the fort at Lahore were covered with all kinds of paintings, including pictures of the Madonna and Jesus. There were romantic scenes in many rooms, and Akbar's bedchamber in Fatehpur Sikri displayed a picture of people in a boat. There was a picture of the Madonna on the wall behind Jahangir's throne in Agra.

Angels were clearly a particular popular subject, as were winged fairies. Shah Jahan's palace had friezes with angels around the ceilings, as did Jahangir's bedchamber in the fort at Lahore. Ebba Koch has referred to these as a 'Solomon-like programme of birds and angels'.

These decorations would appear to be incompatible with the Islamic prohibition on representational art; however, as early as the Umayyad period, the hunting lodge of Qusayr ʿAmra in Jordan was decorated with pictures of vanquished, or soon to be vanquished, princes and beautiful ladies. In a Timurid pavilion in Herat, Babur also saw pictures portraying the heroic deeds of a few of his Timurid relatives. Five centuries earlier, Sultan Masʿud from Ghazna had a pavilion in Herat painted with (apparently extremely sensuous) depictions of Yusuf and Zulaykha.

During the golden age of the Mughals, such portrayals appear to have been quite usual. Akbar's foster brother, Mirza ʿAziz Koka, adorned his garden pavilion in Agra with beautiful murals. In 1620 Jahangir went still further, renovating a picture gallery in a garden in Kashmir with portraits of his forefathers Humayun and Akbar and other members of the ruling house, as well as a portrait of himself and Shah ʿAbbas. There was also a second row of portraits of the great *amirs*.[7]

There are also references to sculptures, for instance the caravansary which Nur Jahan had constructed between 1618 and 1620, with depictions of people and animals carved on the sandstone facade of an entrance gate (as had earlier been carried out in Fatehpur Sikri). Jahangir had marble statues made of Rana Amar Singh of Udaipur and his son Karan, to be placed under the *jharoka* window in Agra.[8]

Another important feature was the use of tiles to cover inner and outer walls of mosques as well as secular buildings. The entrance to the great mosque at Thatta (Sind), constructed by Shah Jahan, is a beautiful example of extremely complex tile overlay, with innumerable stalactite niches on the ceiling, which create an overhead effect almost like a false sky. Fine pottery decoration appears to have been especially popular in the western part of the Mughal empire. Holy tombs in Sind and the Punjab were covered with blue and white tiles, whilst those in the Punjab were covered with colourful geometrical patterns or fine tendrils, with strong yellow predominating. A particularly beautiful example is the Gulabi Bagh in Lahore, built by Dai anaga, Shah Jahan's *amah*. One of the most beautiful tiled buildings from the Mughal era is the Wazir Khan mosque in Lahore, which was built in 1634 by Wazir Khan of Chiniot, who was the governor of the Punjab at the time. It is decorated with arabesques and sayings from the Qur'an, which are evidence of an interesting architectonic programme.[9]

The most important example of all is the fort at Lahore, the outer walls of which are decorated with hundreds of brilliant coloured tiles. The work was begun in 1624, and took ten years to complete. It provides a glimpse of life within the fortress, depicting elephant fights, which would have taken place in the side of the fort facing the Ravi river, as well as knights and falconers, messengers, and much more besides, including the angels which were so popular at that time. Strangely enough, early travellers paid little attention to this colourful tile mural.[10]

*Pietra dura* was an even more elegant technique of inner and outer wall decoration, which had its heyday during the time of Jahangir and Shah Jahan. Semi-precious stones were inlaid in marble so that buildings resembled large treasure chests. Flowers and tendrils were created with the finest colour shadings, and tiny indentations were made in the marble into which the appropriate stones – often miniscule – were inserted. (Today little boxes and plates made with this technique are available for sale in souvenir shops in Agra and Delhi.) The most beautiful example of this kind of building adornment is the mausoleum which Nur Jahan had built for her father, I'timad ad-daula, in Agra, which puts the visitor in mind of the following verses:

Stone flowers inlaid in marble,
Surpassing the reality in hue, if not in scent.

Quite realistic scenes could be created using the *pietra dura* technique, such as the mosaic behind Shah Jahan's *jharoka* throne in Delhi, which is surrounded by bird motifs, and depicts Orpheus playing his lyre.[11]

RELIGIOUS BUILDINGS

In 1652, in the reign of Shah Jahan, the governor of Delhi had Nizamuddin Auliya's small mausoleum, which is the spiritual centre of Delhi, remodelled into its present form with white marble and a beautifully vaulted cupola. There are many references to the construction of mausoleums for holy men and the remodelling of existing structures during this period, among them Mian Mir's small, elegant burial place in Lahore. The yellow-brown marble building which was constructed in Gwalior for the great mystic Muhammad Ghauth Gwaliari (died 1562) is a particularly beautiful example from the early Mughal period. Its *jalis* even appear to some extent to be a reflection of the teachings of the holy man buried within it, which combined astrological and mystical ideas. The elegant mausoleum of Shah Daulat (died 1616), built in Maner, near Patna, displays the developments to this type of mausoleum in the intervening half century.

The most important religious buildings were, of course, mosques; however, there are not nearly as many of them in the central regions of the empire as might be expected.[12] Akbar's great mosque in Fatehpur Sikri, with its huge court surrounded by cells, became a model for the enormous buildings erected by his descendants

Juma Masjid Dehli

113. Delhi's Friday mosque, watercolour, leaf from an album of drawings by a Punjabi artist, *c.* 1890.

in Delhi and Lahore. Jahangir had no large mosques built, but his son, who had a passion for building, made up for this with numerous mosques in the centre of the empire and also in the provinces. After succeeding his father in 1628, he had a mosque constructed in Agra in fulfilment of a vow. Sind also has him to thank for the wonderful Thatta mosque with its blue tile work (1644–57). At the far end of the line of cliffs on which the fortress of Asirgarh is located, a magnificent, if less well known, building of the same name towers above the surrounding landscape, which was built by Shah Jahan in gratitude for the hospitality he received there during his *hijra*. Burhanpur obviously has a great many mosques, but one of them is especially interesting. Although it was constructed during the time of the preceding dynasty, *khankhanan* ᶜAbduʾr Rahim extended and modernised it. It now displays Islamic religious inscriptions in the Sanskrit language.

The great Friday mosque in Delhi is part of Shajahanabad. It is set in extensive grounds, and stands about 9 m above street level. With its three red and white striped domes and its large courtyard, almost one hundred square metres in area, it is typical of late Mughal architecture.

The Badshahi Mosque, built by Aurangzeb a few decades later (1673–74) in Lahore, displays similar features. There is a very large courtyard, big enough to accommodate tens of thousands of believers for prayers, five open *iwans* pointing out the direction to pray in, and inner halls decorated with delicately painted stucco. Some of the eighty rooms surrounding the court served as schoolrooms, and others as accommodation for devout visitors. In both cases, the mighty entrance gateways, although smaller than the one at Fatehpur Sikri, characterize the entire structure. There are long flights of steps leading up to them, so that the physical ascent matches the spiritual ascent which is the goal of the prayers.

114. *The court of the Pearl Mosque at Agra*, 1825-30, watercolour, from an album of drawings of Mughal monuments.

In almost all cases, the fortress-palace complexes and the mighty mosques form a single unit, symbolically linking state and religion.

There was one more type of mosque created by the Mughal princes, i.e. a small white marble mosque located in the interior of a residence known as a *Moti Masjid*, 'Pearl Mosque' (1662), or, as in Agra, *Nagina Masjid*, 'Jewel Mosque' (1630). These are delicate white marble buildings with graceful domes, sometimes almost Rococo in appearance, which were easily accessible for the ruler and his household. Aurangzeb had a palace mosque of this type constructed in Delhi.

The women of the court also had mosques constructed, such as the one near the fort in Agra built by Jahanara, and a small mosque by the riverside wall of the Red Fort in Delhi donated by her niece Zinat un-nisa, which also displays the three typical late seventeenth-century striped domes. Mosques were also donated by *mansabdar*s (e.g. Wazir Khan), and even endowed by

non-Muslim members of the Mughal household, such as the large mosque by Man Singh in Rajmahal, Bengal.

SECULAR BUILDINGS

There are many secular buildings worthy of note. One particular Mughal contribution to architecture was the *hammam*, the bathhouse, which followed the standard Near Eastern pattern with a room, or perhaps several, for undressing and dressing, the cold room, and the bathing room itself.

The hot water was brought in through terracotta piping. There were also plentiful latrines. Fatehpur was known for the large number of *hammams* there. Not only the rulers, but also wealthy benefactors had *hammams* built in their cities of residence, which were often of considerable architectonic beauty. Asaf Khan, Jahangir's

115. Plan of *khankhanan* ʿAbduʾr Rahim's public bath houses in Burhanpur (1607–08).

brother-in-law, had a very beautiful bathing facility built in Agra; and the one built by *khankhanan* ʿAbduʾr Rahim in Burhanpur is very famous.[13]

Because of the Mughals' extensive trading activities, important trading routes were built between the habours and the capital city, and between the most important centres for the production of goods and agricultural produce. These routes were also important militarily. Babur was the first to build a road between Agra and Kabul. The huge Grand Trunk road built by Sher Shah has already been mentioned. Akbar and Jahangir had routes surveyed and milestones placed at intervals of one *kos* (approximately two miles, or three kilometres). The milestones, according to Babur and others, were often decorated with horns. In Jahangir's time, water fountains were placed at three *kos* intervals, and several rulers and *amir*s had caravansaries built for the convenience of travellers, with numerous guestrooms of various sizes, as well as stables for animals, and storage space for goods. These caravansaries were often architectonically very beautiful, such as the one established by the

*khankhanan* ʿAbduʾr Rahim between Burhanpur and Asirgarh, with its elegant pointed bow construction. Travellers often complained about the state of the roads; however, that does not lessen the value of these facilities. One of their specialities were the *bulghur-khana* (no longer in existence), at which free food was given to the poor, so very important in times of famine.[14]

Finally, bridges were built to improve connections between the important cities, One significant bridge was constructed in Jaunpur during Akbar's time by his *khankhanan* Munʿim Khan (1569).

## MUGHAL GARDENS

Gardens were among the most substantial features of Mughal architecture.[15] After Babur had taken Kabul in 1509, his first act was to construct a garden, the *Bagh-i wafa*, 'Garden of the Faithful'. He also restored Ulugh Beg's garden in Istalif, near Kabul. Miniatures in the *Baburnama* depict him overseeing his gardeners as they prune, sow, plant tree striplings and carry corn seed in their shovels.[16] He planted plane trees, orange trees, lemons and pomegranates, and created a small watercourse in marble. Three generations later, Jahangir referred to his seven gardens in Kabul, three of which, called *shahr ara*, 'city adornments', had been laid out by Babur's aunt Shahrbanu. India seemed to Babur uncivilised, because it had no well-kept gardens – a lack which he and his successors certainly remedied.

The Timurids displayed a particularly strong love of gardens, perhaps in common with all Turkish peoples. Whenever Timur brought a new wife home, he had a special garden created for her.[17]

Akbar made the first great Mughal garden, the *Nasim Bagh*, near Dal Lake, in 1597 in Kashmir. Kashmir became the Mughals' ideal garden land, whether for the famous *Nishat Bagh*, laid out by Asaf Khan, or the *Shalimar Bagh* of Kashmir, which was founded by his brother-in-law Jahangir in 1619. The enormous Shalimar Garden in Lahore, which clearly displays the Mughals' conception of the ideal garden, was named after the one in Kashmir. Like Mughal palaces and castles, it is divided into three areas: one for the general public, one for the elite, and one for the family itself. The Persian architect ʿAli Mardan Khan had to construct a canal more than 100 miles long to bring water from the foothills into Lahore to water this garden.

The Shalimar Garden in Kashmir has an elegant black marble pavilion on the third level. Because it was laid out on hilly ground, it was easy to construct water courses with small falls. However, when the Shalimar Garden in Lahore was being laid out during Shah Jahan's time, it had to be artificially terraced so that small waterfalls could be created.

Almost all Mughal gardens utilize the Persian principle of *char bagh*, 'four gardens', the central element being a large water container, or a fairly extensive pond, with a number of streams running into it. Between the flowerbeds are raised footpaths to give a good view of the grounds and the flowers. The paths are often covered with artistically arranged tiles or bricks, and pavilions are located in picturesque spots, favourite locations being the central platform of a lake or pond. This was also a popular site for mausoleums, so as to provide a preview of the bliss of heaven for the deceased, 'in gardens with rivers flowing by' (*Sura* 2:25 and many other passages).

There is an especially lovely example of one such pavilion in Shaykhupura, near Lahore: the Hiran Minar (1607–20), a memorial to Jahangir's beloved gazelle, is next to a pond, with a sort of marble dam across it providing access to the pavilion – an ideal place for evening concerts, as evinced in many miniatures.

Sometimes tree-houses were built in the branches of suitable trees, primarily for use during hunting expeditions; however, they are also seen in the illustrations to romantic prose or poetry.

The rulers were not alone in their love for gardens. The ladies of the court were enthusiastic creators of gardens, and the nobility also took part in laying them out. After his victory over the Gujaratis, the *khankhanan* ʿAbduʾr Rahim built the Fathbagh, 'Victory Park', in Ahmedabad. He also adorned his long-time residence 'Burhanpur' with a number of gardens to which even the general public were allowed access, which was very unusual.

His colleague Man Singh is credited with creating the Wah Gardens near Hasan Abdal, on the old route from Lahore to Srinagar. The pavilions, ponds and irrigation system of these gardens have recently been renovated.[18] This romantic setting is said to have provided the Irish writer Thomas Moore with the inspiration for his famous poem *Lalla Rookh* (1817). There are some

116. 'Flowers and insects beneath gold clouds', *c.* 1635, gouache with gold on paper, from the Grindlay's Bank Dara Shikoh Album.

beautiful white marble pavilions by the Anasagar Lake in Ajmer, a favourite place of pilgrimage for Mughal rulers. The pavilions were built by Jahangir, and renovated by his son in 1636. They used to be wonderfully illuminated during festivals.

Nevertheless, Kashmir was the ideal location for Mughal gardens. Following Jahangir's visit there in 1620, many garden projects were initiated, although not all were actually carried out. The court nobility also vied with the garden-loving rulers in Kashmir: the Zafarabad Garden created by Zafar Khan is an especially interesting result of this rivalry. Zafar Khan, an excellent governor of Kashmir, who was married to one of Mumtaz Mahal's nieces, wrote about his gardens in a Persian *mathnawi*. A few of the miniature illustrations to the text record the fact that Shah Jahan once paid a visit to the park. The Persian poet Saʾib also lived nearby for some time.[19]

The plane trees of Kashmir were particularly lovely, especially in the autumn when their leaves turned golden yellow. Jahangir's painters loved to depict these magnificent trees, the five-pointed leaves of which traditionally reminded poets of hands 'reaching for a wine goblet' (i.e. a red rose or tulip). Pictures show the vast array of different flowers, such as roses, jasmine and the related *champa*, which was very popular in Kashmir, as well as in Lahore, Agra and Delhi. Jahangir's court painter Nadir al ᶜasr painted more than a hundred pictures of Kashmiri flowers, some of them individual portraits of especially impressive and majestic flowers, others floral decorations in albums, surrounding the actual picture. In each case, the flowers were drawn and painted very realistically. The innumerable poems about gardens, and descriptions of gardens in Mughal poetry, all testify to the extent to which the Mughal rulers and their subjects loved gardens.

Above all others, it is roses which feature in the verses by Mughal poets, for their beauty in gardens symbolizes fleeting happiness:

> The same in shape and form are
> Joy and pain – the rose:
> Call it an open heart . . .
> Call it a broken heart.

This was written by Mir Dard. His contemporary Azad Bilgrami also viewed gardens as symbols of the impermanence of life:

> Only with age do we appreciate
> Scent and colour.
> The young bud: ignorant,
> And still blind . . .

117. Attributed to Bhawani Das, *The Mughal Dynasty from Timur to Aurangzeb, c.* 1707–12, watercolour and gold on paper.

# Epilogue

The Mughal dynasty in India began and ended with poetry, and the emperors who ruled during the intervening period, with few exceptions, had the most highly developed aesthetic sensibilities of any rulers of the world. Within the space of a few decades they developed a style which harmonized everything created by the human hand, from great cities to the tiniest jade needles used to secure turbans. It was a form of art which almost always remained in contact with nature. The emperors were mad about flowers and animals, and these were the subjects of their poetical images and forms, whether a crystal bowl in the shape of a mango, or a jade goblet metamorphosing from a flower into a she-goat.

The kings were thoroughgoing romantics, always striving after the unattainable: Babur, the poet-conqueror, was obsessed by dreams of an empire worthy of his forefathers. Akbar was obsessed by his ideal of an Indian utopia for Hindus and Muslims alike, and Aurangzeb, who almost destroyed the empire with his quixotic ideas, was destroyed by his obsession with conquering the Deccan.

This was written by Stuart Cary Welch in his first book on Mughal art, *Paintings and Precious Objects* (1963). It was the Mughal rulers' mentality, their gift of harmonizing nature and art, and their refined sense of beauty, which made India into a wonderland admired from far and wide, at least in the two centuries from the reign of Babur to that of Aurangzeb. Mughal came to signify wealth and beauty, and this also found expression in Europe – such as Dinglinger's masterpiece of the goldsmith's art in Dresden, and the strange pictures by Willem Schellinks, both of which embody European fantasies of the sensuous orient, which become widespread thanks to the influence of *Tales of One Thousand and One Nights* only a few decades later.

'Agra and Lahore of the Great Mughals' became bywords for wealth, pomp and power. The literature of the Mughal empire was of course inaccessible to the West, although it sometimes seems to be easier to translate the verses of the English poet John Donne into the Persian of his contemporaries at the Mughal court, than into modern German; the Metaphysical poets of the early seventeenth century would have been delighted by the literary conceits of their Indian counterparts.

However, not everyone was enchanted by this illustrious vision. British merchants, European diamond dealers and artists also reported on less savoury aspects of the Mughal empire. The poverty of the general population was in sharp contrast to the luxury of their rulers. Whereas miniature paintings depict luxurious velvet and silk fabrics, and costly jewels, when it came to the ordinary people, 'What can one say about the clothing of the masses, when their sole garment consists of nothing but a cloth wrapped around their hips? And what of their housing, when their rude huts are nothing but a place to sleep?' wrote Moreland.

Yet these millions of people had an unsurpassed ability to create amazing works of art with tools which appear extremely primitive today. The mighty Mughal buildings were constructed without the use of wheelbarrows – the building materials had to be carried to the construction site, as can be seen from miniature illustrations in the chronicles. Using the simplest of tools, Mughal jewellers created the finest jewellery, which cannot be replicated even with the most sophisticated techniques available today. Who today could weave the fabric described as 'woven air'? Or string eight threads through a poppy seed? The techniques used by many of the Mughal master artists are scarcely conceivable – it is impressive enough today just to observe a man at work in a busy street in Hyderabad, in the Deccan, stringing a chain of the finest pearls in no time at all, holding the fine thread in place with his big toe. Just as Jahangir's painters were able to copy English paintings so well that they could scarcely be identified as counterfeits, there are craftsmen in the subcontinent who create incredible copies of European utensils, such as silverware, today.

The more time one spends on the subcontinent, the more aware one becomes of the presence of the Mughals – indeed the manners and customs of the upper classes seem to have hardly changed in many respects.

Characters from the time of the Mughals seem to come to life the more one reads from historical sources, especially since many Mughal historians seem to be able to present their heroes and villains to us so vividly that they appear like our contemporaries, sharing with us their reasons for making appointments or dismissals, or allocating rewards or punishments. Many political developments, especially during the time of Jahangir and Nur Jahan, clearly arose out of personal predilections. Nur Jahan, the Persian possessed of almost limitless power, and her influential family, especially her brother Asaf Khan, were far from universally popular with the important officials. Men were obviously promoted to a higher rank after distinguishing themselves on the field of battle or, more rarely, in administration. However, marriage into the imperial family could also set someone's career on an upward course. The influence of 'foster brothers' was an important one in this respect.

Few of the high ranking *mansabdars* were completely without faults – at least not in the view of Bayram Khan, who fell victim to the intrigues of Maham anaga, whilst his son, the *khankhanan* ʿAbduʾr Rahim, who was a highly esteemed patron, an accomplished army general, poet and translator, was later criticised by later chroniclers for his slyness – 'he seeks to defeat his enemies under the cloak of friendship'.

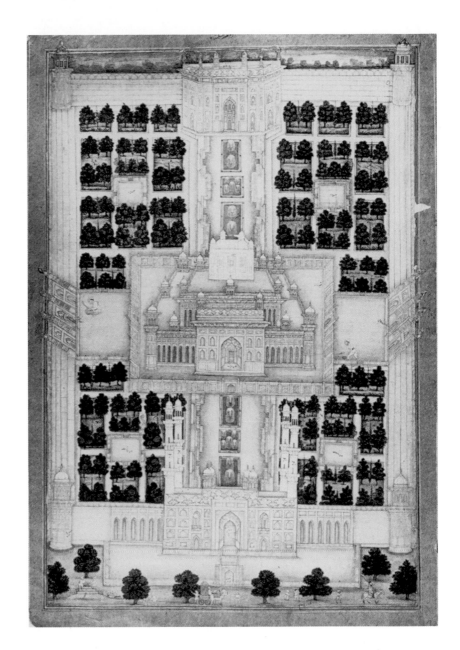

118. A 19th-century engraving of Akbar's tomb in Sikandra.

We are presented with a colourful mosaic of humanity made up of many human races: the brave Turks, who are however considered somewhat unintelligent by some historians; elegant Iranians (especially from Shiraz), oriental-looking Hazaras from Afghanistan, gallant Rajputs, and very many others. Simple souls who only lived to serve the rulers, wily politicians who switched sides whenever it was to their advantage, generous *mansabdar*s who paid their soldiers regularly, sometimes out of their own pockets, and others who wielded their power brutally – all appear on the stage of history.

Here is one, who 'for all his simple mindedness, was very good natured', whereas another was 'strongly built and tall, but well known for his stupidity and ignorance'. One of his colleagues is described as 'a model of faithfulness and steadfastness, who would not be swayed by the slings and arrows of fortune'. In contrast, 'the chief occupations' of another were 'indulging his lusts and eating and sleeping', and he was naturally surrounded by women. Many a *mansabdar* 'with his own hand chopped through the root of his happiness with an axe', and then had to 'wander through the desert of failure'. This could also happen when 'a group of heartless fellows threw the dust of disloyalty into the face of loyalty', in other words, ungrateful to their benefactors, they secretly plotted rebellion and then attacked someone 'whose brain was full of a thousand vexations, like a wasps' nest', and could consequently easily be deceived. Small causes could lead to great effects: 'small discordances blossomed in the garden of his mind', so that he might become dangerous for his – real or imagined – enemies. Many a 'two-faced, forked-tongued person', 'thrived in the daily market of intrigues and trouble making'. If his antics were too wild, the ruler might decide that the troublemaker 'should be relieved of the burden of his scheming head', and 'let the discolouration of arrogance in his cheeks grow pale' (not 'red-faced', which is the Persian expression for 'honoured').

There must have been some very unpleasant men among the officials during Jahangir's time. The chronicler describes one, who was 'a terrible example of contempt for God, full of evil', whose pleasure was limited to 'hearing the sound of the whip', and one of his contemporaries, who was

governor of Bengal (1608), always had a hundred *hafiz* (who knew the Qur'an by heart) in his retinue, who recited the Qur'an at home and on the march, like a hundred trumpeters 'making so much noise 'that the inhabitants of the regions they marched through 'exploded with fury'. Even during prayers he sometimes gave the command to hang or whip someone. There must have been a similar tyrant during the time of Shah Jahan who was up to his tricks in the Deccan, for when 'the news of his death was received, there was no confectioner in Burhanpur whose goods had not all been distributed amongst the inhabitants out of gratitude' (sweets were given out as a sign of pleasure). And so he became, like many of his colleagues, 'a wanderer in the vast realm of non-being'.

However, these brief characterisations of a few of the less lovable individuals in the Mughal period should not detract from the greatness and beauty of this era. The achievements of the early rulers are unforgettable. Their legacies are their magnificent buildings, the unrivalled beauty and wide range of their artworks, and the verses by Mughal poets in many different languages. A great deal may appear alien, even unacceptable to modern readers: however, it should be borne in mind that every age has its own laws, and that an advanced oriental culture in an earlier period of history should not be judged by the standards of the late twentieth century. We should instead be glad to follow the lead of Milton, who blessed the newly created Adam with a vision of the most magnificent pomp and the most illustrious culture, and he found this unique beauty and power...

in the Agra and Lahore of the Great Mughals.

# References

## ONE: Historical Introduction

There is a very large number of works on the history of the Mughals. British academics have translated and published the most important Persian sources, so the writings of Bada'uni, Abu'l Fazl, Jahangir and Samsam ad-daula, among many others, are easily accessible, even though it is necessary to compare them with the original works, especially on the subject of religion. Elliott and Dowson's *History of India as Told by its Own Historians* is an extremely useful overview.

There is an immense amount of pictorial documentation on the Mughal era; it is so vast that I abandoned my intention to include references throughout the text to publications containing Mughal miniatures. R. Weber's comprehensive work, *Porträts und historische Darstellungen in der Miniaturensammlung des Museums für Indische Kunst Berlin*, gives a good overview.

### ZAHIR UD-DIN BABUR

Babur's memoirs provide the foundation. There are many translations (see Bibliography). Quotations are taken from the edition by Wheeler M. Thackston (Washington, DC, 1996), which gives the Chaghatay and Persian text along with the translation. The illustrations are from H. Sulaiman, *Miniatures of Baburnama*.

1 Mutribi, trans. Foltz, *Conversations with Emperor Jahangir*, p. 87.
2 Subtelny, 'Babur's Rival Relations'.

3 *Baburnama*, pp. 263ff., 389, 396, 400.
4 Sulaiman, no. 24 (*Bagh-i wafa*); Goswamy and Fischer, *Wunder einer goldenen Zeit*, ills. 34–35.
5 Sulaiman, no. 92.
6 Sulaiman, no. 94.

### NASIR UD-DIN HUMAYUN

As well as the official historiographies, the most important sources are Gulbadan's *Humayun nama* and Jauhar Aftabji's *Tadhkira*.

1 Hindal was the son of Dildar; Kamran and Askara (born 1516) were the sons of Gulrukh.
2 Aftabji, pp. 45, 51.
3 Gulbadan, pp. 163, 167.
4 Beveridge, *Journal of the Royal Asiatic Society* (January 1897).
5 Chester Beatty Library, Dublin, 39.57; Beach, *The Imperial Image*, no. 12a.
6 Shyam, *Mirza Hindal*.
7 Akbar was in Delhi eleven times – nine times visiting Humayun's grave 'to fortify his heart': Koch, 'The Delhi of the Mughals prior to Shahjahanabad'.

### JALAL UD-DIN AKBAR

There is a vast literature, from Noer to A. Hottinger; Hans Much has produced a delightful translation, K. A. Nizami has produced a critical study; see also Vincent Smith, L. Binyon, I. H. Qureshi, K. P. Menon and the numerous publications on Fatehpur Sikri and on painting of the early Mughul period.

1 *Tuzuk*, I. p. 24.

2  The idea about dyslexia came from Ellen Smart. See also Mahfuz ul-Haqq, 'Was Akbar "utterly unlettered"?', and Thomas W. Arnold, *Bihzad* (London, 1931), which has an example of Akbar's writing in a note in the 'Zafarnama'.

3  *A'in*, III, p. 432.

4  *Akbarnama*, p. 37; Brand and Lowry, *Akbar's India*, no. 2.

5  *A'in*, III; compare also no. 77; also Peter Hardy, 'Abu'l Fazl's Portrait of the Perfect Padshah'. The idea that every step, every action of a holy man has a deeper significance and an effect in the higher spheres is also held by the Chassids.

6  The portrait of Abu'l Fazl: Chester Beatty Library, Dublin, 2. 134–5.

7  Regarding *khankhanan* ᶜAbdu'r Rahim, see Orthmann, *Der Han-i hanan ᶜAbdor Rahim*; Naik, *Khankhanan and his Literary Circle*; Schimmel, *Ein Kunstmäzen zur Moghulzeit*; also *A Dervish in the Guise of a Prince*; also, *The Khankhanan and the Sufis*; M. N. Haq, *The Khankhanan and his Painters*. The most important source is Nihawandi, *Ma'athir-i rahimi*. Portraits in Kühnel and Goetz, *Buchmalereien*, no. 23a; *The Emperors' Album* (a picture of him in old age in the Freer Gallery of Art, Washington, DC), ill. 20. He also appears in many *durbar* scenes, such as 'The Weighing of Prince Khurram'.

8  Regarding Chitor: Bada'uni, II, p. 107f.; 'Akbarnama', II, p. 475; Horn, *Das Heer- and Kriegswesen*; Nizami, *Akbar*, App. XIII; there is a picture in Brand and Lowry, *Akbar's India*, no. 4.

9  See Bada'uni, II, p. 183; the heads of the commanders were conveyed to the ruler in boats; 'Akbarnama', p. 427.

10 Regarding Fatehpur Sikri, see Brand and Lowry, *Fatehpur Sikri: A Sourcebook*; Petruciolli, *Fatehpur Sikri, La città del sole e delle acque*; Rizvi and Flynn, *Fatehpur Sikri*. The oldest picture: E. W. Smith, *Architecture of Fatehpur Sikri*. Habib, *Akbar and his India*, nos. 15–16: construction of Fatehpur Sikri.

11 Bada'uni's observations in II, pp. 262, 211; III, pp. 128, 367.

12 Samsam ad-daula, *Ma'athir al-umara*, I, p. 543.

13 The *mahzar* is dealt with thoroughly in all works on the time of Akbar, among them Bilgrami, Akbar's *mahzar* of 1579; Aziz Ahmad, *Akbar – hérétique ou apostate?*

14 Regarding ᶜAbdul Nabi, see Shamsham ad-daula, *Ma'athir al-umara*, I, p. 44.

15 *Akbarnama*, III, p. 778.

16 Nizami, *Akbar*, p. 13.

17 Regarding this development, see Zebrowski, *Deccani Painting*; Michell, ed., *Islamic Heritage of the Deccan*.

18 C. Ernst, *Eternal Garden: Mysticism, History and Politics in a South Asian Sufi Center*. R. Burhanpuri, *Burhanpur ke Sindhi auliya*.

19 *Akbarnama*, 1163ff. For Asirgarh, see M. M. Hasan, *The Fall of Asirgarh*.

20 A. Ghani, *Persian Language and Literature at the Mughal Court*, III, p. 238. Mirza ᶜAziz Koka was said to be beside himself with joy on hearing of the murder of Abu'l Fazl. The chronogram composed to commemorate Abu'l Fazl's death is *Tigh-i iᶜjaz-i nabi Allah sar-i baghi burid*, 'The Sword of the Miraculous Power of the Prophet of God struck off the head of the Rebel'. Abu'l Fazl appeared to the author in a dream and said that his chronogram really ought to be *banda Abu al-fadl*, 'The servant (of God) Abu'l Fazl'.

21 Welch, *A Flower From Every Meadow*, p. 101.

NURUD-DIN JAHANGIR
See Beni Prasad, *History of Jahangir*.

1  Welch, *A Flower From Every Meadow*, p. 101.

2  Iraj's grave is in Burhanpur; Koch, *Mughal Architecture*, no. 78.

3  Beach, *The Imperial Image*, no. 18c. R. Seth, 'Life and Times of Malik Amber'; and 'Malik Amber: an Estimate'.

4  Cover picture of Beach, *The Imperial Image*; both rulers seated together, *ibid.*, no. 17c.

5  Kanboh, *ᶜAmal-i salih*, p. 203.

SHAH JAHAN
B. P. Saksena, *History of Shahjahan of Delhi*. Beach and Koch, *King of the World*. This edition of the *Windsor Padshahnama* gives the best portrayal of the

splendour of the Mughal era.

1 Kanboh, ʿAmal-i salih, p. 449.
2 The overseer of the Shalimar Garden in Lahore wrote a book on the construction of gardens and agriculture, Falahnama; one of the 1,251 manuscripts by his descendents in 1835, in the Royal Asiatic Society, London, Pers. 212.
3 The scene has been dramatically portrayed: Beach and Koch, King of the World, no. 29; S. Kalim, Diwan, p. 358 (mathnawi).
4 See the section on Sufism in chapter Four. Dara Shikoh is often portrayed in the company of wise men, e.g. S. C. Welch, Imperial Mughal Painting, p. 36.
5 Samsam ad-daula, Maʾathir al-umaraʾ, II, p. 305.
6 Ibid., I, p. 679.
7 There is a lyrical description of the fight over the succession to the throne by Muradbakhsh's poet laureate Bihishti-yi Shirzai in his ʿAshubnama-yi Hindustan, Marshall, Moghuls in India, no. 362.

## AURANGZEB ALAMGIR

Jadunath Sarkar, History of Aurangzeb, 5 vols. Z. Faruqi, Aurangzeb and his Times. Athar Ali, The Mughal Nobility under Aurangzeb. Syed Hashimi, The Real Alamgir. I. Topa, Political Views of Emperor Aurangzeb. J. H. Bilimoria (ed.), Ruqaʾat-yi ʿalamgiri or Letters of Aurangzeb.

1 Beach, The Grand Mogul, p. 19.
2 The Kubrawi Sufi Hamadani also reported that he ate the material for sewing caps, as it contained nothing that was forbidden by the law.
3 Naqvi, History of Mughal Government and Administration. p. 220.
4 Regarding the Firangi Mahal and later developments, see Jamal Malik, Gelehrtenkultur in Nordindien. The comments that Aurangzeb made to Bernier about the necessity of a modern education, which are often quoted, appear to have been Europeanised by Bernier.
5 In this connection, see Dirk Syndram, Der Thron des Grossmoguls. Menzhausen, Am Hofe des Grossmoguls.

## THE TWILIGHT OF THE MUGHAL EMPIRE

W. Irvine, Later Mughals, 2 vols. Jadunath Sarkar, The Fall of the Mughal Empire. Percival Spear, Twilight of the Mughals.

1 Also S. C. Welch in Imperial Mughal Painting, p. 30.
2 Weber, Porträts, no. 82.
3 Picture of the Barha Sayyids in The Emperors' Album, nos. 21, 61.
4 Weber, Porträts, no. 28.
5 Irvine, Later Mughals, II, p. 2. A more positive portrayal: Z. U. Malik, The Reign of Muhammad Shah. Portrait in Weber, Porträts, no. 32. In the Garden: Life at Court, no. 70; S. C. Welch, Imperial Mughal Painting, no. 39; during lovemaking: Life at Court, no. 71.
6 Related in Ahmad Ali, Twilight in Delhi.
7 Ahmad Shah, in Welch, A Flower From Every Meadow, ill. 68.
8 Weber, Porträts, no. 87.
9 Russell and Khurshidul Islam, Three Mughal Poets, p. 32; Jadunath Sarkar, 'Ahmad Shah Abdali in India'.
10 Sprenger, Catalogue . . . of the Libraries of the King of Oudh.
11 Schimmel, Gedanken zu zwei Porträts Shah ʿAlams II. Weber, Porträts, no. 44; Berlin, 'Albumblätter', no. 59; Welch, Room for Wonder, no. 43. The poem in S. M. Ikram, Armaghan-i Pak, p. 319.
12 Welch, Room for Wonder, no. 45: 'Akbar II receiving the British Residents'.
13 Welch, Room for Wonder, no. 52; S. C. Welch, Imperial Mughal Painting, p. 30, no. 40; Goswamy and Fischer, Wunder einer Goldenen Zeit, p. 105; INDIA!, p. 284, on the deathbed, ibid., p.287.

## TWO: At Court

The most detailed descriptions of all duties and ceremonies are by Abuʾl Fazl, Aʾin-i Akbari. There is also a great deal of information in Jahangir's Tuzuk, also in the Shamsham ad-daula, Maʾathir al-umaraʾ. British travellers, especially Sir Thomas Roe, provide detailed descriptions of customs and regulations at court. There is a useful overview of the time of Shah

Jahan in *Life in the Red Fort*. There are numerous pictures of Akbar and his successors in the *durbar*.

THE *DURBAR*: An Audience with the Great Mughal
1 Shamsham ad-daula, *Maʾathir al-umaraʾ*, I, p. 354.
2 *Ibid.*, I, p. 831; compare *ibid.*, II, p. 188.
3 Schimmel, *Islamic Names: An Introduction*: Garcin de Tassy, 'Mémoire sur les noms propres'.
4 Shamsham ad-daula, *Maʾathir al-umaraʾ*, I, p. 562.

OFFICES
1 Concerning the seal, see Gallop, *The Genealogical Seal*; also Weber, *Porträts*, no. 81ff., which the author clearly referred to. Picture of the ruler with the seal: Shah Jahan, in Goswamy and Fischer, *Wunder einer goldenen Zeit*, no. 43; Jahangir shooting Malik Amber (Beach, *The Imperial Image*), no. 18c etc.

DIPLOMATIC RELATIONS
1 Riazul Islam, *Indo-Persian Relations*.
2 There are numerous illustrations of ambassadors to the Mughal court, e.g. in M. Beach and E. Koch, *King of the World*, no. 17; *Life at Court*, no. 13. The Mughal embassy of Shah ʿAbbas has been well documented by the painter Bishndas.
3 There are many depictions showing an ambassador – or high-ranking visitor – being supported at the waist in the course of a taslim, e.g., Berlin, 'Albumblätter', no. 29, Beach and Koch, *King of the World*, nos. 6–7 etc. Welch, *Paintings*, no. 3.
4 Particularly clear concerning the customs relating to gift-giving: Beach and Koch, *King of the World*, no. 19, in which the Portuguese who settled in Hooghly arrive with their packages of presents.
5 Riazul Islam, *Indo-Persian Relations*, p. 236.

THE TRAVELLING COURT
Ansari, *The Encampment of the Great Mughals*. Beach and Koch, *King of the World*, give an overview of Shah Jahan's journey: movements of the imperial camp during the reign of Shah Jahan.
1 Regarding *bargah*, see *Aʾin*, no. 21; Pant, *Economic History under the Mughals*, p. 180.
2 Especially informative is P. A. Andrews, *The Generous Heart or the Mass of Clouds: The Court Tents of Shah Jahan*.
3 *INDIA!*, no. 165.

## THREE: The Empire

RANK AND STATUS
Abdul Aziz, *The Mansabadari System and the Mughal Army*. Naqvi, *History of Mughal Government and Administration*. Abuʾl Fazl provides, as always, the most important details.
1 All officials were included in the army roll call, and had to employ the requisite number of soldiers. Badaʾuni (II, p. 230), as a preacher and translator, had the rank of a 20-*zat* commander and a fief of 1,000 *bigha* = 2877m². This was scarcely adequate to keep him at court, yet according to custom he also had to give the ruler a *pishkash* on festive occasions, which in his case was the considerable sum of 40 rupees. Because he failed to fulfil the obligations of a 20-*zat* commander, i.e., he did not keep five horses, he had only one elephant, six camels and one carriage; he retained his impoverished fief to the end of his days, whereas Abuʾl Fazl fulfilled his obligations and was called to active duty towards the end of his life. At that time, shortly before the conquest of Asirgarh, he had a monthly income of 14,000 rupees, from which he naturally had to pay for the upkeep of his men and horses. This state of affairs might also have contributed to Badaʾuni's great resentment of Abuʾl Fazl.
2 Shamsham ad-daula, *Maʾathir al-umaraʾ*, I, p. 679.
3 I am grateful to Dr Z. A. Shakeb for this information.
4 Badaʾuni, II, p. 221.

MARTIAL ARTS AND WARFARE
Irvine, *The Army of the Indian Moghuls*. Horn, *Das Heer- und Kriegswesen der Grossmoguls*. Pictures of weapons during the time of Akbar in: *Aʾin*, XII–XVI, and in numerous miniatures. M. K. Zaman, 'The Use of Artillery in Mughal Warfare'.
1 *Aʾin*, III, p. 45l.

2 *Baburnama*, pp. 663, 705.

3 Schimmel, *Tagebuch eines ägyptischen Bürgers*, p. 126f.

4 Kalim, *Diwan*, p. 74.

5 Several illustrations depict the way a rifle was supported on the shoulder of an elephant driver or a servant; Sulaiman, *Baburnama*, pp. 19, 20; Beach and Koch, *King of the World*, no. 33; S. C. Welch, *Imperial Mughal Painting*, no. 38.

6 Numerous pictures from the time of Jahangir and Shah Jahan portray helmets with a large elegant egret feather. A particular fine example of a deluxe armbrace is in: INDIA!, ill. 213.

7 As in the battle of Samugarh, Welch, *Indian Drawings and Painted Sketches*, no. 21; Beach, *The Grand Mogul*, no. 65.

8 Brand and Lowry, *Akbar's India*, no. 4; there are also numerous illustrations of the battle of Ranthambhor, e.g. in *Life at Court*, no. 6.

9 As in Horn's description in *Das Heer- und Kriegswesen*, p. 120f.

10 Badaʾuni, II, p. 107; 'the *Fathnama-i Chitor*' by Nizami, *Akbar*, Document no. XIII.

## PUNISHMENT

1 *Tuzuk*, I, pp. 19–20; the chain also appears in allegorical portrayals of Jahangir, such as the picture of him shooting at poverty: *Life at Court*, no. 24.

2 Shamsham ad-daula, *Maʾathir al-umaraʾ*, II, p. 38.

3 Regarding Mindil, see F. Rosenthal, *Four Essays on Art and Literature in Islam*.

4 Kanboh, ʿ*Amal-i salih*, p. 324.

5 Beach, *The Grand Moghul*, no. 3. He is not identified; however, the inscription on the miniature makes it clear that it is of Abuʾl-Maʾali. A picture of him being arrested is in the Chester Beatty Library 2.94.

6 Shamsham ad-daula, *Maʾathir al-umaraʾ*, I, pp. 621–2.

7 *Tuzuk*, I, p. 175.

8 Ibid., p. 104.

9 Ibid., pp. 68–9.

10 Shamsham ad-daula, *Maʾathir al-umaraʾ*, II, p. 76.

11 Goswamy and Fischer, *Wunder einer Goldenen Zeit*, no. 83.

## ECONOMY

Habib, *The Agrarian System of Mughal India*. All the works by Irfan Habib are important on the subject of economic history. Moosvi, *The Economy of the Mughal Empire*. Moreland, *The Agrarian System of Moslem India*. Moreland, *India at the Death of Akbar*. Moreland, *From Akbar to Aurangzeb*. Pant, *Economic History of India under the Mughals*.

The conversion tables in Hinz, *Masse und Gewichte*, are unfortunately inadequate for the situation in India, as the rates of exchange between different currencies, also for weights and measures, were subject to frequent change.

1 Smith, *Lower-class Uprisings in the Mughal Empire*.

2 Kalim, *Diwan*, pp. 355–61.

3 Kanboh, ʿ*Amal-i Salih*, p. 418ff.

## TRADE

The same sources as for the section on 'Economy'. The works of Abuʾl Fazl are fundamental for the time of Akbar also.

1 Pant, *Economic History of India*, p. 159.

2 The Museum of the Armenian Church in Isfahan-Julfa has a few items, for instance fabrics, which provide evidence for the existence of trade relations between India and Armenia.

3 Re: the use of ʿud, Aloe wood, see Qaddumi, *Book of Gifts and Rarities*, on ʿud.

4 *Tuzuk*, I, p. 93, see also II, p. 139.

5 Richards, *Documents*, p. 53.

6 Muʾtamad Khan Bakhshi, *Iqbalnama-i Jahangiri*, p. 243. Compare Dietrich, *Ein Arzneimittelverzeichnis*, p. 47, concerning saffron, which 'is so enjoyable, that the surfeit of pleasure leads to madness' (Razi).

7 *Tuzuk*, I, p. 150.

## FOUR: Religion

For a general overview, see Schimmel, *Islam in the Indian Subcontinent*. Rizvi, *Religious And Intellectual History of the Muslims in Akbar's Reign*. I. H. Qureshi, *The Muslim Community of the Indo-Pak Subcontinent*. M. Mujeeb, *The Indian Muslims*. Garcin de Tassy,

*Mémoire sur les particularites de la religion musulmane dans l'Inde.* S. R. Sharma, *The Religous Policy of the Mughal Emperors.* Attar Singh, ed., *Social-Cultural Impact of Islam on India.*

1 An apposite portrayal: Shah Jahan receiving the religious orthodoxy, S. C. Welch, *Imperial Mughal Painting*, pp. 31–2; Jahangir at his prayers in ʿidgah: Berlin, 'Albumblätter', no. 19. For Jahangir and Sheiks: Beach, *The Grand Mogul*, no. 13.

2 *Der Diwan des Hafis*, ed. H. Brockhaus, no. 47.

NON-ISLAMIC RELIGIONS

HINDUISM

Thomas W. Arnold, *The Preaching of Islam.* Friedmann, *Medieval Muslim Views on Indian Religions.*

1 Jawamiʾ al-kilam, in Schimmel, *Gesang und Ekstase*, p. 88f.

2 Badaʾuni, II, p. 383.

3 *Ibid.*, II, pp. 164, 361; see also Ghani, *Persian Literature at the Mughal court*, III, p. 261, on Birbal.

4 Badaʾuni, II, p. 227; Shamsham ad-daula, *Maʾathir al-umaraʾ*, I, p. 245.

5 Shamsham ad-daula, *Maʾathir al-umaraʾ*, I, p. 644.

6 Shamsham ad-daula, *Maʾathir al-umaraʾ*, II, p. 183.

7 A particularly beautiful portrayal of *yogis* is the one of five *yogis*, S. C. Welch, *Imperial Mughal Painting*, no. 24; also in Beach, *The Grand Mogul*, p. 120, no. 41; Colnaghi, no. 103.

8 *Tuzuk*, I, p. 355f.; he met him in the 11th, 13th and 14th year of his reign. S. Chughtay, 'Emperor Jahangir's interviews with Gosain Jadrup'.

9 Aʾin, III, p. 440.

10 Badaʾuni, III, p. 495, on Nauʾi. Picture: Losty, *The Art of the Book in India*, no. 81: Manuscripts of the British Library, London, no. 2839; Bibliothèque Nationale, Paris, Suppl. Persan 769; Chester Beatty Library, Dublin, Catalogue, pp. 268–9.

11 Example in Brand and Lowry, *Akbar's India*, no. 30.

12 *Tuzuk*, II, pp. 281, 224, 355; 102, 254, 227.

13 Re: Dara Shikoh, see Hasrat, *Dara Shikoh*; Qanungo, *Dara Shikoh*; Göbel and Gross, *Sirr-i akbar*; Massignon and C. Huart, *Les entretiens de Lahore*; Massignon and A. M. Kassim, *Un essai de bloc islamo-hindou au XVII siècle*; Gadon, *Dara Shikoh's Mystical Vision of Hindu-Muslim Synthesis.*

14 For example, Jackson, in Troll, ed., *Muslim Shrines in India*, p. 110.

15 Badaʾuni, II, p. 335; *Tuzuk*, I, p. 361; a miniature of Jahangir celebrating Holi in the Chester Beatty Library, Dublin, 3.14.

JAINS

Prasad, *Jahangir and the Jains.*

PARSEES

D. Shea and A. Troyer, *The Dabistan or School of Manners*, 3 vols. R. P. Karkaria, *Akbar and the Parsees.* J. J. Modi, *The Parsees at the Court of Akbar.*

JEWS

Fischel, *Jews and Judaism at the Court of the Moghul Emperors in Medieval India.* Hashimi, 'Sarmad'. Ezekiel, *Sarmad, Jewish Saint of India.*

SIKHS

Stronge, ed., *The Arts of the Sikh Kingdoms.*

1 Vaudeville, *Kabir*, vol. I; There is a picture in Schimmel, *Islam in India and Pakistan*, XVIa.

2 The first complete translation, albeit not without errors, is by Ernst Trumpp, *The Adi Granth.*

3 Smith, *The Crystallization of Religious Communities in Mughal India.*

CHRISTIANS

Maclagan, *The Jesuits and the Great Mughal.* Faruqi, 'The First Jesuit Mission to the Court of Akbar'. Camps, 'Persian Works of Jerome Xavier, a Jesuit at the Mogul Court'. Wellecz, *Akbar's Religious Thought Reflected in Mogul Painting.*

1 Schimmel, *Islam in India and Pakistan*, no. XII; see Wellesz, *Akbar's Religious Thought*, ill. 33; Brand and Lowry, *Akbar's India*, no. 18.

2 It is impossible to provide a comprehensive bibliography of portrayals with Christian themes here; there are numerous pictures of the birth of Christ, of Mary and the Infant; of the Crucifixion and the Last Judgment, for the most part based on European models.

3  A fairly harrowing account of the conquest of
   Hooghly is in Shamsham ad-daula, *Ma'athir al-
   umara'*, II, p. 493.

## ISLAMIC SECTS
### THE MAHDAWIYYA

Bada'uni, III, pp. 73–7 provides a sympathetic picture
of the Mahdawis. Rizvi, *Muslim Revivalist Movements
in Northern India in the 16th and 17th Century*. Ansari,
*Sayyid Muhammad Jawnpuri and his Movement*.

### THE RAUSHANIYYA

Rizvi, *The Rawshaniyya Movement*. Malik, 'Sixteenth
Century Mahdism: the Rawshaniyya Movement
among Pakhtun Tribes'.

1  Shamsham ad-daula, *Ma'athir al-umara'*, II, p. 601.

### THE NUQTAWIS

Siddiqui, *Nuqtavi Thinkers at the Mughal Court*.

1  Bada'uni is strictly opposed to them, compare III,
   p. 284. It is interesting that Paskhwani, the founder
   of the movement, played on the transformation of
   the name *Muhammad* to his own name *Mahmud*, as
   did Ahmad Sirhindi on the transformation of
   *Muhammad* to *Ahmad*. Both men were attempting to
   prove that their names had the same letters – h-m-d
   – as that of the Prophet Muhammad, and that they
   were thereby closely connected to him.

## SHI'I SECTS
### THE ISMA'ILIS

*Daftari, History of the Ismailis*. Khakee, 'The "dasamo
avatar" of the Satpanthi Isma'ilis and the
Imamshahis of Indo-Pakistan'. Asani, *The bhuj
niranjan, an Ismaili Mystical Poem*.

1  Richards, 'Document Forms for Official Orders of
   Appointment in the Mughal Empire', p. 59.

### THE NURBAKHSHIS

Mirza Ali Haydar Dughlat, *Tarikh-i rashidi*.

### THE TWELVER SHI'A

Hollister, *The Shia of India* (unsatisfactory). Gramlich,
   *Die schiitischen Derwischorden*, 1–3. Rizvi, *A Socio-*

*Intellectual History of the Ithna Ashari Shiis in India*.

## SUFISM

Schimmel, *Mystische Dimensionen des Islam*. Subhan,
   *Sufism, its Saints and Shrines*. Rizvi, *A History of
   Sufism in India*. Arnold, *Saints, Muhammadan, in
   India*. Schwerin, *Heiligenverehrung im indischen Islam*.

1  Schimmel, al-Halladsch, *Märtyrer der Gottesliebe*;
   Schimmel, 'The martyr mystic Hallaj in Sindhi folk
   poetry'.

2  Regarding Ibn ᶜArabi, see Addas, *The Quest for the
   Red Sulphur*.

3  Bada'uni, *Najat ar-rashid*, p. 190.

4  Foltz, *Mughal India and Central Asia*, p. 239.

5  *Baburnama*, pp. 653, 807; he met Ghauth Gwaliori
   in 1529.

6  See Nath, 'The Tomb of Shaikh Muhammad
   Ghauth at Gwalior'.

7  Currie, *The Shrine and Cult of Mu'in al-Din Chishti of
   Ajmer*. Akbar's battle cry was *ya mu'in!*, alluding to
   the name Mu'inaddin (Bada'uni III, p. 74). Re. The
   celebrations in Ajmer: Bada'uni, II, pp. 188, 237ff.

8  Pictures of the Mughal rulers in Ajmer are far from
   rare, e.g., Jahangir in Ajmer 1613 (Rampur) in
   Brown, *Indian Painting under the Mughals*, XX; Shah
   Jahan in Ajmer in Beach and Koch, *King of the
   World*, nos. 41–42; Chester Beatty Library, Dublin,
   2.19. Compare also Tirmizi, *Ajmer Through
   Inscriptions*, for the inscriptions of the different
   rulers.

9  Friedmann, *Shaykh Ahmad Sirhindi*; Fazlur Rahman,
   *Selected Letters of Shaikh Ahmad Sirhindi*.

10 *Tuzuk*, II, pp. 91, 161, 276.

11 Marshall, *Moghuls in India*, no. 1203, mentions 260
   letters by Pir Ma'sum. Nizami, 'Naqshbandi
   influence on Mughal Rulers and Politics'.
   Schimmel, 'The Golden Chain of "Sincere
   Muhammadans"'.

12 Baljon, *Religion and Thought of Shah Wali Allah
   Dihlawi (1703–1762)*; Baljon, *Ta'wil al-ahadith*; the
   translation of the *hujja* by Marcia Hermanson, *The
   Conclusive Proof of God*. The Shah Waliullah
   Academy, Hyderabad (Sind), under the
   directorship of Ghulam Mustafa Qasimi, has

published numerous works and publications by Shah Waliullah.

13 *Tuzuk*, II, p. 34. Yaqut (died 1298) was the greatest master of classical Arabic calligraphy.

14 Eaton, *Sufis of Bijapur*. Lawrence, 'Seventeenth Century Qadiriyya in Northern India'.

15 Mian Mir is frequently portrayed, e.g. in the Los Angeles County Museum of Art, 1, 69, 24.287; a typical drawing is in Schimmel, *Islam in India and Pakistan*, no. XXVa.

16 De Krémer, 'Molla Shah et le spiritualisme oriental'. The quotation 'When poverty is absolute, it becomes God' seems to have been especially favoured by the Qadiris; it appears on a Qadiri writing tablet in my possession.

17 Murata, *The Mysteries of Marriage*.

RELIGIOUS CUSTOMS

For the general development: Jafar Sharif and Herklots, *Islam in India*.

1 *Akbarnama*, p. 519; *Aʾin*, III, p. 441.

2 In this connection see Kanboh, ʿ*Amal-i salih*, p. 285.

3 Re: *maulud* poems see Schimmel, *And Muhammad is His Messenger*; Asani, *Celebrating Muhammad*.

4 Horovitz, 'A List of Published Mohammedan Inscriptions of India'.

5 Ghalib, *Kulliyat-i farsi*, vol. V, *qasida*, no. 9. See 'Die schöne Darstellung: Frauen beim Astrologen': Goswamy and Fischer, *Wunder einer Goldenen Zeit*, no. 58.

6 Falk and Digby, nos. 1–8.

7 *Tuzuk*, I, p. 269.

8 *Ibid.*, p. 43; see also *Akbarnama*, p. 1052.

9 Shamsham ad-daula, *Maʾathir al-umaraʾ*, I, p. 319ff.

10 The devout were received on Saturday and Thursday, state officials on Sunday and Tuesday, and 'Moon-like Youths' on Monday, when beautiful music would be played.

11 Shamsham ad-daula, *Maʾathir al-umaraʾ*, p. 375ff.

12 Bankipore Catalogue, I, pp. 231, 259.

13 Jauhar Aftabji, p. 115.

14 'Ruqaat-yi ʿalamgiri', no. LXXVIII.

15 Shamsham ad-daula, *Maʾathir al-umaraʾ*, p. 319ff. Mirza ʿAziz Koka does seem to have been interested

in fortune telling and astrology, as a *kitab as-saʾat*, an illustrated work of astrology, was pro-duced for him when he was staying in Hajipur. Goswamy and Fischer, *Wunder einer Goldenen Zeit*, ill. 84.

FIVE: Women at Court

A good overview is Rakha Misra, *Women in Mughal India*. Gulbadan's *Humayun nama* is a very important as well as entertaining source for the first few decades of Mughal rule. Babur's meeting with his elder sister is portrayed in Sulaiman, *Baburnama*, no. 7.

1 *Aʾin*, II, p. 574.

2 See *Taʾrikh-i Sher Shah* in Elliott and Dowson, IV, p. 343.

3 Badaʾuni, II, p. 206; *Aʾin*, II, p. 489, counts the number of women in the Mughal household who participated in a pilgrimage; among them were several of Humayun's widows and Akbar's wives. They were accompanied by Rumi Khan Ustad Chelebi, a Turk.

4 Shamsham ad-daula, *Maʾathir al-umaraʾ*, I, p. 328. Compare also *Tuzuk*, I, p. 252.

5 Jauhar Aftabji, p. 31.

6 Chester Beatty Library, Dublin, 2.101, shows Akbar greeting his mother. Compare Shamsham ad-daula, *Maʾathir al-umaraʾ*, I, II, p. 212. Mirza ʿAziz Koka was strongly reproached by Akbar for having left India without informing his mother: Nizami, *Akbar*, Document no. VIII.

7 A portrait of the elegant Abuʾl-Maʾali is in Goswamy and Fischer, *Wunder einer Goldenen Zeit*, no. 6.

8 Beveridge, 'Maham Anaga'. 'Über ihre Moschee': Koch, *Mughal Architecture*, p. 56.

9 For example, Shamsham ad-daula, *Maʾathir al-umaraʾ*, I, pp. 170, 389, 741, 603.

10 Regarding the convoluted relationships between the Mughal house and the Arghuns, see Shamsham ad-daula, *Maʾathir al-umaraʾ*, II, p. 226ff.

11 Shamsham ad-daula, *Maʾathir al-umaraʾ*, II, p. 54.

12 Findly, *Nur Jahan*; Findly, 'Nur Jahan's Embroidery

Trade and Flowers of the Taj Mahal'.

13 Shamsham ad-daula, *Maᵓathir al-umaraᵓ*, II, p. 1072.

14 Choudhuri, 'Mumtaz Mahal'; see the detailed depictions in Kanboh, *ᶜAmal-i salih*, p. 445ff.

15 De Krémer, 'Molla Shah et le spiritualisme oriental'. Compare also a work in the British Museum, London, in Jahanara's handwriting, *Muᵓnis al-arwah*.

16 Kanboh, *ᶜAmal-i salih*, p. 400.

17 See Marshall, *Moghuls in India*, 14, 42 IV, 46 III, IV, VI, 326 II, 685, 1095 I, II, 1224, 1717, 1858; numerous imitations are also listed; Schimmel, *The Triumphal Sun*, last chapter.

18 Kyrklund, *Zib un-nisa*.

19 Chughtay, 'The so-called Gardens and Tomb of Zeb un-nisa at Lahore'.

20 Westbrook, *Dewan of Zeb un-nissa*.

21 Marshall, *Moghuls in India*, no. 1247, no. 711; See also Sprenger, Catalogue, no. 121.

22 Shamsham ad-daula, *Maᵓathir al-umaraᵓ*, I, p. 251f.

23 Goetz, 'The Qudsiyya Bagh at Delhi'.

24 Asher, *Architecture of Mughal India*, p. 376.

25 Gupta, 'Mughalani Begam, the Governor of Lahore, 1754–1756'.

26 Shamsham ad-daula, *Maᵓathir al-umaraᵓ*, I, p. 158, II, p. 306; I, p. 37.

27 *Aᵓin*, II, p. 346.

28 *INDIA!*, no. 186; see also S. C. Welch, *Imperial Mughal Painting*, no. 35. There are many pictures of princesses or pairs of lovers on the riverside terrace, talking or flirting; see Kühnel, *Indische Miniaturen*, nos. 11–13. Welch, *Paintings and Precious Objects*, no. 47; see also Duda, *Die illuminierten Handschriften*, vol. II, especially ill. 488ff. From Cod. Min. 64, fols 55–9.

29 Irvine, *Later Mughals*, III. p. 121.

30 *Tuzuk*, II. p. 110ff.

31 Aurangzeb, *Ahkam*, paras. 10, 16, 20.

32 Shamsham ad-daula, *Maᵓathir al-umaraᵓ*, I, p. 704.

33 Tirmizi, *Edicts from the Mughal Haram*.

34 Jahangir's birthday and Murad's birthday are the best examples of this sort of painted documentation; see S. C. Welch, *Imperial Mughal Painting*, no. 16 (Bishndas); *Life at Court*, no. 10.

Humayun's birthday celebrations, *Baburnama*, no. 45. A charming portrait of an infant prince is in *Life at Court*, no. 22; see also Welch, *Paintings and Precious Objects*, no. 31.

35 Duda, *Die illuminierten Handschriften*, vol. II, ill. 490 (scene of the birth).

36 Reported in Shamsham ad-daula, *Maᵓathir al-umaraᵓ*, II, p. 686.

37 Colnaghi, no. 94.

38 *Life at Court*, no. 60.

39 Shamsham ad-daula, *Maᵓathir al-umaraᵓ*, II, p. 931.

40 The well-beloved lady in a Chaghatay hat in Goswamy and Fischer, *Wunder einer Goldenen Zeit*, no. 66; a similarly impressive influential lady in marbling technique is in *INDIA!*, p. 198.

41 Goswamy and Fischer, *Wunder einer Goldenen Zeit*, no. 21 (Chester Beatty Library, Dublin, 3.60).

42 Haq, *The Khankhanan and his Painters*, p. 622; Frembgen, *Hornhautraspelm aus Sind und Westasien*; On care of the body, see Frembgen, *Rosenduft und Saebelglanz*, pp. 49–51.

43 The school scene is incorrectly bound in the great Akbar-Gulistan, Royal Asiatic Society, London, currently in the India Office in London.

44 *Tuzuk*, I, pp. 380, 384; also p. 241. Kühnel and Goetz, tablet 32, detail 15a; *INDIA!*, no. 85.

45 The way princesses were prepared for bed: Falk and Digby, no. 31.

46 Dallapiccola, *Princesses et courtisanes à travers les miniatures indiennes*. For a contemporary story about an Urdu lesbian, see Ismat Chughtai, trans. U. Rothen-Dubs, *Allahs indischer Garten*. The shocking picture of bacchantes published in *INDIA!*, no. 250, provides a glimpse of female dissolution.

47 In Akhlaq-i Nasiri, Goswamy and Fischer, *Wunder einer Goldenen Zeit*, no. 58.

48 *Aᵓin*, III, p. 425.

## SIX: The Imperial Household and Housekeeping

### TEXTILES

Ansari, 'The Dress of the Great Mughals'. Goetz,

*Bilderatlas zur Kulturgeschichte Indiens.* Abu'l Fazl, as always, describes fabrics and materials in great detail in the *A'in*. Many miniatures are also good sources of information on style and colour of clothing. Unfortunately there is no comprehensive overview.

1 *A'in*, III, p. 440.
2 A picture of Jahangir with – presumably – Nur Jahan shows the emperor in green trousers, plenty of jewellery and his beautiful turban, but without a shirt! Berlin, 'Albumblätter', no. 21.
3 Also Pant, *Economic History*, p. 199.
4 Re: *nadiri*, compare *Tuzuk*, I, p. 377, II, p. 237. The richly embroidered costume, *kurdi*, in the Victoria and Albert Museum, London, gives an idea of the splendour of such jackets. *INDIA!*, no. 137.
5 Ansari, 'The Dress of the Great Mughals', p. 257.
6 As Jahangir himself wrote in *Tuzuk*, I, p. 347; see also II, p. 234.
7 Pelts were imported from Russia as early as the time of Abbasid, and in Mamluk Egypt robes of honour lined with sable or Siberian squirrel were lent. See also Qaddumi, *Book of Gifts and Rarities*, regarding *sammur*.
8 Goswamy and Fischer, *Wunder einer Goldenen Zeit*, no. 71.
9 Berlin, 'Albumblätter', no. 17.
10 Bada'uni, II, p. 248, writes about a man with an extended tail end on his turban who consequently was nicknamed 'comet', because there was a comet in the sky at that time.
11 *A'in*, I, p. 94, no. 31.
12 The best overview of Mughal carpets is Walker, *Flowers Underfoot*.
13 *INDIA!*, pp. 159–60, 112.
14 Walker, *Flowers Underfoot*, ill. 49.
15 *Ibid.*, no. 65.
16 Kalim, *Diwan, Mathnawi*, p. 15; see Schimmel, *Gedanken zu zwei Porträts Shah ʿAlams* II.
17 Smart and Walker, *Pride of the Princes*, no. 62.
18 *Ibid.*, no. 65.
19 There is a pattern-book for chintz decorations in the Victoria and Albert Museum, London, which testifies to the interest of the British in this fabric.

JEWELLERY

The best introduction to Indian jewellery by a jeweller and collector is O. Untracht, *Traditional Indian Jewellery*. Typical Mughal jewellery is illustrated on pp. 343–6.

1 Marshall, *Moghuls in India*, no. 1135; see also Ghani, *Persian Language and Literature*, II, p. 15.
2 Examples from the Islamic middle ages are in Qaddumi, *Book of Gifts and Rarities*, especially *durrah* (large pearls) and *lu'lu'a* (small pearls).
3 Goswamy and Fischer, *Wunder einer Goldenen Zeit*, no. 42, Akbar at the time of Shah Jahan wearing only two rows of pearls, and no other jewellery; see also *ibid.*, no. 188.
4 Title picture of Welch *et al.*, *The Emperors' Album*.
5 *Tuzuk*, II, p. 74.
6 In Aziz Ahmad, *Mirzanama*, p. 105.
7 Colnaghi, no. 119 (*c.* 1640).
8 Illustration of a *jigha* in *INDIA!*, p. 184.
9 Berlin, 'Albumblätter' no. 33, with an important text by Manucci.
10 Stronge, *The Sikh Kingdoms*, on the different jewels.
11 *Tuzuk*, II, p. 195; Stronge, *The Sikh Kingdoms*, ill. 64 and 93.
12 Emeralds: *INDIA!*, pp. 99, 180; Hussa al-Sabah, *The Enigma of the Three Mughal Emeralds*.
13 *INDIA!*, nos. 129, 134.
14 Examples in Untracht, *Traditional Indian Jewellery*, nos. 629, 630; for the importance of nephrite, p. 104.
15 *INDIA!*, no. 127. Keene, 'The Ruby Dagger in the Al-Sabah Collection in the Context of Early Mughal Jewellery'.
16 The different types of daggers, etc., in *INDIA!*, by Spink, also in Haase *et al.*, *Morgenländische Pracht*, nos. 156, 133, 141, 155, 147a, 148.
17 Kalim, *Diwan*, p. 74.
18 *Tuzuk*, II, p. 98.
19 Smart and Walker, *Pride of the Princes*, no. 59; a tortoise: *INDIA!*, no. 172.
20 *INDIA!*, no. 213.
21 Inkwell: *INDIA!*, no. 122.
22 *INDIA!*, no. 172 (Jahangir's opium bowl).
23 Goat bowl: *INDIA!*, no. 167.
24 Mirror: *INDIA!*, no. 175.

25 Akhtar, ed., Qati꜔i, majma꜔a i shu꜔ara,
   introduction, II, p. 38.
26 Zebrowski, Gold, Silver and Bronze from Mughal India,
   is a very important study with wonderful pictures.
27 INDIA!, no. 82; a cabinet with hunting scenes: Smart
   and Walker, Pride of the Princes, ill. 58.
28 There are numerous illustrations with varying
   portrayals of Shah Jahan and later Aurangzeb
   sitting on the peacock throne. See also Shamsham
   ad-daula, Ma꜔athir al-umara꜔, I, p. 397.

KITCHENS AND CELLARS
Ansari, 'The Diet of the Great Moghuls'. Kh. Mustafa,
   Babur's Court in India. A꜔in, no. 24, regarding food,
   cuisine, provisions and crockery at the time of
   Akbar. There were a number of cookery books at
   the time, e.g. the 'Ni꜔matnama-i Nasirshahi' in the
   India Office, with illustrations (MS. 149). As with
   other cookbooks, it contained recipes for
   aphrodisiacs. See INDIA!, no. 78; Life at Court, no. 2.
 1 Schimmel and Welch, A Pocket Book for Akbar,
   p. 105; another miniature of a kitchen is in Welch,
   A Flower from Every Meadow, no. 62 (The feast of
   Hatim).
 2 Sulaiman, Baburnama, nos. 32, 34, 36 and 37 depict
   banquets in Babur's time.
 3 Shamsham ad-daula, Ma꜔athir al-umara꜔, I, p. 127,
   according to which he consumed 22 ser (approximately 19 kg) of meat per day.
 4 Tuzuk, II, p. 219.
 5 A꜔in, no. 24.
 6 Jauhar Aftabji, p. 83.
 7 Tuzuk.
 8 ꜔Aziz Ahmad, Mirzanama, p. 104.
 9 Quoted in Irvine, Later Moghuls, I, p. 108.
10 Tuzuk, I, pp. 423, 427; 116.
11 Ghani, Persian Language and Literature, III, p. 21.
12 Akhtar, ed., Qati꜔i, Majmu꜔a-yi shua꜔ra-i jahangirshahi,
   p. 39.
13 Wikaya-i Asad Beg, in Elliott and Dowson, VI,
   p. 154.
14 Tuzuk, I, pp. 270–71; Beach, The Grand Mogul, p. 109,
   no. 36.
15 Irvine, Later Moghuls, I, p. 403.

DRUGS AND ALCOHOL
 1 The drawing in the Bodleian Library, Oxford,
   Ouseley Add. 1716, fol. 4v, is reproduced in most
   works on the Mughals, likewise the colourful
   portrayal in the Museum of Fine Arts, Boston. See
   S. C. Welch, Imperial Mughal Painting, no.23; INDIA!,
   p. 227, Beach, The Grand Mogul, p. 162, no. 60; Life at
   Court, no. 23.
 2 Kalim, Diwan, p. 66.
 3 Colnaghi, no. 103.
 4 Bada꜔uni, Najat ar-rashid.
 5 Trumpp, Über die Sprache der sogenannten Kafirs, p.
   389.
 6 Baburnama, pp. 395f., 555, 667.
 7 Ibid., p. 485; the illustration in Sulaiman,
   Baburnama, no. 48.
 8 Tuzuk, I, pp. 35–6; also Beach, The Grand Mogul, p. 33.
   Among the victims of alcoholism were the son of
   Parvez (son of Jahangir), the son of Mirza Hakom,
   the sons of Man Singh and the khankhanan ꜔Abdu꜔r
   Rahim, a grandson of Shaykh Salim Chishti, also
   Zayn Khan Koka – to name only the most
   prominent.
 9 Kanboh, ꜔Amal-i salih, p. 137f.
10 Shamsham ad-daula, Ma꜔athir al-umara꜔, II, p. 773,
   ibid., II, p. 511.
11 Ibid., II, p. 672.

RECREATION AND ENTERTAINMENT
 1 Foltz, Mutribi, pp. 51, 53; compare the picture of a
   similar festival in the Muraqqa꜔ of St Petersburg,
   p. 38.
 2 Tuzuk, I, p. 97.
 3 Ruqaat-yi ꜔alamgiri, LXXXVIII.
 4 This scene is frequently portrayed, for example on
   the cover of Rogers, Mughal Miniatures.
 5 Kanboh, ꜔Amal-i salih, p. 525ff.
 6 Beach and Koch, King of the World, contains a large
   number of miniatures of the wedding celebrations
   of Dara Shikoh and Aurangzeb; such festivities are
   frequently portrayed.
 7 Welch, Room for Wonder, no. 40.
 8 Brown, Indian Painting, XLIX; see also Ettinghausen,
   Tanz mit zoomorphen Masken.

9   The verse is taken from the *Diwani- Shams-i Tabriz*, ed. B. Furuzanfar, Taheran 1338 SH/1959, no. 1348.

10   Goswamy and Fischer, *Wunder einer Goldenen Zeit*, no. 49; Jahangir Album: Kühnel and Boetz, fol. 24a; Schimmel and Welch, *A Pocket Book for Akbar*, p. 78.

11   Nihawandi, *Ma'athir-i rahimi*.

12   *Tuzuk*, I, p. 368; the number of animals killed during the course of a hunt is also mentioned in other places. Numerous miniatures depict hunting scenes, especially rulers fighting lions. They also portray lions being carried away hung by their paws from a pole. Regarding hunting, see also Moreland, *India at the Death of Akbar*, p. 25; Verma, *Flora and Fauna in Mughal Art*.

13   Shamsham ad-daula, *Ma'athir al-umara'*, I, p. 668.

14   Babur often refers to wrestling matches, e.g. *Baburnama*, pp. 776, 768, 770, 775, 800. Rogers, *Mughal Miniatures*, no. 63. There is a well-known miniature of Akbar as a child overcoming his cousin in a wrestling match (see Brand and Lowry, *Akbar's India*, no. 1).

15   Musical processions are frequently portrayed: Brown, *Indian Painting*, p. xxxi; the 'Windsor Padshahnama' in particular contains some wonderful scenes of these.

16   *INDIA!*, no. 106.

17   For this portrait see Brend, *The Emperor Akbar's 'Khamsa' of Nizami*, ill. 16.

18   Welch, *Imperial Mughal Painting*, no. 28.

19   *Tuzuk*, I, p. 203.

20   Royal Asiatic Society, London, Pers. no. 211 with 64 miniatures.

21   Re: card games in the Islamic middle ages, see also Mayer, *Mamluk Playing Cards* (Leiden 1971).

MEDICINE

1   Bada'uni, III, p. 382. For doctors in general, also Akbar's court doctors, see *A'in*, II, no. 71ff.

2   Russell and Khurshidul Islam, *Three Mughal Poets*, p. 49.

3   Medical works are listed in Marshall, *Moghuls in India*, nos. 1142, 1912, 284, 1580, 1696, 1424, 1040 in the order in which they are referred to in the text.

4   Royal Asiatic Society, London, Pers., nos. 195–7; Marshall, *Moghuls in India*, no. 408, mentions a *tibb-i Aurangzebi*.

5   *Baburnama*, pp. 705, 724, 772; miniatures in Sulaiman, *Baburnama*, nos. 16, 88; see also Haase et al., *Morgenländische Pracht*, ill. 183a.

6   The Egyptian poet al-Busiri (died 1296) composed his 161-verse ode in Arabic in honour of the Prophet after he had cured him by means of a dream in which he threw his striped Yemeni coat, the *burda*, over him. This poem has acquired the status of a sacred text throughout the Islamic orient, and even in south India it is still recited on certain occasions.

7   *Tuzuk*, II, p. 213f. Fayzi is also supposed to have suffered from asthma, Shamsham ad-daula, *Ma'athir al-umara'*, I, p. 513.

8   *Tuzuk*, II, p. 202.

9   Kalim, *Diwan*, p. 47.

10   Shamsham ad-daula, *Ma'athir al-umara'*, II, p. 378.

THE ROLE OF ANIMALS

S. P. Verma, ed., *Flora and Fauna in Mughal Art*.

1   *Baburnama*, p. 316. Prof. Dr Clas Naumann, Director of the Museum König in Bonn, confirmed that they were in fact flamingos, having himself seen flamingos in the area of Afghanistan visited by Babur.

2   Elephants were a favourite subject of Mughal artists, whether spraying themselves during bathing (Berlin, 'Albumblätter', no. 23), or playing together, or being hunted from trees (Smart and Walker, *Pride of the Princes*, no. 4c); there is a beautiful picture of a family of elephants in Goswamy and Fischer, *Wunder einer goldenen Zeit*, no. 63; see also Frembgen, *Der Elefant bei den Moghul*, and Das, *The Elephant in Mughal Painting*.

3   Meer Hassan Ali, *Observations on the Mussulmans*, p. 88. Muhammad al-Yamani ash-Shirwani, *al-manaqib al-haydariyya*.

4   Kalim, *Diwan Ruba'i*, no. 29.

5   Athar Ali, *The Mughal Nobility under Aurangzeb*, p.29.

6   Horn, *Das Heer- und Kriegswesen der Grossmoguls*, p. 57.

7   Asad Beg, 'Wikaya', in Elliott and Dowson, VI, p.

150. One Akbar *man* was 25,115 kg; however, it could also be a smaller quantity.

8  Brown, *Indian Painting*, LVI, with yak tails; Sulaiman, *Baburnama*, no. 89.

9  *Tuzuk*, II, p.193; compare *ibid.*, I, p. 289, II, p. 79, also II, p. 4, I, p. 432. Ghani, *Persian Language and Literature*, III, p. 29.

10  Welch, *Imperial Mughal Painting*, nos. 12–13; also *Akbarnama*, II, p. 234, and *Tuzuk*, I.

11  Often published, including as a dust-jacket cover for Goswamy and Fischer, *Wunder einer Goldenen Zeit*.

12  Spink, no. 72.

13  Brend, *The Emperor Akbar's 'Khamsa' of Nizami*, ill. 10; Beach, *The Grand Mogul*, 43, no. 4; execution by elephants. Verma, *Flora and Fauna*, p. 43, ill. 7; p. 128, ill. 6.

14  Bada'uni, III, p. 242ff., III, p. 282.

15  Goswamy and Fischer, *Wunder einer Goldenen Zeit*, no. 17; this is a frequent theme.

16  Camel fight by ʿAbduʾs Samad: Goswamy and Fischer, *Wunder einer Goldenen Zeit*, ill. 19 and elsewhere; camel fight beneath the *jharoka* window: Spink, no. 71.

17  Welch, *A Flower From Every Meadow*, no. 55.

18  Miskin, buffalo fight: INDIA!, no. 103.

19  Yak, painted by Abuʾl-Hasan Nadir az-Zaman: Welch, *A Flower From Every Meadow*, no. 61, and Beach, *The Grand Mogul*, p. 171, no. 169. Mountain sheep: Verma, *Flora and Fauna*, no. 12.

20  Cheetahs can be seen in the miniature of ʿAbduʾr Rahim as a child being presented to Akbar.

21  Concerning this remarkable assertion, see Schimmel, *A Two-Colored Brocade*, p. 193.

22  Hadi Hasan, *Qasim Kahi*.

23  Goswamy and Fischer, *Wunder einer Goldenen Zeit*, no. 62; Canby, *Princes, poètes et paladins*, no. 99: Salim catches a cheetah; also Colnaghi, no. 16. The scene with Akbar's 'promoted' cheetah in Verma, *Flora and Fauna*, p. 99, no. 3.

24  Ram: INDIA!, p. 108; ram fight: Sulaiman, *Baburnama*, no. 93.

25  Kühnel, *Indische Miniaturen*, no. 7.

26  Canby, *Princes, poètes et paladins*, no. 114.

27  A few beautiful ivory cages: Spink, no. 92.

28  Title picture of Welch, *Imperial Mughal Painting*; see also Beach, *The Grand Mogul*, p. 140, no. 17, work by Ustad Mansur. INDIA!, p. 144. Akbar's *farman* against the killing of peacocks is in Nizami, *Akbar*, no. XV.

29  *Tuzuk*, II, p. 201; illustrations in Welch, *Imperial Mughal Painting*, no. 27, Spink, no. 70.

30  Turkey cock, painted by Mansur, in Welch, *Imperial Mughal Painting*, no. 27.

31  Squirrel, in the India Office, London, often reproduced, e.g., in INDIA!, no. 141, and in Welch, *Imperial Mughal Painting*, no. 25.

32  A typical example of Noah's Ark is in Welch, *Imperial Mughal Painting*, no. 9.

## EIGHT: Languages and Literature

Schimmel, *Islamic Literatures of India*. Bausani, *Storia delle letterature del Pakistan*. Sprenger, *A Catalogue . . . of the Libraries of the King of Oudh*.

For the forms, see Schimmel, *Stern und Blume*; idem, *A Two-Colored Brocade*. Thiessen, *A Manual of Classical Persian Prosody*. Rückert and Pertsch, *Grammatik, Poetik und Rhetorik der Perser*.

Numerous translations from Indo-Islamic literature are in Schimmel, *Die schönsten Gedichte aus Pakistan und Indien*.

### ARABIC

Brockelmann, *Geschichte der arabischen Literatur*, especially vol. II. M. Ishaq, *India's Contribution to the Study of Hadith Literature*. Zubaid Ahmad, *The Contribution of Indo-Pakistan to Arabic Literature*. M. Y. Kokan, *Arabic and Persian in Carnatic*. Muid Khan, *The Arabian Poets of Golconda*.

1  *Sawatiʿ al-ilham* was printed in 1306/1888 in Lucknow (see Schimmel, *Islam in India and Pakistan*, 'Iconography', XXVIa). A certain Lutfullah Muhandis produced a work titled 'Sihr-i halal' in 1659, which is likewise completely undotted. Marshall, *Moghuls in India*, no. 997. Bada'uni remarked that Akbar had the Arabic alphabet simplified, replacing consonants that are difficult

for non-Arabs to pronounce with easier ones (II, p. 340). The Shah of Iran attempted something similar.

2  Marshall, *Moghuls in India*, no. 200, Arabic commentary on the Koran; no. 198, *Kunst der Koranrezitation*; no. 1657, *Najat al-qari*, 'Deliverance of the Reciter of the Koran'; no. 1248, *Nujum al-furqan*, an index of the Koran, compiled for Aurangzeb.

## TURKISH

Eckmann, *Tschagatayische Literatur*. Schimmel, *Turk and Hindu*. Eaden, *Babur Padishah the Poet*.

1  See also Losty, *The Art of the Book*, p. 84, no. 77; the manuscript is in the Royal Collection at Windsor Castle.

2  See also Fakhri Harawi, *Raudat as-salatin wa jawahir al-ᶜajaᵓib*.

3  Badaᵓuni, III, p. 266, on Bayram Khan's poetry. The elder brothers of Shamsaddin Atga, the Khan Kalan who died in 1575, also wrote verses in Persian and Turkic, Shamsham ad-daula, *Maᵓathir al-umaraᵓ*, II, p. 155.

4  There is an older translation by Mirza Payanda Hasan-i Ghaznawi, see Marshall, *Moghuls in India*, no. 1227.

5  *Akbarnama*, p. 535; Jauhar Aftabji, pp. 42, 45, 71, 75, 106.

6  Nizami, *Akbar*, p. 218; Kanboh, ᶜ*Amal-i salh*, I, 32.

7  Shamsham ad-daula, *Maᵓathir al-umaraᵓ*, I, p. 558f.

8  Irvine, *Later Mughals*, II, p. 57.

9  For Azfari see Abbas, *Azfari Gurgani*, *Safarnama*.

10  Marshall, *Moghuls in India*, no. 669, contains a reference to a grammar of Turkic, 'Haft akhtar', by a Hindu, Kasib Birbal.

## SANSKRIT-HINDI

Jagannath Panditrey, *Sanskrit under Mohammedan Patronage*.

1  Ghani, *Persian Language and Literature*, III, p. 269.

2  *Ibid.*, III, p. 219, for Tulsi Das.

3  There is a whole series of Hindi publications dealing with *khankhanan*'s Hindi poetry; see the bibliography by Naik, ᶜ*Abduᵓr-Rahim Khan-i khanan and his Literary Circle*, p. 551f.

4  Marshall, *Moghuls in India*, nos. 740, 874, 1773 refer to Hindi works.

5  Further Sanskrit works are in Marshall, *Moghuls in India*, 827, 1437, 1512, 1727, 1825, 945, 1774.

6  See also Pramod Chandra, *The 'Tutinama' of the Cleveland Museum of Art and the Origins of Mughal Painting*.

7  Seyller, 'The Freer Ramayana'.

8  The scene from the *Harivamsa* has often been published: INDIA!, no. 109; Losty, *The Art of the Book*, ill. 102; S. C. Welch, *Imperial Mughal Painting*, no. 10.

## PERSIAN

Ghani, *Persian Language and Literature at the Mughal Court*. E. G. Browne, *A Literary History of Persia*, especially vol. III. Ethé, *Neupersische Literatur*. Rypka, *History of Iranian Literature*; J. Marek, *Persian Literature in India*. Sadarangani, *Persian Poets of Sind*. Heinz, *Der 'indische Stil' in der persischen Literatur*. Syed Abdullah, *Adabiyat-i farsi men hinduon ka hissa* (the contribution of Hindus to Persian literature).

1  The manuscript of the version of the *mathnawi* of Amir Khusrau completed by Hafiz is kept in the Tashkent Academy of Science.

2  Hadi Hasan, *The Unique Divan of Humayun Badshah*.

3  Nihawandi, *Maᵓathir-i rahimi*.

4  Browne, *A Literary History of Persia*, III, p. 255.

5  Hadi Hasan, *Qasim-i kahi*; re. him, see also Badaᵓuni, III, p. 242; *Akbarnama*, I, p. 566.

6  Kalim, *Diwan*, several; a bespectacled man in Jahangir's *durbar* portrayed in Goswamy and Fischer, *Wunder einer goldenen Zeit*, ill. 37.

7  Ettinghausen, *The Emperor's Choice* (title picture); the verse: Ikram, *Armaghan-i pak*, p. 318.

8  For the following century see Schimmel, *Gedanken zu zwei Porträts*.

9  Someone who managed to prove that the title *Jahangir* had the same numerical value as *Allahu akbar*, i.e., 289, received a robe of honour, a horse, money and land.

10  Rückert produced a brilliant translation and interpretation of this difficult work; the examples are on pp. 235ff., 240ff., 253.

11 Shihabi-yi mu^camma^i went to Babur with the historian Khwandmir on 18 September 1528.

12 Rückert and Pertsch, *Grammatik*, p. 316ff. on this subject: Shams Anwari Alhoseyni, *mo^camma and lughaz*; compare also Marshall, *Moghuls in India*, nos. 214, 497.

13 There are manuscripts of the dictionaries by Jamaladdin Inju in many libraries, e.g. in Cincinnati (Smart and Walker, no. 55) and in Dublin in the Chester Beatty Library. Another very important dictionary is the *Farhang-i rashidi* by ^cAbdu^r Rashid Tattawi.

14 Abidi, 'Chandra Bhan Brahman'.

15 For Bedil, see Bausani, *Note su Mirza Bedil*; Heinz, *Der indo-persische Dichter Bidil*; Siddiqi, *The Influence of Bedil on the Indo-Persian Poetic Tradition*.

### Pashto

Raverty, *Selections from the Poetry of the Afghans*. Abdul Hayy Habibi, *Pata khazana*. Olaf Caroe and E. B. Howell, *The Poems of Khushal Khan Khattak* (Peshawar, 1963). Caroe's studies on the Pathans are groundbreaking.

### Sindhi

Schimmel, *Sindhi Literature* (Wiesbaden, 1974).

1 *Qadi Qadan jo kalam*, ed. Hiran Thakur.

2 Rashdi, *Amin-al-Mulk Mir Ma^csum-i Bhakkari*.

3 Sajida Alvi, *Religion and State During the Reign of Mughal Emperor Jahangir*. Idem, *Mazhar-i Shahjahani*.

4 Jotwani, *Shah Abdul Karim*. Also, *Miyan Shah ^cInat Qadiri* in the early 18th century belongs in this context.

5 Schimmel, *Shah Inayat of Jhok*.

6 Sorley, *Shah Abdul Latif*. Schimmel, *Pain and Grace* (Part 2). There are numerous editions of the 'Risala' since it was first edited in 1866 by the German missionary Ernst Trumpp. The most accessible is the edition by K. Advani (Bombay, 1958). There is a vast amount of Sindhi literature on Shah ^cAbdul Latif.

7 In the series of Sindhi Folk Literature edited by N. B. Baloch, the *maulud* contain numerous songs about the 'Bridegroom Muhammad'; also the *munajatun* and *mu^cjiza* testify to the great veneration of the Prophet in Sind. Schimmel, *And Muhammad is His Messenger*; Asani, *Celebrating Muhammad*.

8 Schimmel, Translations and Commentaries of the Koran.

9 Sachal Sarmast, *Risalo Sindhi*, and *Siraiki Kalam*.

### Punjabi

L. Ramakrishna, *Panjabi Sufi Poets*. In addition, J. Fück, *Die sufische Dichtung in der Landessprache des Panjab*.

1 In this genre, see Vaudeville, *Les songs des douz mois*.

2 There are numerous translations by Bullhe Shah (also by other Punjabi Sufis) in English; however, none are satisfactory. Pakistani translators usually ignore the expressions which originate from Hinduism.

3 For spinning songs, see Eaton, *Sufis of Bijapur*. Shah Abdul Latif used this form in the 'Risalo' in the Sur Kapa^iti.

### Urdu

Garcin de Tassy, *Histoire de la Littérature Hindoue et Hindoustani*, 3 vols. Sadiq, *History of Urdu Literature*. Schimmel, *Classical Urdu Literature*.

1 Russell and Khurshidul Islam, *Three Mughal Poets*.

2 For Mir see Schimmel, *Pain and Grace*, part I.

3 Sadiq, *History of Urdu Literature*, p. 123.

4 Ghalib, *Kulliyat-i farsi*, 17 vols; *Urdu Diwan*, ed. Hamid Ahmad Khan. Russell, *Ghalib: Life and Letters*. Schimmel, *A Dance of Sparks*. Eadem, *Rose der Woge, Rose des Weins* (translations). There is an extensive secondary literature on Ghalib.

## NINE: The Arts

### The Ruler's Library

Abdul Aziz, *The Imperial Library of the Mughuls*; Losty, *The Art of the Book in India*, chap. III.; see also Minorsky, *Calligraphers and Painters* ref. Qadi Ahmad.

1 Goswamy and Fischer, *Wunder einer Goldenen Zeit*, no. 53.

2 See pages from the *Akhlaq-i Nasiri* in Goswamy and Fischer, *Wunder einer Goldenen Zeit*, ills. 11, 13, 55, 56, 57, 58.

3 Illustrations of the Central Asian past are in Goswamy and Fischer, *Wunder einer Goldenen Zeit*, no. 48.

4 From *Anwar-i suhayli*, INDIA!, p. 93. Also see Qaisar, *Visualization of Fables in the Anwar-i Suhayli*.

5 Royal Asiatic Society, London, Pers. 258 (1581).

6 A page from Amir Khusrau's 'Duval Rani Khizr Khan' in INDIA!, no. 92. A copy was also made of the Diwan of Amir Khusrau's friend Hasan Dihlawi in 1602 for Prince Salim; at the end of the manuscript is a portrait of the calligrapher Mir ᶜAbdallah Mushkinqalam, father of Salih Kanboh. Beach, *The Grand Mogul*, p. 39, no. 1; see Schimmel, *Islam in India and Pakistan*, no. XXVIb. An excellent manuscript of the works of Amir Khusrau was produced for *khankhanan* ᶜAbduʾr Rahim; it contains a long contribution by the owner. Berlin, Staatsbibliothek, MS or Fol. 1278.

7 Brend, *The Emperor Akbar's 'Khamsa' of Nizami*.

8 Losty, *The Art of the Book in India*, p. 74; the manuscript is in The Royal Asiatic Society, London. Mustafa Khan, Governor of Thatta, sent a *Shahnama* to Jahangir (*Tuzuk*, II, p. 232), Shah Jahan received in 1637 an enormous manuscript of the *Shahnama* by ᶜAli Mardan Khan, which is now in Bankipur. See Marshall, *Moghuls in India*, no. 472.

9 Spink, no. 60; Yusuf and Zulaykha, 1609.

10 *Akbarnama*, II, p. 455; compare Rizvi, *Religious and Intellectual History*, p. 335.

11 *Tuzuk*, II, p. 95; for the quotation from Anwari, see Schimmel and Welch, *A Pocket Book for Akbar*, p. 4.

12 Eggert, *Der Hamza-Roman*. The original was taken in 1739 by Nadir Shah. This work was the only item out of the entire booty that Muhammad Shah wanted back. Only about one-tenth of the 1,500 pages survive. Seyller stresses – with good reason – the necessity for an early start to work on the *Hamzanama*. For the recitation, see ᶜAbdun nabi-yi Qazwini, *Dastur al-fusaha*, in Marshall, *Moghuls in India*, no. 52.

13 Maneri, *The Hundred Letters*, trans. Paul Jackson.

14 A manuscript of Sanaʾis 'Hadiqat al- haqiqat' in the Chester Beatty Library, Dublin.

15 Schimmel, *The Triumphal Sun*, p. 269ff.; Sprenger, *Mathnawi-Kommentare*, nos. 361–74.

16 Badaʾuni, III, p. 421.

17 Losty, *The Art of the Book*, no. 68.

18 Schimmel, *Calligraphy and Islamic Culture*. A particularly beautiful example of an inscription from Bengal is in INDIA!, p. 74.

19 Schimmel, Introduction to Welch et al., *The Emperors' Album*.

20 *Eadem*, ref. the *shamsa* at the beginning of the Album; also Welch, *Imperial Mughal Painting*, no. 30

21 Dust-jacket of Losty, *The Art of the Book*. Numerous portrayals of writers appear in the marginal illustrations or earlier albums, e.g. Jahangir's albums in Berlin, and the *Muraqqaᶜ-yi Gulshan*.

22 INDIA!, no. 150; dust-jacket of Schimmel, *Calligraphy and Islamic Culture*.

23 Badaʾuni, III, p. 429f.; compare Goswamy and Fischer, *Wunder einer Goldenen Zeit*, no. 19 in the text.

24 For the *khatt-i baburi* see Azimjanova, *Données nouvelles sur l'écriture Baburi* in *Baburnama* (Bacqué-Gramon).

25 Colnaghi, no. 12 (1607). There is calligraphy in his hand on the back of every picture.

26 Berlin, 'Albumblätter', no. 28 (with erroneous translation). Specimens of his copies of the Koran are in Berlin, Staatsbibliothek, MS orient. Quart 2092: *Suras* 36, 48, 67, 78.

27 Ghulam Muhammad Dihlawi Raqim, *Tadhkira-i khushniwisan*, ed. Hikayat Husain, Calcutta, Bibliotheca Indica, provides an overview up to Akbar II; however, Bahadur Shah Zafar was known especially for his writing pictures.

PAINTING

The literature on Mughal painting is vast. Numerous books, some of them wonderfully illustrated, have appeared since the works of Martin and Brown; catalogues of great exhibitions in the USA, UK and Switzerland; the catalogues of the treasures of the great European and oriental libraries are also becoming available. In addition there are numerous independent works on the nature and history of certain themes, portrayals of individual artists, and much more.

1 The so-called 'Houghton *Shahnama*', ed. Martin Dickson and S. C. Welch (Cambridge, MA, 1981, 2 vols), was produced in the time of Shah Tahmasp in Iran. A small convenient edition is Welch, *A King's Book for Kings: The Shah-namah of Shah Tahmasp* (NY, 1972).

2 The 'House of Timur' (British Museum, London, 1913-2-8-11), *c.* 1555, has often been published and analysed. See INDIA!, no. 84.

3 Brown, *Indian Painting*, chap. on Islamic Culture; p.182ff.

4 An overview of portraits of painters is in Beach, *The Grand Mogul*: Balchand, p. 95; Payag, p. 151, no. 13; Daulat and Govardhan, p. iii; Bishndas, p. 108, no. 8. Also, Manohar, p. 131, no.10; Bichitr, p.102, no.7; Daulat, p.113, no.9. Further examples are Brend, *The Emperor Akbar's Khamsa*, ill. 47; S. C. Welch, *Imperial Mughal Painting*, no. 19: Daulat and ʿAbduʾr Rahim; *Gulistan* of The Royal Asiatic Society: at the end - Manohar and Shirinqalam. There is also a self-portrait by Kesudas. Additional portraits and self-portraits are in the marginal paintings of the *Muraqqaᶜ-yi gulshan*, Teheran.

5 Father and son: Basawan and Manohar, Aqa Riza and Abuʾl-Hasan; uncle and nephew: Bishndas and Nanha; brothers: Payag and Balchand.

6 *Tuzuk*, I, p. 40.

7 Brend, *The Emperor Akbar's Khamsa*, no. 39; a similar picture is in the marginal decoration of Jahangir's album in Berlin: Kühnel and Goetz, Ia.

8 See Mutribi Samarqandi, trans. Foltz, p. 76.

9 In this connection, Weber, *Porträts und historische Darstellungen*.

10 ʿAdil Shah: *Tuzuk*, II, p. 36; *Qutb ul-mulk: ibid.*, II, p. 90.

11 Beach, *The Imperial Image*, no. 180; compare also the portrayal of Jahangir shooting at poverty in *Life at Court*, no. 24; the chain of righteousness is also depicted.

12 Dust-jacket illustration of Beach, *The Imperial Image*; Welch, *Imperial Mughal Painting*, no. 21.

13 Ettinghausen, *The Emperor's Choice*; Welch, *Imperial Mughal Painting*, no. 22 and often; also on the dust-jacket of Gascoigne, *The Mughals*.

14 Dust-jacket of Welch *et al.*, *The Emperors' Album*.

15 Love scenes: Kühnel, *Indische Miniaturen*, nos. 15–17; S. C. Welch, *Imperial Mughal Painting*, no. 35; Beach, *The Grand Mogul*, p. 98, no. 31; idem, image, no. 22; Canby, *Princes, poétes et paladins*, no. III.

16 Muhammad Shah on a sedan chair made up of girls: INDIA!, 182; Muhammad Shah in the act of making love: Dallapiccola, *Princesses et courtesans*, p. 23; *Life at Court*, no. 71.

17 A beautiful portrayal of *yogis* by Govardhan is in Welch, *Imperial Mughal Painting*, no. 33; Beach, *The Grand Mogul*, no. 65.

18 Welch, *Indian Drawings and Painted Sketches*, no. 65; Beach, *The Grand Mogul*, p. 167, no. 65.

19 Farrukh Beg's hermit: INDIA!, p. 147. Rogers, *Mughal Miniatures*, no 69. For the artist see Skelton, *The Mughal Artist Farrokh Beg*.

20 Koch, *Jahangir and the Angels*.

21 Goswamy and Fischer, *Wunder einer Goldenen Zeit*, no. 25.

22 Kühnel and Goetz, *Buchmalereien*, is the first overview of the Jahangir album and the marginal paintings; Swietochowski examines the arrangement of the marginal paintings in Welch *et al.*, *The Emperors' Album*. Examples of marginal paintings are in Yetta Godard, *Muraqqaᶜ-yi gulshan*; also Beach, *The Grand Mogul*, p. 49; Bussagli, *Indian Miniatures*, no. 61; there are some especially good examples in Smart and Walker, *Pride of the Princes*.

23 Goswamy and Fischer, *Wunder einer Goldenen Zeit*, no. 61.

24 Kalim, *Diwan*, pp. 71, 73; also Schimmel's Introduction in Welch *et al.*, *The Emperors' Album*.

25 Miniatures of Shahi's *Diwan* are scattered in several collections.

26 Vaughan, *Mythical Animals in Mughal Art*.

27 Del Bonk, *Reinventing Nature: Mughal Composite Animal Painting*; the picture of Schellinks is no. 13 in this work.

28 Hickmann, Introduction to *Indische Albumblätter*.

29  Duda, *Das Millionenzimmer*.

BUILDINGS AND GARDENS

Koch, *Mughal Architecture*. K. and C. Fischer, *Indische Baukunst islamischer Zeit*. Volwahsen, *Islamisches Indien*. C. Asher, *The Architecture of Mughal India*. Ansar, *Palaces and Gardens of the Mughals*.

1  Begley has devoted a series of works and papers to the Taj Mahal. See also Chughtay, 'Is there a European Element in the Construction of the Taj Mahal?'

2  A miniature showing the construction of the Red Fort in Agra is in *Life at Court*, no. 5. The *Baburnama* also contains pictures of construction works.

3  Bada'uni, II, p. 203ff. for the building of the Ibadatkhana; Brand and Lowry, *Fatehpur Sikri*; *eidem, Akbar's India*; in which ills. 15 and 16 show the construction of the place; see also A. Rizvi and V. J. Flynn, *Fatehpur Sikri*.

4  Kalim, *Diwan*, p. 371. Ctesiphon, known in the Islamic world as Mada'in, is the mighty ruined castle of the Ghassanid prince Nu'man near Baghdad, which is a frequent theme of Muslim poets.

5  For Lahore: Waliullah, *Lahore*; Quraeshi, *Lahore: The City Within*.

6  Numerous miniatures testify to the wall paintings in Moghul palaces, e.g. in 'Disputing Doctors', one can see European pictures, archangel with sword, *puttos* treading a wine press; in another MS, Pers. 61, fol. 28v, in the Bodleian Library, Oxford, there are fairies in fashionable lappets; animals lying peaceably together is a frequent theme. Ebba Koch has studied these pictures.

7  *Tuzuk*, II, p. 162; compare Vogel, *Tile-Mosaics of the Lahore Fort*, p. 63.

8  *Tuzuk*, I, p. 332, for the stone figures.

9  For Wazir Khan and his construction projects, see Shamsham ad-daula, *Ma'athir al-umara'*, II, p. 981; F. Dodd, *Wazir Khan*.

10  Vogel, *Tile-Mosaics of the Lahore Fort*.

11  Koch, *Shah Jahan und Orpheus*.

12  Desai, *Mosques of India*, a very concise overview. Jaffar, 'Mahabit Khan's Mosque in Peshawar'.

13  Koch, *Mughal Architecture*, p. 68. Mohammad, *Hammams in Medieval India*.

14  *Tuzuk*, II, pp. 73, 75; In 1616, six *bulghurkhana* were read, a further 24 were supposed to be built, *Tuzuk*, p. 205.

15  MacDougall and Ettinghausen, *The Islamic Garden*; Mahmood Hussain et al., *The Mughal Garden*.

16  Sulaiman, *Baburnama*, no. 24.

17  Golombek, *Timur's Garden*.

18  Mahmoud Hussain et al., *The Mughal Garden*, containing documentation on the Wah gardens.

19  Shamsham ad-daula, *Ma'athir al-umara'*, II, p. 1014, re Zafar Khan, whose *Mathnawi*, which is illustrated with a few fine miniatures (see Losty, *The Art of the Book*, no. 83) has yet to be published.

# Glossary

*ābdār*  attendant in charge of the drinking room

*ābla*  pustule, blister

*āchār*  fruit or vegetable pickle

*āftābgīr*  parasol, part of the royal insignia

*ahadī*  soldier, immediately subordinate to the ruler, usually not part of the normal military hierarchy; specialist. Many craftsmen and artists were *ahadī*

*ahadipan*  attitude of an *ahadī* who fails to discharge his duties; *ahadi* = laziness

*ajrak* (Arab. *azraq*, blue)  hand-blocked cotton fabric with dark blue, red and white pattern

*akhbārāt-i darbār-i mu*ᶜ*allā*  court bulletin

*akhtabey*  chief stablemaster

*āltamghā*  'red stamp', royal seal; grant of land under royal seal in perpetuity

ᶜ*alam*  standard (for *amīrs* of upwards of 1000-*zāt*)

*alif*  first letter of the alphabet; cipher for Allāh; sign standing for slimness

*amīr, umarā*ᶜ  designation of an official above 500-*zāt*

*ankus*  elephant stick in the form of a cross

ᶜ*arz chahra*  presentation of petitions (chancellery)

*ashrāf*  Muslim immigrants in India from Arabia, Iran and Central Asia claiming noble descent

*asp*  horse; *du aspa* soldier with responsibility for two horses; *nim aspa* soldier or *ahadī*, who has to share a horse with another; *sih aspa* soldier with responsibility for three horses

*atbegi*  marshal; very high-ranking *amīr* in charge of the royal stables, falcons and related facilities (for hunting leopards, etc.)

*auqaf* pl. of *waqf*  tax-free charitable foundations for the benefit of Muslims, towards maintaining schools, libraries, dispensaries etc.

*ayma*,  fief; fallow land bequeathed by ruler as a reward or favour at a very low rent for cultivation

*bahādur*  hero

*bakhshī*  paymaster; also inspector or secretary

*balda*  town (as an administrative unit)

*banyā*  Hindu merchant or shopkeeper

*bar begi*  the person who presents petitions at court, also *mir* ᶜ*arż*

*bārāmāsah*  love poetry which expresses the feelings of a woman throughout the twelve months of the year

*barg bahā*  'price of a betel leaf', salary of the princesses

*basmala*  the saying, 'In the name of God', with which every activity has to commence; *basmala kā dulhā* 'bridegroom of the *basmala*', a boy who is introduced to the Qur'an for the first time at the age of four months and four days

*bhakti*  Hindu devotion; *bhakta* devotee or adherent of Hindu mysticism or folk religion

*bhang*  *cannabis sativa*; intoxicating drink prepared from the leaves of the hemp plant

*bīdaulat*  'miserable wretch', Jahangir's epithet for Shah Jahan after 1622

*bīghā*  a measure of a third of an acre

*bihārī*  style of Arabic calligraphy somewhat square and often coloured; popular in India for copying Qur'āns, especially during the 14th and 15th centuries

*bīstī*  commander of 20-*zāt*

*bitikchī*  military scribe or secretary; also head clerk or chief registrar

*budūh*  apotropaic numerological formulae wherein the Arabic letters b = 2, d = 4, u = 6, h = 8

*bughrā*  quadrangular pastries prepared with sweet or savoury fillings

*bulghurkhāna*  'house of shredded wheat'; public kitchen

*burunsuz*  'noseless', dishonoured

*burqa^c*  women's clothing which covers the entire body, including the head, with a grille covering the eyes

*būta*  pattern of buds on fabric, especially shawls and carpets

*buyutāt*  ('of houses'), royal workshops and departments of the household; account of household expenses in the palace and also the workshops and studios

*chandal mandal*  a board-game invented by Akbar

*chapātī*  flat unleavened bread prepared on a griddle and a staple even today in the subcontinent

*charas*  intoxicant prepared from the flowers and dew of the hemp plant

*chārbāgh*  ('four gardens') garden divided into four sections by watercourses, with raised footpaths to permit a view over the flower beds, often with a pavilion in the centre

*chatr*  parasol, insignia of the kingdom

*chauḍoli*  sedan chair

*chaupar*  ancient board-game for four players using pawns and cowrie shells

*chaupasi*  game of dice

*chilla*  forty days' seclusion, common among Ṣūfīs; also period of mourning, especially among Shī^c īs

*chīnīkhāna*  room in the palace for storing porcelain and glass

*chūbīn rawatī*  the royal seal (in the camp)

*chūnā*  shiny polished mortar

*dahsāla*  tax on agricultural produce calculated decadally according to the average yield

*dāʾira*  tambourine

*dāl*  split pulses, an important staple food

*dām*  copper coin, 1/40 th of a rupee during Akbar's reign

*dār al-khilāfa*  seat of the caliph

*durbār*  imperial audience, state reception

*dārugha*  superintendent, chief inspector; prefect of a town or village

*darśan*  ('vision') a view of the ruler; someone 'had *darshan*' means 'he was blessed by a view of . . .'

*dhikr*  'recollection' especially repetition of the names of God and religious formulae

*dhimmīs*  non-Muslims deemed as 'people of the Book' (Christians, Jews, Zoroastrians, Sabeans, and in India, Hindus) who were exempt from military duty because of payment of the *jizya*; the *dhimmī* administer their own affairs under their own religious leader

*dhotī*  loincloth worn by Hindus

*dhrupad*  oldest surviving genre of north Indian classical vocal music

*digambara*  'clothed in air', naked Jain ascetics

*dih bāshi*  commander of more than ten

*dīn-i ilahī*  the syncretic movement founded by Akbar from elements of various traditions; however, it was really intended to be a private matter rather than an alternative to the major prevailing religions.

*diwālī*  'Row of Lamps'; Hindu New Year and the most significant celebration in India

*dīwān*  (in the provinces) official in charge of revenue collection

*dīwān*  sitting or meeting room; chancery

*dīwān-i ^c āmm*  hall of public audiences; ceremonial place for general assembly and receptions

*dīwān-i khaṣṣ*  hall of private audience

*dīwān-i kull*  financial secretariat; *dīwān-i khāliṣa* office of accountant-general; *dīwān-i tan* office dealing with the salaries of *manṣabdar*s and princesses

*dīwān-i maẓālim*  office dealing with matters of jurisprudence which are not covered by the *sharī^c a* (holy law)

*doha*  tetrametric couplet, usually edificatory, with two rhyming verses and with a caesura as the end of each first hemistich

*dūpyāzā*  rich meat stew with double the quantity of onions added to spices and yoghurt

*ektārā*  long-necked, single-stringed musical instrument

*fālnāma*  book of omens used as an oracle, often

lavishly illustrated

*faluda* soft pudding; flummery

*farmān* decree concerning appointments; imperial order; *farmān-i bayāzī* urgent edict; *farmān-i thabtī* charter concerning an especially important appointment

*farr-i īzadī* 'divine glory' (Avestan *khwarena*), divinely bestowed fortune or splendour that accompanies the ruler (in this case Akbar)

*farrāshkhāna* room for storing furniture, carpets, wall hangings, etc. *farrāshdār* chamberlain

*farsakh* a distance of approx 6.2 km.

*fatāwā-yi ʿālamgīrī* treatise of legal judgments compiled under Aurangzeb

*fatwā* legal judgment; strictly speaking a *responsum*

*fīl* elephant; in chess, bishop

*firnī* milk-based rice pudding

*ganjifa* a card game

*gaz* a measurement equivalent to a yard; *ilāhī gaz* = 33 inches or approx. 80 cm

*ghazal* 'lyric', love poem in mono-rhyme usually not longer than 14 verses

*ghāzī* Muslim frontier fighter; honorific bestowed on ruler for achieving victory in a battle against infidels

*ghee* clarified butter

*ghurāb* corvette

*ghuslkhāna* 'bathing room', area of the palace for confidential and private meetings

*ginān* devotional songs of the Ismāʿīlis in Sindhi, Gujarati, etc.

*gulālbār* red fabric fence around the imperial pavilion in the encampment

*gulpāshī* long-necked silver bottle for pouring rose-water

*gulzār* rose-garden style of Arabic writing, wherein the letters are filled with flowers or other motifs

*gurmukhī* 'script uttered by the Gurū', developed by Sikhs for their scriptures and later standardized as the script of modern Punjabi in India

*ḥabs-i dam* holding the breath during meditation and recollection

*ḥabs-i firangi* 'the European prison'; in later poetry, the temporal world

*al-hādi* 'the guide', one of the 99 names of Allāh

*ḥadith* 'saying, tradition' regarding the words and sayings of the Prophet Muhammad, transmitted orally

*ḥāfiẓ* 'preserver', someone who knows the Qurʾān by heart

*ḥalīm* a heavy stew of meat, spices and pulses

*halqa be-gūsh* 'ring in the ear', badge of servitude

*hama ūst* 'everything is He'; *hama az ūst* 'everything is from Him', both mystical formulae

*hammām* Muslim bath house

*ḥaqīqat* 'truth'; for the Raushaniyya sect, 'contemplation of God'

*harisa* thick paste or *potage* of pounded meat and cereal

*holī* Hindu spring festival during which people spray coloured water and powder on each other

*howda* sedan chair frame for riding on elephants

*hujjat Allāh* 'proof of God'

*hukm* order, imperial edict

*humā bird* ancient Iranian mythological bird symbolizing good fortune and supposed to live on bones alone; anyone on whom its shadow falls is supposed to become king.

*huqqa* water-pipe

*huwa* 'He', God

*ibāḥatiyān* 'lapsed', religious groups which do not follow the official religious (orthodox Sunnī) line

*ʿīdgāh* place of assembly, where prayers are held during the two great festivals

*ʿid ul-fitr* feast marking the end of Ramaḍān, *ʿid ul-aḍḥā* feast on the day of sacrifice during the month of pilgrimage, *hajj*)

*ijtihād* 'exercise of independent judgement' for certain problems outside the scope of the four traditional Sunni schools of law; also practised by Shīʿīs

*ilāhī-Āra* way of reckoning time, introduced by Akbar in 1556 during *Nauruz*, the vernal equinox

*ʿilm ladunī* 'knowledge from Me' (*Sura* 18:60) mystical, intuitive knowledge imparted by Allāh

*iltmish* experienced light cavalry in the centre front of the army

*imāmbārā* building in which Shīʿīs store their paraphernalia for the Muḥarram Festival

*inʿam* revenue; gift; grant of rent-free land

*ʿishqbāzī* 'love game', Akbar's term for the antics of fantail pigeons

*ishrāq* 'illumination', the philosophy of enlightenment of Shihābuddīn as-Suhrawardī, in which God is conceived of as 'The Light of Lights'

*īwān* vaulted, arched hall which opens out into an inner courtyard with a raised floor; the vaulted area round the central yard of a mosque

*jadhba* 'attraction'; mystical rapture

*jagat guru* 'teacher of the world'

*jāgīr* rent-free grant; *jāgīrdār* one who possesses a *jāgīr*

*jālī* carved latticework in front of windows or corridors

*jālīnus az-zamān* 'Galen of the time' – a prominent doctor's honorific

*jāma* overgarment; long gown tied double-breasted and folded into plaits

*jharokā* the window through which the masses could get a glimpse of the ruler

*jīgha* turban ornament

*jizya* poll tax paid by *dhimmīs*

*jauhar* self-immolation by Rajput women, after the conquest of the kingdom in order to escape capture

*kārd* long, straight knife with a single cutting edge

*kārkhāna*, pl. *kārkhānahā* workshop; factory; studio, *atelier* of the palace

*karori* revenue officer

*kashkūl* goblet or bowl in the shape of a boat

*katar* dagger with two handles

*khalīfa* 'successor, deputy'; caliph, head of Islamic (Sunnī) community

*khamyāza* 'yawning', endless longing or infinite thirst (as expressed in Indo-Persian poetry)

*khān* chief, lord, leader; honorific for nobles and warriors, especially of Afghan or Turkish lineage

*khanjar* curved dagger

*kharājī-land* land won by conquest in early Islam where inhabitants had to pay a certain tax, *kharaj* 'yield, produce'

*khaṭṭ-i bāburī* a style of writing invented by Babur

*khichrī* dish of rice, spices and split lentils

*khilaʿ* robe of honour

*khūrak-filān-i ḥalqa* tax collected as 'food for the elephants'

*khwānsālār* head chef

*khwarena* see *farr*

*kīf* opium or other drugs

*kīmkhwāb* velvet worked with gold; also brocaded silk

*kōkā* foster brother; *kōkī* foster sister

*kos* measurement of length, equivalent to approximately 2 miles

*kotwāl* magistrate

*kror (crore)* = 10 million (100 lakhs = 1 crore)

*kūh-i nūr* Kohinoor 'Mountain of Light'; a famous diamond among the Crown Jewels in London

*kundan* Indian technique of using thin 24-carat gold for setting precious or semi-precious stones

*kurnish* salutation performed to the sovereign in an audience

*lakh* = 100,000

*laʿl* ruby; termed accurately 'spinel'

*landey* Pashto poem consisting of 9 plus 13 syllables

*langar* soup kitchen in a dervish monastery, Sikh or Hindu temples

*lashkar-i duʿā* 'prayer army', members of the population who do not work or fight, pensioners

*lassi* sweetened or salted drink of yoghurt diluted with water

*lauḥa* 'sheet, tablet', single page of calligraphy

*laylat ul-qadr* 'night of power', the night of the first revelation of the Qurʾān on approximately 27 Ramaḍān;

*madad-i maʿāsh* 'income support', pension or revenue allocated for the upkeep of charitable institutions or pious scholars

*maghribī* style of Arabic writing used in north Africa

*maḥaldār* representative of the women's quarters of the palace; watchman of a quarter

*mahākavīrāy* poet laureate

*maḥal* 'place', palace; also post or district

*mahārāj* maharajā

*mahd-i ʿulyā* 'the highest cradle', title of the ruler's spouse

*māhi-yi marātib* distinction for *amīrs* of more than 7,000-*zāt*; also conferred on princes and other nobles who wielded the insignia of a fish and two spheres

*mahout* elephant driver

*mahtābī* place for nocturnal conversations in the imperial camp

*maḥżār* decree, especially Akbar's decree of 1579

*maᶜjūn* paste, electuary; usually mixed with opium

*malbūs-i khāṣṣ* a robe of honour bestowed for special merit, which had been worn by the ruler himself

*malfūẓāt* treatises of sayings, reports or apothegmata about Ṣūfī preceptors

*malik ash-shuᶜarā* 'king of poets', an honorific

*malik at-tujjār* 'king of merchants'

*malikā-i jahān* 'queen of the world', title for the wife of the ruler

*man (maund)* measurement of weight, usually 40 *ser* = approximately 80 lb or 37.324 kg. This varied in different parts of India.

*mandīl* pocket handkerchief; white cloth which a condemned man or sinner places around his neck as a sign of submission during a hearing

*manṣabdār* an official of rank

*maᶜrifat* 'gnosis'; mystical knowledge marking the transition from 'station' to 'state'

*marthiyya* dirges commemmorating the martyrdom of Ḥusayn ibn ᶜAlī in Kerbela

*Maryam makānī* 'in the place of Mary'; *Maryam-i zamānī* 'the Mary of the age'

*masīḥ ad-dīn- al-mulk-, az-zamān* 'Messiah of the religion'; 'Messiah of the realm'; 'Messiah of the age': titles for doctors.

*mast* intoxicated; in the case of elephants, especially lively

*mathnawi* 'doubled one', a long narrative poem in rhyming couplets with a common metre

*maulūd* poem celebrating the Prophet's birthday

*melā chirāghān* 'fair of lamps'; celebrated on the last Saturday of March in Lahore honouring Mādhōlāl Ḥusayn, a Punjabi mystic

*mihmāndār* officer responsible for guests, head of protocol

*mirᶜadl* chief justice

*mirᶜarż* overseer, chief petitioner in the *durbār*

*mīr bakāwal (bakāwalbegi)* director of the kitchen; *mīr baḥr* admiral; *barr* superintendent of the

forests; *-manzil* quartermaster general; *-munshī* Chief Secretary; *-sāmān* head steward; *-shikār* chief huntsman; *-tuzak* master of ceremonies

*mīrzā* title of the Tīmūrid princes; later also 'nobleman'; originally 'son of a great lord'

*mlēcha* barbarian, unclean (as Hindus regarded non-Hindus or foreign invaders)

*muhr* standard gold coin of almost 100% purity weighing 169 grains

*muᶜammā* puzzle, especially name riddle or acrostic

*mufarriḥ* drug which 'gladdens the heart'

*muftī* one empowered to promulgate *fatwās*

*muḥtasib* market overseer; censor

*mujaddid* 'renewer (of the religion)', supposed to appear at the beginning of every Islamic century

*munshī* secretary

*mustaufi* chief auditor; head clerk

*mutᶜa* temporary marriage, which according to Shīᶜī law can be contracted for a matter of hours or even longer; frowned upon by Sunnīs

*nādirī* special robe of honour with short sleeves

*nard* backgammon

*naskh* cursive handwriting

*nastaᶜliq* 'hanging' form of writing evolved in Persia which spread to Turkey and India; slanting, with differentiated ground and hair strokes

*nauba* band of drummers and fifers who played during fixed hours at the gates of the palace

*nauratan* 'nine jewels', Akbar's nine most outstanding courtiers

*nauruz* 'new day', the beginning of the Iranian year at the spring (vernal) equinox

*nāẓir* overseer

*nāżr (nadhr)* sacrifice

*nishān* 'sign'; seal, stamp, decree; standard, banner

*nuqta* diacritical point

*padma-i muraṣṣaᶜ* 'the bejewelled lotus', highest order

*pān* betel leaf; *pāndān* elegantly made metallic boxes for storing the ingredients for preparing *pan*: betel leaves, areca nuts, lime paste, etc.

*panchāyat* 'assembly of five'; village council in Hindu communities

*pargana* sub-district

*parmnarm* extremely soft cashmere shawl

*parwāncha* order, permit, license

*pashmīna* fine cashmere shawl

*patkā* ceremonial sash, the ends of which are often richly embroidered

*payjāma* loose trousers

*pīshkash* gift or tribute presented by those of inferior status to their superiors

*pūst* spicy opium mixture

*qabā* long overgarment for men

*qabūlī (qablī)* pilaf made from rice and chickpeas

*qadam rasūl* footprint of the Prophet in stone

*qāḍī* judge

*qahwa* coffee

*qāʾim az-zamān* 'he who will rise of the Age', Ṣūfī title for one who remains resolute

*qamargāh* hunting grounds: an encircling border about ten miles wide within which the game is driven together in the middle of the enclosure, where it can easily be shot

*qānāt* tent enclosure made of red patterned material for the emperor

*qānūn* table zither; trapezoid dulcimer played with two plectra

*qaṣīda* a long poem, normally an ode, with a mono-rhyme

*qayyūm* 'the eternally existing', one of the names of Allāh; name of Sirhindī and three of his descendants

*qāz-i Ḥusaynī* 'Ḥusayn's goose', flamingo

*qitᶜa* 'fragment'; bridging phrase in a *ghazal* lacking the first two rhyming hemistichs

*qoshuq* Turkish verse form

*qurbat* 'nearness'; for Ṣūfīs, ethical proximity to Allāh through gnosis, obedience, etc.

*qūrbegi* one who wears the imperial insignia

*qūshbegi* chief falconer

*quṭb* 'pole, axis'; for Ṣūfīs the highest member of the mystical hierarchy

*rabāb* Arab fiddle; bowed instrument with two or three strings; national instrument of Afghanistan

*raḥmat* compassion, as manifested by prophets; also monsoon rain

*rāi* lower honorary title for Hindus

*rākhī* thread or band tied around the wrist by sisters to their brothers (Hindu brothers' day festival)

*rammāl* geomancer

*rānā* honorary title for Hindu generals or chieftains

*rauẓa-i munawwara* 'the illuminated garden'; Muḥammad's mausoleum in Medina; also the Taj Mahal

*rekhta* 'mixed', early form of Delhi Hindi-Urdu; macaronic verse wherein Persian vocables were added on a Hindi template or vice versa

*rīḥānī* 'basil-like'; fine form of *naskh*, often used for Qurʾānic writing

*riqāᶜ* large form of Arabic writing often used for documents

*rubāᶜī* quatrain with the rhyming pattern *aaba*; also epigram

*rumāl* embroidered cloth for wrapping gifts

*sābād* 'dragon', method of besieging in warfare

*sabk-i hindī* the 'Indian style' of Persian poetry

*ṣadr as-sudūr* chief judge who is an authority on religious law and responsible for managing *waqfs* (endowments)

*safina* 'boat', portable anthology of Persian verse bound on the short side and carried in one's turban's fold or sleeve

*sāg* spinach

*ṣāḥibat az-zamāni* 'the female ruler of the age', title for the wife of the ruler

*ṣāḥib qirān* 'Lord of the auspicious planetary conjunction'; Shah Jahan's epithet

*sajdā* prostration

*sanad* authority original or delegated to confer privilege, fief or charter

*sanbusa (samosā)* deep-fried savoury pastries

*sanyāsi* Hindu ascetic

*sāqīnāma* small *mathnawī* which begins with an appeal

*sāqī* 'cupbearer'

*sarāpa* 'from head to foot'; three-piece robe of honour

*sarāparda* walls of a tent

*sarkār* district; also chief overseer, supervisor

*sarpācha* thick stew made from the head and trotters of a sheep

*sarpati* oval turban fastening made from precious stone(s)

*sarpēch* turban ornament; *-yamani* turban ornament

for *manṣabdārs* of more than 3,000-*zāt*

*satī* (suttee)  self-immolation by Hindu widows

*sayf-i hindī*  Indian sword

*suyurghāl*  'favour, reward'; grant of land, city or province to an *amīr* who in lieu was obliged to provide a fixed number of troops on demand

*sayyid*  lineal descendants of Muhammad through ᶜAlī and Fāṭima

*sehra*  a veil of flowers or pearls worn by a bridegroom

*ser*  measurement of weight, approximately 2 lbs

*shab-i barāt*  full moon night on the 14/15 Shaᶜbān, month preceding Ramaḍān, and celebrated with prayers and fireworks in the subcontinent; it is the night when the destinies of Muslims for the coming year are said to be determined and sins forgiven

*shāhburj*  inner room of the palace where confidential discussions were held

*shahrāshub*  poem concerning people or events which 'stirred up the town'

*shāhtūs*  'ring shawl'; finest cashmere shawl

*shalwār qamis*  baggy trousers and long overblouse, typical dress for Muslim females of the subcontinent, also worn by men; it is the national dress of both men and women in Pakistan

*shamshērbāz*  'sword player', acrobat

*sharbatji*  official responsible for the supply of beverages

*shāsh*  sash

*shaykh ul-islām*  the highest appointed official responsible for interpreting the religious law (*shariᶜa*)

*shikasteh*  'broken'; derivative form of *nastaᶜliq* which while difficult to read became popular for daily and bureaucratic purposes

*shikōh*  splendour

*shish kebāb*  spit-roasted meat cubes infused with spices

*shīsh maḥal*  'glass palace'; room in which the walls are covered with numerous tiny mirrors

*shīsha-i ḥalabi*  Aleppan glass, of which the finest flasks and goblets were made

*sīharfī*  'thirty-letter poem'; 'Golden Alphabet' or abecedarian odes composed in Punjabi, Sindhi and other vernaculars by Ṣūfīs or folk poets

*sipand*  wild rue; it is burned to ward off the evil eye

*śivrātri*  night of the new moon and Hindu festival in honour of Lord Shivā

*sōraṭā*  tetrametric couplet in Indian poetry

*ṣūba*  province; *ṣūbedār*  provincial governor

*sūfiyāna*  'the Ṣūfī Way'; for Akbar it denoted a vegetarian diet and frequent fastings

*sukūnat*  'quietness'; for the Raushaniyya, striving to incorporate the qualities of God

*ṣulḥ-i kull*  'peace with all', Akbar's religio-political ideal

*sulṭān-i ᶜādil*  'the just sultan', who rules wisely

*suwār*  cavalry officer; the ideal number of horses which should be kept by a *manṣabdār*

*śwetambara*  'white robed' Jain monks

*taḥwīldār*  *manṣabdārs* responsible for gifts and expenses of ambassadors

*taj-i ᶜizzatī*  Humayun's turban, folded in a special way

*takauchiah*  pointed skirt which is often seen in pictures from the time of Akbar

*taᶜlīq*  'hanging'; early slanting version of writing with short verticals, broad horizontals and exaggerated natural length used in chancelleries

*tanbūr*  long-necked string instrument

*tankhwāh*  pension

*tappa*  see *landey*

*taqiyya*  dissimulation of religious convictions for fear of persecution; historically practised by the Shīᶜa

*ṭarīqa*  'path'; for Ṣūfīs the fraternity or order in the mystical way; second stage in the threefold path

*tariqa muhammadiyya*  the 'Muḥammadan path', mystical fundamental movement founded in India by Nāṣir Muḥammad ᶜAndalīb

*tarjīᶜ band, tarkīb band*  strophic poem of *ghazals* of equal length united either by a repeated or alternating verse

*tarkhani*  thick soup

*tasbīḥ*  prayer beads, generally with 99 pearls for the 99 beautiful names of Allāh; glorification of Allāh

*taslim*  bowing down before the ruler

*tauḥīd*  declaration of the oneness of God; for some Ṣūfis, unification of the self with God

*thuluth*  'one-third'; heavy, cursive style of writing where one-third of the letter slopes

*toquz*  'nine'; later, denoted gifts, because according to

Turkish custom, gifts were brought in groups of nine or in ninefold amounts

*töre* obligatory customs and traditions of the steppes

*ṭughrā* imperial signature, an image of a royal title created from calligraphy; a closed shape or mirror-image

*tümän tugh* banner of a commander of 10,000 troops

*turk* in Persian poetry, the young, fair, or beloved

*tūshakjī* official handling the expenses and equipment of responsible servants

*tuyugh* four-lineTurkish verse

*tuzuk* institution, document

*ᶜūd* aloe wood, burned as incense for its beneficial aroma

*ulus* tribe, small nation

*ummi* 'illiterate', epithet of the Prophet, who was regarded to have been *ummi*, as the possession of intellectual knowledge would have meant that he was not a pure vessel to receive the final revelation

*urdu-yi muᶜallā* 'the exalted camp'; the cantonment of Mughal Delhi

*ᶜurf* customary law

*ᶜurs* 'wedding', death anniversary of a saint commemorated as one whose soul has been 'wedded' to God

*ᶜushri-land* tithe paid for Muslim-owned property and land

*uṣūl al-fiqh* principles of jurisprudence

*uzuk* the state seal

*vīnā* double-bodied string instrument

*waḥdat ash-shuhūd* 'unicity of contemplation' and *waḥdat al-wujūd*, 'unicity of finding being', interchangeable among Indian Ṣūfīs and intensely discussed by later mystics

*wakīl* administrator of the imperial household, including land, workshops etc.

*walī*, pl. *auliyāʾ* 'friend (of Allah)', holy man or saint

*wāqī ᶜanawīs* court chronicler who records the entire proceedings during sittings

*wasī* 'heir', Shīᶜīte designation for ᶜAlī, as heir of the Prophet

*wazīr* vizier, minister or adviser to the sovereign

*wuṣlat* unification; for the Raushaniyya renunciation of everything worldly

*yād dāsht* memoirs

*yakhnī* lamb shank soup; spice stock (like bouquet garni) used for pilafs

*yalpōst* covering for a horse's mane

*yāqūt* corundum

*yüzbāshī* commander of one hundred

*zamīn* 'ground', form of poem which is imitated exactly

*zamīnbus* kissing the ground during the *durbār*

*zanāna* the women's quarters of the palace

*zardā* sweetened rice pilaf infused with dry fruits, cream and condiments; a festive dish

*zāt* personal numerical rank of an officer

# Bibliography

Abbas, Sayyid Ali, *Azfari Gurgani, Safanama Dihli se Madras tak* (Lahore, 1963)

Abdul Alim, *Hindustan men arabi adab aur ulum-i islamiyyat ki tadris o tahqiq* (Lucknow, 1956)

Abdul Aziz, *Arms and Jewellery of the Indian Mughals* (Lahore, 1947)

—, *The Imperial Library of the Mughals* (Lahore, 1967)

—, *The Mansabdari System of the Mughal Army* (Delhi, 1972)

—, *Thrones, Tents and their Furniture used by the Indian Mughals* (Lahore n.d.)

Abdul Hamid Lahawri, *Padshahnama*, Bibliotheca Indica, 3 vols (Calcutta, 1866–72)

Abdul Haqq, Maulwi, *Urdu ki nashw u nama men sufiya-yi kiram ka kam* (2nd ed, Delhi, 1988)

Abdul Hayy, *Gul-i rana* (Azamgarh, 1923; 2nd ed 1945)

Abdullah, Dr Syed, *Adabiyat-i farsi men hinduon ka hissa* (Delhi, 1942)

Abdur Rahim, 'Mughal Relations with Central Asia', *Islamic Culture*, 11 (1938)

—, 'Mughal Relations with Persia', *Islamic Culture*, 8 (1935); *Islamic Culture*, 9 (1936)

Abidi, S.A.H., 'Chandra Bhan Brahman', *Islamic Culture*, 40

Abul Fazl, *Akbarn amah: History of the Reign of Akbar, including an Account of his Predecessors*, trans. from the Persian by H. Beveridge, 3 vols (Calcutta, 1897–1921; repr. 1977)

—, *The Aʾin-i Akbari*, trans. from the original Persian by H. Blochmann and H. S. Jarrett, 3 vols (Calcutta, 1927–49; 2nd edn corrected and further annotated by D. C. Phillott and Jadunath Sarkar)

Adi Granth *see* Trumpp

Aftab, Shah Alam II, *Nadirat-i Shahi* (Urdu-Hindi, Punjabi), ed. Initiaz Ali Arshi (Rampur, 1944)

Aftabji, Jauhar, *Tadhkirat al- waqiʿat: The 'tezkereh al-vakiat' or Private Memoirs of the Moghul Emperor Humayun, Written in the Persian Language by Jouhar, a Confidential Domestic of His Majesty*, trans. Major Charles Stewart (London, 1832), extracts in Elliott and Dowson, III

Ahkam-i Alamgiri (ed.), *Jadunath Sarkar* (London, 1926)

Ahmad, Ali, *Twilight in Delhi* (2nd edn, Oxford, 1966)

Ahmad, Imtiaz, 'The *ashraf–ajlaf* Dichotomy in Muslim Social Structure in India', *Indian Economic and Social History Review*, 111 (1966)

Ahmad, Maulana, ibn Qadi Thatta, *Tarikh-i alfi*, in Elliott and Dowson, V

Ahmad, N., 'Some Cultural and Literary Remains of Emperor Humayun's Visit to Iran', *Indo-Iranica*, XXVIII (1975)

Ahmad, Q. M., 'Was Bairam Khan a Rebel?', *Islamic Culture*, 21 (1947)

Akhtar, Salim (ed.), *The Majmua al-shuʿara-i Jahangirshahi by Qatiʿi* (Karachi, 1979)

Akimushkin, Oleg F., *Il murakka di San Pietroburgo: album di miniature indiane e persiane del XVI–XVIII secolo e di esemplari di calligrafia di Mir Imad al-asani* (Milan, 1994)

Alamgir Aurangzeb, *Ruqʿat-yi ʿalamgiri* (Lucknow, 1901); ed. Sayyid N. A. Nadwi (Azamgarh, 1940)

Alexander, David, *The Arts of War: Arms and Armour of the 7th to 19th Century*, Nasser D. Khalili Collection of Islamic Art (London, 1992)

Ali, Hafiz Mohammad Tahir, 'Shaikh Muhibbullah of Allahabad', *Islamic Culture*, 47 (1973)

Alsdorf, Ludwig, 'Das Mogulreich von Babur bis Shahjahan', in E. Waldschmidt (ed.), *Geschichte Asiens* (Munich, 1950)

Alvi, M. A., and A. Rehman, *Jahangir the Naturalist* (New Delhi, 1968)

Alvi, Sajida S., 'Mazhar-i Shahjahani and the Mughal Province of Sind: A Discourse on Political Ethics', in Dallapiccola and Zingel, *Indian Regions* (Stuttgart, 1993)

—, 'Religion and State during the Reign of Mughal Emperor Jahangir: Nonjuristical Perspectives', *Studia Islamica*, 69 (1989)

Ambar, V. B., 'Shah Jahan's Rebellion and Abdur Rahim Khan Khanan', *Journal of Indian History*, Golden Jubilee issue (1974)

Ameer Ali, Syed, 'Islamic Culture under the Moghuls', *Islamic*

Culture, 1 (1927)

Amir Khusrau, *Diwan-i kamil*, ed. M. Darwish (Teheran, 1964)

—, *Duwal Rani Khidr Khan*, Facsimile edition (Lahore, 1975)

Andalib, Muhammad Nasir, *Nala-i Andalib*, 2 vols (Bhopal, 1890–91)

Andrews, Peter A., 'The Generous Heart or the Mass of Clouds: The Court Tents of Shahjahan', *Muqarnas*, 4 (1987)

Ansari, Bazmee [A. S.], 'Sayyid Muhammadjawnpuri and his Movement', *Islamic Studies*, 11 (1963)

Ansari, Mohammad Azhar, 'The Dress of the Great Mughals', *Islamic Culture*, 31 (1957)

—, 'The *abdar khanah* of the Great Mughals', *Islamic Culture*, 33 (1959)

—, 'The Diet of the Great Mughals', *Islamic Culture*, 33 (1959)

—, 'Palaces and Gardens of the Mughals', *Islamic Culture*, 33 (1959)

—, 'Social Conditions at the Court of Akbar and its Influence on Society', *Islamic Culture*, 33 (1959)

—, 'The Haram of the Great Mughals', *Islamic Culture*, 34 (1960)

—, 'The Hunt of the Great Mughals', *Islamic Culture*, 34 (1960)

—, 'Amusement and Games of the Great Mughals', *Islamic Culture*, 35 (1961)

—, 'Court Ceremonies of the Great Mughals', *Islamic Culture*, 35 (1961)

—, 'Some Aspects of Social Life at the Court of the Great Mughals', *Islamic Culture*, 36 (1962)

—, 'The Encampment of the Great Mughals', *Islamic Culture*, 37 (1963)

—, *Social Life of the Mughal Emperors, 1526–1707* (New Delhi, 1983)

Ansari, Muhammad Abdul Haq, *Sufism and Sharia: A Study of Shaikh Ahmad Sirhindi's Effort to Reform Sufism* (Leicester, 1986)

Anwari-Alhosseini, Shams, *Logaz und Moᶜamma. Quellenstudien zur Kunstform des persischen Rätsels* (Berlin, 1986)

Arnold, Thomas W., *The Preaching of Islam: A History of the Propagation of the Muslim Faith* (London 1896; 1913)

—, 'Saints, Muhammadan, in India', in, Hastings, *Encyclopedia of Religion and Ethics* (1907), vol. XI

—, *Painting in Islam*, With a New Introduction by Basil W. Robinson (New York, 1965)

Arnold, Thomas W., and J.V.S. Wilkinson, *The Library of Sir Chester Beatty: A Catalogue of the Indian Miniatures*, 3 vols (London, 1936)

Asani, Ali S., *The 'Bujh Niranjan': An Ismaili Mystical Poem* (Cambridge, MA, 1991)

Asher, Catherine B., *The Architecture of Mughal India* (Cambridge and New York, 1992)

—, 'Babur and the Timurid *char bagh*: Use and Meaning', *Environmental Design*, IX (1994), p. 11

Aslah, Muhammad, *Tadhkirat-i shuᶜara-i Kashmir*, ed. S. H. Rashdi, 5 vols (Karachi, 1967–68)

Athar Ali, M., *The Apparatus of Empire: Awards of Ranks, Offices and Titles to the Mughal Nobility (1574–1658)* (Delhi, 1985)

—, *The Mughal Nobility under Aurangzeb* (Bombay, 1970)

Atil, Esin, *The Brush of the Masters: Drawings from Iran and India*

(Washington DC, 1978)

Attar Singh (ed.), *Socio-cultural Impact of Islam on India* (Chandigarh, 1976)

Azad, Abul Kalam, *India Wins Freedom* (Bombay, 1959)

Azfari *see* Abbas

Azimjanova, A., 'Données nouvelles sur l'écriture Baburi', in Baqud-Gramond, *Le livre de Babur* (Paris, 1978)

Aziz Ahmad, *Studies in Islamic Culture in the Indian Environment* (London, 1964)

—, *An Intellectual History of Islam in the Subcontinent* (Edinburgh, 1969)

—, *The British Museum Mirzanama and the Seventeenth-Century Mirza in India*, IRAN XIII (London, 1975)

—, 'Akbar – hérétique ou apostate?', *Journal Asiatique* (1961)

—, 'Religious and Political Ideas of Shaikh Ahmad Sirhindi', *Rivista degli Studi Orientali*, XXXV (1961)

—, 'Political and Religious Ideas of Shah Waliullah of Delhi', *The Muslim World*, 52 (1962)

—, 'Sufismus und Hindumystik', *Saeculum*, 15(1964)

Babur, Zahiruddin, *Baburnama* (Chaghatay, Persian and English) 3 vols, ed. Wheeler M. Thackston Jr. (Cambridge, MA, 1993). Translated into English, A. S. Beveridge, *The Baburnama Translated, Edited and Annotated* (1921); French, Pavet de Courteille (Paris 1871); Jean Louis Baqué-Gramond, *Le Livre de Babur* (Paris 1978); German, Wolfgang Stammler, (Zürich 1982); Turkish, Resit Rahmati Arat, (Ankara 1943–46); and Russian, Azimjanova. Hamid Sulaiman published the 'Miniatures of Baburnama' that can be found in the British Museum (Tashkent, 1970)

Babur, *Aruz risalasi*, ed. J. A. Stebelov, Facsimile edition (Moscow, 1972)

—, *Eine Ausgabe seiner Lyrik in russischer übersetzung* (Tashkent, 1982)

Badaʾuni, Abdul Qadir ibn Mulukshah, *Muntakhab attawarikh*, ed. W. N. Lees, Maulwi Kabiruddin and Maulwi Ahmad Ali (Calcutta 1864–1868); translation, vol. I, G. Ranking; vol. II, W. H. Lowe; vol. III, T. W. Haig (Calcutta 1884–1925; repr. Patna, 1972)

—, *Najat ar rashid*, ed. Sayyid Muiʾnul Haqq (Lahore, 1972)

Baljon, J.M.S., 'Characteristics of Indian Islam' in *Studies in Islam* (Amsterdam, 1975)

—, *Religion and Thought of Shah Wali Allah Dihlawi (1703–1762)* (Leiden, 1986)

—, *A Mystical Interpretation of Prophetic Tales by an Indian Muslim, ʾTaʾwil al-ahadith* (Leiden, 1973)

Bannerje, S. K., *Humayun Badshah*, 2 vols (Lucknow, 1941)

Baqir, Muhammad, *Lahore, Past and Present* (Lahore, 1952)

Barani, Ziyauddin, *Tarikhi Ferozshahi*, ed. Sayyid Ahmad Khan (Calcutta 1860–62)

Bausani, Alessandro, *Storia delle letterature del Pakistan: Urdu, Pangiâbî, Sindhi, Pascʾtô, Bengali pakistana* (Milan, 1958)

—,'Contributo a una definizione del 'stila indiano' della poesia persiana', *Annali dell' Istituto universitario orientale di Napoli* n.s., 7 (1957)

—, 'Indian Elements in Indo Persian Poetry', in *Orientalia Hispanica* I (1974)

—, 'Note su Mirza Bedil' *Annali dell' Istituto universitario orientale di Napoli* n.s., 6 (1955–56)

Bayani, Mehdi, *Tadhkirai khushnivisan (nasta*ᶜ*liq nivisan)*, 3 vols, (Teheran, 1966, 1967, 1969)

Bayazid Biyat, *The Memoirs*, ed. Hidayat Husayn, Bibliotheca Indica (Calcutta, 1941)

Bayram Khan, *The Persian and Turki Divan*, ed. M. Sabir and S. H. Rashdi (Karachi, 1971)

Beach, Milo C., *The Imperial Image: Paintings for the Mughal Court* (Washington DC, 1981)

—, *The Grand Mogul: Imperial Painting in India, 1600–1660* (Williamstown, MA, 1978)

—, 'Mughal and Rajput Painting', in *The New Cambridge History of India* (Cambridge, 1992)

—, *Early Mughal Painting* (Cambridge, MA, 1987)

—, 'Jahangir's *Jahangir Nama*', in Stoler and Miller (eds), *The Powers of Art*

—, *The Adventures of Rama* (Washington, Freer Gallery of Art, 1983)

—, 'Govardhan, Servant of Jahangir', in MARG, ed. Das (1982)

—, with Ebba Koch: *King of the World: The Padshah nama, an Imperial Manuscript from the Royal Library Windsor Castle* (London, 1997)

Bedil, Mirza, Abdul Qadir: *Kulliyat*, 4 vols (Kabul, 1962–65)

Begley, Waine, 'The Myth of the Taj Mahal and a New Theory of its Symbolic Meaning' in *The Art Bulletin* (1979)

—, with Z. A. Desai, *The Taj Mahal: The Illumined Tomb*, The Aga Khan Program for Islamic Architecture (Seattle and London, 1989)

Bernier, François, *Travels in the Mogul Empire, AD 1656–1668*, trans. A. Constable, revised V. A. Smith (London, 1916)

Beveridge, H., 'Maham Anaga', (1899)

—, 'Humayun', *Journal of the Royal Asiatic Society* (1897)

—, 'Was ᶜAbd ur-Rahim the Translator of Babar's Memoirs into Persian?' in *Imperial and Asiatic Quarterly Record* (1900)

Bhakkari, Farid, *Dhakhirat alkhawanin*, ed. Moin ull Iaq (Karachi, 1961)

Bilgrami, Mir Ghulam Ali Azad, *Subhat almarjan fi athar Hindustan* (1886, new edn 1992)

—, *Khizana-yi* ᶜ*amira* (Lucknow n.d., c. 1890)

Bilgrami, Rafat, 'The Ajmer *waqf* under the Mughals', *Islamic Culture*, 52 (1978)

—, 'Pushkar Grants of the Mughals', *Islamic Culture*, 57 (1983)

—, 'Akbar's *mehzar* of 1579', *Islamic Culture*, 47 (1973)

—, *Religious and Quasireligious Departments of the Mughal Period 1556–1707* (New Delhi, 1984)

Bilimoria, Jamshid H., *Ruqᶜat-yi* ᶜ*alamgiri* or *Letters of Aurangzeb* (Bombay, 1908)

Binney, Edwin, *Indian Miniature Painting from the Collections of Edwin Binney III* (Portland, OR, 1973)

Binyon, Lawrence, and T. W. Arnold, *The Court of the Grand Moguls* (London and New York, 1921)

—, *Akbar* (New York, 1932)

Biruni, Abu Rayhan al, *Kitab fiʾl Hind* in *Alberuni's India*, ed. E. Sachau (London, 1887); translated E. Sachau (London, 1888 and 1910)

Blake, Stephen R., 'Courtly Culture under Babur and the early Mughals', *Journal of Asian History*, 20 (1986)

—, *Shahjahanabad: The Sovereign City in Mughal India 1639–1739* (Cambridge, 1991)

Brand, Michael, 'Mughal Ritual in pre-Mughal Cities: The Case of Jahangir in Mandu', *Environmental Design* (1991) (ed.) *Fatehpur Sikri*, MARG (Bombay, 1987)

—, and Glenn Lowry, *Fatehpur Sikri: A Sourcebook* (Cambridge, MA, 1985)

Brend, Barbara, *The Emperor Akbar's 'Khamsa' of Nizami* (London, 1995)

Brockelmann, Carl, *Geschichte der arabischen Literatur*, vols 3 (1898), and supplementary edition, as well as the second revised supplementary edition (Leiden, 1937ff). Vol. 2 is the most useful for India.

Brown, Percy, *Indian Painting under the Mughals, AD 1550 to AD 1750* (London, 1924, repr. New York, 1975)

Browne, Edward G., *A Literary History of Persia* (Cambridge, 1921), many reprints. Vol. 3 is the most important regarding Mughal literature.

Bukhari, Y. K., 'The *bayaz* Presented to Humayun by Shah Tahmasp of Persia', *Islamic Culture*, 42 (1968)

Bullhe Shah, *Diwan*, ed. Faqir M. Faqir (Lahore, 1960)

Burhanpuri, Rashid, *Burhanpur ke Sindhi auliya* (Karachi, 1957)

Bussaglio, Mario, *Indian Miniatures* (London and New York, 1969) (Eng. edn from *La miniature Indiana* (Milan, 1966)

*The Cambridge History of India*, vol. 4, 'The Mughal Period' (Cambridge, 1937)

Camps, Arnulf, 'Persian Works of Jerome Xavier, a Jesuit at the Mogul Court', *Islamic Culture*, 35 (1961)

Canby, Sheila (ed.), *Humayun's Garden Party: Princes of the House of Timur and the Dynastic Image*, MARG (Bombay, 1994)

—, *Princes, poètes et paladins. Katalog der Ausstellung indischer und persischer Miniaturen aus der Sammlung von Prinz und Prinzessin Sadruddin Aga Khan* (Geneva, 1999)

—, 'The Horses of Abd us-Samad', in *Mughal Masters* (ed. Das), MARG, (Bombay, 1998)

Chandarbhan Brahman, Munshi, *Chahar chaman* (Bombay, 1853)

Chandra, Moti, *The Technique of Mughal Painting* (Lucknow, 1949)

Chandra, Pramod, *The Tutinama of the Cleveland Museum of Art and the Origins of Mughal Painting*, 2 vols (Graz, 1976)

Chandra, Satish, *Parties and Politics at the Mughal Court 1707–1740* (New Delhi, 1972)

Chaudhari, *Muslim Patronage to Sanskrit learning* (Calcutta, 1942)

Chopra, P. N., *Life and Letters under the Mughals* (New Delhi, 1976)

Chowdhuri, Jogindra Nath, 'Mumtaz Mahall', *Islamic Culture*, 9

(1936) pp. 373–381

Chughtay, Abdullah, 'Emperor Jahangir's interviews with Gosain Jadrup and his portraits', *Islamic Culture*, 36 (1962)

—, 'The so-called Gardens and Tombs of Zeb un-nisa at Lahore', *Islamic Culture*, 9 (1936)

—, 'Is there a European element in the construction of the Taj Mahal?', *Islamic Culture*, 14 (1941)

Colnaghi, P. and D., et al.., *Persian and Mughal Art* (London, 1976)

Crane, Howard, 'The patronage of Zahir al-Din Babur and the origins of Mughal architecture', *Bulletin of the Asia Institute* 1 (1987)

Crowe, Sylvia, et al., *The Gardens of Mughal India: a history and guide* (London, 1972)

Currie, P.M., *The Shrine and Cult of Mu<sup>c</sup>in al-Din Chishti of Ajmer* (Delhi, 1989)

Dale, Stephen E., '"Steppe Humanism": The autobiographical writings of Zahir al-Din Muliammad Babur, 1483–1530', in *International Journal for Middle Eastern Studies*, 22 (1990)

Dallapiccola, Anna Livia, *Princesses et courtisanes à travers les miniatures indiennes* (Paris, 1978)

—, and Stephanie ZingelAvé Lallemant (eds), *Islam and Indian Regions* (Stuttgart, 1993)

Dani, Ahmad H., *Muslim Architecture in Bengal* (Dacca, 1961)

Dara Shikoh, *Majma' albahrain: 'The Mingling of Two Oceans'*, Persian text with English translation, ed. Mahfuz ul-Haqq ( Calcutta, 1929; repr 1982)

—, *Sirr-i akbar*, Tara Chand and M. Jalali Naini (eds) (Teheran, 1961)

—, *Sakinat al-auliya*, ed. M. Jalali Naini (Teheran, 1965)

—, *Risalai haqnuma, Majma' al-bahrain, Upnekhat mundak*, ed. M.Jalali Naini (Teheran, 1956)

Dard, Khwaja Mir, <sup>c</sup>*Ilm ul-kitab* (Delhi, 1310 h/1892–93)

—, *Urdu Divan* ed. Khalil ar-Rahman Daudi (Lahore, 1962)

Das, Ashok Kumar, *Mughal painting during Jahangir's time* (Calcutta, 1978)

—, *Dawn of Mughal Painting* (Bombay, 1982)

—, *Splendour of Mughal Painting* (Bombay, 1986)

—, 'The Elephant in Mughal Painting', in *Flora und Fauna*, MARG, ed. Verma (Bombay, 1999)

—, 'An Introductory Note on the Emperor Akbar's Ramayana and its Miniatures', *Facets* (ed. Skelton)

—, 'Daswant: His Last Drawing in the *Razmnama*, in MARG (ed. Verma)

—, 'Farrukh Beg: Studies of Adorable Youths and Venerable Saints', in MARG (ed. Verma)

—, 'Bishndas, "unequalled in his Age in Taking Likenesses"' in MARG (ed. Verma)

—, *Mughal Masters: Further Studies*, MARG (Bombay, 1998)

Das, Syamali, 'Flora and Fauna in Mughal Carpets' in MARG (ed. Verma)

Del Bonk, Robert, 'Reinventing Nature: Mughal Composite Animal Painting' in MARG (ed. Verma)

Desai, S. N., *Life at Court: Art for India's Rulers, 16th to 18th Centuries* (Boston, 1985)

Desai, Ziauddin A., *Mosques of India* (Delhi, 1966)

—, *Epigraphia Indica, Arabic and Persian Supplements* (Delhi, 1969)

—, *Studies in Indian Epigraphy*, 3 vols (Mysore, 1975–78)

Digby, Simon, *Encounter with Jogis in Indian Sufi Hagiography*, Lecture (mimeographed), School of Oriental and African Studies (London, 1970)

—, 'The Mother-of-pearl Overlaid Furniture of Gujarat: The Holdings of the Victoria and Albert Museum', in *Facets*, ed. Skelton

Duda, Dorothea, 'Die Kaiserin und der Grossmogul. Untersuchung zu den Miniaturen des Millionenzimmers im Schloss Schönbrunn' in Karin K. Troschke, *Malerei auf Papier und Pergament in den Prunkräumen des Schlosses Schönbrunn* (Vienna, 1995)

—, 'Die illuminierten Handschriften der Österreichischen Nationalbibliothek' *Islamische Handschriften*, I, II (Wien, 1983)

Dughlat, Ali Haydar, *Ta<sup>ɔ</sup>rikhi Rashidi: A History of the Moghuls of Central Asia* (English edition by N. Elias and E. Denison Ross, 1895)

Eaton, Richard, *Sufis of Bijapur* (Princeton, 1977)

Eckmann, J , 'Die tschagatayische Literatur' in *Philologiae Turcicae Fundamenta*, II (Wiesbaden, 1960)

Edwardes, S. M., and H.L.O. Garrett, *Mughal Rule in India* (London, 1930)

Edwards, C. C., 'Relations of Shah Abbas the Great with the Mughal Emperors Akbar and Jahangir' JAOS, 35 (1915)

Egger, G., *Der Hamza-Roman* (Wien, 1969)

Ehlers, Eckhart, and Th. Krafft *Shahjahanabad/Old Delhi. Tradition and Colonial Change* (Stuttgart, 1993)

Elliott, Sir Henry M., and J. Dowson (eds), *The History of India As Told by its Own Historians*, 8 vols (London, 1867–1877, repr. 1966)

Ernst, Carl, *Eternal Garden: Mysticism, History and Politics in a South Asian Sufi Center* (Albany NY, SUNY, 1992)

Ethé, Hermann, 'Neupersische Literatur', in W. Geiger and E. Kulin, *Grundriss der iranischen Philologie*, vol. 2(Strassburg 1896, 1904)

—, *Catalogue of the Persian Manuscripts in the Library of the India Office*, 2 vols (Oxford, 1903, repr. 1985)

Ettinghausen, Richard, 'The Emperor's Choice' in *De Artibus Opuscula* XL: Festschrift for Erwin Panofsky (New York, 1961)

—, *Paintings of the Sultans and Emperors of India in American Collections* (New Delhi, 1961)

—, 'The Dance with zoomorphic masks and other forms of entertainment seen in Islamic art', in Makdisi, George, (ed.) *Arabic and Islamic Studies in honor of H.A.R. Gibb* (Cambridge, MA, 1965)

Ezekiel, I. A., *Sarmad: Jewish Saint of India Radhe Soami Sassanay Beas* (Punjab, 1966)

Fakhri Harawi, *Raudat assalatin wa jawahir al-<sup>c</sup>aja<sup>ɔ</sup>ib*, ed. S. H. Rashdi (Hyderabad, 1968)

Falk, Toby, and Mildred Archer, *Indian Miniatures in the India*

*Office Library* (London, 1981)

—, and Simon Digby (eds), *Colnaghi Catalogue: Paintings from Mughal India* (London, 1979)

Fani Kashmiri, Muhsin, *Diwan*, ed. G. L. Tikku (Teheran, 1964)

Fani Muradabadi, *Hindu shuᶜara ka natiya kalam* (Lyallpur, 1962)

Farooqi, Anis, 'Painters of Akbar's Court', *Islamic Culture*, 48 (1974)

Faruqi, K. A., 'The First Jesuit Mission to the Court of Akbar', *Islamic Culture*, 55 (1981)

Faruqi, Zahiruddin, *Aurangzeb, his life and times* (Delhi, 1935, repr. 1972)

*Fatawa-yi Alamgiri*, 6 vols, (Bulaq, 1276, (AH 1859))

Fazlur Rahman, *Selected Letters of Shaikh Ahmad Sirhindi* (Karachi, 1968)

Findly, Ellison Banks, *Nur Jahan, Empress of Mughal India* (New York and Oxford, 1993)

—, 'Nur Jahan's Embroidery Trade and Flowers of the Taj Mahal', in *Asian Art and Culture, Indian Textiles and Trade* (Washington DC, 1990)

Fischel, Walter J., 'Jews and Judaism at the court of the Moghul emperors in medieval India', *Islamic Culture*, 25 (1951)

Fischer, Klaus and Christa, *Indische Baukunst islamischer Zeit* (Baden-Baden, 1967)

Folsach, Kjeld von, *et al.* (eds), *Sultan, Shah and Great Mughal* (Copenhagen, 1996)

Foltz, Richard C., *Mughal India and Central Asia* (Karachi, 1998)

—, 'Two Seventeenth century Central Asian Travellers to Mughal India', *Journal of the Royal Asiatic Society* (1996)

Foster, William (ed.), *Early Travels in India 1583–1619* (Delhi, 1921, repr. 1985)

Frembgen, Jürgen (ed.), *Rosenduft und Säbelglanz. Islamische Kunst und Kultur der Moghulzeit* (Munich, 1996)

—, 'Der Elefant bei den Moghul' in *Rosenduft und Säbelglanz* (1996)

—, 'Hornhautraspeln aus Süd und Westasien Beitrag zur islamischen Badekultur', in *Münchner Beiträge zur Völkerkunde* 4 (1990)

Friedmann, Yobanan, *Shaykh Ahmad Sirhindi An Outline of His Thought and a Study of his Image in the Eyes of Posterity* (Montreal and London, 1971)

—, 'Medieval Muslim Views on Indian Religions', *Journal of the American Oriental Society* 95 (1975)

Fück, Johann, 'Die sufische Dichtung in der Landessprache des Panjab', *Orientalistische Literaturzeitung* 43 (1940)

Gadon, Elinor, 'Dara Shikuh's mystical vision of Hindu–Muslim Synthesis', in *Facets* (ed. Skelton)

Gallop, Annabel Teh, 'The Genealogical Seal of the Mughal Emperors of India', *Journal of the Royal Asiatic Society* (1999)

Garcin de Tassy, J. H., *Mémoire sur les particularités de la religion musulmane dans l'inde, d'après des ouvrages hindoustanis* (Paris, 1874)

—, *Historie de la littérature Hindoue et Hindoustani*, 3 vols (Paris, 1870–1872)

—, 'Mémoire sur les noms propres et les titres musulmans' *Journal Asiatique* V (1854)

Gascoigne, Bamber, *The Great Moghuls* (London, 1971)

Ghalib, Mirza Asadullah, *Urdu Divan*, ed. Hamid Ahmad Khan (Lahore, 1969)

—, *Kulliyati farsi*, 17 vols (Lahore, 1969)

Ghani, Abdul, *Persian Language and Literature at the Mughal Court*, 3 vols (Allahabad, 1939)

—, *Life and works of Abdul Qadir Bedil* (Lahore, 1960)

Gladston, W. E., 'Perspective and the Moghuls', *Islamic Culture*, 5 (1932)

Glück, Heinrich, *Die indischen Miniaturen des HamzaeRomanesim Österreichischen Museum für Kunst und Industrie und in anderen Saminlungen* (Leipzig, 1925)

Godard, Yedda A., 'Les marges du murakkaᶜ gulshan', in *Athari, Iran* 1 (1936)

Godden, Rumer, *Gulbadan* (London, 1980)

Göbel-Gross, Erhard, *Sirr-i akbar. Die UpanishadÜbersetzung Dara Shikohs* (Marburg, 1962)

Goetz, Hermann, *Bilderatlas zur Kulturgeschichte Indiens in der Grossmogulzeit* (Berlin, 1930)

—, 'The Qudsiya Bagh at Delhi', *Islamic Culture*, 26 (1952)

Goitein, S. D., 'Letters and Documents on the India trade in medieval times', *Islamic Culture*, 37 (1963)

Golombek, Lisa, 'Timur's Garden: The Feminine Perspective', in Mahmoud Hussain *et al.*, *The Mughal Garden*

Goswarny, B. N., and Eberhard Fischer, *Wunder einer Goldenen Zeit. Malerei am Hofe der MoghulKaiser. Indische Kunst des 16 und 17 Jahrhunderts aus Schweizer Sammlungen* (Zürich, 1987)

Graham, Gail Minault, 'Akbar and Aurangzeb – Syncretism or Separatism in Mughal India', in *Muslim World* 59 (1969)

Gramlich, Richard, *Die schütischen Derwischorden*, 3 vols (Wiesbaden, 1965–81)

Guirero, R., *Jahangir and the Jesuits*, trans. C. H. Payne (London, 1930)

Gulbadan, *Humayun-nama. History of Humayun*, ed. and trans. Ann S. Beveridge (London, 1902); Turkish translation by A. Yelgar (Ankara, 1944)

Gupta, Hari Ram, 'Mughlani Begam, the Governor of Lahore 1754–1756', *Islamic Culture* (1956)

Haase, ClausPeter, Jens Kröger and Ursula Lienert (eds), *Morgenländische Pracht. Islamische Kunst aus deutschem Privatbesitz* (Hamburg, Museum für Kunst und Gewerbe, 1993)

Habib, Irfan, 'Mansab Salary Scales under Jahangir and Shahjahan', *Islamic Culture*, 59 (1985)

—, *The Agrarian System of Mughal India 1556–1707* (Bombay, 1963)

—, *An Atlas of the Mughal Empire* (Delhi, 1982)

—, (ed.), *Akbar and his India* (Delhi, 1997)

—, (ed.), *Medieval India* I, *Researches in the History of India 1200–1750* (Delhi, 1992)

Hadi Hasan, 'The Unique Divan of Humayun Badshah', *Islamic Culture*, 24 (1951)

—, *Mughal Poetry: its cultural and historical value* (Aligarh, 1952)

—,'Qasimi Kahi: His life, time, and work', *Islamic Culture*, 27 (1953) Persian edition (Kabul, 1976)

Haque, Enamul, *MuslimBengali Literature* (Karachi, 1957)

Hardy, Peter, 'Abu'l Fazl's Portrait of the Perfect *Padshah*: A Political Philosophy for Mughal India or a Personal Puff for a Pal?' in Troll (ed.), *Islam in India* 11, (1985)

—, *Historians of Medieval India* (London, 1960)

Hasan, M. Mazhar, 'The Fall of Asirgarh', *Islamic Culture*, 51 (1977)

Hashimi, Syed, 'The Real Alamgir', *Islamic Culture*, 2 (1928)

Hashmi, B. A., 'Sarmad', *Islamic Culture*, 7 (1933), *Islamic Culture*, 8 (1934)

Hasrat, Bikramajit, *Dara Shikuh: Life and works* (Calcutta, 1953)

Heinz, Wilhelm, *Der indische Stil in der persischen Literatur* (Wiesbaden, 1974)

—, 'Der indo-persische Dichter Bidil, Sein Leben und Werk', in *Ex Orbe religionum: Studia Geo Widengren* vol. 11 (Leiden, 1972)

Hermansen, Marcia (trans.), *The Conclusive Proof from God: Shah Wali Allah of Delhi's Hujjat Allah albaligha* (Leiden, 1996)

Hickmann, Regina, and Volkmar Enderlein (eds), *Indische Albumblätter. Miniaturen und Kalligraphien aus der Zeit der Moghulkaiser* (Leipzig, 1979)

Hinz, Walther, *Islamische Masse und Gewichte, umgerechnet ins metrische System* (Leiden and Cologne, 1970)

Hodgson, Marshall G. S., *The Venture of Islam: Conscience and History in a World Civilization*, 3 vols (Chicago 1974)

Hollister, John N., *The Shia of India* (London, 1953)

Horn, Paul, *Das Heer und Kriegswesen der Grossmoguls* (Leiden, 1894)

Horovitz, Josef, 'A List of published Mohammedan Inscriptions of India', in *Epigraphia indo-moslemica*, 11 (Calcutta 1909–10)

Hottinger, Arnold, *Akbar der Grosse. Herrscher über Indien durch Versöhnung der Religionen* (Zürich and Munich, 1998)

Hoyland, J. A., 'The Empire of the Great Mogol', trans. De Laets, *Description of India 1630* (Bombay, 1928)

Husain [Khan], Yusuf, *L'inde mystique au Moyen Age* (Paris, 1929)

—, 'An Arabic Version of the Amrtkunda', *Journal Asiatique* CCXIII (1928)

—, 'Shah Muhibbullah of Allahabad and his Mystical Thought', *Islamic Culture*, 28 (1954), pp. 341–357

Husain, Rashid, 'Some notable translations rendered into Persian during Akbar's time', *Islamic Culture*, 55 (1981)

Hussa al-Sabah, Shaikha, 'The Enigma of three Mughal Emeralds in the alSabah Collection', *Newsletter IV of the Dar alathar*, (Kuwait, 1996)

Ibn Hasan, *The Central Structure of the Mughal Empire* (Delhi 1936; repr. 1980)

Ihsan, Abu'l-Fayd, *Raudat al-qayyumiyya*, Ms. in the Asiatic Society of Bengal, Calcutta

Ikram, S. M., *Muslim Civilisation in India* (New York, 1964)

—, *Muslim Rule in India and Pakistan* (Lahore, 1966)

—, *Rudi kauthar* (Lahore, 1969)

—, (ed.), *Armaghani Pak* (Karachi, 1954)

Imtiaz Ahmad, 'Mahabat Khan, khan-i khanan', *Islamic Culture*, 52 (1978), pp. 157–171

Inayat Khan, *The Shah Jahan Nama*. Abridged history of the Mughal emperor Shah Jahan, compiled by the royal librarian. The nineteenth century manuscript translation of A. R. Fuller, ed. and compiled by W. E. Begley and Z. A. Desai (Delhi, 1990)

The Indian Heritage, *Court Life and Arts under Mughal Rule* (London, 1982)

'Indian Painting of the Mughal Period' in *Islam – painting and the arts of the book*, The Keir Collection (London, 1976)

Iqtidar Alam Khan, 'The nobility under Akbar and the development of his religious policy', *Journal of the Royal Asiatic Society* (1968)

—, *Political Biography of a Mughal Noble, Munᶜim Khan Khan-i Khanan, 1497–1575*, (New Delhi, 1973)

—, 'Nature of gunpowder artillery in India during the sixteenth century – a reappraisal of the impact of European gunnery', JRAS (April, 1999), pp. 27–34

Iqtidar Husain Siddiqui, 'Nuqtavi thinkers at the Mughal court, A study of their impact on Akbar's religious and political ideas', *Islamic Culture*, 72 (1998), pp. 65–84

Irvine, William, *Later Mughals*, ed. Jadunath Sarkar, 2 vols (Calcutta, 1922)

—, *The Army of the Indian Moghuls, its organisation and administration* (London, 1903; repr. Delhi, 1952)

Ishaq, M., *India's Contribution to the Study of Hadith-literature* (Dacca, 1955)

Jafar Sharif and Herclots, *Islam in India* (Oxford, 1921; repr. 1972)

Jaffar, S. M., 'Mahabat Khan's mosque in Peshawar', *Islamic Culture*, 14 (1940)

Jahanara, Tochter Shah Jahans, *Risala-i muʾnis al-arwah* (British Museum, MS from the collection of Colonel George William Hamilton)

Jami, *Abdur Rahman, Haft Aurang* ed. Agha Murtaza and Mudarris Gilani (Teheran n.d., c. 1972)

Jhairazbhoy, R. A., 'Early Fortifications and Encampments of the Mughals', *Islamic Culture*, 31, (1957)

Jotwani, Motilal, *Shah Abdul Karim* (New Delhi, 1970)

Kalim, Abu Talib, *Diwan*, ed. Partaw Baydai (Teheran, 1957)

Kambuh, Muhammad Salih Lahori, ᶜ*Amal-i Salih Shahjahannama*, Bibliotheca Indica, 3 vols (Calcutta 1912–1946)

Kanwar, H.I.S., 'Ali Mardan Khan', *Islamic Culture*, 47 (1973)

Karkaria, R. P., 'Akbar and the Parsees', *Journal of the Royal Asiatic Society of Bombay*, 19 (1897)

Kazimi, Masoom Raza, 'Humayun in Iran', *Islamic Culture*, 43 (1969)

Keene, H. G., *The Turks in India* (Delhi, 1972)

Keene, Manuel, 'The Ruby Dagger in the Al-Sabah Collection, in the context of early Mughal jewellery', *Newsletter, Dar al-Athar al-islamiyya IV*, (Kuwait, 1996)

Kerimov, K., *Sultan Muhammad y ego skolo* (Moskow, 1970)

Khakee, Gulshan, 'The Dasa Avatara of the Satpanthi Ismailis and the Imamishahis of Indo-Pakistan', PhD diss. (Harvard University, 1972)

Khan, A. R., 'Gradation of Nobility under Babur', *Islamic Culture*, 60 (1986)

Khatak, Sarfaraz Khan, *Shaikh Muhammad Ali Hazin: His Life, Times, and Works* (Lahore, 1944)

Khwandamir, *Qanun-i Humayun*, trans. B. Prasad (Calcutta, 1940)

Kirmani, Wanis, *Dreams Forgotten: An Anthology of Indo-Persian Poetry* (Aligarh, 1984)

Koch, Ebba, *Mughal Architecture: An Outline of its History and Development (1526–1858)* (Munich, 1991)

—, *Shah Jahan and Orpheus* (Graz, 1988)

—, 'Jahangir and the angels: Recently discovered wall-paintings under European influence in the Fort of Lahore', in J. Deppert (ed.), *India and the West*, (New Delhi, 1983)

—, 'Notes on the painted and sculptured decoration of Nur Jahan's pavilions in the Ram Bagh (*Bagh-i nur afshan*) at Agra', in *Facets* (ed. Skelton)

—, 'The Delhi of the Mughals prior to Shahjahanabad as Reflected in the Pattern of Imperial Visits', in *Festschrift Nurul Hasan* (Delhi, 1993)

—, 'The Influence of the Jesuit Mission on Symbolic Representation of the Mughal Emperors', in Troll (ed.), *Islam in India*, I (Delhi, 1982)

—, *The Architectural Form*, in MARG (Bombay, 1987)

Kokan, M. Yusuf, *Arabic and Persian in Carnatic*, (Madras, 1974)

Krémer, A. de, 'Molla Shah et le spiritualisme oriental', in *Journal Asiatique*, XXXIII (1869)

Krishan, H. Y., 'European Travellers in Mughal India', *Islamic Culture*, 21 (1947)

Kühnel, Ernst, *Indische Miniaturen aus dem Besitz der Staatlichen Museen zu Berlin* (Berlin, 1937)

—, and Hermann Goetz, *Indische Buchmalerei aus dem JahangirAlbum der Staatsbibliothek zu Berlin* (Berlin, 1924)

Kyrklund, Willy, *Zeb un-nisa (Drama)* (Stockholm, c. 1978)

Lal, K. S., *The Mughal Harem* (New Delhi, 1988)

Lane-Poole, Stanley, *Medieval India under Muhammadan Rule* (London, 1917)

Law, Narendra Nath, *Promotion of Learning in India during Muhammadan Rule* (Bombay, 1916)

Lawrence, Bruce B., *Notes from a Distant Flute* (London and Teheran, 1978)

—, 'Seventeenth-century Qadiriyya in Northern India', in Dallapiccola and Zingel (eds), *Islam and Indian Regions*

—, (ed.), *The Rose and the Rock: Mystical and rational elements in the intellectual history of South Asian Islam* (Durham, NC, 1979)

Leach, Linda York, *Indian Miniature Paintings and Drawings* (The Cleveland Museum of Art, Catalogue of Oriental Art I (Cleveland, OH, 1986)

—, *Mughal and other Indian Paintings from the Chester Beatty Library*, 3 vols (London 1995–1998)

Lentz, Thomas W., and Glenn Lowry, *Timur and the Princely Vision: Persian Art and Culture in the 15th Century*, Los Angeles County Museum of Art (Los Angeles, 1989)

Losty, Jeremiah R., *The Art of the Book in India* (London, 1982)

Lowry, Glenn, *Humayun's Tomb: Form, Function, and Meaning in Early Mughal Architecture*, *Muqarnas*, IV (1987)

—, and Susan Nemazee, *A Jeweller's Eye: Islamic Art of the Book from the Vever Collection* (Washington DC, 1988)

MacDougall, Elizabeth B., and Richard Ettinghausen (eds), *The Islamic Garden* (Dumbarton Oaks, Washington DC, 1976)

Maclagan, Sir E., *The Jesuits and the Great Mughal* (London, 1932)

Macneal, Alina, 'The Stone Encampment (Fathpur)' in *Environmental Design*, IX (1994)

Mahfuz ul-Haq, 'The *Khankhanan* and his Painters, Illuminators, and Calligraphists', *Islamic Culture*, 5 (1931),

—, 'Discovery of a Portion of the Original Illustrated Manuscript of the *Ta'rikh-i alfi*, Written for the Emperor Akbar', *Islamic Culture*, V (1931)

—, 'Was Akbar "utterly unlettered"?', *Islamic Culture*, 4 (1930)

Mahmoud Hussain, Abdul Rahman, and James L. Wescoat Jr. (eds), *The Mughal Garden: Interpretation, Conservation, and Implications (Proceedings of a symposium in Lahore)* (Rawalpindi, Lahore and Karachi, 1996)

Malik, Jamal, *Islamische Gelehrtenkultur in Nordindien. Entwicklungsgeschichte und Tendenzen am Beispiel von Lucknow* (Leiden, 1997)

—, 'Sixteenth-century Mahdism: The Rawshaniyya Movement Among Pashtun tribes', in Dallapiccola and Zingel (eds), *Islam and Indian Regions*

Malik, Zahir Uddin, *The Reign of Muhammad Shah, 1719–1748* (Bombay, 1977)

Maneri, Sharafaddin, *The Hundred Letters,* trans. Paul Jackson (New York, 1980)

Manucci, Niccolao, *Storia do Mogor*, trans. William Erskine, 4 vols (Calcutta, 1907, repr. New Delhi, 1981)

—, (abridged), *Memoirs of the Mogul Court* (London, n.d.)

Marek, Jan, 'Persian Literature in India', in Rypka, *History of Iranian Literature* (Dordrecht, 1968)

MARG publishers, Bombay. Each volume, with its own guest editor, contains important studies on Indian, Mughal and Deccani art.

Marshall, D. N., *Mughals in India: A bibliographical Survey, Vol I manuscripts* (Bombay, 1967)

Martin, F. R., *The Miniature Paintings and Painters of Persia, India, and Turkey, from the 8th to the 18th century* (London, 1912)

Massignon, Louis, and A. M. Kassim, 'Un essai de bloc islamo-hindou au XVII siécle, l'humanisme mystique du Prince Dara', *Revue des Études Musulmanes* 63 (1926)

—, et Clément Huart, 'Les entretiens de Lahore', *Journal Asiatique* 209 (1926)

*Masterpieces of Islamic Art in the Hermitage Museum* (Kuwait, 1990)

Masum Nami, Sayyid Muhammad Bhakkari, *Ta'rikh-i Sind*, best known as *Taʾrikh-i Maʿsumi*, ed. U. M. Daudpota (Poona, 1938)

Mayer, L. A., *Mamluk Playing Cards* (Leiden, 1971)

Meer Hasan Ali, Mrs, *Observations on the Mussulmans of India, descriptive of their Manners, Customs, Habits and religious opinions*, 2 vols (London, 1832)

Melikian-Shirvani, A. S., 'Mir Sayyid: Ali Painter of the Past and Pioneer of the Future', in MARG, ed. Das (Bombay, 1998)

Menon, K. R., 'The Personality of Akbar', *Islamic Culture*, 1 (1927)

Menzhausen, Joachim, *Am Hofe des Großmoguls* (Leipzig, 1965)

Michell, G., *Islamic Heritage of the Deccan*, MARG (Bombay, 1986)

Minorsky, Vladimir, *Calligraphers and Painters: A Treatise by Qadi Ahmad, Son of Mir Munshi* (Washington DC, 1959)

Mir Moazam Husain, *Dara (an Epic Poem)*, (Hyderabad n.d., c. 1980)

Misra, Rekha, *Women in Mughal India, 1526–1748* (Delhi, 1967)

Modi, J. J., *The Parsees at the Court of Akbar, Journal of the Royal Asiatic Society*, 21 (1902–4)

Mohan Singh Diwana, *An Introduction to Panjabi Literature* (Amritsar, 1955)

Moosvi, Shireen, *The Economy of the Mughal Empire* (Bombay, 1989)

—, 'The Evolution of the *Mansab* System under Akbar until 1596/7', *Journal of the Royal Asiatic Society* (1981)

Moreland, William H., *The Agrarian system of Moslem India* (1929, repr. Delhi, 1988)

—, *India at the death of Akbar: An economic study* (repr. Delhi, 1989)

—, *From Akbar to Aurangzeb: A study in Indian economic history* (reprinted Delhi, 1988)

Moynihan, Elizabeth B., *Paradise as a Garden in Persia and Mughal India* (New York, 1986)

Mubad Shah, *Dabistan-i madhahib* (Würzburg, 1809)

Mubarak Ali, *The Court of the Great Mughals based on Persian Sources* (Lahore, 1986)

Much, Hans, *Akbar, der Schatten Gottes auf Erden* (Dachau n.d., c. 1925)

—, *Mughal Painters and their Work: A Biographical Survey and Comprehensive Catalogue* (Delhi, 1994)

Muhammad, K. K., 'The Houses of the Nobility in Mughal India', *Islamic Culture*, 60 (1986)

—, 'Hammams in medieval India', *Islamic Culture*, 62 (1988)

Muid Khan, *The Arabian Poets of Golkonda* (Bombay, 1963)

Mujeeb, M., *The Indian Muslims* (Montreal and London, 1966)

—, *Islamic Influence on Indian Society* (Meerut, 1972)

Murata, Sachiko, 'The Mysteries of Marriage', in L. Lewisohn (ed.), *The Legacy of Mediaeval Persian Sufism* (London, 1992)

Mustafa, Khurshid, 'Babur's Court in India', *Islamic Culture*, 30 (1956)

Muʿtamad Khan Bakhshi, Muhammad Sharif, *Iqbalnama-yi Jahangiri*, ed. Maulvi Abdul Hayy, Maulvi Ahmad All and William Nassau Lees, Bibliotheca Indica, (Calcutta, 1865)

Mutribi Samarqandi, al-Asamm, *Khatirat* (Karachi, 1977) transla tion R. Foltz, *Conversations with Emperor Jahangir* (Costa Mesa, CA, 1998)

Nadvi, Abdul Hayy, *Gul-i raʿna* (Azamgarh 1364 AH/1945)

Nadvi, S. A. Zafar, 'Libraries during Muslim Rule in India', *Islamic Culture*, 19 (1945); *Islamic Culture*, 20 (1946)

Nadwi, Sayyid Sulaiman, 'Literary Relations between Arabia and India', *Islamic Culture*, 6 (1932), *Islamic Culture*, 7 (1933)

—, 'Commercial Relations of India with Arabia', *Islamic Culture*, 7 (1933)

—, 'Religious Relations between Arabia and India', *Islamic Culture*, 8 (1934)

Naik, C. R., *ʿAbduʾr Rahim Khan and his literary circle* (Ahmedabad, 1966)

Naimuddin, Sayyid, 'Some Unpublished Verses by Babur', *Islamic Culture*, 30 (1966)

Nami, Mir Maʿsum *see* Maʿsum

Naqvi, H. Q., *History of Mughal Government and Administration* (New Delhi, 1972)

Nath, R., 'The Tomb of Shaikh Muhammad Ghauth at Gwalior', in *Studies in Islam*, II (1978)

—, 'Mughal Hammam and the Institution of Ghusal Khana', *Islamic Culture*, 44 (1970)

—, *History of Mughal Architecture* (New Delhi, 1982)

Nauʿi, *Suz u Gudaz*, English version by Mirza Y. Dawud and Dr A. K. Coomaraswamy (London, 1912)

Nayeem, M. A., 'Two Coronations of Aurangzeb', *Islamic Culture*, 54 (1980)

Nazir Ahmad, Shamsul ʿulamaʾ Hafiz, 'Note on the Library of ʿAbduʾr Rahim Khan Khanan, the First Prime Minister of the Emperor Akbar', *Journal of the Department of Letters*, University of Calcutta, 16 (1927)

Naziri, Muhammad Husain, *Diwan*, ed. M. Musaffa (Teheran, 1961)

Nihawandi, Abdul Baqi, *Maʾathir-i rahimi*, ed. M. Hidayat Husain, 3 vols (Calcutta 1910–1931)

Nizami, Khaliq Ahmad, *Some Aspects of Religion and Politics in India During the 13th Century* (Bombay, 1961)

—, *Akbar and Religion* (Delhi, 1989)

—, *On History and Historians of Medieval India* (New Delhi, 1983)

—, 'Naqshbandi Influence on Mughal Rulers and Politics', *Islamic Culture*, 39 (1965)

Nizamuddin Ahmad Bakhshi, *Tabaqati Akbari*, ed. B. De and Maulana Hidayat Husain (Calcutta, 1913–40), trans. B. De and B. Prashad (Calcutta, 1927f)

Noer, Graf F. A. von (= Prinz Friedrich August of SchleswigHolstein), *Kaiser Akbar*, 2 vols (Leiden 1880–1885)

Nou, JeanLouis, and Amina Okada, *Taj Mahal: Imprimerie Nationale* (Paris, 1993)

Orthmann, Eva, *Abdorrahim Hane Hanan, 964–1036/1556–1627, Staatsmann und Mäzen* (Berlin, 1996)

Pal, Pratabaditya (ed.), *Master Artists of the Imperial Mughal Court*, MARG (Bombay, 1991)

—, et al., *The Romance of the Taj Mahal*, Los Angeles County Museum (London, 1989)

Pant, Chandra, *Nurjahan and her Family* (Allahabad, 1978)

Pant, D., *Economic history of India under the Mughals*, with an introduction by Dr V. K. Saxena (New Delhi, 1930)

Petruccioli, Attilio, *Fatehpur Sikri, La citta del sole e delle acque: The City of Sun and Waters* (Rome, 1984)

—, 'The Process Evolved by the Control Systems of Urban Design in the Moghul Epoch in India: The Case of Fatehpur Sikri', in *Environmental Design* 1 (1984)

—, 'Gardens and Religious Topography in Kashmir', in *Environmental Design*, IX (1994)

Pinder-Wilson, Ralph, 'An Illustrated Mughal Manuscript from Ahmadabad', in D. Barrett *et al.* (eds), *Paintings from Islamic Lands* (Oxford, 1969)

Plantyn's *Royal Polyglot Bible*, pub. 1569–1572 for Philip II of Spain

Polier, Antoine Louis Henri, *Shah Alam II and his Court*, ed. P. C. Gupta (Calcutta, 1989)

Prasad, Beni, *History of Jahangir* (London, 1922, repr. Allahabad, 1940)

Prasad, Pushpa, 'Jahangir and the Jains', *Islamic Culture*, 56 (1982)

Qaddumi, Ghada H., *Book of Gifts and Rarities* (Cambridge, MA, 1996)

Qadi Ahmad *see* Minorsky

*Qadi Qadan jo kalam*, ed. Hiro Thakur (Delhi, 1978)

Qaisar, A.J., 'Visualization of fables in the *Anwar-i Suhaily*', in Verma (ed.) *Flora and Fauna*, MARG (BOMBAY, 1999)

Qamaruddin, *The Mahdawi Movement in India* (Delhi, 1985)

Qani, Mir ᶜAli Shir, *Makli nama*, ed. and annotated S. H. Rashdi (Hyderabad, 1967)

—, *Maqalat ash-shuᶜara*, ed. S. H. Rashdi (Karachi, 1957)

—, *Tuhfat alkiram*, ed. S. H. Rashdi (Hyderabad, 1971)

Qanungo, Kalika Rayan, *Dara Shikoh* (Calcutta, 1935)

Qatiᶜi *see* Akhtar

Quraeshi, Samina, *Legacy of the Indus* (New York, 1974)

—, *Lahore: The City Within* (Singapore, 1983)

Quraishi, A. Q., *Mazhar Janjanan aur unka Urdu kalam* (Bombay, 1961)

Qureshi, Ishtiaq Husain, *The Muslim Community of the IndoPak Subcontinent* (Gravenhage, 1963)

—, *Akbar, the Architect of the Mughal Empire* (Karachi, 1978)

—, *The Administration of the Mughal Empire* (Patna, n.d.)

—, 'The *Pargana* Officials Under Akbar', *Islamic Culture*, 16 (1942)

Ramakrishna, Lajwanti, *Panjabi Sufi Poets* (London and Calcutta 1938, reprinted Delhi, 1975)

Raqim, Ghulam Muhammad Dihlawi, *Tadhkira-yi khushnivisan*, ed. M. Hidayat Husain, Bibliotheca Indica, (Calcutta, 1910)

Rashdi, Sayyid Husamuddin, *Arnin al-mulk Mir Maᶜsum-i Bhakkari*, 944 AH–1014 AH (Hyderabad, 1979)

Raverty, G. H., *Selections from the Poetry of the Afghans* (London, 1862)

Ray, *Humayun in Persia* (Calcutta, 1948)

Raychaudhuri, Tapan, and Irfan Habib, *The Cambridge Economic History of India vol. 1, c. 1200–C.1750* (Cambridge 1989, repr. Delhi, 1991)

Riazul Islam, *Indo-Persian Relations* (Teheran, 1970)

—, *A Calendar of Documents of IndoPersian Relations (1500–1750)*, 2 vols (Teheran, Karachi 1979–1982)

—, *et al.* (ed.), *Central Asia: History, Politics and Culture* (Karachi, 1999)

Richards, John F., *The Mughal Empire* (Cambridge, 1993)

—, *The Imperial Monetary System of Mughal India* (Delhi, 1987)

—, *Document Forms for Official Orders of Appointment in the Mughal Empire: Translation, Notes and Texts* (Cambridge, 1986)

Rizvi, S. Athar Abbas, *A History of Sufism in India*, 2 vols (New Delhi 1978, 1982)

—, *Religious and Intellectual History of the Muslims in Akbar's Reign, with Special Reference to Abu'l Fazl* (New Delhi, 1975)

—, *Muslim Revivalist Movements in Northern India in the Sixteenth and Seventeenth Century* (Agra, 1965)

—, *A Socio-intellectual History of the Ithna Ashari Shiis in India*, 2 vols (New Delhi, 1986)

—, *Shah Wali Allah and his Time* (Canberra, 1980)

—, 'The Rawshaniyya movement' in *Abr Nahrain*, 6 (1965–66); 7 (1967–68)

—, and V. J. Flynn, *Fatehpur Sikri* (Bombay, 1975)

Robinson, Basil W., 'Shah Abbas and the Mughal Ambassador Khan Alam: The Pictorial Record', in *Burlington Magazine* (Feb. 1972)

Robinson, Francis, 'Scholarship and Mysticism in Early 18th Century Awadh', in Dallapiccola and Zingel (ed.), *Islam and Indian Regions*

Roe, Sir Thomas, *The Embassy of Sir Thomas Roe to the Court of the Great Mogul, 1615–1619*, ed. William Foster, 2 vols, (London, 1899; repr. 1923)

Rogers, J. Michael, *Mughal Miniatures* (London, 1993)

RothenDubs, Ursula (ed. and trans.), *Allahs indischer Garten. Ein Lesebuch der Urdu-Literatur* (Frauenfeld, 1989)

Rückert, Friedrich, *Grammatik, Poetik und Rhetorik der Perser*, ed. Wilhelm Pertsch (Leipzig, 1874; repr. 1966)

Rumi, Jalaladdin, *The mathnawi-yi ma'nawi*, ed. and trans. Reynold A. Nicholson, 6 vols with 2 vols of commentary (London and Leiden, 1925–40)

Russell, Ralph, *Ghalib, the Poet and his Age* (London, 1972)

—, and Khurshidul Islam, *Three Mughal Poets*, with an introduction by A. Schimmel (Cambridge, MA, 1968)

Rypka, Jan, *History of Iranian Literature* (Dordrecht, 1968)

Sabahuddin, 'The Postal System during the Muslim rule in India', *Islamic Culture*, 15 (1944)

Sachal Sarmast, *Risalo Sindhi*, ed. Othman Ali Ansari (Karachi, 1958)

—, *Siraiki kalam*, ed. Maulvi Hakim M. Sadiq Ranipuri (Karachi, 1959; repr. 1981)

Sadarangani, H. S., *Persian Poets of Sind* (Karachi, 1956)

Sadiq, M., *History of Urdu Literature* (Oxford, 1964; repr. Delhi, 1984)

Saksena, Banarsi Prasad, *History of Shahjahan of Delhi* (Allahabad, 1932, reprinted 1976)

Saksena, Ram Babu, *A History of Urdu Literature* (Allahabad, 1927)

Salik, A. Majid, *The Muslim Culture of Medieval India* (Lahore, 1968)

Shamsham ad-daula *see* Shahnawaz

Sangar, S. R., 'Piratical Activities in Jahangir's time', *Islamic Culture*, 22 (1948)

Sanial, S. C., 'The Newpapers of the Later Mogul Period', *Islamic Culture*, 2 (1928)

—, 'Some legends of Fatehpur Sikri', *Islamic Culture*, 2 (1928)

Sarkar, Sir Jadunath, *History of Aurangzeb*, 5 vols, (Calcutta, 1912; repr. Bombay 1972–74)

—, *Mughal Administration* (Calcutta, 1924)

—, *The Fall of the Mughal Empire*, 4 vols (Calcutta, 1950)

—, *The Life of Mir Jumla* (New Delhi, 1972)

—, 'An Original Account of Ahmad Shah Durrani's Campaigns in India and the Battle of Panipat', *Islamic Culture*, 7 (1933)

—, *Anecdotes of Aurangzeb and Historical Essays* (Calcutta, 1912)

—, 'Ahmad Shah Abdali in India', *Islamic Culture*, 6 (1932)

Sauda, Mirza Rafiuddin, *Kalam-i Sauda*, ed. Khurshidul Islam (Aligarh, 1965)

Schimmel, Annemarie, *Al-Halladsch, Märtyrer der Gottesliebe* (Cologne, 1968)

—, *Von Ali bis Zahra. Namen und Namengebung in der islamischen Welt* (Munich, 1990)

—, *Tagebuch eines ägyptischen Bürgers: Auswahl aus der arabischen Chronik des Ibn Iyas* (Tübingen, 1985)

—, *German Contributions to the Study of Pakistani Linguistics* (Hamburg, 1951)

—, *And Muhammad is His Messenger. The Veneration of the Prophet in Islamic Piety* (Chapel Hill, NC, 1985)

—, *Islam in the Indian subcontinent* (Leiden, 1980)

—, *Islam in Indo-Pakistan* (Leiden, 1982)

—, 'Islamic Literatures of India – Sindhi Literature – Classical Urdu Literature', in J. Gonda, *History of Indian Literature* (Wiesbaden 1973, 1974, 1975)

—, *Mystische Dimensionen des Islam*, (English edn Chapel Hill, 1975; German edn Cologne, 1985)

—, *Der Islam im indischen Subkontinent* (Darmstadt, 1983)

—, *Calligraphy and Islamic Culture* (New York, 1984)

—, *The Triumphal Sun: A Study of the Life and Works of Jalaladdin Rumi* (Albany, NY, 1992)

—, *Pain and Grace: Studies in Two Mystical Writers of 18th Century Muslim India (Mir Dard and Shah Abdul Latif)* (Leiden, 1976)

—, 'Babur Padishah the Poet, with an Account of the Poetical Talent in his Family', *Islamic Culture*, 34 (1960)

—, 'Turk and Hindu: A Poetical Image and its Application to Historical Fact', in S. Wyonis (ed.), *Islam and Cultural Change in the Middle Ages* (Wiesbaden, 1975)

—, 'Turkish Influences in the Indian Subcontinent', in Riazul Islam *et al.* (ed.), *Central Asia: History, Politics, and Culture* (Karachi, 1999)

—, 'Gedanken zu zwei Porträts Shah Alams II', in U. Haarmann and P. Bachmann (eds), *Festschrift für H. R. Roemer* (Wiesbaden, 1982)

—, 'The Golden Chain of "Sincere Muhammadans"', in Bruce Lawrence (ed.), *The Rose and the Rock*

—, 'Some Notes on the Cultural Activities of the First Uzbek Rulers', *Journal of the Pakistan Historical Society* 8 (1960)

—, 'Mughals, 6. Religious Life', in *Encyclopedia of Islam*, 2nd edn

—, 'The Martyr-mystic Hallaj in Sindhi Folk Poetry' *Numen* 9 (1963)

—, 'A Note on the Poetical Imagery in the *sabk-i hindi*', in *Hakeem Abdul Hameed, Felicitation volume*, ed. Malik Ram (Delhi, 1981)

—, 'Khankhanan ⁼Abduʾr Rahim. Ein Kunstmäzen zur Moghulzeit', in Frank Lothar Kroll (ed.), *Wege zur Kunst und zum Menschen* (Bonn, 1987)

—, 'A Dervish in the Guise of a Prince: Akbar's Generalissimo Khankhanan Abdurrahim', in B. Stoler-Miller (ed.), *The Powers of Art Patronage in Indian Culture* (Oxford, 1992)

—, 'Translations and Commentaries of the Quran in the Sindhi Language', *Oriens* xv (1963)

—, *Pearls from the Indus: Essays on Sindhi Culture* (Hyderabad, 1986)

—, *A Dance of Sparks: Studies in Ghalib's Imagery* (New Delhi, 1979)

—, *Rose der Woge, Rose des Weins. Aus Ghalibs Dichtung* (Zürich, 1971)

—, 'Shah Inayat of Jhok', in *Liber amicorum: Festschrift C. J. Bleeker* (Leiden, 1969)

—, 'Persian Poetry in the Indo-Pakistan Subcontinent', in Ehsan Yar-shater, *Persian Literature* (Albany, NY, 1988)

—, *Die schoristen Gedichte aus Indien und Pakistan. Translations* (Munich, 1997)

—, *Die Träume des Kalifen: Traum und Traumdeutung in der islamis-chen Welt* (Munich, 1998)

—, and S. C. Welch, *A Pocket Book for Akbar: Anvari's Divan* (New York, NY, 1983)

Schwerin, Kerrin Gräfin, *Heiligenverehrung im indischen Islam*, *Zeitschrift der Deutschen Morgenländischen Gesellschaft* 126 (1976)

Seth, D. R., 'Malik Amber: an Estimate', *Islamic Culture*, 19 (1945)

—, 'Life and Times of Malik Amber', *Islamic Culture*, 31 (1957)

Seyller, John W., 'The Freer Ramayana and the Atelier of Abd al-Rahim', (Harvard PhD Dissertation, 1986)

—, 'A dated Hamzanama Illustration', in *Artibus Asiae* LIII (1993)

Shafi, Muhammad, 'The Shalimar Gardens of Lahore', *Islamic Culture*, 1 (1927)

Shah Abdul Latif Bhitai, *Risalo*, ed. Kalyan Advani (Bombay, 1958)

Shahnawaz Khan Shamsham ad-daula and ⁼Abd al-Razzaj, *The maʾathir al-umara*, 3 vols (Calcutta, 1888–96)

Shakeb, Ziauddin Ahmad, *Mughal Archives* vol. I (Hyderabad, 1977)

—, *A descriptive catalogue of the Batala collection of Mughal documents 1527–1757* (London, 1990)

Sharar, Abdul Halim, *Lucknow, the Last Phase of an Oriental Culture* (London, 1975)

Sharma, S. R., *The Religious Policy of the Mughal Emperors* (London, 1940, 2nd edn 1995)

—, *A Bibliography of Mughal India* (Bombay, 1941)

Shea, David, and A. Troyer, *The Dabistan or School of Manners*, 3 vols (Paris, 1843, repr. New York, 1901)

Shyam, Radhey, 'Honors, Ranks and Titles under the Great Mughal', *Islamic Culture*, 46 (1972)

—, 'Mirza Hindal', *Islamic Culture*, 45 (1971)

Siddiq Khan, M., 'A Study in Mughal Land Revenue System', *Islamic Culture*, 12 (1938)

Siddiqui, Abdul Maffid, 'Makhduma-yi jahan. A great ruler of the Deccan', *Islamic Culture*, 17 (1943)

Sirhindi, Ahmad, *Selected letters*, ed. Fazlur Rahman (Karachi, 1968)

Skelton, Robert, 'The Mughal Artist Farrokh Beg', in *Ars Orientalis* II (1957)

Andrew Topsfield, Susan Stronge, Rosemary Crill (eds), *Facets of Indian Art: A symposium held at the Victoria and Albert Museum* (London, 1986)

Smart, Ellen, and Daniel S. Walker, *Pride of the Princes: Indian Art of the Mughal Era in the Cincinnati Art Museum* (Cincinnati, 1985)

Smith, Edmund W., 'Akbar's tomb at Sikandra', *Archeological Survey of India*, vol. 35 (Allahabad, 1903)

—, *The Moghul Architecture of Fatehpur Sikri* (Allahabad, 1899)

Smith, Vincent, *Akbar the Great Mogul 1542–1605*, (Oxford, 1917, repr. Delhi, 1966)

Smith, Wilfred Cantwell, 'Lower-class uprisings in the Mughal Empire', *Islamic Culture*, 20 (1947)

—, 'The Crystallization of Religious Communities in Mughal India', *Yadnamaye Iran-e Minorsky* (Teheran, 1969)

—, 'Solomon, Jahangir and his Artists', *Islamic Culture*, 3 (1929)

—, 'The Sword of Aurangzeb', *Islamic Culture*, 8 (1934)

Sorley, Herbert T., *Shah Abdul Latif of Bhit* (Oxford, 1940)

Spear, Percival, *Twilight of the Mughals: Studies in Late Mughul Delhi* (Cambridge, 1951; repr. Karachi, 1973)

—, (ed.), *Oxford History of India* (Oxford, 1958)

Sprenger, Aloys, *A catalogue of the Arabic, Persian and Hindustany Manuscripts of the Libraries of the King of Oudh*, vol. I (Calcutta, 1854, reprinted Osnabrück, 1979)

Srivastava, A. L., *Akbar the Great*, 3 vols (Agra 1962, 1967, 1973)

—, *Social Life under the Great Mughals* (Allahabad, 1978)

Staude, Willhelm, 'Les artistes de la court d'Akbar et les illustrations du Dastani Amir Hamze', in *Arts Asiatiques* II (Paris, 1955)

Steblev, I. V., *Semantike ghazeli Babura (120 Chagatayische Ghazelen untersucht)* (Moscow, 1982)

Stoler-Miller, Barbara (ed.), *The Powers of Art: Patronage in Indian Culture* (Delhi, 1992)

Storey, H., *Persian Literature: A Biobibliographical Survey* (London 1927–1953)

Streisand, Douglas, *The Formation of the Mughal Empire* (Oxford, 1990)

Stronge, Susan (ed.), *The Arts of the Sikh Kingdoms* (London, Victoria and Albert Museum, 1999)

Subhan, John A., *Sufism, its Saints and Shrines* (Lucknow, 1960)

Subtelny, Maria Eva, 'Babur's Rival Relations: A Study of Kinship and Conflict in 15th–16th Century Central Asia', in *Der Islam*, 66 (1989)

Sufi, B. M. D., *Kashmir: A History of Kashmir* (Lahore, 1949)

Sulaiman, Hamid, *Miniatures of Baburnama* (Tashkent, 1970)

Syndram, Dirk, *Der Thron des Großmoguls. Johann Melchior Dinglingers goldener Traum vom Fernen Osten* (Leipzig, 1996)

Talib-yi Amuli, *Diwan*, ed. Tahiri Shihab (Teheran, 1967)

Tara Chand, *The Influence of Islam on Indian Culture* (Allahabad 1946; repr. 1978)

—, 'Dara Shikoh and the Upanishads', *Islamic Culture*, 15 (1941)

Tavernier, Jean-Baptiste, *Travels in India* (1676) trans. V. Ball, ed. W. Crooke (London, 1889: New Delhi, 1977)

Ter Haar, J.G.D., *Volgeling en arfgeenaan von de Profeet. De denkwereld van schaykh Ahmad Sirhindi 1564–1624* (Leiden, 1989)

Tikku, G. L., *Persian Poetry in Kashmir 1339–1846* (Berkeley and Los Angeles, 1971)

Tirmizi, S.A.J., *Ajmer through Inscriptions* (New Delhi, 1968)

—, *Edicts from the Mughal Harem* (New Delhi, 1979)

—, 'Central Asian Impact on Mughal Edicts', in Riazul Islam et al. (ed.), *Central Asia*

Titley, Nora M., 'An Illustrated Persian Glossary of the 16th Century', *British Museum Quarterly* XXIX (196465)

Topa, Ishwara, 'Political Views of Emperor Aurangzeb, based on his letters', *Islamic Culture*, 39 (1965)

Troll, Ch. (ed.), *Islam in India*, vol. I, *The Akbar Mission and Miscellaneous Studies* (New Delhi, 1982)

—, (ed.), *Muslim Shrines in India* (New Delhi, 1989)

Trumpp, Ernest, *The Adi Granth or the Holy Scriptures of the Sikhs, translated from the original Gurmukhi* (London, 1877)

—, 'Über die Sprache der sog. Kafirs im indischen Kaukasus (Hindu Kusch)', in *Zeitschrift der Deutschen Morganländischen Gesellschaft* 21 (1866)

*Tutinama: Tales of a Parrot: Complete facsimile edition in original size of the Cleveland Museum of Art*, ed. Pramod Chandra (Graz, 1977)

Simsar, Muhammad, *The Cleveland Museum of Art's Tutinama* (Graz, 1978)

Untracht, Oppi, *Traditional Jewelry of India* (New York, 1997)

Urfi Shirazi, Muhammad, *Kulliyat*, ed. Ghulamhusayn Jawahin (Teheran, 1961)

Varma, R. C., 'The Tribal Policy of the Mughals', *Islamic Culture*, 25 (1951), 26 (1952)

—, 'The Relations of the Mughals with the Tribes of the Northwest', *Islamic Culture*, 24 (1950)

Vaudeville, Charlotte, *Les chansons des douze mois dans les littératures indoaryennes* (Pondicherry, 1965)

—, *Kabir*, vol. I (Oxford, 1974)

Vaughan, Philippa, 'Mythical Animals in Mughal Art and Imagery, Symbols and Allusions', in *Flora and Fauna*, MARG, ed. Verma

Verma, Som Prakash, *Art and Material Culture in the Paintings of Akbar's Court* (New Delhi, 1978)

—, (ed.), *Flora and Fauna in Mughal Art*, MARG (Bombay, 1999)

—, 'Lal: The Forgotten Master', in MARG (ed. Das) (Bombay, 1982)

—, 'Ensigns of Royalty at the Mughal Court', *Islamic Culture*, 50 (1976)

Vidyalankar, Pandit Vanshidhar, 'Abdur Rahim Khankhanan and his Hindi poetry', *Islamic Culture*, 24 (1950)

Vogel, J. Ph., *TileMosaics of the Lahore Fort* (1920, repr. Karachi n.d., *c.* 1950)

Volwahsen, Andreas, *Islamisches Indien* (Munich, 1969)

Wade, Bonnie C., 'Music Making in Mughal Painting', in *Asian Art and Culture* (Fall 1995)

Wali Ullah Khan, Muhammad, *Lahore and its Important Monuments* (Lahore, 1961)

Waliullah, Shah, *Hujjat Allah albaligha* (Cairo, *c.* 1955)

—, *Tafhimati ilahiyya*, 2 vols, ed. Ghularn Mustafa al-Qasimi (Islamabad, 1970)

Walker, Daniel, *Flowers Underfoot: Indian Carpets from the Mughal Era* (New York, 1997)

Weber, Rolf, *Porträts und historische Darstellungen in der Miniatursammlung des Museums für indische Kunst Berlin* (Berlin, 1982)

Welch, Anthony, and Stuart Cary Welch, *Arts of the Islamic Book: The Collection of Prince Sadruddin Aga Khan* (London, 1982)

Welch, Stuart Cary, *The Art of Mughal India* (New York, 1963)

—, *A Flower from Every Meadow* (New York, 1973)

—, *Imperial Mughal Painting* (New York, 1978)

—, *Indian Drawings and Painted Sketches* (New York, 1975)

—, *Room for Wonder* (New York, 1978)

—, *Paintings and Precious Objects: The Art of Mughal India* (New York, 1963)

—, INDIA! *Art and Culture, 1300–1900* (New York, 1985)

—, and Milo C. Beach, *Gods, Thrones, and Peacocks* (New York, 1965)

—, Annemarie Schimmel, M. Swietochowski, Wheeler M. Thackston Jr., *The Emperors' Album: Images of Mughal India* (New York, 1987)

Wellecz, Emmy, *Akbar's Religious Thought Reflected in Mogul Painting* (London, 1952)

Wescoat, Jr. James L., 'Early water systems in Mughal India', in A. Petruccioli (ed.), *Environmental Design* II (1985)

Westbrook, J. D., *The Dewan of Zeb unnissa* (Lahore, 1913; 2nd edn 1954)

Williams, Rushbrook, *An Empire-builder of the 16th Century: Babur* (London, 1981)

Yamin Khan Lahori, *Molla Shah Lahori almaruf biBadakhshi* (Lahore, *c.* 1976)

Zafarul Islam, 'The Mughal System of Escheat and the Islamic law of Inheritance', *Islamic Culture*, 62 (1988)

—, 'Nature of Landed Property in Mughal India: Views of Two Contemporary Scholars', *Islamic Culture*, 61 (1987)

Zahid Khan, Ansar, 'Ismailism in Multan and Sind', in the *Journal of the Pakistan Historical Society* 23 (1975)

Zaman, M. K., 'The Use of Artillery in Mughal Warfare', *Islamic Culture*, 57 (1983)

Zayn, Shaikh, 'Tabaqati Baburi', in Elliot and Dowson IV, pp. 288ff., trans. Syed Hasan Askari (New Delhi, 1982)

Zeb un-nissa, Dewan *see* Westbrook

Zebrowski, Mark K., *Deccani Painting* (London, 1983)

—, *Gold, Silver and Bronze from Mughal India* (London, 1997)

Zubaid, Ahmad, *The Contribution of IndoPakistan to Arabic Literature* (Lahore, 1968)

# Photographic Acknowledgements

The publishers wish to express their thanks to the below sources of illustrative material and/or permission to reproduce it:

British Library, London, photos © British Library Reproductions: 1 (Oriental and India Office Collections [henceforth OIOC], Richard Johnson Collection MS BL J.1-2), 4 (OIOC MS BL WD2407), 7 (OIOC, Buchanan-Hamilton Collection MS BL Or.1039), 9 (OIOC, MS BL Add. Or.3854), 11 (OIOC, Richard Johnson Collection MS BL J.2-10), 15 (OIOC, MS BL J.2-2), 23 (OIOC, MS BL Add. Or.342), 36 (OIOC, MS BL Add. Or.3129, f.74), 44 (OIOC, Buchanan–Hamilton Collection MS BL Add. Or.1047), 51 (OIOC, Richard Johnson Collection MS BL J.56-1), 54 (OIOC, MS BL Add. Or. 3129, fol.14), 56 (OIOC, Richard Johnson Collection MS BL J.11-22), 81 (OIOC, Richard Johnson Collection, MS BL J.64-34), 82 (OIOC, Richard Johnson Collection MS BL J.14-8b), 86 (OIOC, Richard Johnson Collection MS BL J.4-3), 93 (OIOC, Hardcastle Collection MS BL Add. Or.2603), 94 (OIOC, Richard Johnson Collection MS BL J.60-2), 105 (OIOC, Richard Johnson Collection MS BL J.14-8a), 114 (OIOC, MS BL Add. Or.4189), 116 (OIOC, MS BL Add. Or.3129, f.49v); Chester Beatty Library, Dublin, photos © the Trustees of the Chester Beatty Library, reproduced by kind permission of the Trustees: 16 (CBL In. 34.7), 25 (CBL In. 05 f.53), 26 (CBL In. 05 f.54r), 42 (CBL In. 03.263), 43 (CBL In. 64.25), 52 (CBL In. 07A.4), 79 (CBL In. 15 f.7r), 84 (CBL In. 69.8), 88 (CBL In. 21 f.67r), 91 (CBL In. 22.85, f.83r), 92 (CBL In. 69.14), 101 (CBL In. 07A.15); photos © Christie's Images Ltd 2004 (all sold at Christie's 'Arts of India' sale, 24 September 2003): 28 (lot no. 184), 69 (lot no. 122), 108 (lot no. 75), 112 (lot 120); Cincinnati Art Museum: 70 (gift of John J. Emery, inv. no. 1949.153), 90 (museum purchase with assistance from Mrs Herbert Marcus, inv. no. 1976.28); collection of the author: 83; Dar al-Athar al-Islamiyyah, Kuwait National Museum (al-Sabah Collection), photos © The al-Sabah Collection, Dar al-Athar al-Islamiyyah, Kuwait National Museum: 53 (inv. LNS 2008 J),

58 (inv. LNS 1809 Ja, b), 59 (inv. LNS 1767 J), 60 (inv. LNS 164 J), 61 (inv. LNS 1660 J), 62 (inv. LNS 1210 J), 63 (inv. LNS 36 HS), 64 (inv. LNS 752 J), 65 (inv. LNS 373 HS), 66 (inv. LNS 1802 J), 67 (inv. LNS 368 HS), 68 (inv. LNS 259 HS); Freer Gallery of Art (Smithsonian Institution), Washington, DC: 20 (gift of Charles Lang Freer, F1907.256), 29 (purchase, F1939.50a); photos Madhuvanti Ghose: 6, 48, 111; The Nasser D. Khalili Collection of Islamic Art, photos © The Nour Foundation: 18 (MSS 987), 104 (MSS 663), 117 (MSS 874); Museum für Islamische Kunst, Berlin, photos Bildarchiv Preussischer Kulturbesitz: 46 (I.4596 f.23), 73 (I.4599 f.19), 77 (I.4593 f.42); Museum Rietberg, Zürich, photo Wettstein & Kauf: 12; National Museum, Copenhagen (Ethnology Collection): 80; National Museum of India, New Delhi: 19 (acc. no. 60.1166), 45 (acc. no. 50.14/11), 47 (acc. no. 60.1720), 76, 102 (acc. no. 58.58/31); Rampur Raza Library, India, photos by courtesy of Rampur Raza Library: 40, 55, 97, 98; Royal Asiatic Society, London, photos courtesy of the Royal Asiatic Society: 10 (RAS Collection 018.10), 17 (RAS Collection 053.007), 38 (RAS MS. 269 f 31a), 41 (RAS Persian MS. 239 31, f.531a - on loan to the British Library, London), 95 (COD. 258 RAS, Fol 128a), 96 (RAS Persian MS. 239, f.3b), 107 (Fraser Collection, RAS 018.006), 110 (RAS MS. 092.004a), 113 (RAS MS. 059.006, Herbert Fanshawe bequest); Royal Collection (Royal Library), Windsor Castle, photos Picture Library © 2004, Her Majesty Queen Elizabeth II: 24 (RCIN 1005025, f195a), 71 (RCIN 1005025, f71a); Arthur M. Sackler Art Museum (Harvard University Art Museums), Cambridge, Mass., photo David Mathews/© 2004 President and Fellows of Harvard College: 99 (gift of John Goelet); Arthur M. Sackler Gallery (Smithsonian Institution), Washington, DC, photo courtesy of the Arthur M. Sackler Gallery, Smithsonian Institution: 13 (Smithsonian Unrestricted Trust Funds, Smithsonian Acquisition Program, and Dr Arthur M. Sackler: S86.0406); San Diego Museum of Art, photos courtesy of the San Diego Museum of Art (all Edwin Binney 3rd Collection): 14

(1990:365), 21 (1990:394), 49 (1990:383), 89 (1990:286); photo courtesy Sotheby's (sold at Sotheby's 'Islamic Works of Art, Carpets and Textiles' sale, 20 April 1983, lot no. 263): 57; Staatliches Museum für Volkerkunde, Munich, photo Robert Braunmüller/© Staatliches Museum für Volkerkunde: 106 (Sammlung Preetorius, inv. no. 77-11-313); Staatsbibliothek zu Berlin (Orientalabteilung), photo Bildarchiv Preussischer Kulturbesitz: 5 (Libri picturati A 117, f.24a), 35 (Libri picturati A 117, f.1a), photo Bildarchiv Preussischer Kulturbesitz/ Kösser: 39 (MS or. quart. 2095, f.8b); Victoria & Albert Museum, London, photos © V&A Picture Library: 2 (acc. no. IM 8-1925, Minto Album), 3 (acc. no. IS 37-1972), 22 (acc. no. IS 48-1956, folio 6), 30 (IS.2-1896, f.72), 31, (acc. no. IS 2-1896 66/117), 32 (acc. no. IS 2-1896 67/117), 50 (acc. no. IM 117-1921, bequeathed by Lady Wantage), 72 (acc. no. IM 97-1967, gift of the National Art Collections Fund, purchased from the executors of the late Capt. E. G. Spencer-Churchill), 74 (acc. no. IS 2-1896 61/117), 75 (acc. no. IS 2-1896 62/117), 78 (acc. no. IS 1508-1883, gift of Lt-Col. Sir Raleigh Egerton), 85 (acc. no. IS 18-1947), 87 (acc. no. IM 12a-1925, a Minto Album), 100 (acc. no. IM 4-1929; gift of Lt-Col. Sir Raleigh Egerton), 103 (acc. no. IM 386-1914).

# Index